A Practical Guide to Presenting Asylum and Human Rights Claims

A Practical Guide to Presenting Asylum and Human Rights Claims

Aryan J Stedman, Benjamin Hawkin

Consultant Editor: Manjit S Gill QC

Print on Demand Edition

Tottel
publishing

Published by
Tottel Publishing Ltd
Maxwelton House
41-43 Boltro Road
Haywards Heath
West Sussex
RH16 1BJ

ISBN 13: 978-1-84592-579-6
ISBN 10: 1-84592-579-3

Formerly published by LexisNexis Butterworths

This edition reprinted by Tottel Publishing Ltd 2006

British Library Cataloguing-in-Publication Data.
A catalogue record for this book is available from the British Library.

Typeset by Letterpart Ltd, Reigate, Surrey
Printed and bound in Great Britain by
Marston Book Services, Abingdon, Oxfordshire

Aryan Stedman would like to dedicate this book
to his Dad, John.

Benjamin Hawkin would like to dedicate this book
to his wife Joanna and his daughter Róża.

'It has been said time and again that asylum cases call for consideration with "the most anxious scrutiny" . . . That is not a mantra to which only lip service should be paid. It recognises the fact that what is at stake in these cases is fundamental human rights including the right to life itself.'

Lord Justice Schiemann in *Sivakumar* [2002] INLR 310.

CONTENTS

Table of Cases

A

B

C

D

E

F

G

H

I

J

K

L

M

S

T

U

V

W

X

Y

Z

Table of Statutes

Table of Statutory Instruments

Table of International and European Conventions

Introduction

A LACK OF UNDERSTANDING

In light of the current political climate surrounding asylum applicants it is informative to look at the language used by the media. Unfortunately, the terminology used is lacking in clarity or real definition. While immigration presents an uncomfortable clash between the right of a state to control its own territory and the fundamental rights of the individual, the tone of much of what is said in the public domain is distinctly unhelpful to all concerned – be they refugees, the general public, journalists or politicians.

The terms 'refugee' and 'asylum seeker' have in recent years been increasingly bandied about to such an extent that few without legal training could give an accurate idea of what they mean or to whom they apply. In much the same vein, though more harmfully, those who ought to be better informed still talk freely of 'illegal immigrants' and 'bogus refugees' when speaking of the majority (at times seemingly the entirety) of individuals who come to the United Kingdom to seek its protection.

Insofar as 'illegal immigrant' is used by the media and even politicians to distinguish between 'genuine' and 'bogus' refugees, it is entirely meaningless. There is in fact no legal means for an individual to travel from a country where they fear persecution to the United Kingdom for the purposes of claiming asylum. With very few exceptions every 'genuine' refugee will therefore have been an 'illegal immigrant' from the time they entered until their case was decided. The predicament of those seeking refuge was aptly summarised by Simon Brown LJ in *R v Uxbridge Magistrates' Court, ex p Adimi* [2001] QB 667:

> 'Escapes from persecution have long been characterised by subterfuge and false papers . . . Although under the Convention subscribing States must give sanctuary to any refugee who seeks asylum (subject only to removal to a safe third country), they are by no means bound to facilitate his arrival. Rather they strive increasingly to prevent it. The combined

effect of visa requirements and carrier's liability has made it well nigh impossible for refugees to travel to countries of refuge without false documents.'

The position regarding the use of the term 'refugee' is more complicated. An ordinary member of the public would probably be surprised by the definition of 'refugee' as contained within the Refugee Convention and interpreted by the courts. The legal definition is both narrower and broader than the popularly understood meaning of the word. The examples below, which are not intended to be exhaustive, illustrate the complexity of the issues involved in determining who is a refugee. It does not include:

- those fleeing famine, drought, disease or natural disaster;
- the majority of the victims of a civil war;
- those likely to face serious harm in their own country where that harm is not for reasons of race, religion, nationality, membership of a particular social group or political opinion;
- those who may face serious harm in their own country if there is deemed to be an adequate system of protection in that country.

It can, however, include:

- those fleeing from serious harm who could return to an otherwise safe but famine-, drought- or disease-ridden area of that country;
- those specifically targeted within a civil war;
- those likely to face serious harm because they belong to a social group as large as the entire female population of their own country, or because they are believed to hold a political belief which they do not in fact hold at all;
- those likely to face serious harm in a country which is a Western democracy.

Despite the complexity of the above issues or perhaps through ignorance of them, the media and certain newspapers in particular, continue to perpetuate the mythical notions that:

- it will be immediately obvious (whether by reading the asylum applicant's mind, or some other way is never explained) who qualifies as a 'genuine' refugee and who does not;
- those that do qualify could only ever be the tiniest minority of applicants;

- the vast majority are obviously 'bogus' and can therefore be 'sent straight back where they came from'.

To anyone who has had any experience in this area, this is all quite unreal. Contrary to the widespread assumption, it does not follow that those who do not meet the legal criteria are 'bogus'. It may be that by the time the Home Office make their decision on the asylum claim, months or even years after the applicant arrived in the United Kingdom, the country where he had in fact been tortured has undergone a radical change of government and is now safe to go back to. It would be entirely understandable if such an individual was nevertheless reluctant to return there. To give another example, a woman who has been raped by members of the security forces in her home country may not qualify as a refugee if it was an isolated and indiscriminate act and not likely to recur. That cannot detract from the fact that she is still the victim of a truly abhorrent crime.

THE FIGURES

Although statistics will never reflect such individual grim realities, the most recent annual figures published by the Home Office do however reveal that:

- the total number of asylum applications for 2002, including dependants, was 110,700;
- the most common country of origin for individuals who applied in 2002 was Iraq. In 2001 it was Afghanistan, in 2000 it was again Iraq and in 1999 it was Kosovo (it is no coincidence that these countries have all now been the subject of military intervention by Western powers);
- the other nine most common countries in 2002 were Zimbabwe, Afghanistan, Somalia, China, Sri Lanka, Turkey, Iran, Pakistan and the Democratic Republic of Congo, ie countries where there are repressive regimes, armed conflict or other serious human rights problems;
- the ten most common countries accounted for about 50% of all applications;
- 10% of applications were granted refugee status and indefinite leave to remain by the Home Office;
- a further 25% were granted exceptional leave to remain;

- another 12% were successful on appeal to adjudicators (this figure apparently still does not take into account appeals which were withdrawn on the basis of a grant of exceptional leave to remain, or subsequent appeals to the Immigration Appeal Tribunal).

So in 2002 just over a third of all those arriving in the United Kingdom were from the outset granted refugee status or exceptional leave to remain. Adding to that the cases allowed on appeal by adjudicators means that at the very least 50% of all those arriving in the United Kingdom are formally allowed to stay. This figure may be higher still, given the number of refusals withdrawn on appeal and further appeals to the Tribunal. The true position therefore appears to be that in over half of all cases there are genuine legal, humanitarian or other good reasons for the asylum applicant to be permitted to remain in the United Kingdom.

The above figures do *not* however, take into account the many individuals whose applications were shoddily prepared by their advisers and subsequently refused by the Home Office. Nor do the figures take into account those who were later poorly, even negligently, represented on appeal, or the not insignificant number who were left unrepresented at that stage and had their appeals dismissed when they should in truth have succeeded.

As to those whose claims in the end do fail, the words of Mr Justice Collins in *R (on the application of Q) v Secretary of State for the Home Department* [2003] EWHC 195 (Admin), [2002] 15 LS Gaz R 26, should be borne in mind:

> 'Whether or not in the end they are granted asylum, many of those arriving are vulnerable and may well have suffered serious ill-treatment. Equally, the so-called economic migrants are frequently trying to escape conditions which no one in this country would regard as tolerable.'

RECENT DEVELOPMENTS

Recent topics that have attracted media attention have been the suggestion that terrorists have entered the United Kingdom in the guise of asylum applicants; controversy over the now closed Sangatte camp in France; financial support for asylum applicants; a system requiring the nationals of 16 specified countries to have visas before travelling through the United Kingdom on their way to a third country; and now the long-term implications of the invasion of Iraq. Perhaps more than any other area of the law, the constant media spotlight and political discussion drive frequent changes in parliamentary legislation. Asylum applicants are nearly always portrayed as a 'problem' for which 'radical solutions' are required, such as removing them to off-shore havens for the determination of their claims, only admitting refugees by 'quota', or even, as was recently mooted, the United Kingdom withdrawing from both the Refugee Convention and the European Convention on Human Rights altogether.

THE LEGAL CONTEXT

Increasingly the higher courts are called on to consider the complex legal and policy issues relating to the United Kingdom's consideration of asylum and human rights applications. From the following recent decisions it can be seen that both the Refugee Convention and the European Convention are being restrictively applied:

- In *Horvath v Secretary of State for the Home Department* [2001] 1 AC 489, the House of Lords held that racist violence would only be persecution within the meaning of the Refugee Convention if the state in question was unable or unwilling to offer reasonable protection.
- In *Saad, Diriye and Osorio v Secretary of State for the Home Department* [2001] EWCA Civ 2008, [2002] INLR 34 the Court of Appeal noted, albeit in passing, that there is in fact no requirement under the Refugee Convention for an asylum claim to be determined by a court. While it is difficult to envisage the existing Immigration Appellate Authority being dismantled, it is interesting to note that there is already an increasing reliance on written evidence and submissions and that appeal rights have in some cases been removed altogether (s 115 of the Nationality, Immigration and Asylum Act 2002), while judicial review of refusal of permission to appeal to the Immigration Appeal Tribunal is being replaced by a paper-only statutory review.
- In *S* [2002] INLR 416 the Court of Appeal stated that the fact that the appellants were refugees at the time they left Croatia could not have a critical effect on the outcome of their appeals

and doubted whether there was, as suggested in the earlier case of *Arif v Secretary of State for the Home Department* [1999] INLR 327, CA, an evidential burden on the Secretary of State to show that in such cases it was safe to return.

- In *R (Hoxha) v Special Adjudicator* [2002] EWCA Civ 1403, [2002] INLR 559 the Court of Appeal interpreted Article 1(C)5 of the Refugee Convention and its 'humanitarian exception' narrowly, so as to preclude its application where appellants had not already been recognised as refugees.
- In *R (Saadi) v Secretary of State for the Home Department* [2002] UKHL 41, [2002] 4 All ER 785, the House of Lords held that detention of asylum applicants at Oakington reception centre for the purposes of fast tracking their asylum claims was not a breach of Article 5 of the ECHR.
- In *Ullah v Special Adjudicator* [2002] EWCA Civ 1856, [2003] 1 WLR 770 (appeal to House of Lords pending) the Court of Appeal decided that if an asylum applicant was unable to show that removal would result in a breach of the Refugee Convention or Articles 3 or 8 of the ECHR, the Secretary of State was not obliged in law to consider whether any of the other Articles of the ECHR would be breached. Moreover, in its discussion of Article 3 the Court appeared to come close to re-formulating the test as a balancing exercise.
- In *Sepet and Bulbul v Secretary of State for the Home Department* [2003] UKHL 15, [2003] 1 WLR 856 the House of Lords held that conscientious objection to military service did not of itself give rise to a valid claim under the Refugee Convention.
- In *European Roma Rights Centre* [2003] EWCA Civ 666 the Court of Appeal decided that although the Refugee Convention required a state not to *return* an individual to their home country without consideration of their asylum claim, it was not unlawful for the United Kingdom to take measures such as a pre-entry clearance scheme to prevent individuals *leaving* their home country in the first place.

THE NATIONALITY, IMMIGRATION AND ASYLUM ACT 2002

The Nationality, Immigration and Asylum Act 2002 (the 2002 Act) is the latest piece of primary legislation intended to transform the immigration system. It aims to simplify the appeals process, prevent the use of multiple appeals to delay removal and to introduce a scheme of non-suspensive appeals for asylum or human rights claims deemed 'clearly unfounded'. Controversially, there is a presumption that in some 24 countries (including not only European Union Accession states, but also countries such as Bangladesh, Jamaica and Sri Lanka) there is in general no persecution and that those countries are safe. Claims by residents of these countries will be automatically certified as 'clearly unfounded' unless the Secretary of State is satisfied to the contrary. The effect of such certification is that applicants are denied an appeal in the United Kingdom but may appeal from abroad. The 2002 Act introduces a 'statutory review' process to replace judicial review for appellants who are refused leave to appeal to the Immigration Appeal Tribunal. There is a power to provide for a closure date to prevent multiple adjournments of appeals. The 2002 Act also prevents last minute appeals against purely administrative decisions such as removal directions, although where there is a genuine and substantial change of circumstances a fresh appeal will remain possible.

OUR PURPOSE

This book is not intended as a political analysis of asylum or human rights, or a textbook on substantive immigration law. It is instead an accessible guide to the basic law and procedure relating to asylum and human rights claims. We will therefore not cover immigration issues beyond asylum and human rights, for example entry clearance or asylum support. Similarly, national security cases give rise to complicated procedures beyond the scope of this book.

We aim to demonstrate the importance of adopting a best practice of presenting such cases to the Home Office and to the Immigration Appellate Authority on appeal. In particular we emphasise the evidential and tactical implications of appeals before adjudicators and the Tribunal. Further appeals are treated in less detail and the reader will have to go to other texts in order to prepare the kind of legal arguments that feature in the High Court and the Court of Appeal. We hope however to provide a starting-point for asylum and human rights claims, with a focus on 'front-loading' such cases from the outset. It is no secret that an appellant will have the greatest chance of success before an adjudicator at first instance who acts as both fact-finder and legal arbiter.

Hearings before the adjudicator and the Tribunal can be not only sensitive and highly emotional, but, from a legal perspective, complex and demanding. They require concentration, ability and frequently lateral thinking. Above all, asylum appeals require an awareness and appreciation of the fact that the appellant has more often than not suffered, both physically and mentally.

REPRESENTATIVES

We anticipate that, depending on the experience of the reader, parts of this book will appear simplistic and obvious. There is no avoiding the fact, however, that although s 84 of the Immigration and Asylum Act 1999 and the availability of public funding through the Controlled Legal Representation system have brought about some improvements, the quality of representation in this field still varies widely. To take but one recurring example, it is our experience that a significant number of unsuccessful asylum applicants who made further applications for leave to remain when the Human Rights Act 1998 came into force, had in fact been previously advised that it was 'not necessary' to attend their asylum appeals even though credibility was clearly in dispute. Sadly but unsurprisingly, their appeals were dismissed. The lapse of time and the approach of the Tribunal to subsequent human rights appeals in *Devaseelan v Secretary of State for the Home Department* [2003] Imm AR 1 mean that it can be an uphill struggle to persuade an adjudicator to re-examine their predecessor's findings on credibility and the risk on return.

Well-prepared cases are obviously more likely to be successful than badly-prepared ones. Unfortunately, sometimes less care is taken over an asylum case than a criminal, family or civil case. Although such cases may also involve human rights, if an injustice occurs such clients can at least seek further redress from within the United Kingdom. A failed asylum applicant once removed may literally never be heard of again.

As it is our intention to provide an overview of the whole process of an asylum or human rights claim from the initial application to its final determination on appeal, we are necessarily dealing with a variety of roles: caseworker, solicitor and counsel. Unless there is a need to be more specific, we will use the collective term 'representative' throughout. Whatever the stage of the process and the role of the representative, the primary aim of every representative must be to use their utmost effort to secure the very best outcome for the client that is consistent with their professional integrity. We therefore ask that the reader forgive us for any parts of this book which may seem simplistic, in favour of the accessible and helpful guide we hope it achieves.

Aryan Stedman

Benjamin Hawkin

9 King's Bench Walk,

Temple,

London EC4Y 7DX

CHAPTER 1

Refugee Law

OVERVIEW

In this chapter we are concerned with the legal principles and authorities, both international and domestic, relating to the recognition of refugees. Since the coming into force of the Human Rights Act 1998 on 2 October 2000, all asylum claims should now be coupled with a claim under the European Convention on Human Rights (ECHR). There will inevitably be overlaps of law and fact between the two claims. To avoid any confusion however, we will first cover the issues relevant to an asylum claim. Human rights claims will then be dealt with in Chapter 2, where we will also indicate the areas common to both kinds of claim.

The difficulty with any examination of refugee law is that it is a unique area of practice where international law sits side-by-side with domestic legislation. Moreover, the law itself merges with the decision-making process, which in turn faces the formidable task of evaluating evidence from a witness who is a stranger to this country and its legal traditions. That evidence will concern events that may have taken place over a period of many years in a country far away. The issue for determination will be what may happen when that individual is once again many hundreds or thousands of miles outside this jurisdiction.

Although it is important to consider these and other features of refugee law separately and in detail, all the issues in this chapter are part of a larger picture that must always be viewed as a whole.

BACKGROUND

Historically the term 'refugee' was applied to those who fled their countries, whether to escape religious persecution, to evade a ruler's campaign of repression, or merely to avoid the ravages of civil war. The twentieth century concern to more clearly define 'refugee' arose out of states' administrative need to control the movement of displaced individuals. The first Convention relating to the International Status of Refugees was signed in 1933. The approach at this time was to define 'refugee' by group, on the basis that in general they lacked the protection of their country, rather than to examine individual cases in detail.

The aftermath of the Second World War and the problems created by the many hundreds of thousands of displaced people in Europe saw an end to the general categorising of groups of such individuals as 'refugees' and the beginning of the modern approach of requiring each person to show a risk of persecution. The founding of the United Nations in 1948 was followed by moves to establish a committee to study refugees and stateless individuals and to draft a convention on their status.

THE REFUGEE CONVENTION AND PROTOCOL

The 1951 Convention relating to the Status of Refugees (the Refugee Convention) was initially limited to those claiming to be refugees in Europe as 'a result of events occurring before 1st January 1951'. However, the continuing incidence of refugee problems led to the 1967 Protocol relating to the Status of Refugees, which removed the temporal and geographical limitations and thus greatly widened the application of the original definition.

As a signatory to the Refugee Convention, the United Kingdom has an obligation to consider all applications for asylum made in this country. Each application is examined on its individual merits to determine whether the applicant has demonstrated a well-founded fear of persecution in his or her country of nationality for one of the reasons set out in the Convention. These are reasons of race, religion, nationality, membership of a particular social group or political opinion.

General definition of refugee

This is found in Article 1A(2) of the Refugee Convention, as amended by the Protocol:

> 'Owing to well-founded fear of being persecuted for reasons of race, religion, nationality, membership of a particular social group or political opinion, is outside the country of his nationality and is unable, or owing to such fear, is unwilling to avail himself of the protection of that country; or who, not having a nationality and being outside the country of his former habitual residence as a result of such events, is unable or, owing to such fear, is unwilling to return to it.
> In the case of a person who has more than one nationality, the term "the country of his nationality" shall mean each of the countries of which he is a national, and a person shall not be deemed to be lacking the protection of the country of his nationality if, without any valid reason based on well-founded fear, he has not availed himself of the protection of one of the countries of which he is a national.'

The second paragraph makes plain that if the individual fearing persecution is also a national of another country they will be expected to seek the protection of that country first. Claiming asylum is therefore a last resort, as will also be seen when looking at the issues of protection and internal relocation.

Prohibition on expulsion or refoulement

Those that qualify as refugees become entitled under the Refugee Convention to a variety of rights and benefits. The most important of these are:

(i) the right not to be expelled from the country of refuge, ie the United Kingdom, as contained in Article 32(1) of the Refugee Convention:

> 'The contracting states shall not expel a refugee lawfully in their territory save on the grounds of national security or public order.'

(ii) the even more critical right not to be returned to the country of persecution, as laid down by Article 33(1):

> 'No contracting state shall expel or return ("refouler") a refugee in any manner whatsoever to the frontiers of territories where his life or freedom would be threatened

> on account of his race, religion, nationality, membership of a particular social group or political opinion.'

The principle of non-refoulement is therefore the obligation on a country not to return an asylum seeker to a country where they will suffer persecution. There are exceptions to both these rights and these will be examined later under 'Exclusion from the refugee convention' and 'National security issues'.

DOMESTIC LAW

Although the Refugee Convention is not incorporated, ie has not been made a part of English law by statute, its provisions are nevertheless given effect in domestic law. The United Kingdom recognises the right to claim asylum, Rule 328 of the Immigration Rules HC 395 states:

> 'All asylum applications will be determined by the Secretary of State in accordance with the United Kingdom's obligations under the United Nations Convention and Protocol relating to the Status of Refugees. Every asylum application made by a person at a port or airport for the United Kingdom will be referred by the Immigration Officer for determination by the Secretary of State in accordance with these Rules.'

Rule 329 provides that neither an applicant nor their dependents will be required to leave the United Kingdom until the claim has been determined or certified as a Third country case. Rule 334 also states:

> 'An asylum applicant will be granted asylum in the United Kingdom if the Secretary of State is satisfied that:
> (i) he is in the United Kingdom or has arrived at a port of entry in the United Kingdom; and
> (ii) he is a refugee, as defined by the Convention and Protocol; and
> (iii) refusing his application would result in his being required to go, (either immediately or after the time limited by an existing leave to enter or remain) in breach of the Convention and Protocol, to a country in which his life or freedom would be threatened on account of

> his race, religion, nationality, political opinion or membership of a particular social group.'

Where an asylum claim is refused by the Home Office, s 69 of the Immigration and Asylum Act 1999 (the 1999 Act) gives a right of appeal to an independent adjudicator. Where the refusal of asylum took place on or after 1 April 2003, s 82 of the Nationality, Immigration and Asylum Act 2002 (the 2002 Act) gives a similar right of appeal.

ISSUE UNDER THE REFUGEE CONVENTION

Taking Articles 1A(2), 32(1) and 33(1) of the Refugee Convention together in combination, the issue in the vast majority of asylum claims and subsequent appeals will be:

> 'If returned to country X, will the appellant have a well-founded fear of persecution on account of their race, religion, nationality, membership of a particular social group or political opinion?'

Expressed this way, the test appears deceptively straightforward. However, it is in the interpretation of the constituent parts of this definition and the decision-making process itself, that the difficulties become apparent.

Interpretation of Refugee Convention

As the Refugee Convention is an international treaty, its provisions must be interpreted by the Courts in accordance with Article 31 of the Vienna Convention on the Law of Treaties (1980):

> '(1) A treaty shall be interpreted in good faith in accordance with the ordinary meaning to be given to the terms of the treaty in their context and in the light of its object and purpose.
>
> (2) The context for the purpose of the interpretation of a treaty shall comprise, in addition to the text, including its preamble and annexes:
>
> (a) any agreement relating to the treaty which was made between all the parties in connection with the conclusion of the treaty;

(b) any instrument which was made by one or more parties in connection with the conclusion of the treaty and accepted by the other parties as an instrument relating to the treaty.

(3) There shall be taken into account, together with the context:
(a) any subsequent agreement between the parties regarding the interpretation of the treaty or the application of its provisions;
(b) any subsequent practice in the application of the treaty which establishes the agreement of the parties regarding its interpretation;
(c) any relevant rules of international law applicable in the relations between the parties.

(4) A special meaning shall be given to a term if it is established that the parties so intended.'

Another essential guide to the interpretation of the Refugee Convention and the requirements of the decision-making process itself, is the 'Handbook on Procedures and Criteria for Determining Refugee Status', published by the United Nations High Commissioner for Refugees (the UNHCR Handbook).

Refugee Convention as 'living instrument'

The Court of Appeal observed in *R v Immigartion Appeal Tribunal, ex p Shah* [1998] INLR 97 that:

> 'Unless it is seen as a living thing, adopted by civilised countries for a humanitarian end which is constant in motive but mutable in form, the Convention will eventually become an anachronism.'

In *Horvath v Secretary of State for the Home Department* [2001] 1 AC 489 the House of Lords stated:

> '. . . the best guide to the meaning of the words used in the Convention is likely to be found by giving them a broad meaning in the light of the purposes which the Convention was designed to serve . . .

> . . . the Convention purpose which is of paramount importance for a solution of the problems raised by the present case is that which is to be found in the principle of surrogacy. The general purpose of the Convention is to enable the person who no longer has the benefit of protection against persecution for a Convention reason in his own country to turn for protection to the international community.'

The House of Lords held in *R v Secretary of State for the Home Department, ex p Adan and Aitseguer* [2001] 2 AC 477, that the Refugee Convention can only have one 'true autonomous and international meaning'. In *Sepet and Bulbul v Secretary of State for the Home Department* [2003] 3 All ER 304, [2003] UKHL 15, the House of Lords recently confirmed:

> 'It is plain that the Convention has a single autonomous meaning, to which effect should be given in any and by all member states, regardless of where a decision falls to be made: *R v Secretary of State for the Home Department, ex p Adan* [2001] 2 AC 477, HL. It is also, I think, plain that the Convention must be seen as a living instrument in the sense that whilst its meaning does not change over time, its application will.'

ANXIOUS SCRUTINY

The principle of anxious scrutiny is one that is now continually referred to in the assessment of asylum and human rights claims. It is the acknowledgment that such cases involve allegations that an individual's basic human rights will be threatened if they are forcibly sent to another country, and that if they are not given conscientious and thorough consideration beforehand, the consequences for that individual could be both tragic and impossible to undo. This concept was referred to by the House of Lords in *Bugdaycay v Secretary of State for the Home Department* [1987] AC 514, and in the recent case of *R (on the application of Sivakumer) v Immigration Appeal Tribunal* [2001] EWCA Civ 1196, [2001] All ER (D) 322, (upheld by the House of Lords) the Court of Appeal stated:

> 'It has been said time and again that asylum cases call for consideration with "the most anxious scrutiny" . . . That is not a mantra to which only lip service should be paid. It recognises the fact that what is at stake in these cases is fundamental human rights including the right to life itself. That degree of scrutiny is called for to a heightened degree in a case such as this where it is accepted that the appellant has been tortured for alleged involvement in political crimes.'

Anxious scrutiny therefore requires a very careful examination of the individual facts of the case and an equally careful consideration of evidence relating to the country of return – the more so where an individual has already suffered persecution there. This is not simply a requirement of the decision-making process itself, but also of all representatives. The task of reaching the right decision in an individual case is one that is shared between the individual, the representatives, the Home Office and, where applicable, the adjudicator.

Burden and standard of proof

It is a general principle of litigation that the party that brings a case must prove it. The burden of proof in respect of an asylum claim is likewise on the applicant and it will be for them to make out their case to the Home Office or to an adjudicator by demonstrating that they have a well-founded fear of persecution for one of the five Convention reasons.

However, it is a unique feature of asylum cases that the applicable standard of proof is far lower than the criminal standard of 'beyond a reasonable doubt' and lower than the civil standard of 'more probable than not'. The low standard of proof and the principle of anxious scrutiny can be regarded as two sides of the same coin. The lower standard of proof acknowledges that asylum seekers are in a far less advantageous position than other litigants and that this must be taken into account in the assessment of their claims.

The UNHCR Handbook states at paragraph 196:

> '. . . an applicant may not be able to support his statements by documentary or other proof, and cases in which an applicant can provide evidence of all his statements will be the exception rather than the rule. In most cases a person fleeing from

> persecution will have arrived with the barest of necessities and very frequently without personal documents. Thus, while the burden of proof in principle rests on the applicant, the duty to ascertain and evaluate all the relevant facts is shared between the applicant and the examiner. Indeed, in some cases, it may be for the examiner to use all the means at his disposal to produce the necessary evidence in support of the application. Even such independent research may not, however, always be successful and there may also be statements that are not susceptible of proof. In such cases, if the applicant's account appears credible, he should, unless there are good reasons to the contrary, be given the benefit of the doubt.'

The definition of the lower standard of proof has been the subject of a number of judicial decisions. In the leading case of *R v Secretary of State for the Home Department, ex p Sivakumaran* [1988] AC 958, the House of Lords held:

> 'Bearing in mind the relative gravity of the consequences of the court's expectation being falsified either in one way or the other . . . A lesser degree of likelihood is, in my view, sufficient.'

The Tribunal decided in *Kaja v Secretary of State for the Home Department* [1995] Imm AR 1 that the lower standard of proof in *Sivakumaran* applied to the assessment of accounts of past events as well as the likelihood of persecution in the future.

In *Karanakaran v Secretary of State for the Home Department* [2000] 3 All ER 449 the Court of Appeal approved *Kaja* and went on clarify its true effect. Unlike in civil litigation, decision-makers were not bound to exclude evidence to which, though not satisfied it was probably true, they were still willing to attach some credence. The Court indicated that this approach should 'be adopted at each stage of the assessment process'.

One of the decisions referred to in *Karanakaran* was that of the High Court of Australia in *Chan Yee Kin v Minister for Immigration and Ethnic Affairs* (1989) 169 CLR 379. The Court held that in order to succeed in a claim for refugee status an applicant should show a 'real chance' of persecution and that even a 10% chance that the applicant would face persecution could satisfy the test.

The case-law shows that the standard of proof can be expressed variously as 'a reasonable chance', 'a reasonable degree of likelihood', 'a real possibility' or 'a real risk'. 'A real risk' emphasises the potential danger in any failure to apply the lower standard of proof.

ELEMENTS OF A CLAIM UNDER THE REFUGEE CONVENTION

As we have already said, a valid claim under the Refugee Convention requires an individual to have 'a well-founded fear of persecution on account of their race, religion, nationality, membership of a particular social group or political opinion'. We now look at the individual elements of that definition, which for the sake of convenience we have taken in the following order:

(i) Persecution
(ii) Insufficient protection
(iii) Subjective fear
(iv) Current well-founded fear
(v) No internal relocation
(vi) Convention reason

PERSECUTION

General concept

Central to every asylum claim is the individual's fear of persecution if returned to their country, often because they claim to have already experienced persecution there. If the treatment apprehended would not amount to persecution, the claim will fail.

In *Applicant A* (1997) 190 CLR 225, the High Court of Australia pointed out:

> 'By including in its operative provisions the requirement that a refugee fear persecution, the Convention limits its humanitarian scope and does not afford universal protection to asylum seekers. No matter how devastating may be epidemic, natural disaster or famine, a person fleeing them is not a refugee within the terms of the Convention.'

This naturally begs the question: what forms of behaviour and ill-treatment will constitute persecution? Although, as will be seen below, persecution within the meaning of the Refugee Convention must always be assessed in relation to the availability of state protection, what we are concerned with at this stage is what actions are capable of being characterised as persecution. We say 'characterised' because there is no universally recognised definition of persecution. However, we would suggest that the starting-point is the violation or denial, through human agency, of fundamental rights. By 'human agency' we mean that persecution must be brought about directly or indirectly by the state or by non-state agents such as private individuals or groups.

Persecution is primarily an issue of fact and degree that will turn on the evidence put forward in a particular case. However, given its importance to refugee law it has also received significant attention in the higher courts.

The UNHCR Handbook states at paragraph 51:

> 'From Article 33 of the 1951 Convention, it may be inferred that a threat to life or freedom on account of race, religion, nationality, political opinion or membership of a particular social group is always persecution. Other serious violations of human rights – for the same reasons – would also constitute persecution.'

In *Sepet and Bulbul v Secretary of State for the Home Department* [2003] UKHL 15, [2003] 1 WLR 856 the House of Lords observed:

> 'At the heart of the definition lies the concept of persecution. It is when a person, suffering or fearing persecution in country A, flees to country B that it becomes the duty of country B to afford him (by the grant of asylum) the protection denied him by or under the laws of country A. History provides many examples of . . . minorities . . . which have without doubt suffered persecution. But it is a strong word . . . valuable guidance is given by Professor Hathaway (The Law of Refugee Status (1991), page 112) in a passage relied on by Lord Hope of Craighead in *Horvath* . . . "in sum, persecution is most appropriately defined as the sustained or systemic failure of state protection in relation to one of the core entitlements which has been recognised by the international community".'

In *R v Immigration Appeal Tribunal, ex p Jonah* [1985] Imm AR 7 the High Court stated:

> 'the courts must remember that the test of persecution is and must be kept at a high and demanding level.'

The Court applied to the word its ordinary dictionary meaning:

> 'to pursue with malignancy or injurious action; especially to oppress for holding a heretical opinion or belief.'

In *Gashi and Nikshiqi v Secretary of State for the Home Department* [1997] INLR 96 the Tribunal carefully reviewed the authorities and guidance relating to persecution and envisaged that the issue had to be determined by reference to a hierarchy of rights:

(i) Inviolable human rights, such as the right to life and the prohibition against torture and cruel, inhuman or degrading punishment or treatment. A threat to these rights would always be a serious violation amounting to persecution.

(ii) Rights where limited restriction by the state in times of public emergency can be justified, such rights include the right to be free from arbitrary arrest and detention and the right to freedom of expression. A threat to these rights may amount to persecution if the state cannot demonstrate any valid justification for their temporary restriction. If accompanied by other forms of discriminatory treatment, there may be persecution on a cumulative basis.

(iii) Rights which, although binding upon states, reflect goals of social, economic or cultural development and which may be reliant on the adequacy of the state's resources. However, within such constraints a state must still act in good faith and without discrimination. Such rights could include the right to basic education and the right to earn a livelihood. A systematic denial of these rights could lead to such prejudicial consequences to the individual as would amount to persecution within the meaning and spirit of the Convention, particularly where the state has adequate resources and is implementing the rights selectively and in a discriminatory manner.

Seriousness v persistency

In many cases what amounts to persecution will depend on the relationship between two factors: the seriousness of the treatment and its frequency. However, that is not to say that persistency as such is a necessary requirement for persecution and much will depend on the particular applicant and the circumstances they are likely to face. The more serious the conduct is, the less that will be required in the way of persistency for it to amount to persecution. A single incident of ill-treatment can therefore suffice: *Mustafa Doymus* (2000/TH/01748).

Torture

Torture, which may be defined as the deliberate causing of severe mental or physical or mental pain, is prohibited in absolute terms by a number of international treaties, including under Article 3 of the ECHR. The Court of Appeal held in *Demirkaya v Secretary of State for the Home Department* [1999] INLR 441 that torture will always constitute persecution. In *R v Secretary of State for the Home Department, ex p Sarbjit Singh* [1999] INLR 632 the High Court, while declining to give an exhaustive definition of torture, commented:

> 'It connotes conduct which may have a serious or significant affect on the mental or physical well-being of the individual.'

Rape

Commentators have long emphasised the importance of the Refugee Convention recognising the particular kinds of persecution faced by women. For example, rape has often been regarded as sexual rather than violent, and rape committed by security forces as a private act rather than an act of the state. However, it has been recognised that such attitudes must change. A European Parliament Resolution dated 14 November 1996 stated that it was:

> '. . . crucial that sexual violence be recognised as a form of torture, particularly given the use of rape as a weapon of war and the cultural traditions of certain countries which involve gender persecution.'

It was confirmed by the Court of Appeal in *Kacaj* [2001] INLR 354 and *Katrinak v Secretary of State for the Home Department* [2001] EWCA Civ 832, [2001] INLR 499 that rape is capable of amounting to persecution. This must be taken to include male rape as well.

Gender-specific ill-treatment

As well as rape itself, other gender-specific acts are likely to be persecution:

(i) Sexual violence falling short of rape.
(ii) Female genital mutilation (FGM).
(iii) Forced abortion or sterilisation.
(iv) Denial of access to contraception.
(v) Forced prostitution.
(vi) Domestic violence.

Detention

In *Ravichandran v Secretary of State for the Home Department* [1996] Imm AR 97 the Court of Appeal observed:

> 'If the real purpose of these round-ups was to deprive Tamils of their liberty simply out of hostility towards them (ie with "malignancy"), I cannot think that the loss of freedom involved would properly be held insufficient to constitute persecution.'

Although the lawful detention of an individual will not in itself amount to persecution, where the detention is disproportionate in length or the conditions are inhuman or degrading, persecution is likely to be made out.

Other forms of ill-treatment

The UNHCR Handbook states at paragraph 52:

> 'Whether other prejudicial actions or threats would amount to persecution will depend on the circumstances of each case . . . The subjective character of fear of persecution requires an evaluation of the opinions and feelings of the person concerned. It is also in the light of such opinions and feelings that any actual or anticipated measures against him must necessarily be viewed. Due to variations in the psychological make-up of individuals and in the circumstances of each case, interpretations of what amounts to persecution are bound to vary.'

It is important therefore to consider the particular characteristics of the individual. For example, treatment that would not be persecution if meted out to an able-bodied adult male may nevertheless be persecution in the case of an elderly woman, a minor or an individual who already has post-traumatic stress disorder.

Furthermore, even non-persecutory treatment may become persecutory in nature if it is persistent rather than isolated. The Court of Appeal held in *Demirkaya v Secretary of State for the Home Department* [1999] INLR 441 that whilst not every beating would constitute persecution, repeated beatings could well do so. In *Lucreteanu* (12126) the Tribunal accepted that a series of threatening telephone calls amounted to persecution.

Categories of persecution not closed

Applicants for asylum come from a wide range of countries and groups within those countries. The concept of persecution must therefore be an open-ended one, able to take account of a whole range of cultural-specific experiences. This point is expressed by Professor Goodwin-Gill in 'The Refugee in International Law' as follows:

> 'There being no limits to the perverse side of human imagination, little purpose is served by attempting to list all known measures of persecution. Assessments must be made from case to case by taking account, on the one hand, of the notion of individual integrity and human dignity and, on the other hand, of the manner and degree to which they stand to be injured.'

Persecution must be discriminatory

It has been recognised that for treatment to be persecutory there has to be an element of discrimination. In *Islam v Secretary of State for the Home Department, R v Immigration Appeal Tribunal, ex p Shah* [1999] 2 AC 629, the House of Lords explained why this is so:

> '. . . the Convention . . . is concerned not with all cases of persecution, even if they involve denials of human rights, but

> with persecution which is based on discrimination. Discrimination means making distinctions which principles of fundamental human rights regard as inconsistent with the right of every person to equal treatment and respect.'

The importance of the discriminatory element is demonstrated by the decision of House of Lords in *R v Secretary of State for the Home Department, ex p Adan* [1999] 1 AC 293. In this case it was held that a Somali national, who feared return to his country because it was in a state of clan-based civil war, did not have a fear of persecution within the meaning of the Refugee Convention. This was because although there was clearly a real risk he would be injured or killed by an opposing clan, he could not demonstrate that this risk was over and above the 'ordinary risks' of the civil war to other members of his clan. There had to be a 'differential impact': in other words discrimination. Fortunately, differential impact is only required in extreme cases of civil war where law and order have broken down completely and the state has effectively ceased to exist.

The requirement for discrimination was again confirmed by the House of Lords in *Sepet v Secretary of State for the Home Department* [2003] UKHL 15, [2003] 3 All ER 304: 'treatment is not persecutory if it is treatment meted out to all and is not discriminatory'. Contrary to what frequently appears in Home Office Refusal Letters, this does not require that an individual be personally 'singled out'. In *Katrinak v Secretary of State for the Home Department* [2001] EWCA Civ 832, [2001] INLR 499 the Court of Appeal decided that a person can be persecuted by attacks on their spouse or immediate family members. An individual may also face persecution as part of a group: *R v Secretary of State for the Home Department, ex p Jeyakumaran* [1994] Imm AR 45. Nor should discrimination be taken to mean solely unfair or arbitrary treatment of a minority but could for example, relate to all women in the home country: *Islam v Secretary of State for the Home Department, R v Immigration Appeal Tribunal, ex p Shah* [1999] 2 AC 629. In the majority of cases the requirements for discrimination will be satisfied by showing a Convention reason.

Discrimination as persecution

The wider issue of whether discrimination in and of itself can amount to persecution is more controversial. The UNHCR Handbook states at paragraphs 53, 54 and 55:

> 'In addition, an applicant may have been subjected to various measures not in themselves amounting to persecution (eg discrimination in various forms), in some cases combined with other adverse factors (eg general atmosphere of insecurity in the country of origin). In such situations, the various elements involved may, if taken together, produce an effect on the mind of the applicant that can reasonably justify a claim to well-founded fear of persecution on "cumulative grounds". Needless to say, it is not possible to lay down a general rule as to what cumulative reasons can give rise to a valid claim to refugee status. This will necessarily depend on all the circumstances, including the particular geographical, historical and ethnological context.'
>
> '. . . It is only in certain circumstances that discrimination will amount to persecution. This would be so if measures of discrimination lead to consequences of a substantially prejudicial nature for the person concerned, eg serious restrictions on his right to earn his livelihood, his right to practise his religion, or his access to normally available educational facilities.'
>
> 'Where measures of discrimination are, in themselves, not of a serious character, they may nevertheless give rise to a reasonable fear of persecution if they produce, in the mind of the person concerned, a feeling of apprehension and insecurity as regards his future existence. Whether or not such measures of persecution in themselves amount to persecution must be determined in the light of all the circumstances. A claim to persecution will of course be stronger where a person has been the victim of a number of discriminatory measures of this type and where there is thus a cumulative element involved.'

In *Chiver* [1997] INLR 212 the Tribunal on the facts recognised that an inability to obtain employment due to discrimination was persecution. Likewise in *Padhu* (IAT) (12318) the Tribunal accepted that discrimination in respect of accommodation, employment and state benefits was persecution.

In the more recent case of *S* (IAT) (2001/TH/00632) the Tribunal observed:

> 'The harm need not result from violence or loss of liberty. An inability to earn a living or to find anywhere to live can result in destitution and at least potential damage to health and even life. If discrimination against which the state cannot or will not provide protection produces such a result, the Convention can be engaged. A desire to achieve a better life or for economic improvement cannot of itself justify asylum. Nevertheless, the line between the need to escape persecution which results in penury and economic migration is often difficult to draw particularly where, as in these cases, discrimination undoubtedly exists and has led and may well lead to considerable hardship and what caused the individual to come to the United Kingdom may include a desire for economic improvement.'

Although each case will turn on its own particular facts, it seems that for discriminatory treatment not amounting to direct physical harm to be characterised as persecution, there would have to be discrimination on several fronts and/or resulting at the very least in significant hardship. However, human rights standards within the United Kingdom and indeed the international community are not set in stone and are gradually evolving. For that reason, it is hoped that the less obvious forms of harm such as discrimination may become increasingly recognised as persecution in the future, particularly as history shows that discrimination committed or permitted by the state is often a precursor to more sinister policies.

Prosecution or persecution

Home Office Refusal Letters frequently argue that what the applicant fears on return to their country is 'prosecution not persecution'. However, this somewhat glib assertion belies the difficulty in cases where there is a fear of the authorities of the home country, of differentiating between the use and abuse of criminal investigation or legal proceedings against that individual.

The UNHCR Handbook states at paragraphs 56, 57, 58, 59 and 60:

> 'Persecution must be distinguished from punishment for a common law offence. Persons fleeing from persecution or punishment for such an offence are not normally refugees. It

> should be recalled that a refugee is a victim – or potential victim – of injustice, not a fugitive from justice.
>
> The above distinction may, however, occasionally be obscured. In the first place, a person guilty of a common law offence may be liable to excessive punishment, which may amount to persecution within the meaning of the definition. Moreover, penal prosecution for a reason mentioned in the definition (for example, in respect of "illegal" religious instruction given to a child) may in itself amount to persecution.
>
> Secondly, there may be cases in which a person, besides fearing prosecution or punishment for a common law crime, may also have a "well-founded fear of persecution". In such cases the person concerned is a refugee. It may, however, be necessary to consider whether the crime in question is not of such a serious character as to bring the applicant within the scope of one of the exclusion clauses.
>
> In order to determine whether prosecution amounts to persecution, it will also be necessary to refer to the laws of the country concerned. It is possible for a law not to be in conformity with accepted human rights standards. It may not be the law but its application that is discriminatory. Prosecution for an offence against "public order" for example for distribution of propaganda material could be a vehicle for the persecution of the individual on the grounds of the political content of the publication.
>
> In such cases . . . national authorities may frequently have to take decisions by using their own national legislation as a yardstick. Moreover, recourse may usefully be had to the principles set out in the various international instruments relating to human rights.'

Far from being fatal to an asylum claim, prosecution may in fact be strong evidence of persecution, whether directly by the state or at the instigation of non-state agents: *Ameyaw v Secretary of State for the Home Department* [1992] INLR 144. What must be avoided is any assumption that criminal investigation would or would not be persecution. The prosecution must be carefully examined in the context of an individual's account and the relevant country background. The following particular points must be considered:

- Have charges or other proceedings ever been brought?

- If so, in respect of what act or acts?
- Is this an offence under the law of that country?
- Were the act or acts in question actually committed by the individual and if so why?
- Whether or not the individual committed the acts, what other motives are there for the proceedings?
- How has the individual been treated in connection with the proceedings?
- How have the proceedings been conducted?
- What sentence has been imposed: is it lawful; is it commensurate with the offence; is it consistent with that imposed in other such cases?

Ultimately, it will be the effect on the individual that counts. Arbitrary or excessive punishment may well amount to persecution: *R (on the application of Sivakumar) v Immigration Appeal Tribunal* [2003] UKHL 14, [2003] 2 All ER 1097. However, the prosecution must be related to a Convention reason: *T v Immigration Officer* [1996] AC 742, HL.

INSUFFICIENT PROTECTION

An act or actions which are otherwise capable of amounting to persecution can only be regarded as persecution within the meaning of the Refugee Convention if the person concerned can also show that they will not receive proper protection against such conduct. This requirement flows from the principle recognised in Article 1A(2) of the Refugee Convention that it is the duty of every country to protect its own citizens from harm and that the states that signed the Refugee Convention were offering substitute or 'surrogate protection' only. This means that asylum should only be granted to individuals whose own countries were unable or unwilling to provide them with protection.

Protection by whom?

Article 1A(2) refers to 'the protection of that country'. Generally, 'country' will be synonymous with 'state' and protection will therefore be examined by reference to what that state can provide. However, in situations where a state in reality lacks the control of its territory that states are expected to have, argument arises as to whether the individual can access protection within the meaning of the Convention.

In *Dyli v Secretary of State for the Home Department* [2000] INLR 372, the Tribunal was concerned with the claim of an ethnic Albanian from Kosovo (a province of Serbia, itself part of the Federal Republic of Yugoslavia). There had been a civil conflict there in 1998–2000 between ethic Albanian separatists and Serbian forces. In 2000, NATO forces intervened against Serbian security forces to prevent atrocities and ethnic cleansing being perpetrated against ethnic Albanians. This resulted in the withdrawal of Serbian forces in June 1999 and Serbia's power of government over Kosovo passing to the United Nations Interim Administration in Kosovo (UNMIK) assisted by the NATO peace-keeping force (KFOR). The issue arose as to whether UNMIK or KFOR could provide the protection required by Article 1A(2). The Tribunal took a factual approach and decided that UNMIK and KFOR could do so:

> 'The Convention is designed for the benefit of persons who need the protection of the international community because they are at risk of persecution in their own countries. A person who, for whatever reason, has protection in his own country has no basis for fear of persecution . . . How it is achieved, whether directly by the authorities of the country or by others, is irrelevant.'

Dyli was followed by the Court of Appeal in *Canaj v Secretary of State for the Home Department* and *Vallaj v Special Adjudicator* [2001] EWCA Civ 782, [2001] INLR 342. However, the distinctive feature of these cases was that in both law and in fact, the role of government and therefore protection was being fulfilled by the United Nations in partnership with NATO.

Where the country in which an individual fears persecution is neither controlled by the government nor by the United Nations or any other recognised international organisation, it has been doubted whether there can be protection within the meaning of the Convention. A recent paper 'Internal Protection/Relocation/Flight Alternative as an Aspect of Refugee Status Determination' by Professor Hathaway and Michelle Foster, commissioned by the UNCHR for the fiftieth anniversary of the Refugee Convention, stated:

> 'The fundamental problem . . . is that none of the proposed protectors, whether it is ethnic leaders in Liberia, clans in Somalia or embryonic local authorities in portions of Northern Iraq, is positioned to deliver what Article 1A(2) of the Refugee Convention requires, namely the protection of a state accountable under international law. The protective obligations of the Convention and Articles 2–33 are specifically addressed to "states". The very structure of the Convention requires that protection will be provided not by some largely unaccountable entity with de facto control, but rather by a government capable of assuming and being held responsible under international law for its actions.'

This view was essentially adopted by the Court of Appeal in *Gardi v Secretary of State for the Home Department* [2002] EWCA Civ 750, [2002] 1 WLR 2755, in the context of the Kurdish Autonomous Area (KAA) of Northern Iraq (although that decision was later set aside for lack of jurisdiction and the case will now be reconsidered by the Court of Session in Scotland). A similar argument will doubtless also be relied on in asylum claims brought by Iraqis reluctant to return to a country where the regime of Saddam Hussein has been overthrown but where interim rule is not under the auspices of the United Nations. At the very least, if those that control a country are not 'accountable under international law', that will be a highly relevant indicator of whether they are equipped and can be trusted to provide the protection contemplated by the Convention.

The standard of protection

The critical issue is of course what level of protection an asylum applicant is entitled to expect in their home state. This will depend on whether the persecution comes from state or non-state agents.

Persecution by the state

The House of Lords in *Horvath v Secretary of State for the Home Department* [2001] 1 AC 489 described persecution by the state or its agents as 'a clear case for surrogate protection by the international community'.

Non-state agents

The UNHCR Handbook states at paragraph 65:

> 'Persecution is normally related to action by the authorities of a country. It may also emanate from sections of the population that do not respect the standards established by the laws of the country concerned. A case in point may be religious intolerance, amounting to persecution, in a country otherwise secular, but where sizeable fractions of the population do not respect the religious beliefs of their neighbours. Where serious discriminatory or other offensive acts are committed by the local populace, they can be considered as persecution if they are knowingly tolerated by the authorities, or if the authorities refuse, or prove unable, to offer effective protection.'

In *Horvath* the House of Lords was concerned with serious and persistent attacks on a Roma citizen and his family by skinheads in Slovakia. It was argued that while the state was not itself carrying out persecution, nor was it providing sufficient protection against the skinhead violence. It was held that:

> '. . . the applicant for refugee status must show that the persecution that he fears consists of acts of violence or ill-treatment against which the state is unable or unwilling to provide protection. The applicant may have a well-founded fear of threats to his life due to famine or civil war or of isolated acts of violence or ill-treatment for a Convention reason which may be perpetrated against him. But the risk, however severe, and the fear, however well-founded, do not entitle him to the status of a refugee. The Convention has a more limited objective, the limits of which are identified by the list of Convention reasons and by the principle of surrogacy.'

The level of protection in such a case was expressed as follows:

> '. . . the application of the surrogacy principle rests upon the assumption that, just as the substitute cannot achieve complete protection against isolated and random attacks, so also complete protection against such attacks is not to be expected of the home state. The standard to be applied is therefore not that which would eliminate all risk and would thus amount to

> a guarantee of protection in the home state. Rather it is a practical standard, which takes proper account of the duty which the state owes to all its own nationals.'

The House of Lords also approved the Court of Appeal's description of what such a practical standard should entail:

> '. . . there must be in force in the country in question a criminal law which makes the violent attacks by the persecutors punishable by sentences commensurate with the gravity of the crimes. The victims as a class must not be exempt from the protection of the law. There must be a reasonable willingness by the law enforcement agencies, that is to say the police and courts, to detect, prosecute and punish offenders.'

Since *Horvath* was decided the Home Office and even adjudicators have been quick to assume in non-state agent cases, particularly involving Roma, that if there is indeed a criminal justice system in a particular country, then that is in itself a sufficiency of protection. That is not what *Horvath* says.

The Court of Appeal pointed out in *Noune v Secretary of State for the Home Department* [2001] INLR 526 that it is not enough that the authorities are doing their inefficient or incompetent best. What has to be examined in each and every case is whether there has been and would be an ability and willingness by their state to provide practical protection for that particular individual.

In cases where the state is able to provide protection, an unwillingness to do so would have to be demonstrated. Often this will depend on whether the applicant has complained about the persecutory acts against them and the response of the authorities to those complaints. In *Havlicek* (2000) (IAT) (2000/TH/01448) the Tribunal stated:

> 'The point made that the respondent had sought protection does not help the appellant [the Secretary of State]. It was precisely because he had sought but had failed to get protection from the police that the special adjudicator found in his favour. This showed, he said, that the protection on offer was not effective. Indeed, if the respondent had not sought the protection of the police, his claim would almost certainly have failed because he had not demonstrated any ground for his

> alleged inability or unwillingness to avail himself of the protection which was available.
> . . . The fact that the protection available has not proved effective in individual cases cannot of itself establish a claim for asylum. The fact that individual police officers are lazy or incompetent or unwilling to carry out their duty does not establish that the state is unable to provide the necessary protection. Furthermore, it must be recognised that a prosecution can only be based on evidence and it may in many cases be very difficult to obtain sufficient evidence to launch prosecutions. However, the state can only provide the necessary protection through its agents, in this case the police. If the police are unwilling to act when they should and there is no means of making them do their duty, there may be shown an inability to provide the necessary protection.'

In *Skenderaj v Secretary of State for the Home Department* [2002] EWCA Civ 567, [2002] INLR 323 the Court of Appeal held that:

> '. . . if the state cannot or will not provide a sufficiency of protection, if sought, the failure to seek it is irrelevant. And that is so whether the failure results from a fear of persecution or simply an acceptance that to do so would be futile.'

The Court of Appeal decided in *Wierzbicki v Secretary of State for the Home Department* [2001] Imm AR 602 that whilst 'sufficiency of protection' was an imprecise test, it remained the correct approach to assessing the risk of persecution by non-state actors.

Other cases

In *Svazas v Secretary of State for the Home Department* [2002] EWCA Civ 74, [2002] Imm AR 363 the Court of Appeal considered that there will be cases in which the persecution is not by non-state agents or strictly speaking, by the state either but rather by agents of the state who are acting outside their proper authority. The Court concluded that the standard of protection must vary by degree according to where in the range between state and non-state persecution the facts of the case place it:

> 'If discriminatory brutality is found to be too widespread to be written off as delinquent activity of the sort that could

> occur in any system, the paradigm will shift away from the *Horvath* end of the spectrum towards the less explored class of state agents who take advantage of their power but do not act on behalf of the state: in ordinary parlance, a police force whose members are out of control. Even in such a context a practical standard of protection does not require a guarantee against police misconduct, but it does, as Professor Hathaway says, call for timely and effective rectification of the situation which is allowing the misconduct to happen . . . this is a different model of protection from that which on authority is called for by the Convention when the source of the fear of persecution is people whom the state has to police but who themselves do not deploy or therefore abuse the state's own power. How different will depend on the state of affairs disclosed by the evidence.'

It was further pointed out by the Court that the more senior the state agents responsible for persecution, the more likely it was that the state had failed to offer adequate protection.

SUBJECTIVE FEAR

The individual must have a personal fear of persecution. The UNHCR Handbook at paragraph 37 perhaps places too much emphasis on this element of the claim:

> 'Since fear is subjective, the definition involves a subjective element in the person applying for recognition as a refugee. Determination of refugee status will therefore primarily require an evaluation of the applicant's statements rather than a judgement on the situation prevailing in his country of origin.'

In the vast majority of cases where the individual is accepted as having given a credible account, the subjective fear will also be accepted as being present. However, as discussed below there is an objective aspect to the fear requiring it to be well-founded and it is this which will generally be in dispute.

The Tribunal in *Gashi and Nikshiqi v Secretary of State for the Home Department* [1997] INLR 96 recognised the problem of dwelling too long on subjective fear:

'. . . the meaning of "fear" . . . we take . . . from The Concise Oxford Dictionary:

> "an unpleasant emotion caused by exposure to danger, expectation of pain; danger; likelihood (of something unwelcome); feel anxiety or apprehension about."

Whilst there may be occasions when an adjudicator so completely disbelieves everything an appellant says (the situation contemplated by Glidewell LJ in *Kingori*) that he does not even accept that his claim to fear the consequences he states await him.

But the adjudicator is in fact usually also finding that the situation which awaits his return – both personal and background – does not, viewed objectively, give rise to any reasonable likelihood of persecution.

Conversely Professor Jackson says in *Radivojevic* where it is shown there is a serious possibility of persecution then it may well be difficult to refuse an application on the ground he has no actual fear.

An adjudicator should we think, first, give his objective assessment, based upon the oral testimony, his evaluation of the available information in the domain and any specific documentation of which he is aware. If he accepts there is objective fear, to hold nonetheless fear in any sense of the word is absent, is hard to contemplate.'

CURRENT WELL-FOUNDED FEAR

This is the objective aspect of the fear. The UNHCR Handbook states at paragraph 38:

'To the element of fear – a state of mind and a subjective condition – is added the qualification "well-founded". This implies that it is not only the frame of mind of the person concerned that determines his refugee status, but that his frame of mind must be supported by an objective situation. The term "well-founded fear" therefore contains a subjective and an objective element, and in determining whether well-founded fear exists, both elements must be taken into consideration.'

This requires the decision-maker to step back from the individual's account and look at it within the broader picture of the situation in that country. The decision-maker then has to consider whether the individual's subjective fear is made out to the extent that there is a 'real risk' rather than merely an apprehension of persecution on return. If there is then the fear is a 'well-founded fear'. Typically this will require recourse to objective evidence such as human rights reports and press articles concerning the country circumstances.

In *Adan v Secretary of State for the Home Department* [1999] 1 AC 293, the House of Lords held that a fear of persecution would only be well-founded if it was current. An historic fear, even if well-founded at the time it was held, was insufficient if it was no longer well-founded at the date of decision or appeal.

INTERNAL RELOCATION

The concept of internal relocation, otherwise described as internal flight, can be regarded as going hand-in-hand with the issue of protection. Just as an asylum claim will fail if the individual cannot show that the authorities would be unwilling or unable to protect them against acts of persecution, so it will also fail if there is a region of the country where they would be safe from persecution and to which it would be reasonable for them to go and live.

The UNHCR Handbook deals with the issue of internal relocation at paragraph 91:

> 'The fear of being persecuted need not always extend to the whole territory of the refugee's country of nationality. Thus in ethnic clashes or in cases of grave disturbances involving civil war conditions, persecution of a specific ethnic or national group may occur in only one part of the country.'

In such situations, a person will not be excluded from refugee status merely because he could have sought refuge in another part of the same country, if under all the circumstances it would not have been reasonable to expect him to do so.'

Internal relocation typically, though not exclusively, arises in cases of persecution by non-state agents. There are two considerations:

(i) Is internal relocation safe?
(ii) Is internal relocation otherwise reasonable?

Safety

It is an obvious requirement of internal flight that it should not amount to 'jumping out of the frying-pan and into the fire' by itself involving a real risk of persecution. Therefore in the great majority of cases involving state persecution, internal relocation will simply not arise, because the entirety of the home country will be under the control of the government. However, there will be cases where parts of the country are not under government control for example, because they are occupied by rebel groups or factions. This of course immediately raises the issue of whether 'protection' under the Convention is possible at all. In any event, there would have to be an extremely careful consideration of the nature of those in control of that territory, of whether the individual would face persecution at their hands or would even be permitted to enter that territory at all. And there may well still be a risk of persecution from state agents operating within that territory. In the clear majority of cases where persecution is by the state, internal relocation to non-state held territory will be unsafe because the individual will be returned by airline to the capital city or another main city, which will usually be government-held and from which movement undetected by the authorities will be difficult.

Where persecution would be solely at the hands of non-state agents who have a presence only in certain parts of the home country, internal relocation is more likely to be a safe option. However, in these cases the decision-maker must carefully assess the realities of exactly where in their country the individual would be returned to and whether they would be able to travel without danger to (and enter) the 'safe' part of the country. Even a lack of presence of non-state agents does not automatically mean safety for the applicant, particularly if they are known to have sympathisers or informers in the 'safe' part of that country.

The question of internal relocation becomes more difficult when there is an issue about when and where the Secretary of State proposes to remove an individual to. There has been significant legal debate about this recently. In *Gardi* (IAT) (2001/TH/02997) the Tribunal dealt with the position of ethnic Kurds from the Kurdish Autonomous Area (KAA) in Northern Iraq. The Secretary of State proposed to remove them 'to Iraq at a time and date to be notified'.

However, the only scheduled airline was to Baghdad where it was accepted that they would have a well-founded fear of persecution from the regime of Saddam Hussein. For that reason the Secretary of State undertook not to return the appellants to Baghdad or any other part of government-controlled Iraq. The Secretary of State was unable to return anyone directly to the KAA and could not say when he would be able to do so. The Tribunal held that if there was no fear of persecution in the home area, ie the KAA, the issue of internal relocation did not arise and the appellants could not be considered refugees.

In considering any danger that is involved in internal relocation, the standard of proof is the same as for the other elements of the claim, ie is there a 'real risk'? Moreover, any harm likely to occur during internal flight need not be persecution for a Convention reason, merely of a level sufficient to constitute 'inhuman and degrading treatment' within the meaning of Article 3 of the ECHR.

Reasonableness

Even if internal relocation is deemed to be safe, it must still be reasonable in all the circumstances of the case. The Court of Appeal decided in *Robinson v Secretary of State for the Home Deparment* [1997] INLR 182, that the reasonableness or otherwise of internal relocation was inseparable from the overall decision of whether an individual was entitled to refugee status. The Court took note of the decision of the Federal Court of Australia in *Randhawa* (1994) 124 ALR 265, in which it was said:

> 'If it is not reasonable in the circumstances to expect a person who has a well-founded fear of persecution in relation to the part of a country from which he or she has fled to relocate to another part of the country of nationality it may be said that, in the relevant sense, the person's fear of persecution in relation to the country as a whole is well-founded.'

The Court in *Robinson* also considered the kinds of factors that would make internal relocation unreasonable:

(i) the financial, logistical or other practicalities of whether the 'safe' region of the country is reasonably accessible;

(ii) whether travelling to or staying in the 'safe' region would expose the individual to 'great physical danger' or 'undue hardship';
(iii) if life in the 'safe' region fails to meet 'basic norms of civil, political and socio-economic human rights'.

The reasonableness test now most frequently cited in asylum appeals is that given by the Federal Court of Canada in *Thirunavukkarasu v Minister of Employment and Immigration* (1994) 109 DLR (4th) 682:

> '. . . would it be unduly harsh to expect this person, who is being persecuted in one part of his country, to move to another less hostile part of the country before seeking refugee status abroad?'

'Undue harshness' was amplified in the judgment to include an individual having to cross battlefields or having to live in isolation from civilisation, such as in mountains, desert or jungle. It was further stated that a dislike of the weather, a lack of friends or relatives or suitable employment in the 'safe' region would not make internal flight unduly harsh.

In *Karanakaran v Secretary of State for the Home Department* [2000] 3 All ER 449 the Court of Appeal described the 'undue harshness' test as tempering the requirement that an asylum applicant seek internal relocation with 'a small amount of humanity'.

Recent developments

The concept of internal relocation was developed in the case of *Refugee Appeal No. 71684/99* [2000] INLR 165, in which the New Zealand Refugee Status Appeals Authority took account of 'The Michigan Guidelines' written by Professor Hathaway and contributed to by other leading academics. The Appeals Authority held:

(i) There was no conceptual basis for a 'reasonableness' element in the assessment of internal relocation, as the issue was not to be considered in isolation from the definition of refugee in Article 1(A)(2) of the Refugee Convention.
(ii) Where the issue of internal relocation arose, the necessary question was whether the individual could genuinely access

meaningful domestic protection against persecution, serious harm, or a denial of civil, political and socio-economic rights found in the Refugee Convention.

(iii) Internal relocation would only be found to exist where relocation eliminated a real risk of persecution for a Convention reason, where it would not otherwise create a real chance of serious harm giving rise to a risk of return to the original site of persecution and where the local conditions met the standard of protection prescribed by the Refugee Convention.

(iv) Where relocation was found to eliminate a real chance of persecution, this had to be a durable rather than merely transitory state of affairs. This would depend on whether the fear was of state agents, who had the ability to act on a nationwide basis, or of non-state agents whose threat might be localised. Where the state was unwilling or unable to offer proper protection, it had to be considered whether this too was nationwide or localised.

Refugee Appeal No. 71684/99 was described by the Court of Appeal in *Canaj v Secretary of State for the Home Department* and *Vallaj v Special Adjudicator* [2001] EWCA Civ 782, [2001] INLR 342, as being of 'great interest' and it was recommended for citation in any case in which internal relocation was in issue.

The above must all now be read subject to *AE v Secretary of State for the Home Department* [2003] EWCA Civ 1032, a further and very recent decision by the Court of Appeal. The Court reviewed the various authorities and held:

(i) In the light of the numerous legislative changes since *Robinson* was decided, including the Human Rights Act 1998, it was important to distinguish between:
- the right to refugee status under the Refugee Convention;
- the right to remain under the ECHR;
- considerations which would be relevant to the grant of leave to remain for humanitarian reasons.

(ii) In considering whether internal relocation was reasonable, the comparison to be made was between conditions in the asylum applicant's home area and the area to which relocation would take place; not between conditions in the United Kingdom and the area of relocation.

Burden of proof

The Court of Appeal in *Karanakaran v Secretary of State for the Home Department* [2000] 3 All ER 449 held that in considering the reasonableness of internal flight, no question of burden or standard of proof arose:

> 'The question is simply whether, taking all relevant matters into account, it would be unduly harsh to return the applicant . . . '

CONVENTION REASON

The final element of the claim is that the persecution would be for one or more of the reasons of race, religion, nationality, membership of a particular social group or political opinion. In *Applicant A* (1997) 190 CLR 225 the High Court of Australia pointed out:

> '. . . by incorporating the five Convention reasons the Convention plainly contemplates that there will even be persons fearing persecution who will not be able to gain asylum as refugees.'

However, the UNHCR Handbook at paragraphs 66 and 67 recognises that it would be unrealistic and unfair to require too high a degree of precision in the identification of the Convention reason(s):

> 'It is immaterial whether the persecution arises from any single one of these reasons or from a combination of two or more of them. Often the applicant himself may not be aware of the reasons for the persecution feared. It is not, however, his duty to analyse his case to such an extent as to identify the reasons in detail.
> . . . It is evident that the reasons for persecution under these various headings will frequently overlap. Usually there will be more than one element combined in one person, eg a political opponent who belongs to a religious or national group or both, and the combination of such reasons in his person may be relevant in evaluating his well-founded fear.'

It is thus recognised that although persecution must be for one of the five Convention reasons, it need not be solely for such reason but may include a mixture of reasons and motives for those reasons. The House of Lords in *R (on the application of Sivokumar) v Secretary of State for the Home Department* [2003] UKHL 14, [2003] 1 WLR 840 decided:

> 'So long as the decision-maker is satisfied that one of the reasons why the persecutor ill-treated the applicant was a Convention reason and the applicant's reasonable fear relates to persecution for that reason, that will be sufficient. Ex hypothesi any such reason will be an operative reason for the persecution . . .'

In *Sepet v Secretary of State for the Home Department* [2003] UKHL 15, [2003] 1 WLR 856, the House of Lords stated that the Convention reason:

> '. . . is the reason which operates in the mind of the persecutor and not the reason which the victim believes to be the reason for the persecution . . . there may be more than one real reason. The application of the test calls for the exercise of an objective judgement. Decision-makers are not concerned . . . to explore the motives or purposes of those who have committed or may commit acts of persecution, nor the belief of the victim as to those motives or purposes . . .'

It was further stated in *Sepet and Bulbul* that even where the persecution is for reasons which do not in fact apply to the victim, the belief of the persecutor is nevertheless still the key:

> '. . . where the reason for the persecution is or may be the imputation by the persecutors of a particular belief or opinion (or, for that matter, the attribution of a racial origin or nationality or membership of a particular social group) one is concerned not with the correctness of the matter imputed or attributed but with the belief of the persecutor: the real reason for the persecution of a victim may be the persecutor's belief that he holds extreme political opinions or adheres to a particular faith even if in truth the victim does not hold those opinions or belong to that faith.'

In *Montoya* [2002] INLR 399 the Court of Appeal held that the Tribunal were correct to concentrate not on the political beliefs of the persecutors but on their perception of the appellant's political beliefs.

Race

Race is perhaps the most common basis for discrimination and it is therefore unsurprising to find it as the first of the Convention reasons. The UNHCR Handbook at paragraph 68 encourages a purposive interpretation of race:

> '. . . to include all kinds of ethnic groups that are referred to as "races" in common usage. Frequently it will also entail membership of a specific social group of common descent forming a minority within a larger population. Discrimination for reasons of race has found world-wide condemnation as one of the most striking violations of human rights. Racial discrimination, therefore, represents an important element in determining the existence of persecution.'

Paragraph 69 recognises that:

> 'Discrimination on racial grounds will frequently amount to persecution in the sense of the 1951 Convention. This will be the case if, as a result of racial discrimination, a person's human dignity is affected to such an extent as to be incompatible with the most elementary and inalienable human rights, or where the disregard of racial barriers is subject to serious consequences.'

Paragraph 70 states that mere membership of a racial group will not in itself be sufficient to make out a claim under the Convention, unless the group is affected by particular circumstances.

We would also suggest that 'race' must cover individuals of mixed ethnicity, a feature for example in many asylum claims arising out of the Ethiopia–Eritrea conflict, where the polarisation of the two countries on ethnic lines resulted in mass deportations from both sides not only of citizens of Eritrean or Ethiopian birth but also those of or perceived as being of mixed parentage.

Religion

Historically, much persecution and repression has been on religious grounds. The UNHCR Handbook at paragraph 71 emphasises that:

> 'The Universal Declaration of Human Rights and the Human Rights Covenant proclaim the right to freedom of thought, conscience and religion, which right includes the freedom of a person to change his religion and his freedom to manifest it in public or private, in teaching, practice, worship and observance.'

Paragraph 72 states that persecution:

> '. . . may assume various forms, eg prohibition of membership of a religious community, of worship in private or in public, of religious instruction, or serious measures of discrimination imposed on persons because they practise their religion or belong to a particular religious community.'

Paragraph 73 points out that that mere membership of a particular religious community will not normally be sufficient to qualify an individual as a refugee. In practice, the majority of cases will concern either severe discrimination against followers of a particular religion or sect so as to amount to persecution, or else punishment for conversion or proselytisation.

Nationality

Nationality as a Convention reason is not used in its traditionally limited sense, as the UNHCR Handbook makes clear at paragraph 74:

> '. . . "nationality" in this context is not to be understood only as "citizenship". It refers also to membership of an ethnic or linguistic group and may occasionally overlap with the term "race". Persecution for reasons of nationality may consist of adverse attitudes and measures directed against a national (ethnic, linguistic) minority and in certain circumstances the fact of belonging to such a minority may in itself give rise to a well-founded fear of persecution.'

Paragraph 75 illustrates this by reference to situations of conflict between ethnic/linguistic groups within the territory of the same state and suggesting that where such conflict also involves political movements:

> 'It may not always be easy to distinguish between persecution for reasons of nationality and persecution for reasons of political opinion . . .'

Paragraph 76 makes the valid point that although persecution on grounds of nationality is most likely to be feared by a national minority, it may also be feared by a majority group in a country where there is a dominant minority, eg holding the key positions in government.

Particular social group

Inevitably this Convention reason is relied on when a claim does not satisfy the other more clear-cut reasons. Consequently 'particular social group' has been the most-litigated Convention reason. The authorities make clear that this is not a 'catch-all' for those who do not fall into any of the other categories.

The UNHCR Handbook at paragraph 77 offers a broad definition of particular social group:

> '. . . normally comprises of persons of similar background, habits or social status. A claim to fear of persecution under this heading may frequently overlap with a claim to fear of persecution on other grounds, ie race, religion or nationality.'

Paragraph 78 suggests that:

> 'Membership of such a particular social group may be at the root of persecution because there is no confidence in the group's loyalty to the Government or because of the political outlook, antecedents or economic activity of its members, or the very existence of the social group as such, is held to be an obstacle to the Government's policies.'

Paragraph 79 states that unless there are special circumstances mere membership of a particular social group will not justify refugee status.

The unifying feature of all the Convention reasons is recognition of and protection against discrimination. This is particularly apparent in the courts' approach to what can and cannot constitute a 'particular social group'. The United States Board of Immigration Appeals decided in *Re Acosta* (1985) 19 I & N 211 that the members of a social group must share:

> '. . . an immutable characteristic . . . that either is beyond the power of an individual to change or that is so fundamental to his identity or conscience that it ought not to be required to be changed.'

The Convention's stance against discrimination equally requires that the group must be capable of being identified other than merely by reference to the suffering of persecution: *Secretary of State for the Home Department v Savchenkov* [1996] Imm AR 28. It was also thought that the group must possess a degree of 'cohesiveness' or 'common impulse'.

All of these issues were extensively reviewed in *Islam v Secretary of State for the Home Department, R v Immigration Appeal Tribunal, ex p Shah* [1999] 2 AC 629 by the House of Lords. In this case it was not disputed that the two women faced persecution in Pakistan from their husbands and that there would not be protection from the police or from the courts. The question was whether this would be persecution for the Convention reason of particular social group. It was held:

(i) That women in Pakistan constituted a particular social group because the human rights reports showed that in general women in that country faced many forms of discrimination, particularly in matters of sexual conduct and access to justice and this was clearly contrary to the principles of equal treatment and respect recognised by the Refugee Convention.
(ii) There was no requirement of interdependence or cohesiveness for a particular social group.
(iii) Although not all women in Pakistan feared persecution there was no need to define the social group in this case in narrower terms: the persecution feared by the appellants on a personal level became persecution for a Convention reason as it was because they were women that the state was unable or unwilling to protect them.

What is very clear from *Shah* and *Islam* is that whether or not a group of people who share a common characteristic are to be considered a particular social group within the meaning of the Convention will be dependant on the facts of the case, not least the characteristics of the individual; the nature of the group as a whole; their individual and shared experiences; and attitudes towards them by the persecutor and the authorities. Although cohesiveness is not a requirement it can still of course help prove the existence of a particular social group. A perception of membership of such a group would be sufficient to make out a Convention reason.

The other interesting feature of this case is that the Convention reason emanated not from the persecutors but from the lack of protection by the state. This underlines the importance of both considering each element of a claim sequentially at first and then cumulatively in the final analysis.

In *Skenderaj v Secretary of State for the Home Department* [2002] EWCA Civ 567, [2002] INLR 323 the Court of Appeal held that where the persecutors were non-state agents, discrimination was not a necessary ingredient to establishing a particular social group.

Political opinion or imputed political opinion

In common with religion, this Convention reason recognises the importance of freedom of expression. Whereas religion is concerned with the holding and expression of spiritual beliefs, political opinion covers views and acts pertaining to government and society at large. The UNHCR Handbook sets out the following principles at paragraphs 80–86:

(i) Having political opinions is not sufficient to make out a claim for Refugee status. The applicant must hold views which are critical of the powers that be and are not tolerated by them. The applicant must also have come to the attention of the authorities. This may depend on the profile of the applicant and the strength of his opinions.

(ii) Adverse measures by the state are rarely on the basis of 'opinion' but rather alleged criminal acts committed against the state. This requires the decision-maker to examine whether political opinion is at the root of the applicant's acts.

(iii) There may be cases in which the individual has not yet expressed his political views or come to the attention of the authorities, but where this is likely to occur sooner or later. If so, there is a fear of persecution for reasons of political opinion.

(iv) Likewise, it is not necessary for an applicant to show that the authorities were aware of his opinions before he fled. The simple act of refusing to seek state protection or to return to his country may reveal his political views and result in persecution. This consideration particularly arises with the refugee 'sur place'.

(v) In cases of prosecution there must be a consideration of whether the prosecution is for a political opinion or a politically-motivated act. If the latter and the act is punishable under the criminal law, such prosecution is not in itself persecution.

(vi) However, prosecution may be an excuse to punish the individual for his political views. Excessive or arbitrary punishment will amount to persecution. (In *R (on the application of Sivakumar) v Secretary of State for the Home Department* [2003] UKHL 14, [2003] 1 WLR 840, the House of Lords held that the phrase 'will amount to persecution' is too strong and that 'may' should be substituted for 'will'.)

By including the reason of 'imputed' political opinion the Convention also protects those who their persecutors perceive, whether rightly or wrongly, to hold particular political beliefs. There has been much debate on the issue of what kinds of views can be recognised as 'political' within the meaning of the Convention. In cases of persecution by the state or its agents, a government seeking to quell those it perceives to be critical of or in opposition to its policies or activities will almost inevitably be imputing political opinion.

The 'starred' Tribunal decision of *Gomez* [2000] INLR 549 considered the position of non-state actors. The Tribunal commented:

> '. . . one cannot easily see how differences they may have with someone they persecute could be described as political unless they themselves have or express a political ideology or set of political objectives, i.e. views which have a bearing on the major power transactions relating to government taking place in a particular society. That is to say, the Tribunal doubts that the Refugee Convention ground of political opinion was meant to cover power-relationships at all levels of society. It may well make sense to speak in other contexts of the "politics of the family" or of "sexual politics" taking place

> between two persons, but to engage the Convention these power relationships must in some way link up to major power transactions that take place in government-related sectors such as industry and the media. Put another way, politics at the "micro" level must in some meaningful way relate to politics at the "macro" level.'

The Tribunal further pointed out:

> 'As well as the need to adopt a broad definition of the term "political" there is also a need to recognise that the term is a malleable one. In the nature of politics, the boundaries between the political and the non-political shift in historical time and place . . . the nature of the power relationships and transactions that compose what is political vary from society to society. Sometimes political opinion may be located in a particular type of expression or activity, e.g. wearing western clothes in a highly fundamentalist Muslim country with strict social mores; sometimes not. In society A where trade unions adopt a combative posture towards the government, membership of a trade union may be tantamount to holding a political opinion; in society B it may not be so. The risk of extortion threats from a criminal gang will not normally be on account of political opinion, but in some societies where criminal and political activities heavily overlap, the picture may be different. Persons who hold posts in governmental agencies of the state at central or local level will not normally be capable of having political opinions attributed to them by groups opposed to the government. But if for example there is a major armed conflict going on between the authorities and guerrilla groups (e.g. Islamic fundamentalists in Algeria in the 1990s) then it may be that they will have attributed to them the political opinion of being on the government's side rather than the fundamentalist Islamic side (*Doufani* (14798); see also *Woldemichael* (17663)).'

The Tribunal warned against determining such context-specific issues by reference to fixed distinctions between for example 'political' and 'criminal', 'political' and 'economic' or 'political' and 'personal'. In certain circumstances even 'neutrality' could constitute political opinion.

OTHER EXAMPLES OF REFUGEE CLAIMS

Refugees 'sur place'

The UNHCR Handbook at paragraphs 94, 95 and 96 recognises that refugee status should be conferred upon those who did not leave their country in fear of persecution but who later have reason to fear return. A refugee 'sur place' is therefore one who has a well-founded fear of returning to their state based on events after their departure. A classic example would be where an individual comes to the United Kingdom and is granted leave to enter for the purposes of a visit or to study and during that period of leave there is a military coup in their home country, in the course of which their family members are detained and killed.

Acts committed outside the home country

The activities of an individual which have been carried out since leaving their home, even if done in bad faith, do not preclude them from the protection of the Convention: *Danian v Secretary of State for the Home Department* [2000] Imm AR 96, CA. This is in accordance with the principle that in all cases there must be an evaluation of future risk. Clearly account may also be taken of any acts the applicant may undertake when returned.

Intention to commit acts on return

In *Ahmed v Secretary of State for the Home Department* [2000] INLR 1 the Court of Appeal held:

> 'In all asylum cases there is ultimately but a single question to be asked: is there a serious risk that on return the applicant would be persecuted for a Convention reason? . . . if returned, would the asylum seeker in fact act in the way he says he would and thereby suffer persecution? If he would, then, however unreasonable he might be thought for refusing to accept the necessary restraint on his liberties, in my judgement he would be entitled to asylum.'

Military Service

In *Fadli* [2001] INLR 168 the Court of Appeal held that the Refugee Convention does not confer the status of refugee on a soldier who has a well-founded fear of terrorist attacks against him whilst off-duty. The state would otherwise be unable to provide the very protection for the generality of its citizens which the Convention assumes that it should undertake.

It will normally be argued by the Home Office that refusal to perform military service cannot lead to a finding of persecution because it is the legitimate right of the state to require and enforce compulsory service. In *Sepet v Secretary of the State for the Home Department* [2003] UKHL 15, [2003] 1 WLR 856, it was confirmed that: 'In general the state does have the right to impose upon its citizens an obligation to kill people in war.' The appellants in that case were both Turkish Kurds who claimed asylum on the basis that their objections to military service based on their opposition to the policies of the Turkish government, and consequentially, imprisonment under Turkish military law, would amount to persecution for a Convention reason. The House of Lords held that objection to military service for absolute or partial conscientious reasons did not of itself give rise to a valid claim for refugee status.

However, it was recognised in this decision that there were exceptions to that general rule:

> 'There is compelling support for the view that refugee status should be accorded to one who has refused to undertake compulsory military service on the grounds that such service would or might require him to commit atrocities or gross human rights abuses or participate in a conflict condemned by the international community, or where refusal to serve would earn grossly excessive or disproportionate punishment.'

Failed asylum seekers

There may be circumstances in which the very act of return as a failed asylum seeker to a country will place the appellant in danger. This could be because either it could be known that the applicant claimed asylum abroad and this is regarded with hostility by the authorities, or the regime's human rights record is such that there is a risk that any returnee could be ill-treated: see *M v Secretary of State for the Home Department* [1996] 1 WLR 507, CA.

EXCLUSION FROM THE REFUGEE CONVENTION

Protection not required

Article 1(D) of the Refugee Convention states:

> 'This Convention shall not apply to persons who are at present receiving from organs or agencies of the United Nations other than the United Nations High Commissioner for Refugees protection or assistance.'

Article 1(E) of the Refugee Convention states:

> 'This Convention shall not apply to a person who is recognised by the competent authorities of a country in which he has taken residence as having the rights and obligations which are attached to the possession of the nationality of that country.'

Exclusion by reason of criminal acts

Article 1(F) of the Refugee Convention states:

> 'The provisions of this Convention shall not apply to any person with respect to whom there are serious reasons for considering that:
>
> (a) He has committed a crime against peace, a war crime, or a crime against humanity, as defined in the international instruments drawn up to make provision in respect of such crimes;
>
> (b) He has committed a serious non-political crime outside the country of refuge prior to his admission to that country as a refugee;
>
> (c) He has been guilty of acts contrary to the purposes and principles of the United Nations.'

In *T v Immigration Officer* [1996] AC 742, the House of Lords delivered a restrictive definition of 'political crime' as having to satisfy two requirements: firstly, that the crime was committed for a political purpose namely to overthrow, subvert, or change the government, or to induce it to change its policy (the last being clearly broad); secondly, that there must be a sufficiently close and direct link between the crime and the political purpose. In considering this, the Court would look to the means used, whether the target was military or government or civilian, and in any event whether indiscriminate killing or injury of civilians would have occurred.

In *Gurung v Secretary of State for the Home Department* [2003] Imm AR 115, the Tribunal gave the following points of guidance on the exclusion clauses:

(i) That the exclusion clauses are to be applied restrictively with a focus on past criminal conduct.

(ii) It is for the adjudicator to make specific findings of fact concerning the act or acts that potentially exclude the appellant from the Refugee Convention, and then to explain into which sub-category those events fall. The burden of showing exclusion falls on the Home Office, and the standard of proof namely 'serious reasons for considering', is lower than the balance of probabilities.

(iii) In relation to Article 1(F)(b) the principles in *T* remain valid. Whether or not membership of an organisation would show complicity in proscribed acts will depend on the circumstances, including the organisation's role in society and the individual's role in that organisation. The more frequently the organisation was known to commit terrorism, the more likely that voluntary membership would amount to complicity.

(iv) Where the appellant has personally committed a serious crime such as murder, Article 1(F) is clearly engaged. However, the issue can also arise where an appellant has been a member of an organisation involved in armed struggle:

- Mere membership of such an organisation may not be enough in itself to bring the appellant within the exclusion clauses; personal participation however, in acts contrary to those covered by Article 1(F) is not necessary either. If the organisation is one whose aims and activities are predominantly terrorist in character 'very little more will be necessary'. Where the organisation engages in both political and violent activities, the assessment is more complex.

- The Tribunal have adopted the principle recognised in other jurisdictions that the exclusion clause should also encompass those who provide the physical and logistical support that enables terrorist groups to operate.
- Whilst complicity may arise indirectly it remains essential in all cases that the appellant is a voluntary member of the organisation who fully understands its aims, methods and activities, including any plans to carry out acts contrary to Article 1(F).
- From the above it is clear that in considering an issue of complicity for acts contrary to Article 1(F) both an objective and subjective test needs to be satisfied.

(v) The exclusion clauses are mandatory. Even if the Home Office has not raised exclusion issues, adjudicators were under a duty to consider them where they were obvious, subject to the requirements of procedural fairness.

(vi) It would only be appropriate to determine an exclusion point as a preliminary issue where the evidence strongly pointed to the appellant falling within article 1(F), otherwise the hearing should cover all issues.

(vii) If Article 1(F) is found to apply, adjudicators should only consider the inclusion clause issues when the decision to exclude is finely balanced. However, it will still be necessary to separately consider Article 3, which is absolute in nature.

(viii) Notwithstanding the above the Home Office in considering an asylum claim at first instance should consider both exclusion and inclusion in the decision and give reasons for both in the Refusal Letter.

Clearly, the issue of exclusion under Article 1(F) gives rise to complex questions on which the jurisprudence is still developing.

NATIONAL SECURITY ISSUES

Occasionally, asylum claims may raise what can loosely be termed 'national security' issues. These may arise either during the determination process itself, or after an individual has been recognised as a refugee and granted status in the United Kingdom.

Article 32(2) of the Refugee Convention states:

> 'The expulsion of . . . a refugee shall be only in pursuance of a decision reached in accordance with due process of law. Except where compelling reasons of national security otherwise require, the Refugee shall be allowed to submit evidence to clear himself, and to appeal to and be represented for the purpose before the competent authority or a person or persons specially designated by the competent authority.'

Article 33(2) states:

> 'The benefit of the present provision [the prohibition on refoulement] may not, however, be claimed by a refugee whom there are reasonable grounds for regarding as a danger to the security of the country in which he is, or who, having been convicted by a final judgment of a particularly serious crime, constitutes a danger to the community of that country.'

In respect of Article 33(2), s 72(2) of the 2002 Act states:

> 'A person shall be presumed to have been convicted by a final judgment of a particularly serious crime and to constitute a danger to the community of the United Kingdom if he is—
> (a) convicted in the United Kingdom of an offence, and
> (b) sentenced to a period of imprisonment of at least two years.'

Section 72(3) and (4) of the 2002 Act create the same rebuttable presumption in respect of those receiving equivalent convictions and sentences outside the United Kingdom and those convicted of offences specified or certified by the Secretary of State, whether committed inside or outside the United Kingdom.

Section 23 of the Anti-Terrorism, Crime and Security Act 2001 (the 2001 Act), in conjunction with the Human Rights Act 1998 (Designated Derogation) Order 2001 (by which the United Kingdom derogated from Article 5(1)(f) of the ECHR), provides for the detention of foreign nationals who have been certified as a threat to national security and who are suspected of being international terrorists, where their removal is not for the time being possible. In *A and X v Secretary of State for the Home Department* [2002] EWCA Civ 1502, [2003] 1 All ER 816, the Court of Appeal held that insofar as these measures authorised only the detention of foreign nationals and not British nationals suspected of terrorism, this was not discriminatory so as to breach Article 14 of the ECHR. Non-nationals were not in an analogous situation to British nationals, in that they did not have a right to remain, only a right not to be removed. International law permitted states to distinguish between nationals and foreign nationals, especially in times of emergency.

Other provisions of the 2001 Act permit the substantive consideration of asylum claims of suspected terrorists to be dispensed with, where the Secretary of State certifies that their removal would be conducive to the public good and not in breach of the Refugee Convention. The 2001 Act also allows for the retention of fingerprints taken as part of an asylum claim for ten years, so as to help prevent applicants creating multiple identities for the perpetration of terrorism or serious crime.

Section 4 of the 2002 Nationality, Immigration and Asylum Act empowers the Secretary of State to deprive an individual of British citizenship where satisfied that they have done 'anything seriously prejudicial to the vital interests of the United Kingdom or a British overseas territory'.

If the Home Office raise a national security issue, then the normal asylum procedures are very unlikely to apply. Any decision by the Home Office in respect of such issues will not usually be dealt with by the Immigration Appellate Authority, but by the Special Immigration Appeals Commission (SIAC), in respect of which there are specialised procedures which will not be dealt with in this book.

CESSATION

Article 1(C) of the Refugee Convention sets out circumstances in which persons cease to qualify for international protection: voluntary re-availment of protection from the country of nationality; voluntary re-aquisition of old nationality; acquisition of new nationality and protection from that country; voluntary re-establishment in the country where persecution was feared; change in circumstances giving rise to recognition as a refugee.

Paragraph 135 of the UNHCR Handbook states that:

> ' "Circumstances" refer to fundamental changes in that country, which can be assumed to remove the basis of the fear of persecution. A mere – possibly transitory – change in the facts surrounding the individual refugee's fear, which does not entail such major changes of circumstances, is not sufficient to make this clause applicable. A refugee's status should not in principle be subject to frequent review to the detriment of his sense of security.'

This principle was approved in *Arif v Secretary of State for the Home Department* [1999] INLR 327. The Court of Appeal held that where it was accepted that but for delay in processing the application an appellant would have qualified as a refugee, the burden shifted to the Home Office to show that there was a sufficiently fundamental and durable change in circumstances in the home country so that the appellant would no longer be entitled to asylum.

In more recent cases such as *Canaj v Secretary of State for the Home Department* and *Vallaj v Special Adjudicator* [2001] EWCA Civ 782, [2002] INLR 342, the Court of Appeal has limited the effect of *Arif* to cases where it was accepted that the appellant had previously qualified as a refugee. In *S* [2002] INLR 416 the Court of Appeal held that the fact that the appellants were refugees at the time they left Croatia could not have a critical effect on the outcome of their appeals and doubted whether there was an evidential burden on the Secretary of State to show that in such cases it was safe to return. In the light of these decisions the principle in *Arif* can perhaps be regarded as another way of posing the question: is there (still) a real risk of persecution?

Similarly, the 'compelling reasons' exception to Article 1(C)(5), described in paragraph 136 of the UNHCR Handbook as 'the humanitarian principle . . . that a person who – or whose family – has suffered under atrocious forms of persecution should not be expected to repatriate', has also been restrictively interpreted to apply only to those who have already been formally recognised as refugees: *R (Hoxha) v Special Adjudicator* [2002] EWCA Civ 1403, [2003] 1 WLR 241.

THE DECISION-MAKING PROCESS

The Court of Appeal held in *Ravichandran v Secretary of State for the Home Department* [1996] Imm AR 97 that:

> '. . . the question whether someone is at risk of persecution for a Convention reason should be looked at in the round and all the relevant circumstances brought into account. I know of no authority inconsistent with such an approach and, to my mind, it clearly accords both with paragraph 51 of the UNHCR Handbook and with the spirit of the Convention.'

It was further decided by the Court of Appeal in *Ravichandran* that the critical date in any asylum appeal is the date of the hearing itself, rather than the date of the decision under appeal.

In *Karanakaran v Secretary of State for the Home Department* [2000] 3 All ER 449, the Court of Appeal gave invaluable guidance on the correct approach to determining an asylum claim:

> 'The issues for a decision-maker under the Convention (whether the decision-maker is a Home Office official, a special adjudicator, or the Immigration Appeal Tribunal) are questions not of hard fact but of evaluation: does the applicant have a well-founded fear of persecution for a Convention reason? Is that why he is here? If so, is he nevertheless able to find safety elsewhere in his home country? Into all of these, of course, a mass of factual questions enters: What has happened to the applicant? What happens to others like him or her? Is the situation the same as when he or she fled? Are there safer parts of the country? Is it feasible for the applicant to live there? Inseparable from these are questions of evaluation: Did what happened to the applicant amount to persecution? If so, what was the reason for it? Does what has been happening to others shed light on the applicant's fear? Is the home situation now better or worse? How safe are the safer places? Is it unduly harsh to expect the applicant to survive in a new and strange place . . . ?
> Such decision-makers, on classic principles of public law, are required to take everything material into account. Their sources of information will frequently go well beyond the testimony of the applicant and include in-country reports, expert testimony and – sometimes – specialist knowledge of their own (which must of course be disclosed). No probabilistic cut-off operates here: everything capable of having a bearing has to be given the weight, great or little, due to it.

What the decision-makers ultimately make of the material is a matter for their own conscientious judgement, so long as the procedure by which they approach and entertain it is lawful and fair, and provided their decision logically addresses the Convention issues. Finally, and importantly, the Convention issues from first to last are evaluative, not factual. The facts, so far as they can be established, are signposts on the road to a conclusion on the issues: they are not themselves conclusions.'

The Court of Appeal in *R (on the application of Sivakumar) v Immigration Appeal Tribunal* [2001] EWCA Civ 1196, [2001] INLR 310 emphasised the importance of not employing too rigid an approach:

> 'The evaluation of the material facts must not be compartmentalised. It is necessary to consider the cumulative effect of the relevant factors.'

CREDIBILITY

Refugee status must be determined on an individual basis, each case being assessed on its own merits and an applicant must show that he individually fears persecution. Credibility cannot be assessed without placing the claim into the context of the background information of the country of origin and a complete understanding of the whole picture. Professor Hathaway has stated that the fact-finding tribunal should be cautious in rejecting as incredible an account by an anxious asylum applicant, whose reasons for seeking asylum may well be expected to contain inconsistencies and omissions.

Paragraph 196 of the UNHCR Handbook states:

> 'Often, however, an applicant may not be able to support his statements by documentary evidence or proof, and cases in which an applicant provides evidence or statements will be the exception rather than the rule. In most cases a person fleeing from persecution will have arrived with the barest necessities and very frequently even without personal documents. Thus, while the burden of proof in principle rests on the applicant, the duty to ascertain and evaluate all the relevant facts is shared between the appellant and the examiner. Indeed in

> some cases, it may be for the examiner to use all the means at his disposal to produce the necessary evidence in support of the application. Even such independent research may not, however, always be successful and there may also be statements that are not susceptible of proof. In such cases, if the applicant's account appears credible, he should, unless there are good reasons to the contrary, be given the benefit of the doubt.'

In *Serban* (IAT) (11771) the Tribunal emphasised that an adverse finding as to credibility should not be based solely on a lack of substantiation.

In the case of *Kasolo* (IAT) (13190) the Tribunal warned of the inherent difficulties in assessing credibility in a 'cross-cultural situation', stating that:

> 'English judges are poorly equipped to judge how a reasonable person from a different country would act in a given situation, let alone one giving evidence through an interpreter.'

In *Muhammad Hussain* (CO/990/1995) the High Court stated:

> 'Credibility is not in itself a valid end to the function of the Adjudicator . . . over-emphasis on the issue of credibility may distort the findings of an Adjudicator.'

It has been suggested that the proper approach is to first consider the account and see whether if it were true the appeal would succeed, and then to proceed to examine it against the background of the country in question. In the case of *Matinkima* (IAT) (14426) the Tribunal rejected the view that credibility is indispensable in asylum appeals, stating that the natural corollary would then be that once an application is not found to be credible, the appeal must be dismissed.

In *R v Secretary of State for the Home Department, ex p Kingori* [1994] Imm AR 539, CA, it was held that once an adjudicator has concluded that an appellant has not been credible, the standard of proof to be applied to determine whether the appellant had a well-founded fear of persecution becomes irrelevant. In *R v Immigration Appeal Tribunal, ex p Ramirez-Espana* [1996] Imm AR 329,

Kingori was confirmed as being applied to cases where the adjudicator 'comprehensively disbelieves' an appellant upon matters material to his asylum claim and not in other cases. The problem with this is that it is understood by the case law that the important issue of credibility is to be assessed in light of the objective country evidence and not in isolation from it. A further difficulty with *Kingori* is that, as decided in *Ravichandran v Secretary of State for the Home Department* [1996] Imm AR 97, CA, an asylum claim is to be considered taking into account all relevant considerations.

In *Kaja v Secretary of State for the Home Department* [1995] Imm AR 1 further guidance was offered on the approach to the evidence. Adjudicators must decide and distinguish between:

(i) evidence they are certain about;
(ii) evidence they think is probably true;
(iii) evidence to which they attach some credence even if they could not go so far as saying it is probably true;
(iv) evidence to which they are not willing to attach any credence.

The Tribunal importantly stated in *Chiver* [1997] INLR 212 that it is perfectly possible for an adjudicator to believe that the appellant is not telling the truth about some matters, has exaggerated the story to make his case better, or is simply uncertain about matters, but still to be persuaded that the centre-piece of the story stands.

It is also worth considering the factors which the Home Office take into account when initially considering an applicant's credibility. Paragraphs 340–342 of the Immigration Rules set out the factors which may be taken to damage an applicant's credibility and lead to the claim being refused. In summary, they are:

- a failure to make prompt and full disclosure of material facts, without reasonable explanation, to assist the Secretary of State in establishing the facts;
- that there has not been an immediate application for asylum on arrival without reasonable explanation;
- that the application was made after the applicant was refused leave to enter, or was otherwise likely to be deported;
- that the applicant has produced manifestly false evidence or has made false representations;
- that the applicant failed without reasonable explanation to produce a passport which was valid or produced an invalid passport and failed to inform an immigration officer that it

was invalid; where the applicant has without reasonable explanation destroyed their passport or other relevant document;
- that the applicant has undertaken activities in the United Kingdom either prior to or after lodging their claim which are inconsistent with their previous beliefs and which are intended either to create or enhance their claim;
- that the applicant has lodged concurrent applications either in the United Kingdom or abroad;
- the actions of anyone acting as an agent of the applicant may also be taken into account.

It is important to note that these points are *not* mandatory and all the evidence must be considered in the round. There may well be good reasons or explanations for an applicant's behaviour.

In *R v Uxbridge Magistrates Court, ex p Adimi* [1999] INLR 490 the Court of Appeal held that Article 31(1) of the Refugee Convention precluded states from imposing penalties on refugees who came directly from territories where they are persecuted, on account of their illegal entry or their production of false documents or delay where this could be attributed to a genuine desire to seek asylum.

The Court considered the issue of direct travel and held that some element of choice was available to an asylum seeker. The court will however look at the length of time and the reason for staying in the intermediate country. Similarly the court will look at the length of time spent in this country if there has not been a claim made on arrival. Again the important thing is if there has been illegal entry, how long the delay was before claiming asylum. One who waits a long period of time before making a claim and without what must be very good reason is bound to have their credibility damaged.

Inconsistencies due to fear and trauma

The UNHCR Handbook at paragraph 198 states:

> 'A person who, because of his experiences, was in fear of the authorities in his own country may still feel apprehensive vis-à-vis any authority. He may therefore be afraid to speak freely and give a full and accurate account of his case.'

In *Alan v Switzerland* [1997] INLR 29 the European Court stated:

> 'The State party has pointed to contradictions and inconsistencies in the author's story, but the Committee considers that complete accuracy is seldom to be expected by victims of torture and that the inconsistencies as exist in the author's presentation of the facts do not raise doubts about the general veracity of his claims, especially since it has been demonstrated the author suffers from Post traumatic Stress Disorder.'

Relevance of past persecution

In its 'Joint Position' the Council of the European Union adopted guidelines for the application of Article 1 of the Convention. Paragraph 3 reads:

> 'The fact that an individual has already been subject to persecution or to direct threats of persecution is a very serious indication of the risk of persecution, unless a radical change of conditions has taken place since then in his country of origin or in his relations with his country of origin.'

Similarly, in *Demirkaya v Secretary of State for the Home Department* [1999] INLR 441, CA, the Court of Appeal stated:

> 'Where evidence of past maltreatment exists, however, it is unquestionably an excellent indicator of the fate that may await an applicant upon return to her home. Unless there has been a major change in circumstances within that country that makes prospective persecution unlikely, past experience under a particular regime should be considered probative of future risk.'

In *Adan v Secretary of State for the Home Department* [1999] 1 AC 293, it was further added that:

> '. . . historic fear . . . may well provide evidence to establish present fear. But it is the existence or otherwise, of present fear which is determinative.'

It was pointed out in *Noune v Secretary of State for the Home Department* [2001] INLR 526 that it was never necessary to have actually suffered harm in the past.

CHAPTER 2

Human Rights Law

In this chapter we discuss the alternative or additional legal regime to the Refugee Convention: making a claim under the European Convention on Human Rights. The similarities and differences between asylum and human rights claims will also be outlined where appropriate.

THE EUROPEAN CONVENTION ON HUMAN RIGHTS

The well-documented atrocities of the Second World War forced the international community to look at ways of protecting fundamental rights and of preventing their violation on such a scale from ever occurring again. This resulted in a number of human rights treaties, including the Universal Declaration of Human Rights adopted by the General Assembly of the United Nations in 1948.

As part of the same human rights advance, the then ten member states of the Council of Europe drafted and adopted the European Convention on Human Rights in 1950. A notable feature of the ECHR, through the establishment of the European Commission of Human Rights in 1954 and the European Court of Human Rights itself in 1959, is that it can be enforced by individual citizens of signatory states petitioning those institutions in Strasbourg.

Since then a vast body of jurisprudence on the applicability and content of the ECHR rights has steadily built up, in the form of full judgments of the European Court, as well as other decisions such as the admissibility of cases, which were formerly made by the Commission but are now taken by the Court. Although the text of the ECHR embodies the minimum human rights standards that could be agreed between the member states at that time, a theme running throughout the subsequent jurisprudence is the recognition that the ECHR must be a 'living instrument', to be interpreted in the light of modern-day society and its constantly progressing notions of human dignity and worth.

Prior to its incorporation, however, use of the ECHR in English courts was fairly limited, for example to the interpretation of statute where ambiguous. Individuals claiming that the government had acted in breach of its human rights were generally left to exercise their right of petition. The practice of 'taking a case to Strasbourg' was arduous, expensive and extremely time-consuming, with complaints that were accepted as admissible taking several or many years before the European Court considered the case and gave judgment. Lawyers, commentators and campaigners long pointed out that forcing its citizens to resort to this process was hardly the best way for the United Kingdom, one of the original signatory states, to honour its commitments under the ECHR.

THE HUMAN RIGHTS ACT 1998

The Human Rights Act 1998, which came into force on the 2 October 2000, finally incorporated the ECHR into domestic law. The Act describes itself as 'An Act to give further effect to rights and freedoms guaranteed under the European Convention on Human Rights' and is of great constitutional significance, placing the task of protecting human rights between parliament and the judiciary.

The incorporated rights

Section 1 lists 'the Convention rights' which are made part of domestic law, namely Articles 2-12 and 14 of the ECHR, Articles 1-3 of the First Protocol and Articles 1 and 2 of the Sixth Protocol.

Obligation to take account of Strasbourg jurisprudence

Section 2(1) states:

> 'A court or tribunal determining a question which has arisen in connection with a Convention right must take into account any–
> (a) judgement, decision, declaration or advisory opinion of the European Court of Human Rights,
> (b) opinion of the Commission given in a report adopted under Article 31 of the Convention,

(c) decision of the Commission in connection with Article 26 or 27(2) of the Convention, or
(d) decision of the Committee of Ministers taken under Article 46 of the Convention,

whenever made or given, so far as, in the opinion of the court or tribunal, it is relevant to the proceedings in which that question has arisen.'

'Court or tribunal' includes adjudicators sitting in the Immigration Appellate Authority (the IAA), the Immigration Appeal Tribunal (the Tribunal), the High Court, the Court of Appeal and the House of Lords. Although s 2(1) sets out a broad range of decisions of the European Court and the European Commission that must be taken into account if relevant, in practice it is the full judgments of the European Court itself that tend to be most frequently cited. There is no Strasbourg equivalent of the doctrine of binding precedent and the European jurisprudence does not strictly speaking bind the domestic courts. However, in *R (on the application of Anderson) v Secretary of State for the Home Department* [2002] UKHL 46, [2003] 1 AC 837 the House of Lords stated:

> 'While the duty of the House under section 2(1)(a) of the Human Rights Act 1998 is to take into account any judgment of the European Court, whose judgments are not strictly binding, the House will not without good reason depart from the principles laid down in a carefully considered judgment of the court sitting as a Grand Chamber.'

Requirement of compatibility

Section 3 requires:

'(1) So far as it is possible to do so, primary legislation and subordinate legislation must be read and given effect in a way which is compatible with the Convention rights.

(2) This section–
  (a) applies to primary legislation and subordinate legislation whenever enacted;
  (b) does not affect the validity, continuing operation or enforcement of any incompatible primary legislation; and

(c) does not affect the validity, continuing operation or enforcement of any incompatible subordinate legislation if (disregarding any possibility of revocation) primary legislation prevents removal of the incompatibility.'

In the event that legislation cannot be read or given effect in a way which is 'compatible', s 4 provides for the remedy of a declaration of incompatibility. However, this can only be done by the High Court, Court of Appeal or House of Lords. In practice this rarely arises as the higher courts can and will go to great lengths to find an ECHR-compatible interpretation of the offending provision.

Duty on public authorities

In addition to requiring the courts to take account of the ECHR case-law, the Human Rights Act also binds all public authorities to act in accordance with its rights, unless required to act otherwise by incompatible legislation. Section 6 states:

'(1) It is unlawful for a public authority to act in a way which is incompatible with a Convention right.

(2) Subsection (1) does not apply to an act if–

(a) as the result of one or more provisions of primary legislation, the authority could not have acted differently; or

(b) in the case of one or more provisions of, or made under, primary legislation which cannot be read or given effect in a way which is compatible with the Convention rights, the authority was acting so as to give effect to or enforce those provisions.

(3) In this section "public authority" includes–

(a) a court or tribunal, and

(b) any person certain of whose functions are functions of a public nature,but does not include either Houses of Parliament or a person exercising functions in connection with proceedings in Parliament.'

'Public authority' includes not only the Immigration Appellate Authority, but also the Home Office and all those carrying out its functions for example, caseworkers and immigration officers.

Remedies and appeals

Section 7 provides the right of an individual to seek recourse for breach of their human rights:

> '(1) A person who claims that a public authority has acted (or proposes to act) in a way which is made unlawful by section 6(1) may–
> (a) bring proceedings against the authority under this Act in the appropriate court or tribunal, or
> (b) rely on the Convention right or rights concerned in any legal proceedings, but only if he is (or would be) a victim of the unlawful act.'

Although s 7(1) creates a separate cause of action, this will rarely be necessary, as a decision to refuse asylum can also be appealed under s 65 of the Immigration and Asylum Act 1999 (the 1999 Act) on the ground that the individual's removal from the United Kingdom would result in their rights under the ECHR being breached. In *R (Kariharan) v Secretary of State for the Home Department* [2002] EWCA Civ 1102, [2003] QB 933 the Court of Appeal held that removal itself gave rise to the right of appeal under section 65 of the 1999 Act, even when removal was pursuant to a decision that had been made prior to the coming into force of the Human Rights Act. Where the decision was made on or after 1 April 2003, s 82 of the Nationality, Immigration and Asylum Act 2002 (the 2002 Act) gives a right of appeal. However, s 7(1) of the Human Rights Act should not be ignored either. In the recent and important case of *R (on the application of N) v Secretary of State for the Home Department* [2003] EWHC 207 (Admin), a Libyan asylum applicant brought a successful claim against the Home Office for a declaration and damages under s 7(1) of the Human Rights Act, on the basis that their maladministration and delay in granting him refugee status to which he was clearly entitled, had caused him psychiatric illness, thereby breaching Article 8 of the ECHR.

THE SUBSTANTIVE ECHR RIGHTS

Below we look at incorporated rights relevant to immigration decisions. Numerous cases have been decided by the European Court on the interpretation and reach of these rights and we will consider the most important of these, in addition to domestic decisions.

ARTICLE 2 – THE RIGHT TO LIFE

Article 2 provides:

'(1) Everyone's right to life shall be protected by law. No one shall be deprived of his life intentionally save in the execution of a sentence of a court following his conviction of a crime for which the penalty is provided by law.

(2) Deprivation of life shall not be regarded as inflicted in contravention of this Article when it results from the use of force which is no more than absolutely necessary:

(a) in defence of any person from unlawful violence;

(b) in order to effect a lawful arrest or to prevent the escape of a person lawfully detained;

(c) in action lawfully taken for the purpose of quelling a riot or insurrection.'

Article 2 recognises, upholds and protects the sanctity of human life. However, in the context of most immigration cases the reality is that a consideration of a future breach of Article 2 will be subsumed by the evaluation of the risk of a breach of Article 3. For example, an unlawful deprivation of life will almost inevitably also involve either torture, or inhuman or degrading treatment.

ARTICLE 3 – THE PROHIBITION OF TORTURE AND INHUMAN OR DEGRADING TREATMENT OR PUNISHMENT

Article 3 requires that:

'No one shall be subjected to torture or to inhuman or degrading treatment or punishment.'

There are three distinct aspects to Article 3:

(i) The right not to be tortured.

(ii) The right not to be subjected to inhuman treatment or punishment.

(iii) The right not to be subjected to degrading treatment or punishment.

Torture

A definition of torture has already been suggested in Chapter 1. Additionally, torture has been defined by the European Court in *Ireland v United Kingdom* (1978) 2 EHRR 25 as 'deliberate inhuman treatment causing very serious and cruel suffering'. In that case, the Court was considering whether various interrogative techniques to which the security forces in Northern Ireland subjected IRA suspects amounted to torture. The methods were: deprivation of food and water; sleep deprivation; noise disruption; hooding; and wall-standing. The Court accepted that these treatments were inhuman and degrading, but decided that the suffering they caused was not of sufficient intensity to justify the 'special stigma' of being classified as torture.

The European Court has found the stripping, tying up and then suspension of a detainee by the arms to be torture: *Aksoy v Turkey* (1996) 23 EHRR 553. The beating, blindfolding, soaking with high-pressure water and rape of a detainee was held to be torture in *Aydin v Turkey* (1997) 25 EHRR 251. In *Selmouni v France* (1999) 29 EHRR 403 the individual was detained by police for several days, during which he was dragged, beaten, urinated over, raped with a truncheon and threatened with a blowlamp and syringe. In finding that the ill-treatment cumulatively amounted to torture, the Court observed:

> '. . . certain acts which were classified in the past as "inhuman or degrading treatment" as opposed to "torture" could be classified differently in the future . . . the increasingly high standard being required in the area of the protection of human rights and fundamental liberties correspondingly and inevitably requires greater firmness in assessing breaches . . .'

Inhuman treatment

The European Court in *Ireland v United Kingdom* defined inhuman treatment as 'intense physical or mental suffering'. In *Selmouni v France* the Court stated:

> '. . . in respect of a person deprived of his liberty, recourse to physical force which has not been made strictly necessary by

> his own conduct diminishes human dignity and is in principle an infringement of the right set forth in Article 3.'

It was found to be inhuman treatment in *Selcuk and Asker v Turkey* (1998) 26 EHRR 477 for security forces to torch the homes of individuals who were forced to watch as this was done.

Threats to use force may be also be sufficient to engage Article 3. The European Court stated in *Campbell and Cosans v United Kingdom* (1982) 4 EHRR 293:

> '. . . provided it is sufficiently real and immediate, a mere threat of conduct prohibited by Article 3 may itself be in conflict with that provision. Thus, to threaten an individual with torture might in some circumstances constitute at least "inhuman treatment".'

In *Kurt v Turkey* (1998) 27 EHRR 373 the anguish and distress caused to a mother by the authorities' continual failure to investigate the whereabouts of her son, who she believed to have been detained by the security forces, was considered to amount to inhuman treatment.

Degrading treatment

This has been described in the recent case of *Pretty v United Kingdom* (2002) 35 EHRR 1 as treatment which:

> '. . . humiliates or debases an individual showing lack of respect for, or diminishing, his or her human dignity or arouses feelings of fear, anguish or inferiority capable of breaking an individual's moral and physical resistance . . .'

It seems that unlike torture and inhuman treatment, degrading treatment may be subjective, it being sufficient if the individual is 'humiliated in his or her own eyes': *Smith and Grady v United Kingdom* (1999) 29 EHRR 493.

What is the threshold?

However, the case-law makes equally clear that such decisions can only provide guidance in any particular case. As always, it is the facts of the case at hand that are what matter. It was emphasised in *Ireland v United Kingdom* (1978) 2 EHRR 25 that:

(i) ill-treatment must reach a minimum level of severity before it breaches Article 3;
(ii) that minimum threshold will be relative in each case, depending on the circumstances, eg kinds of treatment; its duration; the physical and mental effects; the sex, age and state of health of the individual etc.

The relative nature of the threshold is clearly illustrated by the different approaches the European Court took in two 'corporal punishment' cases. In *Tyrer v United Kingdom* (1978) 2 EHRR 1 it was found that the judicial birching of a 15-year-old boy involving three strokes of the birch, although neither torture nor even inhumane, was nevertheless sufficiently humiliating as to be degrading, given that: it took place several weeks after sentence thereby causing the mental anguish of anticipating the violence he was to have inflicted on him; was carried out by total strangers; and was administered to his bare posterior. On the other hand, in *Costello-Roberts v United Kingdom* (1993) 19 EHRR 112 it was found that the slippering of a 7-year-old boy in private and without any severe after-effects did not breach Article 3.

Absolute nature

Article 3 of the ECHR is expressed in unqualified and absolute terms. This means that once it has been established that the threshold of inhuman or degrading treatment or torture has been reached in a particular case, then a breach has been proved. There is no balancing exercise as with other ECHR rights, and so there cannot be reference to factors such as the prevention of crime or immigration control as 'justification' for the ill-treatment. This is so even when the ill-treatment is a punishment carried out under domestic law: *Tyrer v United Kingdom*.

Application to immigration decisions

Article 3 is of central importance in any asylum claim, the European Court having recognised that the fundamental and absolute nature of Article 3 extends to decisions to remove an individual from the jurisdiction of the signatory state altogether.

In *Soering v United Kingdom* (1989) 11 EHRR 439 it was argued on behalf of a German national that his extradition from the United Kingdom to face trial for capital murder in the United States of America would infringe Article 3, because the decision to expel him could result in him being convicted, sentenced to death and then left to languish on 'death row' for six to eight years. In a landmark judgment the Court stated:

> 'Article 3 makes no provision for exceptions and no derogation from what is permissible under Article 15 in time of war or other national emergency. This absolute prohibition on torture and on inhuman and degrading treatment or punishment under the terms of the Convention shows that Article 3 enshrines one of the fundamental values of democratic societies making up the Council of Europe . . .
>
> . . . It would hardly be compatible with the underlying values of the Convention, that "common heritage of political traditions, ideals, freedom and the rule of law" to which the Preamble refers, were a Contracting State knowingly to surrender a fugitive to another State where there were substantial grounds for believing that he would be in danger of being subjected to torture, however heinous the crime committed. Extradition in such circumstances, while not explicitly referred to in the brief and general wording of Article 3, would plainly be contrary to the spirit and intendment of the Article, and in the Court's view this inherent obligation not to extradite also extends to case in which the fugitive would be faced in the receiving State by a real risk of exposure to inhuman or degrading treatment or punishment.'

Underlying the Court's assessment of the scope of Article 3 was the principle that for a state to knowingly send an individual to a country where he faced ill-treatment was akin to the removing state inflicting the ill-treatment itself. Put another way, removal in such circumstances amounted to facilitating or at best turning a blind eye to what was likely to happen in the receiving state and this was contrary to the principles of the ECHR.

In the later case of *Chahal v United Kingdom* (1996) 23 EHRR 413, it was submitted by the United Kingdom that it was entitled to deport a Sikh separatist leader to India, even if this resulted in him being tortured by the security forces, because his continued presence in the United Kingdom was detrimental to national security. In an equally important judgment the European Court held:

> 'Article 3 enshrines one of the most fundamental values of democratic society. The Court is well aware of the immense difficulties faced by States in modern times in protecting their communities from terrorist violence. However, even in these circumstances, the Convention prohibits in absolute terms torture or inhuman or degrading treatment or punishment, irrespective of the victim's conduct . . .
>
> The prohibition provided by Article 3 against ill-treatment is equally absolute in expulsion cases. Thus, whenever substantial grounds have been shown for believing that an individual would face a real risk of being subjected to treatment contrary to Article 3 if removed to another State, the responsibility of the Contracting State to safeguard him or her against such treatment is engaged in the event of expulsion. In these circumstances, the activities of the individual in question, however undesirable or dangerous, cannot be a material consideration. The protection afforded by Article 3 is thus wider than that provided by Articles 32 and 33 of the United Nations 1951 Convention on the Status of Refugees.
>
> . . . It should not be inferred . . . that there is any room for balancing the risk of ill-treatment against the reasons for expulsion in determining whether a State's responsibility is engaged.'

It is therefore clear that if an individual can demonstrate that removal from the United Kingdom would be likely to result in torture or inhuman or degrading treatment or punishment, they will have shown that such removal will be unlawful. Indeed, prior to the Human Rights Act 1998, it was the Secretary of State's own policy to grant exceptional leave to remain to asylum applicants whose claims were refused on Refugee Convention grounds, but in respect of whom there was nevertheless reason to suppose that there was a risk of Article 3 ill-treatment if returned to their own country.

ARTICLE 3 AND ASYLUM – SIMILARITIES AND DIFFERENCES

The starting-point for a comparison between Article 3 of the ECHR and the Refugee Convention is the 'starred' decision of *Kacaj* [2001] INLR 354, in which the Tribunal had to consider a number of issues relating to appeals to adjudicators in which both Conventions were relied on.

The burden and standard of proof

The burden of proof will be on the applicant. As to the standard of proof, the Tribunal in *Kacaj* pointed out that there was very good reason for it to be the same lower standard applicable in refugee cases:

> 'The link with the Refugee Convention is obvious. Persecution will normally involve the violation of a person's human rights and a finding that there is a real risk of persecution would be likely to involve a finding that there is a real risk of a breach of the Human Rights Convention. It would therefore be strange of different standards of proof applied . . . Since the concern under each Convention is whether the risk of future ill-treatment will amount to a breach of an individual's human rights, a difference of approach would be surprising . . .
>
> In our view, the decision of the European Court of Human Rights in *Vilvarajah v United Kingdom* (1991) 14 EHRR 248 provides added support for our conclusion.'

The Tribunal also referred to the decision of the House of Lords in *R v Secretary of State for the Home Department, ex p Sivakumaran* [1988] AC 958 and commented as follows:

> 'The House of Lords found that the test (for establishing whether a person was a refugee) was an objective one and that there has to be demonstrated a reasonable degree of likelihood, or a real or substantial risk, that the person will be persecuted if returned to his own country . . .
>
> . . . When formulating the test that there must be "substantial grounds for believing that the person concerned faced a real

> risk of being subjected to torture or to inhuman or degrading treatment or punishment in the country to which he was [to be] returned", the Court is clearly intending to follow the same approach as was considered correct for the Refugee Convention . . .'

The Tribunal also confirmed:

> 'The words "substantial grounds for believing" do not and are not intended to qualify the ultimate question which is whether a real risk of relevant ill-treatment has been established . . .'

The Court of Appeal recently held in *Hariri* [2003] EWCA Civ 807 that where an applicant could not rely on any individual characteristics to demonstrate a risk of inhuman or degrading treatment, he would have to show that:

> '. . . the situation to which . . .[he] . . . would be returning was one in which such violence was generally or consistently happening.'

Persecution: the same as breach of Article 3?

There is an ongoing legal debate as to whether treatment not amounting to persecution may still be a breach of Article 3 of the ECHR. In *Kacaj* the Tribunal took the view:

> 'Persecution and breaches of Article 3 are not necessarily the same, although we doubt whether treatment which did not amount to persecution could nonetheless cross the Article 3 threshold. We recognise the possibility that Article 3 could be violated by actions which did not have a sufficiently systemic character to amount to persecution, although we doubt that this refinement would be likely to be determinative in any but a very small minority of cases . . .'

In the recent case of *Ullah v Special Adjudicator* [2002] EWCA Civ 1856, [2003] 1 WLR 770 the Court of Appeal stated:

> 'As we read *Soering* and *Chahal* the underlying rationale for the application of the Convention to the act of expulsion is that it is an affront to fundamental humanitarian principles to remove an individual to a country where there is a real risk of

> serious ill-treatment, even though such ill-treatment may not satisfy the criteria of persecution under the Refugee Convention.'

As seen in Chapter 1 'torture' will always amount to 'persecution' and so in this respect, Article 3 and the Refugee Convention are in agreement. However, when we look at 'inhuman' or 'degrading' treatment, it seems that linguistically at least these are plainly not the same as 'persecution'. Not only do they indicate less severe forms of ill-treatment than 'persecution', but they also suggest (as recognised in *Kacaj*) that the ill-treatment need not be persistent in the way that 'persecution' may be. Given the large numbers and endless factual variety of asylum claims, it should not be assumed that the distinctions between the Refugee Convention and Article 3 will only affect 'a very small minority of cases'. In summary, the correct approach may be that while 'persecution' is always likely to be a breach of Article 3, not every breach of Article 3 need amount to persecution.

Protection

The issue of protection was also under consideration in *Kacaj* in the context of a fear of non-state agents. The Tribunal noted that *Horvath v Secretary of State for the Home Department* [2000] INLR 239 was the leading case on protection for non-state agent asylum claims and pointed out that in *Horvath* itself the House of Lords had specifically referred to the recognition by the European Court in *Osman v United Kingdom* (1998) 29 EHRR 245 that the authorities' obligation to protect its citizens had to take account of operational responsibilities and practical constraints, and could not therefore be a disproportionate or impossible duty. The House of Lords had gone on to decide that the standard of protection must be 'a practical standard, which takes proper account of the duty which the state owes to all its nationals'. The Tribunal were of the view that this should also be the standard applicable in Article 3 cases:

> '. . . Since the result will be similar, namely persecution or a violation of a human right, it would be wrong to apply a different approach. We do not read *Horvath* as deciding that

> there will be a sufficiency of protection whenever the authorities in the receiving State are doing their best. If this best can be shown to be ineffective, it may be that the applicant will have established that there is an inability to provide the necessary protection.
>
> . . .
>
> The fact that the system may break down because of incompetence or venality of individual officers is generally not to be regarded as establishing unwillingness or inability to provide protection. In many cases, perhaps most, the existence of the system will be sufficient to remove the reality of risk.'

Kacaj was followed in *Hari Dhima* [2002] INLR 243, in which the High Court stated:

> 'Although Article 3 has a wider application than Article 1(A) of the Geneva Convention, and is absolute in its terms and effect, it clearly allows for the home State, by providing suitable protection, to remove the real risk at which it is directed . . .'

In *Karel Krepel* [2002] EWCA Civ 1265 the Court of Appeal proceeded on the basis that *Hari Dhima* was correctly decided. However, in *Althea Britton* [2003] EWCA Civ 227, the point was left open for future consideration. See also *R (on the application of Bagdanavicius) v Secretary of State for the Home Department* [2003] EWHC 854 (Admin), in which the High Court granted the claimant permission to appeal to the Court of Appeal.

So far as ill-treatment by state agents is concerned, it is submitted that the position is the same as under the Refugee Convention: if a real risk is made out the claim under Article 3 of the ECHR must be allowed.

In cases where the ill-treatment is by state agents acting outside their authority, the situation may be different. In *Ireland v United Kingdom* (1978) 2 EHRR 25 the European Court held that state authorities are 'strictly liable for the conduct of their subordinates'. The words 'strictly liable' could be taken to imply an extremely high or even absolute standard of protection in such cases and this may be different to the standard described in *Svazas v Secretary of State for the Home Department* [2002] EWCA Civ 74, [2002] 1 WLR 1891.

Subjective fear

The position is the same as under the Refugee Convention: where a real risk has been objectively demonstrated, it is extremely difficult to envisage an appeal not being allowed on the basis that there is no subjective fear.

Internal relocation

There is no authority that suggests that the position is not the same as under the Refugee Convention. Where therefore an applicant can show that internal relocation in respect of a fear of Article 3 ill-treatment is neither safe nor reasonable, their claim should be allowed.

No requirement to show discrimination or reason for ill-treatment

To succeed under Article 3 of the ECHR it is only necessary to show a 'real risk' of the requisite treatment. The applicant does not bear the additional burden of having to prove that this would be suffered by reason of their race, religion, nationality, membership of a particular social group or political opinion, or indeed any other particular reason. The establishment of the risk will always be sufficient. So for example, an individual who faced a real risk of indiscriminate physical harm arising out of a full-scale civil war would succeed under Article 3 without the need for demonstrating they would suffer 'differential impact', as was the case under the Refugee Convention in *Adan v Secretary of State for the Home Department* [1999] 1 AC 293, HL. This application of Article 3 was confirmed by the European Court in *Ahmed v Austria* (1996) 24 EHRR 278.

ARTICLE 3 – OTHER KINDS OF CLAIM

The nature of Article 3 is such that it encompasses claims that may not fall under the Refugee Convention at all.

Punishment

In *Tyrer v United Kingdom* (1978) 2 EHRR 1 the European Court held that the very wording of Article 3 implies a distinction between punishment in general and punishment that is degrading. In order for otherwise lawful punishment to be 'degrading', the humiliation or debasement involved must reach a level above the usual element of humiliation associated with punishment in general. This would depend on:

> '. . . all the circumstances of the case and, in particular, on the nature and context of the punishment itself and the manner and method of its execution.'

Detention

Equally, an otherwise lawful term of imprisonment may breach Article 3, if for example:

(i) The manner of its enforcement by the security forces amounts to torture or inhuman or degrading treatment.

(ii) The conditions of detention are themselves inhuman or degrading, due to poor or non-existent food and water, sleeping facilities, heating, ventilation, lighting, sanitation, medical facilities, exercise and contact with the outside world: *Greek Case* 12 YB 1 (1969). In *Dougoz v Greece* (2001) 10 BHRC 306 the European Court held that a period of detention of 17 months in a cell unsuitable for detention for more than a few days amounted to degrading treatment. In *Kalashnikov v Russia* (15 July 2002 unreported), ECtHR, the European Court found that a period of four years and ten months spent in a 'severely overcrowded and insanitary environment' coupled with its 'detrimental effect on the applicant's health and well-being' amounted to degrading treatment.

Medical treatment

In *D v United Kingdom* (1997) 24 EHRR 423 the applicant was in the advanced stages of AIDS and was to be removed to St Kitts in the Caribbean, where he would not be able to access the medical treatment or facilities he was currently receiving in the United Kingdom. It was accepted that removal in these circumstances would shorten his life expectancy and therefore be a breach of Article 3. The European Court held that:

> '. . . removal would expose him to a real risk of dying under most distressing circumstances and would thus amount to inhuman treatment . . .'

In *Bensaid v United Kingdom* [2001] INLR 325 it was argued that an Algerian national suffering from schizophrenia would not receive the medical facilities and support he had in the United Kingdom and was therefore at risk of a relapse, resulting in inhuman and degrading treatment. The European Court accepted in principle that the suffering caused by such a relapse could breach Article 3, but found on the particular facts that the risk of both a relapse and a lack of the necessary care were speculative rather than real.

It is important to understand the effect of these cases. There is no automatic entitlement for an asylum applicant to remain in the United Kingdom merely because they are receiving medical treatment. What must be established in each and every such claim is the existence of a real risk of inhuman or degrading treatment if removed to their home country. The following factors must be considered:

- What is the nature of the illness or condition?
- How would it affect the individual's ability to function and lead a normal and dignified life in their home country?
- Does the individual have responsibility for dependents – how are they affected?
- What kinds of treatment are being received in the United Kingdom, for how long have they been received and how long should they continue?
- Will other kinds of treatment be necessary?
- What will the effects of withdrawal of treatment be?
- Is treatment available in their home country? If so how does it compare to that being received in the United Kingdom?
- Are there any barriers to accessing treatment in the home country?

Inevitably, such issues will require expert evidence and/or inquiries relating to the position in the home country.

Where harm does not emanate from human agency

As the Strasbourg case-law indicates, the central consideration in any Article 3 case will be whether as a result of removal the individual is likely to face consequences that amount to inhuman or degrading treatment. However, unlike persecution within the meaning of the Refugee Convention, the consequences do not have to be brought about by human intervention. The European Court stated in *Bensaid* that it was not:

> '. . . prevented from scrutinising an applicant's claim under Article 3 where the source of the risk of proscribed treatment in the receiving country stems from factors which cannot engage either directly or indirectly the responsibility of the public authorities of that country, or which, taken alone, do not in themselves infringe the standards of that Article. To limit the application of Article 3 in this manner would be to undermine the absolute character of its protection . . .'

Apart from the requirements that there be a real risk that harmful consequences will occur and that these be sufficiently serious, there is no real limit to what kinds of harm can be invoked in an Article 3 claim: *S, D and T* [2003] EWHC 1941 (Admin).

Consequences of successful claim

Whereas a successful claimant under the Refugee Convention is recognised as a refugee, and will benefit from the range of rights specified in Articles 2–33 of the Refugee Convention, an applicant who succeeds under the ECHR, even if irremovable because there would be a breach of Article 3, is only granted the lesser status of exceptional leave to remain for varying periods, though usually four years.

ARTICLE 8 – THE RIGHT TO RESPECT FOR PRIVATE AND FAMILY LIFE

Article 8 states:

> '(1) Everyone has the right to respect for his private and family life, his home and his correspondence.
>
> (2) There shall be no interference by a public authority with the exercise of this right except such as in accordance with the law and is necessary in a democratic society in the interests of national security, public safety or the economic well-being of the country, for the prevention of disorder or crime, for the protection of health or morals, or for the protection of rights and freedoms of others.'

Of the four aspects to Article 8(1) – private life, family life, home and correspondence, most human rights claims will be concerned with the first two. In examining what these concepts include, it must be borne in mind that identifying that private or family life will be interfered with by removal will not in itself be sufficient. Unlike Article 3, Article 8 of the ECHR is qualified and can therefore be restricted in certain circumstances. While Article 8(1) sets out the individual's right to private and family life, Article 8(2) defines when and how this can be interfered with by the state, and in every claim there will be an argument by the Home Office that even if removal would interfere with the individual's private or family life, such interference is both lawful and justified by the United Kingdom's need for effective immigration control. The success or otherwise of the case will depend on where the balance between these considerations lies.

Private life

The European Court has declined to give an exhaustive definition of 'private life', preferring to consider the notion on a case-by-case basis. However, from the case law it is clear that it includes 'the physical and moral integrity of the person, including his or her sexual life': *X and Y v Netherlands* (1985) 8 EHRR 235. In *Niemietz v Germany* (1992) 16 EHRR 97 it was also taken to cover professional or business activities. The concept of private life was described by the European Court in *X and Y v Netherlands* as one that recognised the need:

> '. . . to establish and develop relationships with other human beings, especially in the emotional field for the development of one's own personality . . .'

Family life

This too has been given a flexible and autonomous meaning which is not so much dependent on how domestic law defines the relationship, but rather on the nature and closeness of the ties involved. In *Marckx v Belgium* (1979) 2 EHRR 330 it was stated that a state has a 'positive duty' to permit its citizens to lead 'a normal family life'. Biological ties, such as between a parent and child, will create an immediate presumption that family life exists (*Kroon v Netherlands* (1994) 19 EHRR 263), even where the parent and child live apart (*Boughanemi v France* (1996) 22 EHRR 228). So will a lawful and genuine marriage, despite the fact that the couple are not co-habiting: *Abdulaziz, Cabales and Balkandali v United Kingdom* (1985) 7 EHRR 471.

Family life will also cover 'de facto' family relationships, for example where an unmarried couple live together: *Keegan v Ireland* (1994) 18 EHRR 342. A parent and an adult child may also share family life if there is dependency between them over and above 'the normal emotional ties' (*Advic v United Kingdom* (1995) 20 EHRR CD 125).

Range of relationships

As the definition of family life under Article 8 is concerned with the essence of the relationship rather than its form, it can in principle apply to a whole range of other relationships: children and their grandparents; children and aunts or uncles or other relatives; adoptive or foster families etc. In accordance with the principle that the ECHR is a living instrument, family life has also been found to encompass relationships that have traditionally been ignored by domestic law. In *X, Y and Z v United Kingdom* (1997) 24 EHRR 143 the European Court held there to be family life between a transsexual, his partner and their child conceived through artificial insemination. Although it is likely to be only a matter of time, this approach has not yet been extended to same-sex partners, but such relationships already fall within the ambit of private life in any event: *X and Y v Netherlands*.

Irreducible minimum

Whether family life exists will always be a question of fact and degree: *G v Netherlands* (1993) 16 EHRR CD 38. In *Kugathas v Immigration Appeal Tribunal* [2003] EWCA Civ 31 the Court of Appeal decided that, with the exception of the natural bond between a parent and child, the existence of 'family life' required there to be 'real', 'committed' or 'effective support' between the individuals concerned. This was the 'irreducible minimum' without which no question of any interference under Article 8 would arise. While in principle 'family life' under Article 8 was not limited to family ties within the territory of the state, such a relationship would nevertheless have to attain the irreducible minimum content. Clearly, in determining whether the minimum content of family life is satisfied, regard must be had to all the different features of the relationship, such as the nature and ages of the persons, how their relationship came about, whether they live together all or some of the time, and what degree of contact and emotional or financial support there is between them.

Interference

Where private or family life has been established in a state's territory, there will be few cases in which removal of the individual and their dependents would not interfere with, ie restrict, enjoyment of that private or family life. However, interference is not the same as a breach.

Interference must be lawful

Article 8(2) states that any restriction on the right to respect for private and family life must be 'in accordance with the law'; not arbitrary or unintelligible. However, as this requirement is fairly easily satisfied by the Home Office giving a written decision and/or removal directions referring to the relevant statutory provisions or rules, it will not be an issue in the vast majority of cases.

Interference must pursue a legitimate aim

It is a further requirement of any action resulting in interference, that it be directed towards an objective listed in Article 8(2). Where the Home Office seek to deport a foreign national convicted of a serious criminal offence, any interference with that individual's private or family life in the United Kingdom will obviously be pursuant to ensuring 'public safety', preventing 'disorder or crime' or protecting 'the rights and freedoms of others'. So far as other cases are concerned, although 'immigration control' is not itself expressly stated as an objective in Article 8(2), it has been held by the European Court to be implicit in the need to achieve all of the express objectives.

Interference must be proportionate

Article 8(2) only permits a measure which will interfere with private or family life when, in all the circumstances of the case, it is both necessary in light of the measure's stated aim, as well as proportionate to that aim. The requirement of 'proportionality' recognises that the protection of human rights involves searching for a balance between the rights of the individual and the various needs of society, including the collective rights of other individuals. An otherwise lawful and legitimately-pursued measure will therefore be in breach of Article 8, if the resulting interference with privacy and family life is disproportionate to the wider interests of society. It will be for the state to justify its actions and it is on the issue of proportionality that nearly all cases will turn.

Striking the balance – European cases

Just as the question of whether private or family life itself is in existence will depend on an array of different factors, so too will the issue of whether the removal of an individual would be disproportionate. There will often be a degree of overlap between the two sets of factors, as the case-law shows. The European Court has dealt with Article 8 in an immigration context on numerous occasions and although its decisions have not always been consistent on the relative importance and weight to be attached to the different factors involved in the balancing exercise, the relevant factors themselves recur time and again. In *Boultif v Switzerland* (2001) 33 EHRR 50 the Court considered the case of an Algerian national, who had been married to a Swiss citizen for four years, but was subsequently convicted of offences of violence and possession of firearms. In considering whether the Swiss authorities' deportation of the applicant would breach Article 8, the Court had regard to the following principles:

(i) The nature and seriousness of the offence committed.
(ii) The length of the applicant's stay in the country from which they are to be expelled.
(iii) The length of time since the offence was committed and the applicant's conduct during that period.
(iv) The nationalities of the affected parties.
(v) The applicant's family situation, including the length of the marriage.
(vi) Any other factors relevant to the effectiveness of the couple's family life.
(vii) Whether the spouse knew about the offence at the time of entering into the relationship.
(viii) Whether there were children in the marriage and if so their ages.
(ix) Whether the spouse was likely to encounter difficulties in the applicant's country of origin, and if so the nature of those difficulties.

The Court gave particular weight to the applicant's wife's inability to speak Arabic and it seems, Islamic fundamentalism in Algeria, finding that she would not be able to live there and that the applicant's deportation was therefore disproportionate.

Where a relationship has resulted in children, this will have a significant effect on the balancing exercise. In the case of *Amrollahi v Denmark* (11 July 2002, unreported) (ECtHR), the European Court held that although the applicant had been found guilty and sentenced for a serious drug trafficking offence, his forced return to Iran would be a breach of Article 8 as his Danish wife and their children could not be expected to go with him to Iran, not being Muslim themselves and being unable to speak the Farsi language.

The domestic approach

Domestic decisions on Article 8 have been concerned not only with the balancing exercise itself, but also with the extent to which the courts can or should overrule adverse decisions by the Home Office. The leading case is *R (on the application of Mahmood) v Secretary of State for the Home Department* [2001] 1 WLR 840, in which the Court of Appeal was concerned with a judicial review of the Secretary of State's decision not to grant leave to remain to a Pakistan national who had entered the United Kingdom illegally and had married a British citizen. Although the Human Rights Act was not in force at the time, the Secretary of State had taken into account in making his decision not only the relevant policy DP 3/96, but also the requirements of Article 8. In its review of the Secretary of State's decision, the Court agreed that the conventional *Wednesbury* approach would not sufficiently recognise the fundamental right in issue. However, the Court held that although its role was more intrusive, it was still a supervisory one of considering:

> '. . . whether the decision-maker could reasonably have concluded that the interference was necessary to achieve one or more of the legitimate aims recognised by the Convention . . .'

and must not involve retaking the Secretary of State's decision on the merits.

The Court reviewed the Strasbourg jurisprudence and drew a number of conclusions as to how the balance between the right to respect for private and family life, and immigration control should be struck:

'(1) A state has a right under international law to control the entry of non-nationals into its territory, subject always to its treaty obligations.

(2) Article 8 does not impose on a state any general obligation to respect the choice of residence of a married couple.

(3) Removal or exclusion of one family member from a state where other members of the family are lawfully resident will not necessarily infringe Article 8 provided that there are no *insurmountable obstacles* to the family living together in the country of origin of the family

member excluded, even where this involves a degree of hardship for some or all members of the family.

(4) Article 8 is likely to be violated by the expulsion of a member of a family that has been long established in a state if the circumstances are such that it is *not reasonable* to expect the other members of the family to follow that member expelled.

(5) Knowledge on the part of one spouse at the time of marriage that rights of residence of the other were precarious militates against a finding that an order excluding the latter spouse violates Article 8.

(6) Whether interference with family rights is justified in the interests of controlling immigration will depend on (i) the facts of the particular case and (ii) the circumstances prevailing in the state whose action is impugned.'

(Emphasis added)

The Court decided that the Secretary of State's view that the applicant's family could relocate to Pakistan was reasonable. Moreover, 'firm immigration control' required fairness and consistency and in the absence of exceptional circumstances, individuals in the applicant's position would be expected to return to their country of origin and join the queue for entry clearance.

It was confirmed by the House of Lords in *R (on the application of Daly) v Secretary of State for the Home Department* [2001] UKHL 26, [2001] 2 AC 532, that *Wednesbury* review had no place where fundamental rights are concerned (see Chapter 8). That decision qualified *Mahmood* to the extent that the focus had to be on whether any interference would have a disproportionate effect on the rights contained in Article 8(1), not simply whether the Secretary of State's decision was reasonable.

Unfavourable history

In *Isiko* [2001] INLR 109 the Court of Appeal upheld the Secretary of State's decision to remove the appellants to their home country of Uganda, albeit that this would interfere with the relationship between one of the appellants and his 5-year-old daughter from a previous marriage to a British citizen. The Court emphasised the appellants' 'deplorable' immigration history, including entry by deception, a conviction for rape and a 'baseless' asylum claim. The Court held that:

> '. . . the mere fact that the presence of an individual and his family in this country will not in itself constitute a threat to one of the interests enumerated in Article 8(2) of the Convention does not prevent a decision to enforce a lawful immigration policy which applies in the individual's case from being lawful.'

R (Samaroo) v Secretary of State for the Home Department [2001] EWCA Civ 1139, [2001] UKHRR 1150, concerned a national of Guyana who came to the United Kingdom as a visitor, married a British citizen with children from a previous marriage and was subsequently granted indefinite leave to remain. The couple then had their own child. The appellant was later convicted of being knowingly concerned in the importation of cocaine with a street value of £450,000, sentenced to 13 years imprisonment and recommended for deportation. The Secretary of State made a deportation order and after appealing unsuccessfully to an adjudicator and the Immigration Appeal Tribunal, the appellant made an application for exceptional leave to remain based on good behaviour in prison and family ties in the United Kingdom. This was refused by the Secretary of State and the appellant sought judicial review. It was accepted that deportation would split up the family. The issue was:

> '. . . whether the Secretary of State has struck the balance fairly between the conflicting interests of Mr Samaroo's right to respect for his family life on the one hand and the prevention of crime and disorder on the other.'

Applying *R (Daly) v Secretary of State for the Home Department*, [2001] UKHL 26, [2001] 2 AC 532, the House of Lords held that the Secretary of State had to 'convincingly' justify derogation from a Convention right. However, the Court concluded that the trafficking of class A drugs was in general a very serious offence; given also the appellant's crucial role in the crime and the need for deterrence, the Secretary of State had struck a fair and reasonable balance.

Favourable factors

The necessary implication of cases such as *Isiko* and *Samaroo*, is that where the applicant does *not* have a serious criminal record or history of deceiving the Home Office, it will be that much harder for removal to be convincingly justified. Of course, for reasons already touched on in the Introduction, there will be few cases in which there has not been an unlawful entry into the United Kingdom. However, what needs to be considered is the entirety of the applicant's life and conduct in this country, and even if there has been any *subsequent* deception, the circumstances and reasons for it. This must then be set against the combination of all the favourable factors relevant to the existence of private and family life.

Delay by Home Office

In *Arben Shala* [2003] EWCA Civ 233 the appellant was an ethnic Albanian from Kosovo who arrived in the United Kingdom in 1997, claimed asylum and was granted temporary admission. The Home Office did not interview him until July 2001 and the claim was refused just over a week later. At his appeal reliance was placed on the appellant's relationship with a Czech asylum-seeker who had indefinite leave to remain. They had been cohabiting since 1998 and married in 2001. The adjudicator accepted the appellant had genuine family life in the United Kingdom, but decided he had married at a time when his status in the United Kingdom was unclear and that he would be able to apply for entry clearance from Kosovo. The Tribunal similarly concluded that there would not be a disproportionate interference with Article 8.

In the Court of Appeal it was argued that there was no guarantee that the appellant would only be separated for a short time, and that the Tribunal had ignored the difficulties the appellant would face in Kosovo. Furthermore, that the Secretary of State's delay of over four years in deciding on the asylum claim meant it was unsurprising that the appellant had formed an enduring relationship in the meantime. On the question of proportionality the Court confirmed that the Secretary of State has:

> '. . . a significant margin of discretion before the Court will conclude that he has gone wrong in the relative weight which he has attached to the conflicting interests.'

Account was taken of another Tribunal decision, *Xhacka* [2002] UK IAT 03352 in which an applicant from Kosovo had been in the United Kingdom for two and a half years and had in that time met and married a British woman. The Tribunal held that the appeal under Article 8 should have been allowed by the adjudicator.

The Court of Appeal importantly distinguished between cases where there was a legitimate claim to enter, for example in this case and in *Xhacka* the appellants were at the time refugees, and cases where an individual who having no other legitimate claim to enter or remain, sought to rely on marriage. In allowing the appeal the Court commented that what was needed was an exceptional circumstance, which was present in this case, as the appellant arrived at a time when he would have no doubt been granted four years exceptional leave to remain.

'Effective immigration control'?

Arben Shala was followed in *Ismet Ala* [2003] EWHC 521 (Admin), the High Court commenting that:

> '. . . the consequences of considerable delay (on the part of the Home Office) are a relevant factor in striking the balance.'

Implicit in the reasoning of such decisions is a recognition of the wider principle that when the Home Office meet an Article 8 claim with the argument that an interference with private and family life is justified by the requirement of 'effective immigration control', that expression has to actually *mean* something in the context of the facts of the case. The Home Office cannot plead effective immigration control where, as in *Arben Shala*, their own delay in determining the appellant's asylum claim was the very antithesis of such a policy.

'Effective immigration control' is not therefore an incantation which once uttered will automatically defeat an Article 8 claim: it too has to be looked at in every case on its own merits.

Jurisdiction of an adjudicator

The cases of *Mahmood*, *Isiko* and *Samaroo* were of course all judicial reviews. It was therefore thought that where an applicant faced with an adverse Home Office decision exercised a statutory right of appeal to an adjudicator, that adjudicator would have full jurisdiction to retake the Secretary of State's decision on the merits. In this regard reliance was placed on *B* [2000] INLR 361, in which the Court of Appeal was concerned with an appeal against a decision to deport an Italian national who had lived in the United Kingdom since the age of 7. The appellant had been convicted of serious sexual offences towards his own daughter from marriage to a British citizen. Being a citizen of the European Union, the appellant could only be deported if it was 'proportionate' to do so. On appeal from the Tribunal, the Court of Appeal concluded that the appellant's 36 years of continuous residence in the United Kingdom far outweighed the public interest in deporting him. In so doing, the Court proceeded on the basis that it was entitled to look at the original decision afresh and if it disagreed, substitute its own decision.

However, such an approach was doubted by the Tribunal: *Noruwa* (2000/TH/02345). Likewise in *Blessing Edore* [2003] EWCA Civ 716 the Court of Appeal confirmed and held that an adjudicator should only interfere with the Secretary of State's decision where it could not properly be regarded as proportionate and as striking a fair balance. An adjudicator should not intervene merely because he would have preferred the balance to be struck in the appellant's favour. *Blessing Edore* has the following implications:

(i) Where there are no *factual* disputes in an Article 8 appeal (quite rare), the sole question for the adjudicator is whether the Secretary of State has struck a 'fair balance' between the competing interests of the individual and the state.

(ii) There will be cases in which there is more than one answer to the question of what constitutes a 'fair balance' and in those cases it will more be difficult for an appellant to succeed.

(iii) In Article 8 cases there does not now seem to be a great deal of difference between the scope of High Court judicial review and the jurisdiction of an adjudicator.

Given these far-reaching consequences, it seems likely that this issue will receive further judicial attention in the future.

Step-by-step approach

In *Nhundu and Chiwera* (IAT) (2001/TH/00613) the Tribunal recommended that adjudicators take a step-by-step approach to an Article 8 claim:

> 'The approach taken by the European Court of Human Rights establishes that article 8 is to be analysed according to a step-by-step approach, asking first whether there is an existent private or family life, second whether there is an interference with that private or family life, third whether that interference pursues a legitimate aim, fourth whether it is in accordance with the law and finally whether it is proportionate.'

Tribunal emphasised the particular importance of considering private and family life in combination:

> '. . . the adjudicator should also have considered the question of whether there was existent private life or family life. In this regard he should have borne in mind that the Court views the private life concept as a broad one that includes not only the idea of an 'inner circle' in which individuals may live their personal lives as they choose without interference from the state; it also covers the right to develop one's own personality and to create and foster relationships with others: *Niemietz v Germany* (1992) 16 EHRR 97. *In the context of immigration and asylum cases, the Court has come to view the right to respect for private and family life as a composite right.* This approach requires the decision-maker to avoid restricting himself to looking at the circumstances of "family life" and to take into account also significant elements of the much wider sphere of "private life": *Chorfi v Belgium* 7 August 1996, *Bouchelkia v France* judgment of 29 January 1997 (paragraph 41) , *El Boujaidi v France* 26 September 1997 and *Mehemi v France* 26 September 1997 and *Nasri v France* (1996) 21 EHRR 458. *One consequence of this approach is that a person may be able to establish a protected right under Article 8 either by reference to significant elements of family life or significant elements of private life or a mixture of both.*'
>
> (Emphasis added.)

Health issues

In the case of *Bensaid v United Kingdom* [2001] INLR 325 the European Court importantly stated:

> 'Not every act or measure which adversely affects moral or physical integrity will interfere with the right to respect to private life guaranteed by Article 8. However, the court's case law does not exclude that treatment which does not reach the severity of Article 3 treatment may none the less breach Article 8 in its private life aspect where there are sufficiently adverse effects on physical and moral integrity.
>
> Private life is a broad term not susceptible to exhaustive definition. The court has already held that elements such as gender identification, name and sexual orientation and sexual life are important elements of the personal sphere protected by Article 8. Mental health must also be regarded as a crucial part of private life associated with the aspect of moral integrity. Article 8 protects a right to identity and personal development, and the right to establish and develop relationships with other human beings and the outside world. The preservation of mental stability is in that context an indispensable precondition to effective enjoyment of the right to respect for private life.'

In *Razgar, Soumahoro and Nadarajah* [2003] EWCA Civ 840, the Court of Appeal considered in the light of *Ullah v Special Adjudicator* [2002] EWCA Civ 1856, [2003] 1 WLR 770 (see below), the correct approach to Article 8 claims based wholly or in part on the argument that removal would interfere with the applicant's physical or moral integrity:

> 'We suggest that, in order to determine whether the Article 8 claim is capable of being engaged in the light of the territoriality principle, the claim should be considered in the following way. First, the claimant's case in relation to his private life in the deporting state should be examined. In a case where the essence of the claim is that expulsion will interfere with his private life by harming his mental health, this will include a consideration of what he says about his mental health in the deporting country, the treatment he receives and any relevant

> support that he says that he enjoys there. Secondly, it will be necessary to look at what he says is likely to happen to his mental health in the receiving country, what treatment he can expect to receive there, and what support he can expect to enjoy. The third step is to determine whether, on the claimant's case, serious harm to his mental health will be caused or materially contributed to by the difference between the treatment and support that he is enjoying in the deporting country and that which will be available to him in the receiving country. If so, then the territoriality principle is not infringed, and the claim is capable of being engaged. It seems to us that this approach is consistent with the fact that the ECtHR considered the merits of the Article 8 claim in *Bensaid*. It is also consistent with what was said in paragraphs 46 and 64 of *Ullah*.
>
> The degree of harm must be sufficiently serious to engage Article 8. There must be a sufficiently adverse effect on physical and mental integrity, and not merely on health (*Bensaid* paras 46-48).
>
> There must be substantial grounds for believing that the claimant would face a real risk of the adverse effect which he or she claims to fear: see, for example, *Kacaj* [2001] INLR 354 at para 12 . . .'

In relation to Article 8(2) and the balancing exercise, the Court approved the approach taken by the European Court in *Boultif v Switzerland* (2001) 33 EHRR 50.

Evidence

As will be seen from the above cases, Article 8 claims are invariably concerned with whether or not an applicant and/or their family will be able to carry on private and family life, notwithstanding removal from the United Kingdom. Such an evaluation requires enquiries to be made as to what alternatives are in reality available, such as whether it would be possible to obtain entry clearance from abroad, or whether the family could safely and reasonably be expected to live in the other country: *Soloot* (IAT) (2001/TH/01366). Where removal is likely to result in the severance of contact between a parent and young children, a social worker's report on the impact of this on the children's welfare will be particularly valuable: *Mindoukna* (IAT) (2001/TH/02635).

Article 8 – an overall checklist

Drawing on the above cases, representatives putting forward an Article 8 claim on behalf of their client, should consider whether any of the following apply and if so, what evidence in support can be obtained:

BACKGROUND

- Why do the Home Office intend to remove or deport the applicant?
- How long has the applicant lived in the United Kingdom?
- How did the applicant come to be living in the United Kingdom and what is their immigration history?
- Does the applicant have a criminal record and if so how serious?
- What was the applicant's original purpose in coming to the United Kingdom?

CONDUCT OF HOME OFFICE

- If it was to claim asylum, did the Home Office deal with that application promptly?
- Where there has been delay in determining the application, would the applicant have qualified for Refugee status at the time of the original claim; or was there a policy of exceptional leave to remain or non-return to their country?
- If there has already been an unsuccessful asylum appeal, what favourable or relevant findings were made – was the applicant found credible?
- What steps if any, have been taken to remove the applicant – has there been evasion by the applicant or delay by the Home Office?

PRIVATE AND FAMILY LIFE

- Does the applicant have a relationship?
- If so, when did it commence and was the applicant's partner aware of their immigration status?
- What is the nature and duration of the relationship?
- Is the partner a British citizen, a refugee or do they have leave to remain?
- Are there any children from the relationship?
- If so, how old and have they started school?
- What are the living arrangements for the family unit?
- Are there any children from previous relationships and if so, with whom do they live – is there regular contact?
- Does the applicant, their partner or children have any mental health or other medical condition requiring ongoing treatment which could be difficult or impossible to obtain in the country of return?
- Has the applicant had regular employment in the United Kingdom – does the employer support the applicant's claim?
- Did the applicant make any other contributions to society, such as charity work?
- Does the applicant have any other family-members living in the United Kingdom?
- What friends does the applicant have in the United Kingdom?
- Does the applicant have any other community ties or attachments?

EFFECTS OF REMOVAL

- Will removal break up the family and what effects would this have on those remaining in the United Kingdom, in particular the children ?
- Would removal result in the remaining family-members being reliant on public funds?
- Will the applicant be able to obtain entry clearance from abroad – what difficulties or delay would there be?
- What difficulties are those who are removed likely to face living in the country of return?

OTHER ARTICLES

The other Articles of the ECHR incorporated by the Human Rights Act are:

- Article 4 – the prohibition of slavery and forced labour
- Article 5 – the right to liberty and security (in context of bail see Chapter 3)
- Article 6 – the right to a fair trial (in context of appeal hearings see Chapter 6)
- Article 7 – the prohibition of punishment without law
- Article 9 – the right to freedom of thought, conscience and religion
- Article 10 – the right to freedom of expression
- Article 11 – the right to freedom of assembly and association
- Article 12 – the right to marry
- Article 14 – the prohibition of discrimination

Also incorporated are:

- Article 1 of the First Protocol – the protection of property
- Article 2 of the First Protocol – the right to edication
- Article 3 of the First Protocol – the right to free elections
- Article 1 of the Sixth Protocol – the abolition of the death penalty
- Article 2 of the Sixth Protocol – the requirement that use of the death penalty in time of war be in accordance with the law

Applicability of other rights to immigration decisions

In *Soering v United Kingdom* (1989) 11 EHRR 439 the European Court had stated in respect of the right to a fair trial under Article 6 of the ECHR:

> 'The right to a fair trial in criminal proceedings, as embodied in Article 6, holds a prominent place in a democratic society. The Court does not exclude that an issue might exceptionally be raised under Article 6 by an extradition decision in circumstances where the fugitive has suffered or risks suffering a *flagrant denial* of a fair trial in the requesting country . . .' (Emphasis added.)

In *Devaseelan v Secretary of State for the Home Department* [2003] Imm AR 1, the Tribunal considered the application of Article 6 and also Article 5 to immigration decisions:

> 'It is clear that the Court does not attempt to impose the duties of the Convention on States that are not party to it. It is also clear that the fact that a person may be treated in a manner that would, in a signatory State, be a breach of the Convention does not of itself render his expulsion to another country unlawful, unless either the breach will be of Article 3, or the consequences of return will be so extreme a breach of another Article that the returning State, as one of its obligations under the Convention, is obliged to have regard to them. Following the jurisprudence on Articles 5 and 6, this consequence will only arise if the situation in the receiving country is that there will be a *flagrant denial* or *gross violation* of the rights secured by the Convention. For this reason we have not needed to consider in this determination the precise implications of Articles 5 and 6 within signatory States.
>
> The reason why flagrant denial or gross violation is to be taken into account is that it is only in such a case, where the right will be completely denied or nullified in the destination country, that it can be said that removal will breach the treaty obligations of the signatory State however those obligations might be interpreted or whatever might be said by or on behalf of the destination State.'
>
> (Emphasis added.)

However, the current position in domestic law is the decision of the Court of Appeal in *Ullah v Special Adjudicator* [2002] EWCA Civ 1856, [2003] 1 WLR 770, in which it was held in respect of the right to freedom of religion under Article 9 that:

> '. . . The Refugee Convention and Article 3 of the Convention already cater for the more serious categories of ill-treatment on the ground of religion. The extension of grounds for asylum that Mr Blake and Mr Gill seek to establish would open the door to claims to enter this country by a potentially very large new category of asylum seeker. It is not for the Court to take such a step. It is for the executive, or for Parliament, to decide whether to offer refuge in this country to persons who are not in a position to claim this under the Refugee Convention, or the Human Rights Convention as currently applied by the Strasbourg Court . . . It is not for the courts to make that extension.

> For these reasons we hold that a removal decision to a country that does not respect Article 9 rights will not infringe the HRA where the nature of the interference with the right to practice religion that is anticipated in the receiving state falls short of Article 3 ill-treatment. It may be that this does not differ greatly, in effect, from holding that interference with the right to practice religion in such circumstances will not result in the engagement of the Convention unless the interference is "flagrant".'

The Court then considered the implications of the case for all other Articles of the ECHR apart from Article 3:

> 'Where the Convention is invoked on the *sole* ground of the treatment to which an alien, refused the right to enter or remain, is likely to be subjected by the receiving state, and the treatment is not sufficiently severe to engage Article 3, the English court is not required to recognise that any other Article of the Convention is, or may be, engaged. Where such treatment falls outside Article 3, there may be cases which justify the grant of exceptional leave to remain on humanitarian grounds. The decision of the Secretary of State in such cases will be subject to the ordinary principles of judicial review but not to the constraints of the Convention.'
>
> (Emphasis added.)

At the time of writing, *Ullah v Special Adjudicator* [2002] EWCA Civ 1856, [2003] 1 WLR 770 was granted leave to appeal to the House of Lords and it remains to be seen whether the approach of the Court of Appeal will be found to be the correct.

It is important to appreciate the true effect of the Court of Appeal's judgement in *Ullah and Do*. Where the basis of a claim under an Article of the ECHR other than Article 3 is not 'solely' predicated on the conditions in the receiving country, but on the situation in the United Kingdom or a combination of both, then that claim still falls to be considered: *Bushati* [2002] UK IAT 07423; *Razgar, Soumahoro and Nadarajah* [2003] EWCA Civ 840.

CHAPTER 3

Bail

INTRODUCTION

Individuals entering the United Kingdom and seeking asylum are frequently detained by an immigration officer or the Secretary of State. This has clear implications for their human rights, not least their health and mental well-being, but also their ability to pursue or give evidence in support of their substantive claim (see Appendix 3). Securing bail can therefore be regarded as part of the process of an asylum or human rights appeal. This chapter provides a summary of the legal provisions and procedure concerning bail and considers the key features of a bail hearing before an adjudicator.

In the criminal jurisdiction there is a presumption in favour of granting bail to any defendant. The presumption recognises that any restriction on a person's liberty will have a serious impact on that person and so must be strictly justified. This central principle does not however find such clear recognition in the field of immigration. Although the individuals concerned are *already* likely to have suffered infringements of their fundamental rights, such as torture and detention, the Immigration Acts do not contain any statutory presumption in favour of bail. The UNHCR Guidelines do however refer to 'a presumption against detention' and the general right to liberty under Article 5 of the European Convention on Human Rights has clearly had a significant effect on decision-making in this area.

The powers of detention are confusingly arranged in the various statutory provisions, which are expressed in the broadest terms and contain few references to time limits. As a result, many potential refugees are detained for long periods of time in removal centres and even prisons. The Nationality, Immigration and Asylum Act 2002 (the 2002 Act) repeals the unimplemented automatic bail hearing provisions in Part 3 of the Immigration and Asylum Act 1999, but leaves in place provisions for applying for bail.

The 'legal' starting point when considering bail may be taken from the Immigration Service Instruction (20 September 1994) which states: 'It is the Government's policy that detention should be authorised only when there is no alternative'. The lack of procedural safeguards and time limits to detention can be seen as leading to widespread arbitrary detention, often for indefinite periods. A significant proportion of individuals are detained for many months and in some cases years without any real prospect of removal.

INDIVIDUALS LIABLE TO DETENTION

Below we set out the circumstances in which an individual seeking to enter the United Kingdom can *potentially* be detained under the powers of the Immigration Acts. The power to detain exists: whether or not the power is exercised and how that decision is arrived at will be dealt with further below. The 2002 Act does not affect the categories of individuals who may be detained, it does however extend the powers available to the Secretary of State ie the Home Office, to include situations where they were previously exercised only by an immigration officer. Individuals liable to detention are:

- Persons required to submit to an examination by an Immigration Officer in order to establish:
  - (i) whether they are a British citizen;
  - (ii) if not, whether they require leave to enter the United Kingdom;
  - (iii) if leave is required, whether they have been given leave which is still in force, or they should be given or refused leave,

  may be detained for the purposes of an examination and pending decision to grant or refuse leave to enter (paragraph 16(1), Schedule 2 of the Immigration Act 1971).
- Persons who arrive in the United Kingdom with leave to enter given on a prior occasion, may be detained for the purposes of establishing:
  - (i) whether there has been a change in circumstances since that leave was given such that it should be cancelled;
  - (ii) whether that leave was obtained as a result of false information or a failure to disclose relevant facts;
  - (iii) whether there are medical grounds on which that leave should be cancelled;

(iv) whether it would be conducive to the public good for leave to be cancelled;

and a decision on whether to cancel leave for any of the above reasons (paragraph 16(1A), Schedule 2 of the Immigration Act 1971).

- Persons for whom there are reasonable grounds for suspecting that directions have or may be given for the following reasons:
  (i) they have been refused leave to enter;
  (ii) they are an illegal entrant refused leave to enter;
  (iii) pending a decision as to whether or not to give such directions and pending removal pursuant to such directions;
  (iv) they are seamen or aircrew granted leave to enter to join their ship or aircraft and have overstayed that leave or absconded, or intend to do so, or are reasonably suspected of the same.

  (Paragraph 16(2), Schedule 2 of the Immigration Act 1971.)
  Section 62 of the 2002 Act, which came into force on 10 March 2003, provides that the power in sub-paragraph (iii) above can now be exercised by the Home Office as well as an immigration officer.

- Persons who are not British citizens and who are or are reasonably suspected of:
  (i) having limited leave to enter, failing to observe a condition or overstaying;
  (ii) obtaining leave to remain by deception;
  (iii) family members of the above.

  (Section 10 of the Immigration and Asylum Act 1999; paragraph 16(2), Schedule 2 of the Immigration Act 1971.)
  By virtue of s 62 of the Nationality, Immigration and Asylum Act 2002, the above power can now be exercised by the Home Office as well as an immigration officer.

- Deportation cases:
  (i) where a recommendation for deportation has been made by a criminal court in respect of an individual and they are neither serving a custodial sentence nor are released on bail by any court (paragraph 2(1), Schedule 3 of the Immigration Act 1971);

(ii) where an individual has been given notice of a decision to make a deportation order against them (paragraph 2(2), Schedule 3 of the Immigration Act 1971);
(iii) where a deportation order has been made in respect of an individual and pending their subsequent removal or departure from the United Kingdom (paragraph 2(3), Schedule 3 of the Immigration Act 1971);
(iv) where the Secretary of State has issued a certificate to the effect that an individual is a risk to national security and suspected of being involved with national terrorism, irrespective of whether or not removal or deportation can actually take place (paragraph 16, Schedule 2 and paragraph 2(1), Schedule 3 of the Immigration Act 1971; ss 21 and 23 of the Anti-Terrorism, Crime and Security Act 2001).

- Where the Secretary of State has power to examine a person, or to grant or refuse leave to enter under s 3A of the Immigration Act 1971, pending such an examination, a decision to grant or refuse leave, a decision to set removal directions or removal of such an individual (s 62(2) of the Nationality, Immigration and Asylum Act 2002).

The effect of the changes brought about by the 2002 Act is that decisions on detention can now be taken concurrently with substantive decisions on asylum or human rights claims, and by the same decision-maker. In practical terms this means that someone whose asylum claim has been refused by the Home Office may, in a decision made on the same date by the same official, find that they are detained. The changes therefore can be seen as widening the scope for the detention of asylum applicants.

PERSONS WHO MAY BE GRANTED TEMPORARY ADMISSION OR BAIL

Temporary admission

Temporary admission is a purely technical status given to an individual in order to allow them to be physically admitted into the United Kingdom, rather than be detained. It is to be distinguished from leave to enter or remain, which is the legal right not to be removed for a particular period of time. No such legal right is conferred by temporary admission, which can be withdrawn at any time and the individual detained instead. Temporary admission is rarely granted without the imposition of one or more conditions, commonly restrictions on place of residence and taking up paid employment.

The Home Office Operational Enforcement Manual (2000) suggests, at chapter 38.3, a presumption in favour of granting temporary admission. There must be strong grounds for 'believing that a person will not comply with conditions of temporary admission or temporary release for detention to be justified'. Moreover 'all reasonable alternatives' to detention must be considered before an adverse decision is made.

Making a decision

The Operational Enforcement Manual sets out, in no particular order of importance, the factors which are to be taken into account when making a decision on detention:

- The likelihood and timescale of removal.
- Evidence of previous absconding.
- Evidence of previous non-compliance with temporary admission or bail.
- Has the individual made a determined attempt to breach immigration law, eg by clandestine entry, or in breach of a deportation order?
- Previous history on non-compliance with immigration control.
- Ties in the UK, eg close relatives/dependants, fixed address, employment.
- Progress of case, eg what stage is it at? Does it give the individual an incentive to comply with temporary admission or bail?
- Is the individual a minor?
- Is there a history of torture?
- Is there a history of physical or mental health problems?

Further considerations will apply to those detained at the Oakington Removal Centre. Such detainees comprise of individuals who are from one of the nationalities listed in the regular instructions to staff; whose applications can be considered quickly and a swift decision made, or whose claims are likely to be certified as 'clearly unfounded' under s 94 of the 2002 Act (see Chapter 8).

Bail

Paragraph 22, Schedule 2 to the Immigration Act 1971 makes provision for the release on bail by an immigration officer of at least the rank of Chief Immigration Officer, or by an adjudicator, of *all* the above categories who are liable to detention, save for the following:

- those detained following a recommendation or the making of a deportation order by a criminal court;
- those detained (and who have not appealed) following a notice of detention to make an order for deportation;
- individuals detained under paragraph 16(1), Schedule 2 of the Immigration Act 1971, pending an examination and a decision on leave to enter (until seven days have elapsed since the date of their arrival in the United Kingdom).

Additional cases where the adjudicator may grant bail

By virtue of paragraphs 29(1) and 29(3), Schedule 2 to the Immigration Act 1971, an adjudicator sitting in the IAA (Immigration Appellate Authority) can also bail individuals who have appeals pending against one of the following:

- refusal of entry;
- asylum or human rights appeals against refusal of entry or removal as illegal entrant;
- asylum appeals against removal to a safe third country;
- lawfulness of removal directions or destination;
- notice of intention to make a deportation order.

In general terms it may be stated that detention can only be justified where it is necessary:

- to prevent unauthorised entry, for example:
    - to establish the identity of the applicant and the basis of the claim, or

  - where doubts arise as to the applicant's compliance with conditions to be set;
- to effect removal.

Constraints on the power to detain

The statutory powers noted above must be exercised and interpreted in light of both common law constraints that existed prior to the incorporation of the Human Rights Act as well as those which came after. In *R v Governor of Durham Prison, ex p Singh* [1984] 1 WLR 704 the High Court considered an application for habeas corpus which turned on the length of time that it was appropriate for the Secretary of State to detain an individual pursuant to a deportation order. The Court held that the period of detention was limited to what was 'reasonably necessary' for carrying out that purpose. What is a reasonable time was dependant on the circumstances of the case. Furthermore, the Court concluded that the Secretary of State must take 'all reasonable expedition' to ensure that removal takes place within a reasonable time, failing which detention could become unlawful.

ARTICLE 5 OF THE ECHR

Singh was decided long before the Human Rights Act 1998. The domestic powers to detain an individual must now be read subject to Article 5 of the ECHR, which governs the individual's right to liberty, security and freedom from arbitrary detention.

Article 5 states:

'(1) Everyone has the right to liberty and security of person. No one shall be deprived of his liberty save in the following cases and in accordance with a procedure prescribed by law:
  - (a) The lawful detention of a person after conviction by a competent court;
  - (b) The lawful arrest or detention of a person for non-compliance with the lawful order of a court or in order to secure the fulfilment of any obligation prescribed by law;

(c) The lawful arrest or detention of a person effected for the purpose of bringing him before the competent legal authority on reasonable suspicion of having committed an offence or when it is reasonably considered necessary to prevent his committing an offence or fleeing after having done so;

(d) The detention of a minor by lawful order for the purpose of educational supervision or his lawful detention for the purpose of bringing him before the competent legal authority;

(e) The lawful detention of persons for the prevention of the spreading of infectious diseases, of persons of unsound mind, alcoholics or drug addicts or vagrants;

(f) The lawful arrest or detention of a person to prevent his effecting an unauthorised entry into the country or of a person against whom action is being taken with a view to deportation or extradition.

(2) Everyone who is arrested shall be informed promptly, in a language which he understands, of the reasons for his arrest and of any charge against him.

(3) Everyone arrested or detained in accordance with the provisions of paragraph 1(c) of this Article shall be brought promptly before a judge or other officer authorised by law to exercise judicial power and shall be entitled to trial within a reasonable time or to release pending trial. Release may be conditioned by guarantees to appear for trial.

(4) Everyone who is deprived of his liberty by arrest or detention shall be entitled to take proceedings by which the lawfulness of his detention shall be decided speedily by a court and his release ordered if the detention is not lawful.

(5) Everyone who has been the victim of arrest or detention in contravention of the provision of this Article shall have an enforceable right to compensation.'

Applicability

In *Amuur v France* (1996) 22 EHRR 533 it was held that Article 5 of the ECHR applied to a group of asylum applicants who had not technically entered the territory of France, but were being held in the international zone of the airport. Article 5 therefore protects an applicant from unlawful or arbitrary detention as soon as they are physically within the United Kingdom.

Requirements

For detention to be and remain lawful, Article 5 requires that detention be:

- in accordance with a procedure given in law; and
- for the purposes of preventing an unauthorised entry in to the United Kingdom; or
- whilst steps are being taken to remove that individual from the United Kingdom.

Entry

In the typical immigration bail case, the individual enters the United Kingdom and makes an application for asylum, which for the purposes of Article 5 can be regarded as a request for 'authorised entry' within the meaning of Article 5(1)(f). The process of determining whether that individual's entry should be authorised, is of course the consideration of the asylum claim by the Home Office and any subsequent appeal. Although there are powers for an immigration officer or the Home Office to detain the asylum applicant at any point during those proceedings, the crucial issue in any given case will be whether such detention is both lawful *and* procedurally fair. The same principles apply to other restrictions on liberty, such as conditions of residence and reporting, particularly when these cumulatively start to bear the complexion of detention. Even so, for obvious reasons asylum applicants whose liberty is restricted in such ways without actually being detained are unlikely to take issue.

In 2001, however, the Secretary of State introduced a policy not merely of *restricting* the liberty of asylum applicants in order to examine their claims, but in a particular category of cases *detaining* them altogether. The issue arose as to whether Article 5(1)(f) permitted detention for this purpose. In *R (on the application of Saadi) v Secretary of State for the Home Department* [2002] UKHL 41, [2002] 1 WLR 3131 the House of Lords held that the detention of four Iraqi Kurd asylum applicants at the Oakington Reception Centre was lawful:

(i) Until the Home Office had determined an asylum claim and authorised entry, the entry was 'unauthorised'.
(ii) The detention of asylum-seekers for the purposes of determining their claims therefore fell within Article 5(1)(f).
(iii) Such detention did not require that an asylum-seeker was seeking to enter by evading immigration control.
(iv) Nor did such detention have to be 'necessary' to prevent an unauthorised entry in the sense that no other procedure of determining an asylum claim would be sufficient.
(v) The detention was short-term, in an amenable environment and was both reasonable and proportionate to the aim of dealing with an increasing number of asylum claims.

Removal

The second purpose for which an individual can be detained under Article 5(1)(f) is that of removal, which also includes deportation and extradition.

In the case of *Chahal v United Kingdom* (1996) 23 EHRR 413, the long-term detention of the applicant pending deportation was held to be in accordance with the requirements of Article 5(1)(f). For detention to have been lawful it had to be shown that:

(i) removal was possible;
(ii) steps were being taken to enforce removal;
(iii) such action was being pursued with due diligence.

Procedural requirements

Articles 5(2) and 5(4) are concerned with the procedural fairness of the detention and with the ability to challenge detention. They work in conjunction with each other in so far as it is only when an individual has been informed of the reasons for their detention that they are in a position to effectively challenge their detention in court.

Reasons

The wording of Article 5(2): '. . . shall be informed promptly, in a language which he understands, of the reasons for his arrest . . .' is of particular importance in the context of immigration detention, requiring that the decision and reasons be communicated to the detainee in their own language. Rule 9 of the Detention Centre Rules 2001 (SI 2001/238) makes it a statutory requirement that an individual who is detained must be initially given the reasons for their detention followed by further reasons each month.

Review

A bail hearing before an adjudicator will allow an individual who is being detained the opportunity to argue that they should be released. Such a hearing is a vital safeguard of the right to liberty and in practical terms could be said to comply with Article 5(4). However, an adjudicator does not have jurisdiction to grant a declaration as to lawfulness of detention or damages and consequently this aspect of the right under Article 5(4) remains unsatisfied by a bail hearing. Challenging the actual lawfulness of detention is strictly speaking confined to High Court proceedings, whether judicial review or habeas corpus (see Chapter 8).

Paragraph 3.3 of the Guidance Notes to adjudicators from the Chief Adjudicator states:

> 'Article 5 of the ECHR requires a decision to detain to be reviewed at reasonable intervals (*Bezicheri v Italy* (1989) 12 EHRR 210). At present this can only be done in our jurisdiction by way of repeat applications for bail. What is a "reasonable interval" is a question of fact in each case. The Court said in *Bezicheri* that the nature of the detention on remand called for short intervals before the decision to detain was again considered by the court.'

Proportionality

Where statutory powers are exercised in a way which is incompatible with the ECHR, the decision to detain will be unlawful. Thus, even if the detention is lawful by reference to statutory powers and Home Office policy, there could still be a breach of Article 5. Article 5 requires that any restriction of liberty be *proportionate*, a principle intended to counter arbitrary detention.In the case of *Amirthanathan* [2003] EWHC 1107 judicial review was sought of the Secretary of State's decision to detain an asylum applicant between the refusal of a human rights application and prior to a notice of appeal being lodged, despite the applicant's representatives having already notified the Home Office of their intention to appeal. The applicant was not released until three days after the notice of appeal was lodged. The High Court held that it was 'more desirable for the state to have to wait for the time limit of ten working days to expire, than for an applicant to be detained because he had not yet formally lodged an appeal. In any event, the three days detention after the appeal was made was contrary to the Secretary of State's own policy.

The High Court further held that the detention was a breach of Article 5 of the ECHR, referring to *R (Saadi) v Secretary of State for the Home Department* [2002] UKHL 41, [2002] 1 WLR 3131, to the effect that for the purposes of Article 5, arbitrary detention was not merely irrational detention but also included detention that was disproportionate. Although the right to liberty was not one of the absolute rights such as Articles 2 or 3, it was nevertheless fundamental and concerned an area in which the courts have as much, if not more expertise than the executive. Consequently, only relatively slight deference should therefore be given to the Secretary of State's view on detentions.

SECURING RELEASE

Different considerations arise depending on whether a representative is dealing with an immigration officer or another Home Office official or applying to an adjudicator for bail.

Bail from an immigration officer

Where an individual has been initially detained and is not released on temporary admission, the representative will have to contact the relevant immigration officer, either by telephone in the first instance or by letter thereafter in attempting to secure temporary admission. Such an application will necessarily be expected to deal with the reasons for not granting temporary admission as stated in the Operational Enforcement Manual. The reasons given by the immigration officer should conform to the reasons given for detention in accordance with the Secretary of State's own policy. Experience shows that where a client is able to secure accommodation, half the battle may be won on that basis alone.

Where the request is not acceded to and detention continues, the right to regular review means that repeated requests can and must be made, particularly where there is new evidence or a change in circumstances. Representatives should additionally be aware that when asking for bail the Chief Immigration Officer may demand unrealistically high sums of money, and again negotiation on this point may be crucial in obtaining the client's release.

In *B* (18 December 1997, unreported), QBD, the High Court dealt with a refusal to grant bail to the applicant while his application for asylum was considered. It was held that the policy in respect of bail set out in *Brezinski and Glowacka* (CO/4237/95; CO/4251/95) (19 July 1996) and the powers of detention under the Immigration Act 1971 were used only where there was 'no alternative' and where there were strong grounds for believing that a person would not comply with the conditions of temporary admission. It was stated:

> 'One only restricts a person's liberty if it is *essential* to do so and one judges that by having regard to all the factors that are properly to be considered in a particular case.'
>
> (Emphasis added.)

Factors to be taken into consideration include whether there was any evidence of previous absconding from detention or previous failure to comply with conditions of temporary admission or bail, and whether the applicant has shown a blatant disregard for the immigration laws or has attempted to gain entry by presenting falsified documents. The longer a person has been detained, particularly if it was as a result of a failure on the part of the Home Office to resolve the case, the greater was the onus on the part of the Home Office to justify continuation of detention.

In *Tan Te Lam v Superintendent of Tai A Chau Detention Centre* [1997] AC 97, the Privy Council set out the principles that underlay the lawful detention of persons and the limits to be imposed. First and foremost, detention must only be for a lawful purpose, and must be no longer than is reasonably necessary. The immigration authorities must also act efficiently (and with 'due diligence': *Chahal v United Kingdom* (1996) 23 EHRR 413) to ensure that the purpose of the detention is carried into effect. Where this is not possible in a reasonable amount of time, detention could become excessive and once excessive, would no longer remain lawful.

Bail from an adjudicator

The IAA is for all practical purposes the only form of independent oversight of detention for hundreds of detainees. Clearly, if the applicant has previously been released on temporary admission or bailed either by an immigration officer or by an adjudicator then there will be a history to take into account. Where the applicant has been detained since arrival then the situation is more difficult. It would be wholly wrong for the court to infer from that situation that future non-compliance would naturally follow.

Too often an applicant's method of entry into the United Kingdom is unreasonably held against them. Having gained illegal entry into the United Kingdom, a significant number of asylum applicants claim asylum at a later point whether within weeks or months, or indeed having been apprehended by the police at some later time. Similarly, whether by presenting a false passport, travel document or visa, many asylum applicants use a form of 'deception' to gain entry into the United Kingdom. To allow the detention of such persons simply based on those broadly defined allegations, absent other serious justification, would seem arbitrary and wrong.

THE BAIL HEARING

The bail hearing will commence following the appropriate application notice, which will include the grounds on which the application is made, and where a previous application has been refused any change of circumstances. Bail applications are governed by Part 5 of the 2003 Procedure Rules. The application will be listed for hearing within three working days of receipt (Practice Direction CA6 of 2001). The bail hearing may take place either in isolation from the appeal hearing or at the appeal hearing itself, either in the first instance or as a renewal. Bail applications will be listed for hearing at the hearing centre nearest to where the applicant is being held. The hearing takes place in the same way as any appeal hearing with the Home Office frequently being represented. Where the Home Office are not represented, the hearing will nevertheless proceed, unless the applicant's representative wishes there to be an adjournment.

Chief Adjudicator's guidelines

The guidelines, issued in a revised form in May 2003, are intended to assist adjudicators responsible for hearing bail applications and to achieve uniformity in both procedure and decision-making. The guidelines can be summarised as follows:

- There is a common-law presumption in favour of bail, subject to the restrictions under paragraph 30 of Schedule 2 of the 1971 Act.
- By analogy with the Bail Act 1976, the burden of proving that detention is necessary lies on the Secretary of State, who must show that there are 'substantial grounds for believing' that the applicant if released on bail, whether subject to conditions or not, would fail to comply. 'Substantial grounds for believing' is a higher test than balance of probabilities.
- If the contents of the bail summary are insufficient to meet that standard an applicant will normally be entitled to bail. Where allegations in the bail summary are contested, the Secretary of State should adduce evidence in support including any documents.
- Applications should be dealt with in three stages:
  - (i) Is bail right in principle subject to suitable conditions?
  - (ii) Are sureties necessary?
  - (iii) If so, are the sureties satisfactory?
- Bail applications are required to be listed within three days of the application being received by the IAA.

- The applicant has the right to attend, to be represented and to have an interpreter. Attendance by the applicant should be the rule rather than the exception, especially if there is a dispute on the factual basis on which the Home Office oppose bail.

The bail summary

The 'bail summary' is a document setting out the Home Office's objections to bail and is usually the only 'evidence' produced by the Home Office. The bail summary should always be available at the hearing itself, although under rule 33(2) of the 2003 Procedure Rules, where the application is opposed by the Home Office, then they must file with the IAA and serve on the applicant a written statement of reasons either not later than 2pm the day before the hearing, or if served with notice of the hearing less than 24 hours before that time, then 'as soon as reasonably practicable'.

Conditions

As bail is only very rarely granted without conditions being imposed, it is imperative that the representative discusses with the applicant some of the possible conditions that may be attached to bail, so that they are neither taken by surprise when subjected to them, nor being asked about them in evidence. The consequences of breaching the conditions should also be discussed, including the likelihood of further detention. Conditions of residence and reporting to a local police station are usually appropriate. The frequency is a matter for the adjudicator but twice weekly is a reasonable starting-point (bearing in mind it may well be reduced on a renewal if there has been compliance). Other conditions may be imposed if they are necessary to ensure the applicant answers bail. A prohibition on taking up employment cannot be imposed.

SURETIES

The application notice will contain the full names, addresses, occupations and date of birth of any persons who have agreed to act as sureties, as well as the sum of money they have offered as surety.

The adjudicator will usually warn the sureties that they may forfeit some or all of their money if the applicant fails to attend at the appropriate time and absconds. Under rule 34(1)(a) and (b) the recognisance of the applicant or a surety must be in writing and must state both the amount in which they agree to be bound and that they have read and understood the bail decision and agree to pay that amount of money if the applicant fails to comply with the conditions set out in the bail decision.

The full details of the sureties should be sent to the Home Office on the completed form so that the relevant checks can be undertaken prior to the hearing, including whether the surety has a criminal record, and any previous immigration dealings, for example their address having being used by bailed persons who have absconded. The surety does not have to be a British citizen or settled in this country, but they should bring to court proof of their identity and any other relevant documents.

At the hearing the sureties will need to provide evidence of the money they are putting forward. This can be done by providing recent bank statements. Where the statement shows that there are conspicuous transfers soon or immediately prior to the application, this may raise questions about its legitimacy. One way of dispelling these is for the surety to lodge the money with the applicant's solicitors who can then guarantee by way of undertaking that they hold it for the court. Unless any specific evidence is required, a surety will need to obtain the following personal evidence:

- passport, birth certificate or other document confirming their identity;
- evidence confirming their address, for example tenancy agreement, utility bills, etc.;
- up-to-date bank or building society statements;
- employment and income documents.

It is imperative that the surety attends the hearing. Where for some reason they are unable to attend, a detailed, signed and dated letter from the surety enclosing written evidence proving their identity and other relevant details may be accepted as sufficient by the adjudicator.

No strict requirement for sureties

There is no rule that sureties *must* be given for bail to be secured. In *Lamin Minteh* (1996) 3 ILD the Court of Appeal held that where no sureties had been given it was unlawful for an adjudicator not to grant bail without regard to whether there was any evidence that the applicant was likely to abscond. Reliance was placed on published Home Office policy, to the effect that temporary admission should be granted whenever possible, and that detention in cases such as this should be authorised only where there was no alternative and where there were grounds for believing a person would not comply with the conditions of temporary admission.

In *Brezinski and Glowacka* (CO/4237/95; CO/4251/95) it was said that the starting point was one in which sureties were not required, but where it was not possible to ensure that the conditions would be observed that the use of sureties acted as 'extra ammunition' for an adjudicator to grant bail where he otherwise would not grant it.

Despite these clear statements of principle, adjudicators continue to demand sureties before release, despite being aware that asylum applicants rarely have family or friends who can stand as sureties, and often regardless of whether sureties are even appropriate in the particular circumstances of the case.

Chief Adjudicator's guidelines – sureties

- Sureties are only to be required if an adjudicator cannot be otherwise satisfied that the applicant will comply with any conditions imposed on a grant of bail.
- If sureties are offered it is only exceptionally that an adjudicator is likely to proceed with hearing, unless the adjudicator is of the view that sureties are not required.
- It should be borne in mind that asylum applicants rarely have relatives or friends in the United Kingdom who can act as sureties.
- Adjudicators have no power to require that a bail bond be entered into and cannot require the deposit of a surety. If the money has already been deposited the adjudicator can agree to this before accepted the surety as suitable.

- Where the money has not been deposited, the adjudicator does not arguably have jurisdiction to make the applicant's release conditional upon it, but it would be appropriate to request the sureties to give an oral undertaking to instruct the applicant's solicitors to hold the money on their behalf and to give the IAA an undertaking not to part with it without the express authority of the IAA. The applicant's solicitors will be required to confirm this in writing.
- A recognisance taken from a surety should be realistic and based on their means, not on matters in the bail summary. The amount should be within the sureties' resources, great enough to encourage compliance with their obligations but not so high as to be prohibitive.
- If the adjudicator is considering a very low amount, it should be asked whether a surety is necessary in the first place.
- The amount must always be adequate and sufficient to secure attendance. There is however, no tariff figure, and the sums involved are always a matter for the adjudicator.
- The adjudicator must be satisfied that in the event of forfeiture the payment can and will be made by the surety.
- A member of a charity or church cannot put the funds of such an organisation forward as a surety. They may however be able to give moral force to attendance and in such circumstances the adjudicator may feel bail can be granted without the need for a surety.

Recognisances

An adjudicator is required to take a recognisance from the applicant before they are released on bail. If the applicant has no assets this can be a nominal sum of £10 or less.

REFUSING BAIL

Where an adjudicator refuses bail, brief reasons should be given in court and noted in the Record of Proceedings and a form entitled 'Refusal of Bail' is filled in by the adjudicator but is kept on file. At present there is no requirement for written reasons to be given save for the notice of the decision. However, the adjudicator must keep a record of the evidence, arguments for and against bail, the decision and reasons for it. Where bail is refused there will be the opportunity of making a renewed application for bail.

In the case of *I* [2002] EWCA Civ 888 the Court of Appeal listed a number of factors relevant to a decision to detain pending deportation, but which are also relevant to the issue of detention generally:

(i) the length of detention;
(ii) the obstacles that stand in the way of removal;
(iii) the speed and effectiveness of any steps taken by the Secretary of State to surmount such obstacles;
(iv) the conditions in which the applicant is detained;
(v) the effect of detention upon the applicant and his/her family;
(vi) the risk of absconding;
(vii) the danger that, if released, the applicant will commit criminal offences.

One of the most common reasons for refusing bail is that there is a 'greater than normal risk of absconding' and this is dealt with in greater detail below.

Risk of absconding

The risk of the applicant failing to attend when required to do so, is only one of a number of factors to be taken into account and must be balanced against them. The burden of proof is on the Secretary of State to show that the individual will 'probably abscond'. In the case of *I* [2002] EWCA Civ 888 an Afghani asylum applicant was detained for 15 months pending a recommendation for deportation. The Court of Appeal held that:

> 'The relevance of likelihood of absconding, if proved, should not be overstated. Carried to its logical conclusion, it could become a trump card that carried the day for the Secretary of State in every case where such a risk was made out regardless of all other considerations, not least the length of detention. That would be a wholly unacceptable outcome where human liberty is at stake.'

In *Stefanowicz* (CO/2451/96) the High Court stated that 'any policy that locks up those not immediately going to ground would be ridiculous and irrational'. In *R v Secretary of State for the Home Department, ex p Mendje* [2000] Imm AR 353 the High Court held that there was no obligation on the Secretary of State to show that there was a high degree of probability that the applicant would abscond. It was the balance of probabilities standard.

The Chief Adjudicator's guidelines also provide assistance:

> 'Unless you can find that there is a materially greater than normal risk of the appellant absconding, and cannot be satisfied he would comply with any conditions attached to his bail, and in particular to appear in answer thereto, even if there were satisfactory sureties and recognizances then bail must be granted.'

Continuation of bail

Renewal of bail may be considered as simply a new date to appear before the adjudicator where there is an ongoing appeal with a view primarily to extending, or discontinuing the need for bail depending on the circumstances of the case. Conditions may of course be varied at the renewal hearing, and where there has been compliance with the conditions already imposed, adjudicators are often willing to relax them in favour of the applicant. Both the applicant and the sureties should attend. Where they are unable to attend, the court should be informed in writing and the sureties should give clear written confirmation of their willingness to continue to act as sureties. Where a surety fails to attend and has not given written notice of his intention to continue acting, it will usually be appropriate for the adjudicator to continue bail, given that the applicant has attended. Where there has been a breach by the applicant of one of the conditions then more stringent conditions are likely to be imposed.

Where the renewal hearing is after the hearing of the applicant's appeal, bail is normally granted for a period of six weeks. Following that, where there is an appeal to the Tribunal the applicant will be bailed to appear before that Tribunal or four weeks later in any event.

CONCLUSION

In summary form, the following factors are to be taken into account when considering whether detention is justified:

- Is detention under a statutory power and for the purpose for which the power is given?
- If so has it nevertheless gone beyond a time that is reasonably necessary? Is the exercise of detention reasonable when weighed against the alternative of temporary admission?
- Is the exercise of detention reasonable when weighed against the alternative of temporary admission? If not, has detention nevertheless gone beyond the period of time that is reasonably necessary?
- Has there been a failure to follow Home Office policy?
- Is detention in accordance with Article 5 ECHR ? Is it in reality for a lawful purpose i.e. to prevent unlawful entry or to remove the individual ? Is it procedurally fair ?
- Above all, is detention proportionate and reasonable?

In seeking to obtain bail, the task of the representative is essentially either to demonstrate that the reasons why bail is objected to are invalid, or that further detention is disproportionate or unreasonable. Moreover, although there may be good reasons for detention, these can frequently still be overcome by reference to the underlying principles and policies relating to detention, and by the offering of suitable conditions and sureties.

CHAPTER 4

Instructions and Evidence

HOME OFFICE REFUSALS

As noted in the introduction to this book, the Home Office refuse a large proportion (about 65%) of claims at first instance. A number of these cases are refused because the case was simply not presented properly, for example where the statement was sparse or worse illegible, or important documentary evidence was not translated and so could not be taken into account. In addition, claims frequently include allegations of torture or assertions that removal from the United Kingdom would adversely affect the applicant's health. Such claims are often refused by the Home Office because no supporting medical or psychiatric evidence was provided.

The number of first-instance refusals also includes many non-compliance refusals, ie where the Statement of Evidence Form (SEF) was not submitted in time or at all or where the applicant failed to attend an interview and the Home Office decide that an applicant has failed to establish their claim. Although in many such cases it turns out that the Home Office erred in stating that there was non-compliance and it was in fact their own administrative error, it also has to be said that representatives are often responsible.

GETTING THE BEST START

The aim of this chapter is to emphasise the importance of presenting a claim as strongly and coherently as possible from the very start and maintaining control of it thereafter. The approach of some representatives has all too often been to rely heavily on an automatic right of appeal. However, a case that has started off badly will often require a disproportionate effort to put into order, and without which it will go from bad to worse. This must also be seen in light of the fact that whenever legislative changes occur in this field, they tend to restrict rather than expand appeal rights –

s 94 of the Nationality, Immigration and Asylum Act 2002 (the 2002 Act) being the most recent example.

The goal must always be to avoid the client having to endure the delay, uncertainty and sheer ordeal of an appeal by having their claim succeed at first instance if at all possible. The Home Office do of course frequently make unreasonable decisions based on obvious factual and legal errors, but that only increases the importance of putting forward the strongest possible claim at first instance, so that whatever the basis of refusal, it is not because more could or should have been done for the applicant at that stage.

OVERVIEW OF THE ASYLUM PROCESS

The Immigration and Nationality Directorate (IND) of the Home Office is the department that deals with asylum applications. When an asylum application has been made, whether at the port of entry or after an asylum applicant has entered the country, they will be 'screened' during which their personal details are recorded and their photograph and fingerprints taken. The applicant is then issued with an Application Registration Card, which has replaced the former Standard Acknowledgement Letter, and allows asylum applicants to access the support and other services provided for them. This initial procedure stage is often gone through without the applicant having recourse to legal advice.

Before proceeding further it should be noted that when the applicant arrives in the United Kingdom having already claimed asylum in a European Union country, or can be removed to a designated safe third country, namely one that will not cause the United Kingdom to breach the Refugee Convention, then there will usually not be an in-country right of appeal. We deal with these issues in Chapter 8.

After being screened the applicant will generally be given a Statement of Evidence Form (SEF) in which to set out the basis of their claim. After the completed SEF has been received by the Home Office, the applicant will then usually attend a full asylum interview. The aim of IND caseworkers is to reach a decision on the application within two months. There are three usual outcomes:

- The applicant is recognised as a refugee under the terms of the Refugee Convention and is granted indefinite leave to remain (ILR) in the United Kingdom.
- The applicant is refused asylum, but humanitarian protection (HP) is granted for a limited period under Article 3 of the ECHR or discretionary leave (DL) is granted because there are other compelling reasons for allowing the applicant to stay in this country. The applicant can still appeal against the refusal of asylum to an adjudicator sitting in the Immigration Appellate Authority (IAA).
- Both the asylum and human rights claim are refused, in which case there will normally be a right of appeal to an adjudicator against both decisions.

TAKING INITIAL INSTRUCTIONS

At whatever stage the representative meets the client, whether soon after entry or just prior to removal from the United Kingdom, the importance of obtaining clear and comprehensive instructions is vital. Even if these details already appear in their documents, they still need to be checked with the client.

Personal details

The obvious starting point is to be sure of the client's name, age, address and telephone or mobile number in the United Kingdom. The client will also have a 'port reference number', a 'Home Office reference number or an 'IAA appeal reference number' and these should be given in any subsequent correspondence or communications with the Home Office or IAA regarding their case.

All the client's above details should be recorded on the case file straight away and then checked at every subsequent meeting or court hearing. It must be impressed on the client that any change of address should *immediately* be notified to the representative or, where that is not possible for some reason, then directly to the Home Office. It of course follows that the representative should inform the Home Office and, where applicable, the IAA of any changes of address. A good number of applications to the Tribunal are made on the basis that the applicant was not aware of the date of their appeal and therefore did not attend, only to have their case dealt with by the Adjudicator on paper and dismissed. The anguish and waste of resources this represents could in most cases have been avoided.

The next step is to ask whether the client has any relatives or friends in the United Kingdom and whether they are contactable. Their details must also be obtained and recorded. Subsequent questions should establish the following:

- the client's nationality and ethnicity;
- the client's religious or political affiliations;
- the country and the region from which they originate or were previously living;
- the reasons why they have fled from their country and from whom, and why they fear persecution or a breach of their human rights;
- any other reasons why they cannot return or otherwise should not be forced to leave the United Kingdom.

The initial application

The basis of the claim may well be straightforward and an application for asylum obviously needs to be made if this has not already been done by the client on arrival. Sometimes, however, things are less clear-cut, for example where no fear is manifested by a client who comes from a country where such fear would be well-founded or vice versa. This will obviously require further exploration and instructions.

In other cases a client may be injured, traumatised, mentally ill or suffering from another illness, which will necessitate registering them with a GP if they do not already have one, with a view to being referred to a suitable specialist. In most cases where there are physical problems, these will be known from the outset. However, where the client is suffering from a mental illness this may not be so easily apparent, but signs such as being unresponsive and disengaged should alert the representative to the need for a referral. If they claim to be a minor and age is disputed by the Home Office this too may require an expert report, particularly as the Home

Office policy regarding unaccompanied minors is generally to not interview and to grant discretionary leave until the age of 18.

If the client has already claimed asylum at port or at the Home Office, they will have had a screening interview, been issued with a Registration Card and have been granted 'temporary admission'. A statement of evidence form (SEF) then has to be completed and returned within 12 working days. If the client has come directly to the representative, they should be given a letter of introduction to take to the Home Office and so commence the above procedure.

Claim or appeal pending

There will also be cases where a client has already made an asylum or human rights claim that has been refused and an appeal before an adjudicator or the Tribunal is pending. Clearly the client or his previous representatives will have documentation concerning the nature and status of his appeal and this must be obtained and considered by the new representative as quickly as is possible.

Fresh evidence or change in circumstances

Finally, the client may have previously made an asylum or human rights claim which has been rejected by the Home Office, and has exhausted all of his or her rights of appeal. If the client has further evidence that was not previously available, even if relating to the previous claim, or there is a significant change in either their personal circumstances or the country situation, then the new representative should consider making a fresh asylum or human rights claim to the Home Office. For judicial review of fresh claim refusals, see Chapter 8.

THE SCREENING INTERVIEW

The main purpose of the screening interview is to confirm an applicant's identity, address and mode of entry into the United Kingdom, as well as their eligibility for asylum support. If the representative does not already have a copy of the record of the screening interview, it should be obtained from the Home Office as soon as possible, as it is likely to include information relevant to the claim, such as: whether the client had a passport; what was done with it; what countries were passed through and how long they spent there; and what the client initially said about their reasons for coming to the United Kingdom. The answers recorded in the screening interview must of course be checked against the client's instructions and if there are any inconsistencies they should be dealt with in the SEF.

THE STATEMENT OF EVIDENCE FORM

The SEF is invariably the first written account of the client's asylum claim. The importance and potential repercussions arising from this document are very often overlooked. The SEF will provide a basis on which an immigration officer will question the client at the substantive interview and, together with any other evidence submitted, will constitute the claim to be considered by the Home Office. The SEF will also stand as an evidential document in any subsequent appeal hearing, will be scrutinised by the adjudicator at the appeal and will have a definite impact on the appellant's credibility.

The representative will usually fill in the SEF at their office with the client and interpreter present to give instructions. Regrettably this procedure is frequently rushed and the SEF is often completed by hand and sometimes not checked or read over to the client at all. Even worse, it is not unknown for the basis of a claim to be assumed by representatives on the very scantiest of instructions. In such cases it hardly needs pointing out that what may have been an arguable claim if properly prepared will be effectively ruined from the outset.

The SEF itself does not provide much room for the actual substance of the claim to be written down. The best practice is therefore to complete the necessary boxes for personal and family details by hand, tick the relevant Convention reason(s) and attach a comprehensive stand-alone statement to the back of the SEF. Although this will invariably require obtaining detailed and often lengthy instructions, there is simply no choice in the matter if the client is to be given the best prospects of success in their claim. Time spent at this stage is certainly not wasted. Making sure that a client gives their first account in a chronological, coherent and logical way will also reduce the chances of important details being left out and of there being any inconsistencies with the interview and any further statement prepared for an appeal in the event that the claim is refused.

A major factor in the determination of the claim by the Home Office will be credibility. Refusal Letters frequently cite inconsistencies in the applicant's account as a reason for disbelieving and refusing a claim. Where a representative can refer the adjudicator to what the client said at the very outset of their claim for asylum in the SEF set against what the client subsequently said in written and oral evidence as being consistent, this will greatly resound to the client's credibility. Conversely, any subsequent additions or differences to the evidence contained in the SEF are more likely to have a negative effect on the appellant's credibility.

Language difficulties

It goes without saying that the interpreter should be able to fully understand the client's answers and translate them into English. Another frequent problem in this regard, is dealing with dates given by clients, especially where the dates are not in the Gregorian Calendar and will require conversion. Dates should *always* be double-checked but even more so in the latter scenario to avoid any later problems. Another difficulty is the use of specific terminology. Particular care should be taken when describing technical matters and issues specific to the case. Often there is an inadequate word or no word in the client's language, and therefore descriptive language (instead of chancing the nearest or most literal word) leaving no ambiguity, is a necessity. To give one very obvious example, rather than use the specific term 'persecution' it may be best to ask 'what kinds of problems' the client experienced in their home country.

THE SEF – THE ATTACHED STATEMENT

The statement should be typed and not handwritten. It should start by identifying its maker and confirm that the statement is made to the best of the client's knowledge and belief. The statement should then proceed to explain:

- the applicant's personal and family background;
- a clear, chronological and relevant history of the case: what event or events led to the persecution; the forms of persecution suffered and from whom, for example the state or non-state agents; whether they sought protection; if not then why not; how they came to leave and by what means; if their journey to the United Kingdom involved stopping in or travelling through other countries which are signatories to the Convention; any reasons why they did not claim asylum there; any relevant developments in their country since leaving; any evidence of a continuing adverse interest in the applicant;
- that the applicant is outside the country of their nationality due to persecution or harm suffered and the applicable Convention reason(s);
- details of any significant health problems afflicting the applicant, treatment being received or to be received in the United Kingdom and whether this would be affected by removal to the home country;
- if the applicant has a partner or spouse in the United Kingdom: the partner's own personal details, nationality and immigration status; the background to and length of their relationship; their state of health; whether there are any children and if so, their personal details, length of time in the United Kingdom, schooling, state of health etc.; what effect removal is likely to have on this relationship or family unit; what kinds of problems they will face in the applicant's home country;
- studies undertaken, employment, business or other civic contributions made whilst living in the United Kingdom;
- any other family or friends in the United Kingdom and the nature and strength of these ties;
- the basis for any further human rights considerations.

It is of course acknowledged that these are general objectives, but if kept at the forefront of the representative's mind they will be of great assistance. The statement should be in simple and clear language and should not be any longer than necessary. Great care should be taken, however, to ensure that it is accurate and sufficiently detailed to impress the claim on its reader. The statement must also be truthful insofar as the representative can ensure:

reading the statement back to the applicant and checking each sentence for accuracy is a required practice. For completeness there should be a declaration at the end of the statement that the client has had the statement read back to them in their own language, and it should be signed and dated, and include the interpreter's declaration where appropriate.

If carefully prepared, the SEF statement can be adopted as the principal part of the applicant's evidence-in-chief at any appeal hearing. If the client has maintained their credibility at later stages (which in itself will be much more likely if the SEF statement was true and accurate) it will reduce the scope for cross-examination by a Home Office presenting officer (HOPO) who generally focuses on inconsistencies between statements and documents, with the SEF usually receiving the most attention.

Statements are often protracted by over-emphasis on tangential or irrelevant aspects of a case, or worse are instead seriously lacking in necessary information. The approach should be to concentrate on exploring and explaining the central issues required for a valid claim. Two examples of statements in a fictional case are given below, which we hope demonstrate the 'wrong' and 'right' ways of drafting statements.

The wrong way

I was born in Pakistan. My father is from Multan and I also have 2 older brothers. In 1998 my father arranged for me to get married to a boy. I do not know him and had never seen him in my life, but my father knew his family very well and paid them a large dowry. I felt very upset by this arrangement as I had already met another boy who was one of the neighbours in our village who I loved. When my father found out about this he became very angry and started shouting and hitting me. He said that if I did not forget about my boyfriend, it would bring shame to the whole family. My brother said that I would be in trouble. After a while I decided that I could not bear this anymore as he was a lot older than me. I also knew that the boy's family would become very angry if I did not marry him. In February 1999 his family tried to kidnap me when I was out buying the shopping, to ensure that I got married. I managed to escape and I went to a friend's house. I reported this incident to the police but they did not listen and said that the family would not do this. I stayed with her for two weeks. I left my country in fear of my life and came directly to the UK. I arrived on the 16th of March 1999. I did not claim asylum because my friend in Pakistan told me that I should not, and she gave me an address in Ealing. I stayed with these people for two months but I was treated very badly and forced to do lots of housework in their home. I spoke to some other people who told me that I should claim asylum. My father has written to me saying that I should not return to Pakistan because he would kill me. I have also received a phone call from my elder brother. I am in fear of my life if I were to be returned to Pakistan.

A better way

Statement of Ms Yasmin Khan

1. My full name is Yasmin Khan. I am a female citizen of Pakistan, born on 31 May 1979 and I am 23 years of age. I make this statement in support of my asylum and human rights claim. I confirm that the contents have been read back to me in Urdu and are true to the best of my knowledge and belief.
2. I was born in Lahore, but my family moved to Islamabad when I was five years old. I lived with them until two weeks before I arrived in the United Kingdom. I have a younger sister aged 13 and two elder brothers Ahmed (aged 22) and Asif (aged 24) who are all in Islamabad. After completing secondary school my parents did not allow me to continue with my studies and would not let me go out to work, but they made me stay at home and look after the house.
3. In August 1998 my father arranged for me to get married to a man from our neighbouring village. I did not know him and I had never seen him before. I was simply told that his name was Shahab and that he was a lot older than me. I was told that I had no choice in the matter and that I should make the necessary preparations. My father knew Shahab's father very well, and I believe that my father paid him a large sum of money as a dowry, although I do not know how much.
4. I was extremely upset and distressed by the arranged marriage that I was being forced into, particularly as I had previously formed a relationship with a man named Hassan Iqbal whom I had gone to secondary school with. I had been seeing him for a number of months and I felt very much in love. My father came to know of this relationship and consequently became physically abusive towards me. On one occasion, it was either the 3rd or 4th September 1998, after I had been with Hassan, my father beat me very badly and I was not allowed to leave the house for a month. My father threatened that he would kill me if I did not obey him, and that he would not allow a daughter of his to bring shame on the

family. I could tell by the way he said this that he would seriously harm me if I did not follow his wishes.

5. On the 15th of February 1999, an attempt was made to kidnap me whilst I was at the local shops buying food for the family. I was pulled into a car and a man who I recognised as one of Shahab's work colleagues told me that 'I had better sort my act out and get married or there would be trouble.' At the same time as telling me this he was gripping me around the throat. I struggled and managed to get hold of a bottle from my shopping bag which I smashed over his head. He was forced to let go of me and I got out the car and ran away down an alleyway. I was extremely scared by this incident but I was also very frightened of going home to my family. I decided to leave and went to my best friend Naseem Rasheed's house which is about 4 km away on the outskirts of Islamabad.
6. After two days I felt strong enough to go to the police. I reported the incident to the police and a First Information Report was made. However the police did not really take my complaint seriously. The officer in charge said that he knew of Shahab's family and did not think that they would behave improperly. He said that they did not have time to investigate such matters anyway. I had no confidence in the police and I did not think that they were willing to protect me. I also knew that I could not possibly stay with my family if I wanted to avoid getting married. I went back to stay with Naseem for the next two weeks during which I did not venture out at all but remained at home to avoid any contact with either my own or Shahab's family or friends.
7. Due to these experiences I knew that I was not safe in Islamabad. I could not stay with Naseem indefinitely as she was scared that my family would soon track me down. As a single young woman without employment or money of my own it would be impossible for me to live alone and I did not have any other friends or family elsewhere in Pakistan who I could go and live with in safety. It was only a matter of time before I was made the subject of an honour killing by my family. Apart

from Naseem I had no other person I could go to. I was afraid to even contact Hassan in case that put him in danger. I decided that I must leave Pakistan.

8. Naseem helped me raise some money to pay an agent who could arrange a passport and ticket for me. The agent suggested that the United Kingdom was the best place to go for a woman in my position. With his help I left Pakistan on the 15th of March 1999 and flew directly to the United Kingdom. I did not claim asylum on arrival because I had been advised by the agent not to do so and I trusted him. He also gave me the address of a family in Ealing who he said would look after me.
9. I stayed with the family for two months but I was treated very badly and forced to do demeaning manual work in the home. I was not allowed to go outside. After two months they began to let me go out and I met some other Pakistani women who told me that I should claim asylum. Three days later, on the 28th of May 1999 I made a claim for asylum at Croydon.
10. Since I have been in the United Kingdom I have written to my father to try and explain my feelings and to be reconciled with him. However, in return I have received two letters from him saying that I disgraced the family and if I return to Pakistan he would be forced to kill me. I attach to my statement copies of these letters and the envelopes, as well as certified translations. I have also received a phone call from my brother Asif who threatened that he would kill me if I were to return to Pakistan.
11. I have been in the United Kingdom for over four years now and I feel much safer here. If I were to be returned to Pakistan I am certain that even now I would be subjected to an honour killing, because I am viewed as having brought permanent shame on the entire family.

Signed: Yasmin Khan Dated: 16 July 2003

Interpreter's declaration

I can confirm that I have read the statement back to the applicant in Urdu

Signed: Dated: 16 July 2003

Observations

What is immediately apparent is that the second statement is typed and in numbered paragraphs and therefore easy on the eye. The statement is logical, clear and comprehensive, giving detail where necessary but avoiding surplus information.

As we have said, SEFs are invariably lacking in the information and details which are essential to found a valid asylum or human rights claim. In many cases that proceed to appeal, there remain glaring gaps and omissions in the SEF which have only been rectified at the Home Office interview, a later statement, or indeed in oral evidence. The role of the representative must be a dynamic rather than passive one. Instead of simply listening to an account and reproducing it in written form, a critical and probing approach must be employed. It is tempting to just ask a client 'Tell the story, in your own words, of why you came to the United Kingdom'. In many cases, that may be a reasonable starting point, but it will never be sufficient. At the very least, when an account has been given it should be looked at as a whole.

Does the account make sense?

Is the account coherent and understandable in human terms? Representatives must of course recognise that concepts of what constitutes reasonable human behaviour may differ greatly between countries, societies and cultures. However, it is worth bearing in mind at this point that the immigration officer considering the claim on paper, and even the adjudicator hearing an eventual appeal, will almost inevitably take their own views and life experience as a starting-point. The best way of forestalling such preconceptions is to raise with the client at the first opportunity any aspects of their account that do not on the face of it make sense. The client will frequently be able to provide helpful explanation to put their account in context. It will also be helpful for the representative to have an eye to the objective evidence, which may also assist in making sense of the events described by the client.

Does the account disclose a valid claim?

Does the claim satisfy the necessary legal requirements of an asylum or a human rights claim? Does it disclose for example that the client has a fear of persecution, which is objectively justified, with no reasonable avenue of internal relocation, and for a Convention reason?

Do more instructions need to be taken?

Often an initial account is not merely lacking coherence or detail in certain parts, but lacks any overall sense at all. Different clients will present their stories in very different ways. However, the SEF will not of itself make allowances for this as it is a piece of written evidence that must be capable of standing alone. In order to ensure that the SEF does in fact contain the client's whole case, a probing or inquisitorial approach will often be required. Of course, this should be done cautiously and sensitively, particularly with vulnerable, traumatised or unwell clients.

The end result

The result of the above process should be a statement of the case that alone constitutes a valid claim for asylum or protection under the ECHR. This will impact on the client in two ways. Firstly, it is a good bridge to the interview, which will usually follow the completion of the SEF submitted to the Home Office. Secondly, as already pointed out, it is a concrete evidential document for use in any appeal.

The SEF should be photocopied at least twice, and sent with any enclosures or representations by recorded delivery so as to be guaranteed to reach the Home Office within the requisite time-limit. Proof of posting should always be retained in case there is any future dispute over whether it was received in time or at all by the Home Office.

ORIGINAL EVIDENCE

Original evidence can take many forms:

- birth certificates;
- identity documents;
- death certificates;

- employment or business documents;
- political party membership cards;
- arrest warrants;
- court summonses;
- contemporaneous medical reports;
- letters from relatives in the home country;
- photographs;
- marriage certificates.

Where applicable certified translations of documents should be obtained and copies of both served on the Home Office as soon as available.

The approach of the courts

The assessment by adjudicators and the Tribunal of the genuineness of such documents has the been the subject of two important recent decisions: *Tanveer Ahmed* [2002] INLR 345 and *Oleed* [2003] INLR 179, both of which should be read together. The former is a 'starred' decision of the Tribunal regarding the proper approach to documentary evidence produced by an asylum applicant. The latter is a decision of the Court of Appeal which concerned an appeal by a male Tamil from Sri Lanka who produced an arrest warrant which showed he was wanted by the security forces. This 'tipped the balance' in his favour. The adjudicator accepted on the lower standard of proof that the warrant was authentic and concluded that the appellant would be at risk of persecution by the security forces if returned to Sri Lanka.

What is interesting about *Oleed* is that although the existence of the warrant was consistent with the appellant's account, the warrant's date did not exactly tally with the dates given by the appellant. However, the adjudicator properly applied the lower standard of proof and took this item of evidence into account. The Home Office appealed to the Tribunal, who allowed the appeal. The asylum applicant appealed in turn to the Court of Appeal who in restoring the adjudicator's original determination significantly pointed out that:

> 'To do the former [that is to find that the warrant was not genuine] in the absence of a challenge from the Home Secretary to the authenticity of the warrant would have been a bold step. It is not a step which should in my judgement have been taken, at least not without adequate warning before the hearing so as to permit Mr Oleed to try and find other evidence of authenticity – such as asking the Home Office through the High Commissioner to check with the Magistrates' Court or such as obtaining evidence from his sister.'

Oleed is a positive recognition of three principles:

(i) Documentary evidence of this kind cannot be dismissed without careful consideration and adequate reasoning.

(ii) The Home Office and indeed an adjudicator should not proceed to challenge or doubt such evidence without giving the appellant a fair opportunity to meet such concerns. The more so, we would suggest, if such evidence has been served in good time before the hearing.

(iii) It is wrong to necessarily expect documentary evidence to match an appellant's account in 'chapter and verse' fashion, particularly where, as in this case, the country background provides possible explanations for this.

Ultimately however, the question is whether on the lower standard of proof, the Home Office at first instance or the adjudicator on appeal, can be satisfied of the veracity of the documents. Once this hurdle is cleared, the issue is how relevant they are to the claim and to the question of risk, which will of course very much depend on the facts of the case.

Obtaining corroboration

It is an important principle of refugee law that corroboration is *not* an essential requirement for an account to be accepted. That said, however, it will always be valuable for an applicant to have evidential documents to support their account or parts of it. Where there is a possibility that genuine documents can be obtained, all avenues should be pursued. If the representative is not in a position to do this, for example because the applicant believes that contacting individuals in his home country might put them in danger or exacerbate his own plight if returned, it must be left to the applicant's own judgement. However, the situation in many cases is that obtaining at least one document will simply require effort and time, and the applicant should be encouraged to at least try to obtain any evidence to support their case. If there are credibility problems for example, or the case is finely balanced, it may make all the difference.

Handling documents

Documents are often in original form and perhaps old or fragile. In the criminal and civil jurisdictions, original evidence is very carefully protected and documents and other exhibits are frequently bagged or otherwise protected. By contrast in asylum and human rights cases, which inherently involve much more serious issues, crucial evidence is frequently hole-punched, stapled, torn and written on, and generally not given the care which its importance demands. At the very least, documents should be put in clear plastic envelopes in order to prevent damage or deterioration. Needless to say, every conceivable effort should be made not to lose them.

Similarly, serious consideration has to be given to how these documents are brought to the attention of the Home Office. It is far from unknown for the Home Office to lose not only SEFs but original and irreplaceable evidence as well. We would suggest that the Home Office are served with copies initially, so that they are aware that the evidence exists and is to be relied on. Copies are often sufficient for authentication purposes as well.

The covering letter sent with the documents should indicate that if copies are not sufficient to determine the veracity, then the originals can of course be sent. Should the Home Office require this to be done it is obvious that the documents should be sent by recorded delivery. By the same token, the originals should not be sent to the court, only copies. Original documents should generally be retained on the representative's case file and only taken to court on the day of the appeal hearing. In countless cases original evidence has been either lost or mislaid so that it was not before the court for the appeal. Appellants are understandably distressed by this and it can be difficult to persuade them that their case is going to receive a fair hearing, even if copies are available.

Home Office checks on veracity

Although there is strictly speaking no duty on the Home Office to make their own inquiries as to the genuineness of documents put forward in an asylum claim, in certain cases they can and will do so, for example through the Foreign and Commonwealth Office and the relevant Embassy. Evidence that is open to such checks, for example arrest warrants or court summonses, should be sent to the Home Office under cover of a letter warning that any Home Office inquiries should be made in an anonymous manner that will not reveal the client's whereabouts or that they have claimed asylum and requesting that all correspondence relating to the inquiries is disclosed.

Producing the documents as evidence

Whenever a piece of original evidence is to be relied on, it must be 'put into evidence' in the following way:

- The documents should be referred to chronologically or in logical order in the statement.
- The provenance of the documents should be explained in sufficient detail. Where the documents have been sent to the United Kingdom from abroad, the envelope or packaging in which they came will often be as valuable as the documents themselves and should be retained (a HOPO will frequently try to cast doubt on a document by pointing to the lack of evidence of its origin).
- The relevance of the documents to the applicant's particular case should be fully explained in the statement or, if this has not been possible, at the hearing itself.

MEDICAL REPORTS

Representatives must consider from an early stage whether a medical report should be obtained in support of a claim. A medical report could for example demonstrate that a client's physical condition (wounds, scars, bruising, ongoing pain or other after-effects) are consistent with or indeed highly probative of their claim to having been tortured or physically abused in their home country.

Often due to the ill-treatment a client has suffered they will have symptoms of post-traumatic stress disorder (PTSD) or other related psychological or mental health problems. A psychiatric report will still be necessary if only to detail how this would affect the appellant's ability to give evidence or answer questions at the hearing, and will have a bearing on the adjudicator's assessment of their evidence and therefore their credibility.

Another reason for a medical report would be to demonstrate that the client requires or is receiving a particular type of treatment or medication for an illness or other disorder, and that removal would expose him to serious health consequences. Even if this would not result in a real risk of inhuman or degrading treatment, it may still have an impact on the consideration of the case by the Home Office on compassionate grounds.

We would not, however, seek to suggest a practice of medical reports across-the-board in each and every case. There may be instances where there has been past ill-treatment which will have no bearing on the current risk on return, for example, where the authorities responsible for that ill-treatment are no longer in power. Given that the issue of safety on return must be considered at the date of decision, medical evidence in such a case may not be justified. Whether medical evidence is required will be a matter of judgement for the representative.

Choosing a specialist

The nature and history of the ill-treatment and/or the health problems in a particular case will govern the type of specialist that should be instructed. Many medical reports are effectively ignored by adjudicators because the authors are not sufficiently or suitably qualified or experienced to reach the conclusions they give. In particular, it is expected that reports dealing with torture are written by practitioners with relevant experience, and that a diagnosis of PTSD be made by a consultant psychiatrist. In general, reports should state the position, qualifications and expertise of the expert, confirm their awareness of their duty to the court, before detailing the client's medical history and presentation, describing the clinical examination and findings and then giving reasoned diagnoses and conclusions.

Representatives should therefore exercise some care in their choice of expert. The Medical Foundation for the Care of Victims of Torture is a popular choice, because they are a renowned organisation with obvious expertise. However, in practice the Medical Foundation is in such high demand that it may take many months to get a preliminary assessment pursuant to the Foundation deciding whether to take on the case. A more realistic approach would be for representatives to instruct a practitioner who has recognised expertise in the relevant field. The Law Society Directory of Expert Witnesses is usually a good start, as is asking the Medical Foundation or indeed other representatives to recommend a suitable expert.

It is our experience that adjudicators are reluctant to adjourn hearings in order for medical reports to be obtained, even if steps have already been taken to instruct an expert. Additionally, adjudicators are now restricted by the statutory closure dates for appeal hearings. It is therefore never too early to 'set the wheels in motion' in this regard and ideally, and in accordance with the concept of front-loading a claim, such a report should be obtained as soon as reasonably possible so that it can be considered by the Home Office in determining the application. Once an expert has been instructed, an appointment should be arranged to be attended by the client and an interpreter if necessary. The expert should be provided in advance with the client's SEF, interview and any other statements, as well as the Home Office Refusal Letter if a decision has already been made.

THE HOME OFFICE INTERVIEW

In the majority of cases the applicant will already have completed and submitted an SEF before the interview. Sometimes, however, the Home Office do not issue an SEF but proceed to arrange an interview during which the asylum applicant will be expected to set out for the first time, their claim for asylum or human rights protection. The latter scenario obviously provides a far less cautious and sympathetic opportunity for the applicant to give a coherent and complete account, when compared with making a statement in their own time.

Purpose

The role of the interviewer should be to facilitate the applicant in giving their history; to listen to as well as to abstract the relevant information; and to create an atmosphere that is conducive to the telling of a sometimes very distressing account. A recent IND Protocol (binding on representatives from 1 January 2003) states that the purpose of the interview is to 'obtain facts relevant to the application' and to allow the applicant to 'elaborate on the background to his or her application'. The Protocol states that interviews should be conducted 'objectively and impartially'. This is not always the case in practice however. The interview can instead set off in a wholly disbelieving manner, and can appear designed to catch the applicant out. On the other hand it is sometimes the case that by omitting to ask pertinent questions, the applicant has less opportunity to put forward his case, which can be extremely unhelpful, particularly when the SEF is not fully inclusive. For these reasons it can be a good idea to ask the interviewing officer how long they have spent on reading the case file before the interview begins, and if there are any particular documents which have not been read by them. The Protocol states that the interviewing officer should give the applicant a proper opportunity to explain their account, including dealing with inconsistencies. A poorly-prepared interviewer may not however ask the right questions or in the best manner necessary to bring out the client's evidence. Added to this is the fact that the decision on the claim is often ultimately taken by a person other than the interviewing officer. That third party will not have had the opportunity of seeing and observing the applicant, while purporting to make a decision on their credibility.

Lastly, it is worth bearing in mind that the purpose of the interview is also to ascertain whether the claim discloses any other humanitarian or compassionate factors which could lead to discretionary leave or humanitarian protection being granted. The reality however seems to be at odds with this approach: there are cases which are refused without interview, and a significant number which are due to be rescheduled for one reason or another but are not and instead simply refused on the basis of the SEF.

Fairness

In *Thirukumar and Others* [1989] Imm AR 402 the Court of Appeal stated that interviewing refugee applicants demanded the highest level of fairness. Although there are no statutory provisions regulating the conduct of the interview, it nonetheless has to be conducted objectively and impartially. This is recognised by the Home Office in their policy regarding asylum interviews, the most recent Protocol having been in practice since 1 November 2002:

- The interviewing officer must keep an accurate, verbatim and legible written record, including comments made by the representative, the times of breaks and any difficulties in the course of the interview.
- The applicant must be given the proper opportunity to explain and give details of his claim.
- Where there is no SEF previously submitted, the interviewer should advise the applicant and their representative that they have a period of further time in which to submit further material before a decision is made.
- There is a discretion to read back the record in exceptional cases.
- A copy of the interview is to be given to the applicant.

Tape-recording

In the case of *Mapah* [2003] EWHC 306 (Admin) there was a challenge to the Home Office refusal not to allow asylum applicants to have their interviews tape-recorded by their representatives. A number of points were put forward regarding shortcomings in the current interview procedure, which were said to undermine the high standard of fairness required:

- verbatim records of interview are in reality rarely possible;
- there is no longer a general policy of reading back the record of interview at the conclusion of the interview;
- the interpreters used by the Home Office vary widely in quality and conduct.

Despite these very valid arguments, the Court held that the policy was not unreasonable and met the requisite standard of fairness.

Questioning

In line with what has already been said, questioning at the interview can be robust. The element of surprise posed by the questions combined with the atmosphere of the interview can create a very different environment to that of a solicitor's office. The importance of the SEF statement is now more obvious. It both restricts the scope of questioning and limits the room for error by providing a statement which is comprehensive and detailed and more importantly is recognised by the client as theirs.

A declaration that forms part of the interview states that all the details set out in the SEF do not have to be repeated. It follows that any questioning at the interview should be primarily concerned with information *not* provided in the SEF. In practice however, the Home Office frequently depart from this principle by making adverse credibility comments solely on the basis that as 'fact X' was mentioned as part of the account set out in the SEF, it should have been mentioned in the interview as well. This approach is obviously unfair given that the applicant is being required to answer specific questions rather than make general statements.

The representative's role

Although the client does not have the absolute right to have a representative present at the interview, it seems clear that in the interests of a procedurally fair interview, as well as the interview also being seen to be conducted properly and fairly, very good reasons would have to be given for excluding a representative at the start of an interview – all the more so, given the very limited role of the representative at the interview. Similar considerations apply to representatives' own interpreters. In *R v Secretary of State for the Home Department, ex p Bostanci* [1999] Imm AR 411 it was held that there was no absolute right to have an interpreter present to assist the legal representative where a Home Office interpreter was being used, but that the immigration officer had a discretion which had to be exercised reasonably.

The representative must of course be aware of the basic facts of the client's case so that they are in a position to judge the relevance of the questions and the fairness of the interview. A comprehensive note of the interview will also need to be taken by them in case of a dispute at some later point concerning the accuracy of the written record.

The representative's role is confined to that of an observer, and therefore may not interrupt during the interview or otherwise distract or obstruct it. However, the representative does have the opportunity of making any comment he or she wishes at the end of the interview. If the client or representative have concerns as to the conduct of the interview or the Home Office interpreter, these must be raised at the end so that answers to particular questions can be clarified if necessary or other observations written down in the record of interview.

In most cases this will stand as sufficient testimony of any problems. In some cases it will be insufficient, however, and the interview will have to be interrupted, for example where the questioning becomes hostile or aggressive. In rare cases, the interview may even need to be stopped. It is a judgement call of some significance. One view may be that as the interview is an opportunity for the applicant to expand upon their SEF and to put themselves forward to be tested, that it will always be to their advantage to undergo the interview whatever the circumstances. However, this may not be so if, for example, there is an obvious problem with the interpreter, or the interview is being conducted in a language other than the client's first language. Where the interview has been unfairly conducted and the Home Office insist on taking it into account as evidence in the claim or refuse to arrange another interview, judicial review may be appropriate (see Chapter 8).

Submission of documents at the interview

The interview also provides an opportunity for the applicant to hand in any written evidence. This should be done at the start of the interview. If such evidence has not yet been received or requires translation the Home Office usually give the client five days in which to submit them and should be requested to give further time if necessary.

Failure to attend Home Office interview

Where there has been a failure on the part of the appellant to attend the interview without reasonable explanation then the case may well be refused on non-compliance grounds under rule 340 of the Immigration Rules (HC 395). However, even if such a decision is made it can and should be rectified before the matter proceeds to an appeal by written representations made to the Home Office. Often an interview can be rescheduled. The importance of writing to the Home Office is crucial. Failure to attend an interview is usually because the client has not received a notice: either because it has been lost in the post or because the client has moved address and his representatives have not informed the Home Office. Clients can often be difficult to get hold of in such circumstances, but having made contact speed is vital.

Post-interview submissions

Written representations on the asylum and human rights claim, submitted after the interview and before a decision is made, can be of great assistance, particularly if the implications of the claim will not be immediately apparent on a reading of the SEF and record of interview. This is an opportunity to submit any further documents the client wishes to rely on. Any objective evidence which supports the claim should also be submitted, although being realistic, not in the volume that would be put before an adjudicator.

THE REASONS FOR REFUSAL LETTER

A proportion of claims are granted following the interview and the client will be given a grant of ILR or humanitarian protection. The majority however are refused and the appeal process will begin. As the name suggests, the Reasons for Refusal Letter (the Refusal Letter) sets out in varying degrees of quality and coherence the reasons why the claim has been refused and will usually refer to both the appellant's account and the objective country evidence. One of the main difficulties in dealing with Refusal Letters is that they only very rarely set out what evidence the Home Office accept and that which they do not. Consequently, this leaves the appellant and representatives to prepare for unnecessary or badly-taken points, both in terms of drafting statements and at the appeal hearing itself, meaning a greater waste of time and expense.

All too often Refusal Letters adopt a highly cynical approach and can even be derisory. More significantly, Refusal Letters can be plagued with a number of worrying features that every representative must look out for. The list below relating to 'standard paragraphs' contained within Refusal Letters is not exhaustive and is intended to provide a summary only of particular points to be aware of, namely paragraphs which:

- demand a higher standard of proof than the applicable low standard
- ignore the substance of the claim
- are not based on the appellant's evidence SEF or Home Office interview
- are otherwise factually erroneous
- emphasise the lack of documentation as corroboration
- challenge the authenticity of documentation by general assertion and without referring to the documents themselves
- unreasonably challenge documents which have been submitted at a late stage
- ignore crucial documentary or medical or other specialist evidence
- assert that persecution or torture will not happen again
- over-emphasise minor discrepancies
- unreasonably question the timing of the appellant's departure from their country of origin or their claim for asylum in the UK
- question the appellant not claiming in a third-country
- refer to the appellant as an 'economic migrant' without any reference to the circumstances and characteristics of the appellant.

NOTICE OF APPEAL

Rules 7 and 10 of the 2003 Procedure Rules apply to decisions made after 1 April 2003. Under rule 7(1) the notice of appeal must be given within 10 days after the appellant is served with the notice of decision (unless in detention when it is five days). Where the asylum claim has been rejected but at some later stage is granted discretionary leave for one year or more the time for giving notice of appeal runs from the date of the grant of discretionary leave . The notice of appeal must be signed either by the appellant or the representative, in which case the representative must certify that they have completed the form in accordance with the appellant's instructions.

OUT OF TIME APPEALS

Where the appeal notice is given outside of the time limit the appellant must state in the notice any reasons for the delay and attach any written evidence in support of those reasons. Under rule 10(2) the Home Office may treat the notice as timely if satisfied that by reason of 'special circumstances it would be unjust not to do so'. Where the Home Office treat the application as out of time they must serve the appellant with a notice which is also sent to the Immigration Appellate Authority (IAA) to allow an adjudicator to consider whether or not to extend the time for appealing, again if he is satisfied that due to special circumstances it would be unjust not to do so.

GROUNDS OF APPEAL

The relevant parts of s 84 of the 2002 Act state that the grounds must be on one of the following grounds:

- That the decision is not in accordance with immigration rules.
- The decision is unlawful under s 19B of the Race Relations Act 1976.
- That the decision is unlawful under s 6 of the Human Rights Act 1998 as being incompatible with the appellant's Convention rights.
- That the decision is otherwise not in accordance with the law.
- That the person taking the decision should have exercised differently a discretion conferred by the immigration rules.
- That the removal of the appellant from the United Kingdom in consequence of the immigration decision would breach the United Kingdom's obligations under the Refugee Convention or would be unlawful under s 6 of the Human Rights Act 1998 as being incompatible with the appellant's ECHR rights.

An adjudicator has full fact-finding jurisdiction, is not bound by any adverse credibility or factual comments in the Home Office Refusal Letter and will replace the original decision on asylum and Article 3 of the ECHR with a fresh decision on the merits. Accordingly, the grounds written on the notice should merely reiterate the appellant's case in 2 or 3 short bullet points: little is served by lengthy or repetitive grounds of appeal.

Statement of additional grounds

As the name suggests, this is an addendum document to the notice of appeal, on which should be written any *further* reasons why the appellant considers they should be permitted to remain in the United Kingdom, and which have not previously been mentioned in the SEF statement, interview or post-interview representations. The 'statement of additional grounds' is an integral part of the 'one-stop' appeals process, which envisages that where possible all such issues will be dealt with by one adjudicator in one appeal.

Further representations

It may be the case that the representative, especially if only instructed at this stage, will need to take a global view of the case and not simply assume that it is only the notice of appeal and statement of additional grounds that needs to be lodged. There are a number of circumstances in which further action will be appropriate, for example, a procedural irregularity such as important evidence not being taken into account. There will also be instances where further evidence has come to light. It is important to ensure that, so far as is reasonably possible, the Home Office have considered the *totality* of the claim and the evidence in support *before* the appeal reaches the IAA.

If the Home Office have rejected a cogent and well-prepared case without adequate reasons, they may start off on the defensive before the adjudicator. By the same token, there is obviously a tactical need to avoid a situation in which the HOPO at the appeal hearing can suggest that as certain evidence was not put forward earlier it therefore lacks credibility or should be given little weight because the Home Office have had insufficient time to consider it and/or rebut it. In any event, this kind of preliminary argument effectively puts the appellant on the back foot, even if through no fault of their own, and detracts from the central issues in the case. An appellant will often be emotionally 'fired up' for the hearing at which they hope to give their account, but instead find that it gets adjourned, put back or otherwise does not get off to a very good start. All of this can have a very real effect on an appellant's mental well-being, confidence and ability to give evidence.

COMPLIANCE WITH STANDARD DIRECTIONS

Standard IAA directions require the following documents to be filed with the IAA and served on the Home Office seven days before the date of the full hearing:

- Witness statements of the evidence to be called at the hearing, such statement to stand as evidence in chief at the hearing.
- A paginated and indexed bundle of all the documents to be relied on at the hearing with a schedule identifying the essential passages.
- A skeleton argument, identifying all the relevant issues including Human Rights claims and setting out all the authorities to be relied on.
- A chronology of events.

WITNESS STATEMENTS

If the SEF has been prepared in accordance with best practice, the witness statement will serve to complement it and complete the appellant's evidence-in-chief at the appeal hearing. It is now common practice to produce a witness statement following receipt of the Refusal Letter in order to deal with some or all of the points of refusal. This is of course very important, however if the SEF is cursory or incomplete, the client has not attended interview or the refusal letter has raised major inconsistencies and credibility issues, the witness statement will need to cover a lot more ground and perhaps even set out the appellant's claim fully for the first time.

When drafting witness statements it is always best to err on the safe side, so that the appellant is able to adopt the statement in its entirety at the hearing without any qualification or amendment, and can then be asked a few supplementary questions for clarification purposes.

Drafting the witness statement

As we have said, the statement should deal with the points raised by the Home Office in the Refusal Letter. This must be good practice in so far as Refusal Letters almost always raise issues that are based on evidential issues, factual misunderstandings or language difficulties and which can easily be dealt with in writing. As well as being necessary this is also likely to create a good impression with the adjudicator because it is clear that the appellant upon receiving the Refusal Letter has made timely comment on those parts that he takes issue with.

The guidance we have given on drafting SEF statements is equally applicable here. A particular and frequently occurring problem is 'legal comment', namely comments that go beyond the knowledge of the appellant. The statement can be posed as answers to questions put to the client by the representative but not beyond; for example, it could properly read:

> 'I went to the police and asked them to help me, but they did nothing, they did not even take a statement.'

But should not say:

> 'The police in Nepal are unwilling and unable to offer sufficiency of protection from the ongoing Maoist insurgency in Nepal.'

Nor should witness statements give a generalised commentary on the country situation, including facts and figures, unless this is specifically given by the appellant. Put another way, any factual or legal comment which has not come directly from the appellant's mouth is to be avoided. Such comments can rarely benefit the appellant and are more likely to detract from the authenticity and therefore the credibility of the statement. The statement should be a personal testimony of the facts as the appellant knows them and no more.

As evidence-in-chief

Witness statements are now expected to stand as evidence-in-chief and this places a heavy burden on representatives to get the witness statement absolutely right. More significantly, if an appellant will only be permitted to give evidence in re-examination, which by its nature is more limited in scope, the witness statement needs to be absolutely comprehensive and to deal with each and every aspect of the case.

Despite what we have already said about making SEF statements and witness statements careful and comprehensive, it must nevertheless be recognised that in this area of law more than any other, appellants have an expectation that they will be able to 'tell their story' at the hearing. Whilst this in no way means it will be appropriate for an appellant to repeat everything they have already said in their statements, we feel they should be afforded the opportunity of at least giving some additional oral evidence, rather than being 'attacked' from the outset in cross-examination. It seems that the recent requirement of the IAA that the *totality* of an appellant's evidence except cross-examination to be confined to writing, assumes too literal a comparison with domestic civil litigation and does not take into account the humanitarian context in which these appeals are heard.

Additionally, the directions optimistically suppose that in each and every case a comprehensive and sufficiently detailed statement will have been prepared, and that the adjudicator will in fact have read all the relevant evidence. It is to be hoped that in considering the admission of documentary and oral evidence and their interpretation of the Rules regarding the same, adjudicators will have regard to all the relevant evidence, keeping at the forefront of their minds the obligation to consider the case with the most anxious scrutiny.

Last but by no means least, there will be cases where the appellant does not attend the hearing. A witness statement that deals with all outstanding issues obviously provides the best chance of an appeal dealt with 'on the papers' succeeding.

FURTHER WITNESSES AND EVIDENCE

Witnesses generally fall into two categories:

- those that can give evidence concerning events which have occurred in the appellant's home country;
- those that can give evidence regarding the appellant's activities and ties in the United Kingdom.

Witnesses who fall into either category should have made a statement that has been filed and served in advance of the hearing and may confidently be relied on in evidence. We have already given guidance about witness statements; supporting witness statements however, require some additional considerations.

- Which part of the appellant's claim can this witness give evidence about?
- How probative is that evidence, for example does the witness have direct knowledge of the events in question; if not from where does that knowledge come?
- What is the witness's immigration status in the United Kingdom? Have they for example been granted asylum on the same or a similar factual basis to the appellant's claim?
- Above all, judgement is called for in assessing whether the witness's evidence is going to advance the appellant's case on appeal. For example, if the statement is superficially consistent but differs in key aspects, such as the dates given, this may call into question the credibility of the witness or indeed the appellant.

Where there is a claim under Article 8 ECHR on the basis of marriage or other relationship, a full and detailed witness statement must be taken from the spouse or partner and they should attend the appeal hearing. If children are involved, statements from schoolteachers, social-workers and perhaps even a psychiatrist, to show the effect of removal and/or break-up of the family unit should where possible also be obtained.

Further supporting evidence can also come from a variety of different individuals, for example an appellant's relatives, friends, work-colleagues, members of their church or other acquaintances, the number of which may make the task of drafting separate witness statements for each an onerous one. Also, there may be individuals who want to support the appellant's case but may not be able to attend court. In such cases, signed and dated letters of support written by the individuals themselves may be sufficient, rather than formal statements. This is a matter of judgement in the particular case, but we have in mind here testimony which is unlikely to be contentious or disputed. Such witnesses should whenever possible attend court in case their evidence is disputed at the hearing. In Article 8 ECHR cases particularly, there is an undeniable psychological impact where, for example, five supporting witnesses are physically in court to put faces to the names on their letters of support.

OBJECTIVE EVIDENCE

Most solicitors' firms have standard bundles on the countries they are most concerned with and use these to form the appellant's objective evidence to be submitted to the Home Office and the IAA for the appeal hearing. These vary markedly in quality, and representatives attending the appeal hearing must be aware as part of their own personal preparation exactly what the bundle of objective information contains. As an absolute minimum the bundle should contain the annual Amnesty International, Human Rights Watch and US State Department reports (all available on the internet in 'printer-friendly format'), and where applicable the most recent UNHCR guidelines for that country. These will provide a general picture of the situation in the country as well as dealing with specific groups of persons and any persecution, harassment, discrimination, and human rights breaches that have occurred.

Importance of specific objective evidence

Reliance on these documents alone however, is insufficient for the purposes of a well-prepared case. The need for additional material will depend on the nature of the case, but there will invariably be such a need. The first reason is that only rarely will such general reports be up-to-date, as they are published periodically. Moreover, reports by the Home Office Country Information and Policy Unit (CIPU), which draw on a number of sources of various dates, can also vary greatly in quality and detail and are frequently selective in the information they cite. At worst the CIPU Reports can contain errors and omissions which can be both misleading and fail to address relevant human rights issues in any meaningful way. This emphasises the need for representatives to obtain up-to-date objective country evidence from other independent and established sources.

Use of the internet

In every case therefore a search on the internet is invaluable, and we would say that *all* representatives must have access to the internet for this reason. Care must be taken however of the source of the information. There are a number of credible sources such as the BBC News website or those of human rights organisations. Less high-profile sources are not worthless by any means, but the weight attached to them by the adjudicator may be less. A final point to bear in mind when using internet search-engines, is that there are often different spellings of names of individuals and places and that several permutations may therefore need to be tried.

Electronic Immigration Network (EIN)

A key resource for representatives is the Electronic Immigration Network (EIN), at www.ein.org.uk. This is a subscription website including both substantive law and case-law, as well as country reports and other objective materials. Not only is the website kept extremely up-to-date, but there is a 'Members' Queries' bulletin board allowing any subscribing representative to post up issues on which others may be able to assist.

Country expert evidence

An increasingly used form of evidence for asylum and human rights appeals is that of reports from experts on country conditions. Such experts are usually academics, journalists, or members of human rights organisations with particular knowledge and experience of the country in question. A report may be obtained for three overlapping reasons:

- To demonstrate by reference to the expert's knowledge of that country that the appellant's account is credible.
- To explain why a particular appellant would be at risk of persecution or other forms of harm if returned to that country.
- To provide a more general picture of the country (often referred to as 'generic reports').

It is obviously not every case in which a representative will be justified in incurring the expense of commissioning such a report. However, a good rule of thumb would be to consider doing so where the more general and readily available forms of objective evidence are silent about the particular issues raised in the account. A very good starting-point for finding a suitable expert is the Immigration Law Practitioners Association (ILPA) Directory of Country Experts. This is also a frequent subject for 'Members' Queries' on EIN. The UNHCR and the Foreign and Commonwealth Office may be able to answer enquiries relating to specific issues in a particular country.

The weight to be given by an adjudicator or the Tribunal to a country expert report is bound to depend on the particular expert and the issue on which they have been called to give an opinion. Ultimately, the decision in the case is one that can only be made by the court. However, the Court of Appeal has in the past criticised the Tribunal for failing to give due consideration to expert evidence. In *S* [2002] INLR 416 the Court of Appeal observed, in an appeal from a 'starred' decision on the question of risk in a particular country:

> 'In this field opinion evidence will often or usually be very important, since assessment of the risk of persecutory treatment in the milieu of a perhaps unstable political situation may be a complex and difficult task in which the fact-finding tribunal is bound to place heavy reliance on the views of experts and specialists . . .'

FIRST AND FULL HEARINGS

The IAA 'Notice of First Hearing and Full Hearing' which attaches a Reply to Directions Form is sent to the appellant and their representatives in advance of the first hearing. The notice stipulates that either the appellant or the representative of the appellant must complete and return the Reply Form within seven days or attend the hearing. The Reply Form must confirm whether or not the appellant is in all respects ready to proceed with the hearing. Often this is filled in by representatives without proper regard to the practicalities of presenting the case. Representatives should at the very least consider the following points when filling in the Reply Form or attending the first hearing:

- Are any documents missing from the 'Respondent's bundle' ?
- Is the Home Office interview legible? If not, a specific direction should be sought to obtain a typed transcript prior to the full hearing.
- Does the appellant have any family in the country who have refugee status ? If so, it may need to be established prior to the hearing on what basis or for what reasons such grant was made.
- What kind of interpreter will the appellant need?
- Will the appellant require an all-female court or the hearing to be in private?

It is strongly advisable that representatives carefully consider at this stage whether or not they will be ready at the date of hearing given in the notice. Where applications for adjournments are made on the day of hearing itself, it is always properly pointed out by the adjudicator that the representatives had previously indicated that they were ready to proceed. Where the representative is not ready at this stage for the full appeal they should attend the first hearing and give their reasons, so that time can be extended and the full hearing vacated for a future date. Failure to do so or to properly complete and submit the Reply Form will lead to the appeal being determined on the day.

PREPARATION OF BUNDLES

The Home Office are required when forwarding an appeal to the IAA to serve on the appellant's representatives, the 'Respondent's bundle' containing the SEF and attached statement, the Home Office interview record, any other evidence or representations submitted by the appellant, as well as the Refusal Letter. We suggest that to avoid confusion, the Respondent's bundle be kept separate from the bundle submitted by the appellant's representative and that precious time and money not be wasted on duplication.

The appellant's bundle should comprise of two sections:

- *Subjective evidence* – this should include the appellant's witness statement, other witness statements or letters of support, medical reports and expert evidence, documents with certified translations, as well as any other evidence to be relied on at the hearing. If the Respondent's bundle has left out evidence previously submitted by the appellant in support of the claim, this will have to be included here instead.
- *Objective evidence* – as we have already stated this should include the up-to-date country reports and any other specific evidence. It is important to remember that where the appellant's account relates to incidents occurring a few or more years in the past and the Home Office are challenging the account given, specific objective evidence relating to that time may well be required to substantiate such a claim.

Filing and service of evidence

Rule 48(1) of the 2003 Procedure Rules states:

> 'An adjudicator or the Tribunal may allow oral, documentary or other evidence to be given of any fact which appears to be relevant to an appeal or an application for bail, even if that evidence would be inadmissible in a court of law.'

However rule 48(1) of the 2003 Procedure Rules is qualified by Rule 48(5) which states:

> 'An adjudicator or the Tribunal *must not* consider any evidence which is not filed or served in accordance with time limits set out in these Rules or directions given under Rule 38, unless satisfied that there are *good reasons* to do so.'
>
> (Emphasis added.)

The wording of this provision appear to be more restrictive than the old rule 33(2)(c) which provided that an adjudicator *may* prohibit a party relying on a document, evidence or statement not sent in compliance with directions made by the court. Rule 48(5) therefore puts the onus on the appellant to show good reason why a document or other evidence not served in time should be allowed into evidence. Whilst there may be instances where documents can only be obtained at the eleventh hour, this Rule underlines the importance of representatives putting a case together properly and filing and serving well in advance of the hearing.

Skeleton arguments

These are dealt with separately in Chapter 5.

Chronologies

The drafting of a chronology is part of the standard IAA directions. There is not a great deal that needs to be said about them beyond their purpose and how they should be set out. Adjudicators frequently indicate that chronologies are extremely helpful, especially when writing-up determinations.

A chronology is essentially a list of the key factual events that form the appellant's account, set out in chronological order, starting from the earliest event through to the most recent. A recurring error of representatives is that rather than specify the events that took place in the country of origin, they tend to focus on the sequence of events from the initial asylum application through to the court hearing. Such a chronology will rarely be of any assistance to the adjudicator. Similarly, chronologies that are overly long or detailed are often unhelpful. What is required is a short (usually one page) summary of the main events, rather than a discussion of them.

CONCLUSION

What we hope this chapter has achieved is a recognition of the fact that the prospects of a claim being successful (whether through the Home Office or at the appeal stage) are very much dependent on the care taken in preparation. The focus from the outset must be on the necessary ingredients of a valid asylum or human rights claim and how at every opportunity to present them as strongly as possible. Claims are rejected and appeals ultimately lost in many cases where there has either been insufficient regard to detail, or evidence that could have been obtained was not.

In light of the recent restrictions on rights of appeal and on public funding too, the emphasis in asylum and human rights cases must now be on 'front-loading' the evidence as much as possible. The representative's task, whether prior to the Home Office interview or before an adjudicator, is a highly important one as these stages present the greatest opportunity for a deserving case to be accepted.

CHAPTER 5

Skeleton Arguments

Standard IAA directions require the appellant to produce a skeleton argument for the appeal hearing. The IAA Practice Direction on Trial Bundles (March 2003) states that skeleton arguments (or written submissions) should 'define and confine the area at issue in a numbered list of brief points', and this will be more than adequate given the nature of most appeals.

Well-written skeleton arguments can have the positive effect of crystallising the central issues in a particular case for the adjudicator and will be of great assistance in the presentation of the case. Skeleton arguments really come into their own however, where the factual background is convoluted or where the case turns on a narrow interpretation of the law. Skeleton arguments are of course particularly helpful when making closing submissions. Not only will one provide a route-map for the closing submissions, but will stand as clear proof that specific matters were indeed raised before the adjudicator, should any issue as to this arise on appeal to the Tribunal.

GENERAL GUIDANCE

We suggest that the following points should be considered when drafting a skeleton argument:

- It cannot and should not try to be all-inclusive. An overly long skeleton argument will tend to become bland and have the opposite effect to that which it should achieve, namely clarifying and narrowing the particular issues in the case.
- It should avoid *lengthy* recitals of the common issues of law relevant to all asylum appeals and in which adjudicators are (or should be) well-versed. If the representative considers it necessary to outline basic legal principles applicable to the case, then this should be done in a crisp and concise manner.
- Although a representative may well be able to anticipate the oral evidence that will be given by the appellant at the hearing,

they cannot know what the evidence will in fact be for obvious reasons. For this reason, direct reference to what the appellant may say at the hearing is to be avoided. Where there is a witness statement prepared for the hearing, this can be referred to, but there is a balance to be struck between producing a skeleton that is specific to the case in hand and one that does not become a straitjacket for the appellant.

- The skeleton should be written in a logical order and should emphasise in clear and *sensible* steps why the adjudicator should allow the appeal.

Case law

Drafting a skeleton is part of the normal process of preparing a case in readiness for an appeal. Part of the process will involve an awareness of obtaining up-to-date and relevant case law. The most comprehensive and accessible means is through the EIN (www.ein.org.uk), which provides subscription access to a database of up-to-date Tribunal decisions and judgments of the High Court, Court of Appeal, the House of Lords, and the European Court of Human Rights, as well as decisions from other jurisdictions. All representatives undertaking appeal hearings must have access to the EIN.

'Starred' Tribunal decisions which are binding on adjudicators as well as other constitutions of the Tribunal deal with the most important legal and procedural questions affecting many other cases (the 'starring' system has been approved by the Court of Appeal, see for example *S* [2002] INLR 416). The Immigration Appeal Tribunal Practice Direction No. 10: 'Citation of Determinations', which took effect from 19 May 2003, states that only reported determinations i.e. those with a neutral citation number, may be cited in proceedings before an adjudicator or the Tribunal unless the applicant or a member of his family were party to the proceedings in which the previous determination was issued, or the adjudicator or the Tribunal gives permission. Permission will only be given in exceptional circumstances. It is to be noted however, that Tribunal determinations published up to December 2002 may still be cited at an appeal, although the party relying on that decision must be able to state that it has not been overtaken by a more recent Tribunal decision.

Given the volume of Tribunal decisions and the speed with which situations in, or approaches to a particular country change, it is incumbent on representatives to make a search on the EIN case law database prior to every appeal, if only to find the latest Tribunal views on the country in question. Relevant decisions are also circulated to adjudicators and it is bound to be to the appellant's distinct advantage if the representative is already aware of a decision bearing on their case.

SAMPLE SKELETON ARGUMENTS

To illustrate the process of analysing the issues in a typical case, we show three fictional case-studies with appellants originating from different countries and making differing kinds of claims. For each we have given a summary of the relevant parts of the claim, as if taken from the Refusal Letter and the appellant's own evidence, and on those issues have suggested how the skeleton arguments could be drafted. Skeleton arguments should be served on the Home Office and the Court in advance of the hearing whenever possible, even if sent in by fax the day before the hearing.

We should however point out that in this area of practice the relevant objective evidence is fast-changing as of course is the law itself. Although we have endeavoured to state the law as at 31 July 2003, the skeleton arguments included to demonstrate the presentation of cases (and the grounds of appeal in Chapter 7), should not be taken as definitive regarding the points they seek to argue, but are intended to be illustrative only.

(1) NEPALESE CASE

Summary of evidence and basis of refusal

The appellant is a 30-year-old male from a Maoist stronghold in Nepal. He has been a voluntary and active member of the Maobadi party since 1997 and has participated in numerous meetings and has given financial and other support. In 1998 he was asked to assist in an armed ambush on a police station in which nine Maoist rebels were held captive. He killed a policeman. Prior to this incident the appellant had never been involved in any violence of any nature. Fearing reprisals from the security forces, he left immediately through Kathmandu airport on a forged passport bearing his own name and photograph.

The Secretary of State does not believe the appellant's account, but contends that, even if it is true, he is not entitled to refugee status because Article 1(F) applies so as to exclude him from the Convention, and in any event his fear is of prosecution and not persecution.

Issues

- Credibility
- Exclusion under Article 1(F)
- Fear of state authorities
- Prosecution or persecution
- Refugee Convention ground
- Article 3 ECHR
- Future risk.

IN THE IMMIGRATION APPELLATE AUTHORITY
CASE No.

BETWEEN:

RAM BAHADUR

Appellant

and

THE SECRETARY OF STATE FOR

THE HOME DEPARTMENT

Respondent

SKELETON ARGUMENT

Credibility

1. The facts and history of this claim are amply set out in the appellant's SEF statement, Home Office interview record and further witness statement dated 21 March 2003. The appellant's documented evidence has been clear and unambiguous from the outset and is consistent with the objective material.

Exclusion – the Secretary of State's position

2. It is the Secretary of State's assertion that the appellant is excluded from the protection of the Convention under Article 1(F) in so far as the appellant is wanted by the authorities for a *non-political* crime. Article 1(F) of the Regugee Convention states:

   'The provisions of this Convention shall not apply to a person with respect to whom there are serious reasons for considering that:

   (b) he has committed a serious non-political crime outside the country of refuge prior to his admission to that country as a refugee.'

Exclusion – the appellant's submissions

3. It is not disputed that the appellant has committed a serious crime. The burden of showing exclusion falls on the Secretary of State. The standard of proof of 'serious reasons for considering' is lower than the balance of probabilities. It is for the adjudicator to make specific findings on the nature of the crime and whether it will exclude the appellant from the Refugee Convention, and then to decide into which sub-category those events fall.
4. The Secretary of State does not seek to argue that the appellant's mere membership of the CPN (Maoist) amounts to complicity in serious non-political crimes. In any event, in *Gurung v Secretary of State for the Home Department* [2003] Imm AR 115 the Tribunal considered that the CPN was not such an organisation, having regard to the diverse nature of its activities – political as well as violent. It cannot be reasonably argued that the appellant's membership and activities prior to 1998 could serve to bring him within the exclusion clause Article 1(F)(b).
5. The only issue is whether the killing of the policeman in 1998 is a serious non-political crime. In *T v Immigration Officer* [1996] AC 742, the House of Lords stated that in order to be a political crime an act must:
   (i) be committed for a political purpose i.e. to overthrow, subvert, or change the government, or to force it to change its policy; and
   (ii) be sufficiently closely and directly connected to the political purpose (bearing in mind the means used, whether the target was military or government or civilian, and whether indiscriminate killing or injury of civilians could have resulted).
6. The appellant's evidence is that on 26 July 1998 he along with a number of Maoists were involved in a planned attack on the police station, with the twin aims of freeing a number of comrades and to prevent vital information being extracted from them by interrogation and torture. The appellant's credible and indeed candid evidence was that although he had to kill a policeman,

he felt that this was the price that had to be paid for saving the lives of the nine Maoist prisoners.

Political nature of crime

7. It is submitted that the appellant's actions were clearly part of the Maoist's overall campaign to overthrow the Nepalese government, and that there was a clear nexus between the appellant's actions and that campaign for the following reasons:
   - The nine Maoists had been captured by the police during combat.
   - The objective evidence shows that the police torture and extra-judicially execute captured Maoists.
   - Information obtained by the police would have jeopardised the Maoist campaign.
   - The appellant honestly admits to killing a policeman, but states this was a regrettable but inevitable consequence of such an operation.
   - The appellant's actions were proportionate, in that although the life of a single policeman was unfortunately lost, nine civilian lives were saved.
8. For the above reasons, the Secretary of State has failed to show that there are 'serious reasons for considering' that the appellant is excluded from the Refugee Convention, as the crime was clearly political in nature.

Prosecution v persecution

9. Accordingly, it is submitted that the appellant's asylum claim must be considered in the normal way. The Secretary of State argues that the appellant merely fears prosecution. That position ignores the reality of what the appellant will face on return to Nepal. The objective evidence indicates that individuals who are wanted by the security forces for Maoist activities face prolonged interrogation, detention, torture and frequently extra-judicial execution. There is no question but that such treatment would amount to persecution. The Convention reason is political opinion, because the Maoists are

in vehement opposition to the ruling monarchy and government. Internal relocation is obviously not an option as the appellant will be returned right into the arms of his persecutors.

10. If, contrary to the arguments advanced by the appellant, the adjudicator considers that the exclusion issue is a finely balanced one, the substantive asylum claim and the issues arising under it must nevertheless be considered, given the nature of the appellant's account and the country situation as set out in paragraph 9 above.

Article 3 of the ECHR

11. In the alternative, even if the appellant is deemed to be outside the protection of the Refugee Convention, he nevertheless must succeed under Article 3 ECHR, which is breached if there is a real risk of torture, inhuman or degrading treatment or punishment. The objective evidence in this case shows that any treatment the appellant is likely to suffer on return would amount to torture.

Conclusion

12. For the above reasons this appeal should be allowed, if not under the Refugee Convention then under Article 3 of the ECHR in any event.

Date:

Name:

Address:

Particular points for consideration

- The exclusion issue was perhaps not raised very often in the past, but seems likely to be increasingly relied on in the future. An asylum claim in which it is raised requires very careful preparation – the case law is complex even though still in its early stages – and detailed written argument will usually be necessary.

- Erring on the side of caution, it would always be best to invite the adjudicator to consider the whole picture, even if the adjudicator has decided that the appellant is excluded. We suspect that most adjudicators would hear the whole case in any event.
- It is to be noted that in this case we have very much pinned the Article 3 claim on the likelihood of torture because the objective evidence in this regard is very strong. This is not the kind of case in which the treatment on return should be understated.
- Given the issues arising in this case and dealt with in the skeleton, we did not include any discussion on how the appellant was able to leave Nepal on his own documents, which is probably better dealt with in evidence and submissions.

(2) SOMALI CASE

Summary of evidence and basis of refusal

The appellant is a female from Somalia and is of the Benadiri minority clan. She arrived in 1999 and claimed asylum on arrival. The appellant states that she fears persecution and/or ill-treatment by the majority clans. The history of the claim is that her home in Mogadishu was attacked in 1996 and both her parents were killed. The appellant alleges that she was beaten and raped but managed to escape. She fled to Ethiopia after one week (where she stayed for two weeks) following which she made her way to the Sudan, where after another month she was able to get a flight to the United Kingdom.

The Home Office do not accept that:

- the birth certificate produced by the appellant is genuine;
- the appellant is Somali as claimed;
- the appellant is a member of the Benadiri clan;
- the appellant is credible;
- the appellant was raped.

Issues

- Credibility
- Nationality/ethnicity
- Documentary evidence
- Medical and expert reports.

IN THE IMMIGRATION APPELLATE AUTHORITY CASE No.

BETWEEN:

SAEEDA ALI

Appellant

and

THE SECRETARY OF STATE FOR

THE HOME DEPARTMENT

Respondent

SKELETON ARGUMENT

Background

1. The appellant is a female citizen of Somalia born 23/05/1972 in Mogadishu. She is of the Ashraf, a sub-clan belonging to the Reer Hamar clan, which is itself part of the Benediri tribe.
2. The Respondent refused the claim on the basis that he did not accept that the appellant is a Benadir or even from Somalia. The appellant appeals under section 69(5) of the 1999 Act removal directions having been set for Somalia.

Nationality

3. The first point for consideration must be the appellant's nationality. The burden of proof in demonstrating nationality within the asylum context rests upon the claimant on the lower standard.

Evidence

4. The appellant has submitted an original birth certificate and translation showing her birthplace as being in Mogadishu on 23 May 1972. The birth certificate also shows the name of her mother and father referred to in

her documents and asylum interview. The onus of proving that the birth certificate is genuine rests on the appellant and must be demonstrated on the lower standard of proof. Where the appellant achieves this then the document can properly be relied upon: *Tanveer Ahmed* [2002] INLR 343.

5. The original birth certificate and its translation were served at the Home Office interview (nine months ago). The Respondent has therefore had more than an ample opportunity to consider the document and its authenticity. It is significant that the Respondent has been unable to make any specific comment about this document, other than an extremely generalised assertion that such documents are 'easily obtainable in Mombassa'. That assertion ignores the fact that the appellant did not travel to the United Kingdom via Kenya, but via Ethiopia and the Sudan. In such circumstances and in the absence of any other evidence to the contrary, the adjudicator is invited to accept the document as genuine, and therefore find that the appellant is a Somali national.

Ethnic origin

6. The appellant claimed at her screening interview that she is of the Reer Hamar clan. The appellant's solicitors have requested that an interpreter who is able to speak the same dialect of Somali as the appellant ie Af-Reer Hamar, be made available for the hearing. This in itself will 'speak volumes' about the appellant's ethnic origin.
7. Further in this regard, it is necessary to consider in some detail the appellant's substantive asylum interview. The appellant was asked 12 questions relating to her ethnic origin (Qs 17–28). Particularly telling are questions 17–20 which demanded a specific knowledge of the appellant's sub-clan. Those questions would simply not have been possible to answer correctly had the appellant not originated from this sub-clan. The Court is further

referred to the expert report of Mr Gaveera-Smith dealing with appellant's clan membership. The report concludes:

> 'The appellant's name, appearance, dialect and knowledge of Somalia all lead me to conclude that it is more likely than not that she is a member of the Reer Hamar tribe, Ashraf sub-clan and furthermore that she was born and brought up in Somalia. Mindful of my duty to the Court, I should say that I am aware that there are Ashraf communities to be found outside Somalia, for example in Ethiopia.'

8. It is submitted that this evidence wholly supports the appellant's ethnic origin and nationality.
9. Whilst the expert report properly informs the adjudicator that there are Ashraf communities outside Somalia, its conclusion that it is *more probable than not* that the appellant is Somali satisfies the lower standard of proof to be applied in these cases. The objective evidence shows that members of this ethnic group are likely to be persecuted

Persecution

10. The core of the appellant's claim that that her family was attacked and that she was severely ill-treated is consistent with the objective material. The October 2002 Home Office Operational Guidance Note states that the Benadiri:

> '. . . are likely to be able to establish a need for international protection. The UN has assessed them as persecuted minorities and their situation in Somalia remains, at best, uncertain.'

11. That the appellant did not leave Somalia earlier is not inconsistent with her claim to having been persecuted. The assertion in the Refusal Letter is in contrast with the objective evidence that a significant number of the Benadiri are still living in Somalia at the mercy of the warlords and without the means to leave.

Rape

12. The Secretary of State disbelieves the appellant's account of having been raped because the appellant had failed to mention it at her interview, and only did so in her psychiatric examination. However, the very reason that the appellant was referred to a psychiatrist was that she had become very distressed at the conclusion of the interview, and as result her solicitors made the necessary arrangements to have her seen by a doctor.
13. The adjudicator will note that Dr. Anton Stuart is an experienced psychiatrist with expertise in the field of treating victims of torture. The psychiatric examination provided a far more appropriate and sensitive opportunity for the appellant to give her account, when compared to the atmosphere of the Home Office interview which was in the presence of a male immigration officer. It is therefore not surprising in the least that the appellant felt able to confide in a doctor and did so at the first opportunity. In those circumstances, to draw any negative conclusions as to the appellant's credibility would be unjustified.
14. The adjudicator will also note that the report concludes that the appellant is genuinely suffering from a mild form of PTSD, which can be considered as corroborative of her account of having been persecuted.

Conclusion

15. The Secretary of State's conclusions, both as to the appellant's ethnic origins and the credibility of her account, are both without support and in conflict with the objective evidence. The appellant has made out her claim on the lower standard to have a fear of persecution.

Date:

Name:

Address:

Particular points for consideration

- There were a number of separate challenges made to credibility in this case. We felt it appropriate to deal with each one in sequence.
- There is no specific allegation that the birth certificate is a forgery, although this is implicit in the Home Office's comment that such documents can be easily obtained in Kenya. The Home Office rarely make an allegation of forgery, and we would say that in nearly all cases the issue of forgery is a red herring. The real issue is simply whether on the low standard of proof the document may be considered genuine.
- The value of serving crucial documentary evidence *prior* to the determination of the claim is apparent in this case. Although the two points made about this in the skeleton, namely that the Home Office had plenty of time to authenticate the birth certificate, and their unfounded assertion as to its authenticity are effectively 'jury points' (it would be very difficult to authenticate a Somali document) we feel that they are nevertheless worth making. The adjudicator is a tribunal of fact and law and such points will have a cumulative effect.
- At first blush, it might seem risky to have submitted the expert opinion on the appellant's ethnicity, which allows for some uncertainty regarding the appellant's country of birth. However, on a proper application of the lower standard of proof the report clearly furthers the appellant's case. In reality it might be anticipated that a HOPO would wish to take instructions on a report of this nature.

(3) IRANIAN CASE

Summary of evidence and basis of refusal

The appellant is a 23-year-old male from Iran, who arrived in this country in September 2001 on a visitor's visa valid for six months. After five months he made an asylum and human rights claim on the basis that he feared persecution from the Iranian authorities because of his religious conversion to Christianity. Whilst working as a calligrapher for a local Christian group the appellant became interested in Christianity and was given a copy of the Bible. He attended meetings of the group and converted four months later in March 2001. The authorities eventually became suspicious of his activities and found the Bible at his place of work. The appellant went into hiding before leaving Iran three months later, travelling via Turkey to the United Kingdom. The appellant's Muslim parents remain in Iran and have been harassed by the authorities who seek the appellant. His father was arrested by the authorities and detained for one week during which he was interrogated and beaten. There is no evidence that the appellant practised or spoke publicly about Christianity in Iran. He is now a regular church-goer and has a letter from his local church to that effect. If returned to Iran the appellant says that he would not publicly preach but would make no secret of his newly found faith and would want to tell his friends and family about it.

The Home Office position on refusal of the claim was that:

- the appellant is not a genuine convert;
- the appellant's account is not true and even if it was he is not of on-going interest to the authorities, because he did not proselytise his faith in Iran;
- if returned he would not be prevented from practising Christianity because there are many Christians in Iran;
- the appellant has never been arrested or detained which casts doubt upon the claim as a whole;
- the appellant's immigration history does not support a genuine claim.

Issues

- Credibility

- Convention reason
- Objective evidence
- Future risk.

IN THE IMMIGRATION APPELLATE AUTHORITY
CASE No.

BETWEEN:

AZAD AKBARI

Appellant

and

THE SECRETARY OF STATE FOR

THE HOME DEPARTMENT

Respondent

SKELETON ARGUMENT

History

1. The appellant appeals under section 69(2) of the 1999 Act against a decision of the Home Office refusing to vary his leave and refusal of asylum and human rights claim.
2. The appellant has a well-founded fear of persecution from the Iranian authorities on the basis of his conversion to Christianity.
3. The history of the claim is set out in the following documents: SEF statement (B1 of the Home Office Bundle); record of asylum interview (D1–10 of the Home Office Bundle); appellant's witness statement, pages 1–5 of the appellant's own bundle.

Genuineness of conversion

4. The first and central question is whether the appellant is in fact a genuine convert, and whether he would as a result come to the attention of the authorities in Iran for that reason. The Home Office concede that of a series of 18 questions concerning the history of Christianity during his asylum interview, the appellant was able to answer 14 correctly, but are not satisfied that that this is probative of a genuine conversion, commenting that the

appellant 'could have researched Christianity and come to the interview prepared for such questions'. Not only is this pure speculation but it blatantly contradicts the Home Office practice of interviewing asylum applicants in order to test their accounts. The Home Office do not send an interviewee a set of proposed questions in advance and must be presumed to ask sufficient and relevant questions to properly assess a claim. The adjudicator is therefore invited to ignore this reason for refusal altogether.

5. It is significant that the appellant both underwent his conversion and practised Christianity in Iran. Both of these factors show a genuine faith, but have not been taken into account by the Home Office. The reality of the appellant's faith is further demonstrated by the fact that since his arrival in the United Kingdom, he has been a 'regular and devout worshipper' at the Evangelical Church of Christ in Islington (see letter of Pastor Moses at page 56 of the appellant's bundle.) As the President of the Tribunal confirmed in the case of *Ghodratzadeh* [2002] UKIAT 01867, in this kind of case evidence of conversion from a church in this country is very important.

Objective evidence

6. Whilst non-Muslims are not in general at risk of persecution by the authorities, the situation is very different for those who renounce the Muslim Faith. The US State Department Report 2003 states: 'Apostasy, specifically conversion from Islam, may be punishable by death.' The CIPU report April 2003, makes it abundantly clear at paragraphs 5.58 and 5.59 that an apostate would be at risk:

> '. . . Apostasy, or conversion from Islam to another religion, is not acceptable in Islamic law. It states that an innate-apostate (one whose parents were Muslims and who embraced Islam but later left Islam), if a man, is to be executed. If a woman, she is to be imprisoned for life,

but will be released if she repents. A national apostate (a person converting from another faith, and then reconverting back to the other faith) is to be encouraged to repent and, upon refusal to repent, is to be executed. The most prominent cases of apostasy appear to occur from Islam to Christianity . . .'

'Proselytising apostates (converts who have begun preaching Christianity) are likely to face execution . . .'

Specific fear of authorities

7. The appellant will undoubtedly be considered an apostate, due to his conversion from Islam to Christianity. Whilst the appellant is not intending to proselytise in the strictest sense of the word, his evidence is that he will not keep his Christian beliefs to himself. This is an additional and highly relevant risk factor as it will be likely to bring him to the attention of the authorities that much sooner. The objective evidence demonstrates that if this happens he will face ill-treatment or death. Additionally, the appellant's evidence is that the authorities have shown their continued interest in him by the arrest and detention of his father.

Conclusion

8. There is no doubt that the persecution or ill-treatment the appellant would be expected to face on return to Iran would be on religious grounds and therefore would engage the Refugee Convention. Article 3 of the ECHR is engaged by the same facts and falls to be considered on the same lower standard of proof.

Date:

Name:

Address:

Particular Points for Consideration

- Whilst a potential detraction from credibility in some cases, the fact that the appellant entered the United Kingdom on a visa is not likely to be the central point in this case. Mention of it in the skeleton would be unwise as it would only distract from the issue of conversion and its consequences.
- The credibility of the appellant's conversion was an issue which was required to be confronted head on. Given the credible written evidence, it was appropriate to bring it to the forefront of the adjudicator's mind, with suitable reference to the Home Office interview. If the appellant succeeds on credibility, then given the objective evidence, he is well on the way to succeeding in his appeal.
- The fact that the appellant had not been previously arrested or detained by the Iranian authorities was not a strong point against the appellant and would certainly not prevent a finding in his favour given the ultimate issue of return. As such it could properly be dealt with as a point in submissions if necessary.
- Given the unequivocal country background evidence, quoting extracts from the various reports served to highlight the risk on return and really set the claim in its proper context.

CHAPTER 6

The Appeal Hearing

Asylum and human rights claims deserve and must be treated with the utmost seriousness and professionalism. A client's claim should receive careful attention and comprehensive preparation from the outset, so that if the Home Office refuse the claim, the client will be in the strongest possible position at the appeal hearing.

This first-tier appeal before an adjudicator is crucial. The number of appeals actually allowed at this stage is in the region of 20% and it is without doubt the best opportunity the client will have of succeeding in their case. If unsuccessful, the appellant will face greatly diminished prospects of success in any further appeal. An appeal from an adjudicator to the Immigration Appeal Tribunal (the Tribunal) is now, at least in theory, only on an issue of law and is conditional upon the Tribunal granting permission in the first place. There is no room therefore for any complacency.

In the past few years the emphasis in all asylum appeals has increasingly been on speed and efficiency. Adjudicators are under pressure to hear more appeals, and there is a feeling among representatives that this efficiency drive often makes fairness and justice secondary to expediency. This year there has been a significant increase in the number of appeals being listed on a daily basis, but it is not clear that this has actually led to an increase in efficiency. Overloaded lists result in more cases being adjourned for lack of court time, thus increasing the backlog even more. Any reduction in the quality of determinations is also likely to lead to an increase in the number of cases heard by the Tribunal and those remitted for re-hearing.

The role of the adjudicator

The role of an adjudicator can, on one view, be said to be defined by their powers to make directions and to allow or dismiss an appeal. However, as will be seen later, their role has to be seen in the context of the nature of an asylum or human rights appeal, which although adversarial may nevertheless require a more interventionist approach than would be expected of judges in other jurisdictions.

The adjudicator has the power to consider afresh any determination of a question of fact on which the original decision was made. An adjudicator must allow an appeal insofar as they think that a decision against which the appeal is brought is 'not in accordance with the law (including immigration rules)' or where a discretion exercised in making a decision against which the appeal is brought or is treated as being brought 'should have been exercised differently'. Otherwise, an adjudicator must dismiss the appeal.

The issue of credibility

Before moving on to consider the various aspects of the substantive hearing it is important to look at the fundamental issue of credibility in asylum appeals, as it is regularly at the heart of the adjudicator's task. For the appellant and any other witnesses, this hearing is usually the first and last opportunity to give oral evidence, be found a credible witness and make out a successful case. The adjudicator's function of assessing credibility was discussed in *Hassan v Immigration Appeal Tribunal* [2001] Imm AR 83 in which the Court of Appeal stated:

> 'It is for the special adjudicator to weigh up as best he can, having heard the applicant and looked at the surrounding facts, whether or not he believes what he is being told. It is not required in that context for the special adjudicator to reason out, in respect of every single item of fact or claim, the reason why or why not he considers that particular item to be unfounded. What he must do is look at the position as a whole . . .'

As we have forewarned, a negative credibility finding is notoriously difficult to challenge at a later stage in the appellate system. Representatives must therefore do all they reasonably can to avoid adverse findings being made. That does *not* mean of course that representatives should seek in any way to misrepresent the evidence or mislead the adjudicator. But it does mean they should do their very best to maintain and to advance the appellant's case within the context of an adversarial hearing in which the representative must fight for the client's best interests, whilst maintaining an overriding professional duty to the court system.

Combined appeals

Rule 51 of the 2003 Procedure Rules allows for appeals to be combined where there are two or more appeals pending at the same time. The adjudicator may direct them to be heard together if it appears that:

- there is a common question of law or fact;
- they relate to decisions or action in respect of individuals from the same family; or
- it is desirable for some other reason.

THE PRE-HEARING CONFERENCE

For the representative appearing at the appeal, a conference with the appellant prior to the hearing will almost always be essential. If counsel has been instructed for the appeal, a conference provides the appellant with the opportunity to meet their representative for the first time and to discuss any particular concerns about their case.

If a case has been properly prepared and a full witness statement taken by the solicitors, a conference on the day of hearing may suffice. If not, or if there are issues on which instructions still need to be taken, a conference on the day could be problematic, especially where the solicitors are unable to obtain their own interpreter to attend court. Where there is no interpreter, the representative will have to do their best in a situation where the appellant's command of English can be very poor or often non-existent. A case in which there are serious credibility issues, no witness statement and no interpreter for the conference at court, is highly likely to require an application for an adjournment. Needless to say, the adjudicator will want to know why the case has been allowed to get to the day of hearing in such a state.

For the majority of appellants, the appeal hearing will be their first appearance before *any* court – let alone a foreign court making a decision of such grave importance to their life and those of their dependants. Similarly, other appellants may have had very negative experiences of the authorities and legal system in their own country. The majority are therefore likely to be apprehensive if not nervous, and so telling them that the hearing is relatively informal and that they can ask for a break at any time will help calm nerves. It will also be helpful to explain the actual mechanics of the appeal, in terms of giving evidence-in-chief, producing their documents, being cross-examined, as well as being asked questions by the adjudicator. Many appellants will understandably want the opportunity to give their account and they should be reassured that they will have this opportunity, at the same time being told that much of their evidence is already in written form and will not need to be repeated in full.

The appellant should also be informed that their appeal will be held in open court and that members of the public and even journalists may be present. If the appellant has a particular concern about any of this, it can be raised with the adjudicator.

Hearings in private

Section 108 of the Nationality, Immigration and Asylum Act 2002 and rule 50(2) of the 2003 Procedure Rules, require that where there has been an allegation that a document relied on by a party to an appeal is a forgery and disclosure to that party of a matter relating to the detection of the forgery would be contrary to the public interest, the hearing must be held in private. The adjudicator may also exclude members of the public from a hearing where it is in the interests of public order or national security, or to protect the private life of a party or the interests of a minor (rule 50(4)). Where it is strictly necessary, an adjudicator may also exclude the public to ensure that publicity does not prejudice the interests of justice.

Checking the evidence

It is now standard practice for written statements to stand as the appellant's evidence-in-chief. For this reason it is essential to ensure the client has had these all read to them in their own language and that they agree the contents are true to the best of their knowledge and belief, even where this has already been done or confirmed in the relevant document. Any outstanding contradictions or discrepancies should be raised with the client and their instructions taken on these as well as any new points arising. If there is time before the hearing, any further amendments or evidence can be dealt with in an addendum statement, otherwise these points will have to be covered in evidence-in-chief. Likewise, the representative should check that copies of all the supporting documents such as membership cards, photographs, arrest warrants, etc. as well as any necessary translations are in the bundle. If documents are missing they must be located and copies made for the adjudicator and the Home Office presenting officer (HOPO).

Late submission of documents

There will be occasions when essential documents are unavailable until the day of the hearing and will not therefore have been served in compliance with directions. Copies of these documents must be obtained for both the adjudicator and the HOPO, and it will then be a matter of persuading the adjudicator, pursuant to rule 48(5) of the 2003 Procedure Rules, that there are 'good reasons' to allow the documents into evidence. A practical point to bear in mind is that if more than a few pages are involved the adjudicator may refuse to allow use of the IAA's photocopying facilities and then refuse to admit the documents into evidence because copies have not been made.

PRACTICALITIES

Listing

Cases are often adjourned the day before hearing by the IAA due to unavailability of adjudicators. Late changes of venue are equally common. Appellants and representatives are not always informed in time or even at all. It is always a sensible precaution to ring the IAA 'hotline' (0845 600 0877) the day before the hearing to confirm that the case is still listed and at the same venue.

Arrival at court

An obvious but often overlooked aspect of these cases, is sorting out travel arrangements prior to the day of hearing so that the appellant does not have problems finding the hearing centre. This is often difficult due to the frequent number of listing changes. If the appellant does not attend the hearing or fails to arrive on time, then unless there is a reasonable excuse they run the risk of having the case heard in their absence. The representative and the appellant should arrive at court as early as possible and report to the reception as well as the court usher straight away. This will enable as much time as possible for a conference and discussion with the HOPO, as well as giving the appellant the opportunity to become familiar with the court environment.

The usher

No matter how pressured a representative is feeling, they should always be courteous to the usher. Rudeness or pomposity may be communicated to the adjudicator. Also, it may be the usher that 'rescues' your case by re-arranging the list to give you more time or if you are appearing in more than one court. It should at this stage be pointed out that taking on two full appeals in separate courtrooms is generally to be avoided unless there is good reason. Shuttling between different courtrooms is likely to give both appellants the distinct impression that they are not getting your undivided professional attention. If this situation does arise, counsel's clerk should liaise with the IAA well before the day of hearing to try and have both cases listed before the same adjudicator. It is not unknown for adjudicators to make complaints about 'double-booking' to the Law Society and the Bar Council.

Respecting the appellant

It should go without saying that the appellant must be accorded respect and patience at all times. If there is a delay in their case being called on, the appellant should be kept informed and the representative should not 'wander off' without telling the appellant. Lengthy or overly-friendly discussions with the HOPO or indeed other representatives in front of the appellant are to also to be avoided. This is particularly important when you are meeting the appellant for the first time at court because they are more likely to be worried about their case. Anything that lessens their confidence will be detrimental.

LIAISING WITH THE HOPO

In an increasing number of appeals, the Home Office are not represented at the appeal hearing due to a 'lack of resources': this has its own implications which will be dealt with later. However, when the Home Office are represented by a HOPO or by counsel, a professional discussion at court before the appeal is heard is invariably beneficial. Although we will be using 'HOPO' to refer to both presenting officers and counsel, an important distinction between them is that a presenting officer will often know more about specific Home Office practices and policies, as well as having the power to concede appeals (although exercised very rarely).

Discussing the case

It should be borne in mind that a HOPO will probably have several cases to deal with on the day, so representatives should be patient and economical in their discussion of the case. However, this is also an opportunity to bring to the attention of the HOPO issues which have either been overlooked or not been given proper consideration, and a superior knowledge of the case will now pay dividends. Even seemingly minor points can have the effect of minimising the prospect of an unnecessarily long drawn-out hearing which is unlikely to be productive for the appellant.

A discussion between the representatives may also allow there to be agreement on the issues in the case, particularly where the decision letter is formulaic or unclear. The HOPO may, for example, take the view that credibility is not in dispute and that there will be no cross-examination on the written statements already in existence. If the representative was intending to examine the client on matters not contained within these statements, they will now have to make a judgement about whether doing so is going to further the client's case, given that HOPOs can and do change their mind on cross-examination if they start hearing 'new' evidence.

Representatives should obviously confirm that all documents and bundles have been received and it is often only at this point that the HOPO will serve objective evidence – usually the current CIPU report – and any authorities on which they are relying.

Discretionary leave

Another matter that may need to be raised is whether the Home Office are willing to grant the appellant discretionary leave. This may arise, for example, where irrespective of the outcome of the appeal, the appellant cannot be returned to their home country due to civil war, where there are exceptional or compassionate factors, or simply where the claim is in fact obviously credible and the refusal letter is illogical or very weak.

In cases where discretionary leave has already been granted, an appellant is still entitled to pursue their appeal against refusal of asylum – it is important that those individuals entitled to full refugee status are given a mechanism to put their case: *Saad, Diriye and Osorio v Secretary of State for the Home Department* [2001] EWCA Civ 2008, [2002] Imm AR 471. This is recognised by section 83 of the 2002 Act. Nonetheless in some cases, perhaps where the client is not going to make a good witness and is liable to be found not credible or there is no arguable Convention reason, it may be in the client's best interests to accept the grant of discretionary leave and withdraw their appeal on the understanding a further appeal can be made should the Home Office seek to remove them in the future. Before the expiry of discretionary leave the client can normally apply for an upgrade to indefinite leave to remain (ILR) which is frequently granted. In making the decision of whether to pursue an appeal, the appellant should be aware of the lesser status that discretionary leave entails – the main difference being that there is no right for their immediate family to join them in the United Kingdom, save in exceptional compassionate circumstances.

Certification

From 9 June 2003 the Home Office policy has been to withdraw certificates made under paragraph 9, Schedule 4 of the Immigration and Asylum Act 1999. This allows all appellants whose appeal to an adjudicator is dismissed, to apply for permission to appeal to the Tribunal. This policy coincides with the replacement of judicial review of refusal of permission by the Tribunal with 'statutory review'.

THE COURTROOM

Before entering the hearing room all mobile phones should be turned off. Representatives should also do their best to ensure that the room is ventilated and that the client is supplied with drinking water. If the appellant has any injuries or disabilities, they should be reminded that they can stand up or walk around if sitting for long periods of time becomes uncomfortable. As already mentioned, they should also be told to ask for a break whenever they need one.

Note-taking

Taking a clear and detailed note of the proceedings is, as in any court hearing, obligatory. Although the adjudicator is duty-bound to keep a record of the proceedings, this will never be comprehensive, or necessarily totally accurate. Therefore, a note of a legal ruling, directions, questioning, or the evidence given, may prove crucial in the event of an appeal to the Tribunal. There will be cases where an appeal will be based simply on the dialogue between the adjudicator and the representative and/or the appellant. In such cases the adjudicator is unlikely to be taking a full note of his own comments or questioning.

THE ADJUDICATOR

Adjudicators are independent of the Home Office, being appointed by the Lord Chancellor. An adjudicator must have either legal qualifications or other suitable experience (s 81 of the 2002 Act). There are both full-time and part-time adjudicators, but all will have had a mandatory period of training before being appointed and receive ongoing training as well as bulletins, case law and practice directions. The reality, however, is that adjudicators vary greatly in their knowledge and experience. As a representative's own experience develops so too does their knowledge and familiarity with adjudicators. Whether rightly or wrongly, a significant part of the solution in each case will be about getting on with the adjudicator in a professional way: learning their different methods and ways is often a key aspect of presenting appeals. One way of viewing the task of a representative is in seeking to appeal to an adjudicator's humanity, at the same time as recognising and respecting their judicial role. This is particularly relevant as the adjudicator has the difficult task of judging the credibility of the appellant, which involves an assessment of human behaviour set against the backcloth of the objective country evidence.

It is strongly advised that whatever the circumstances, adjudicators should be treated with the utmost respect and due courtesy at all times. What should always be remembered is that the appellant's interests are paramount and that it is the adjudicator who has the power to allow their appeal.

PRELIMINARY MATTERS

Before the substantive appeal begins there will sometimes be legal or administrative issues that need to be addressed, and these are dealt with below.

Checking bundles and adjudicator's readiness

Most adjudicators will helpfully go through the Home Office and appellant's bundles, checking that they have in their possession all the relevant documents. This will be an opportune time for handing in any additional materials, of which sufficient copies should have been made. By checking through the documents with the adjudicator, representatives can ensure that the adjudicator has read all the documents, including the skeleton argument. Where the adjudicator has not read an essential document, for example a recent statement, this will be a good time to offer a reminder. This avoids an adjudicator hearing the case 'cold' and ensures that they are focused on the basis of the appellant's claim. Furthermore, an adjudicator who is aware of precisely what the issues are will be less likely to tolerate irrelevant and lengthy cross-examination. Representatives should always be prepared to give the adjudicator an outline or summary of the main issues.

Poorly prepared cases

There will be cases where preparation has been shoddy or improperly undertaken and where vital evidence is missing. Depending on the severity of the failings there may be no option other than to seek an adjournment. These are cases in which the representative's assessment is the key: the touchstone is whether the case can proceed without unfairness to the appellant. Where an adjournment can at all be avoided, then an application should not be made, for example if the documentation can be faxed to court, or by getting the case put to the back of the list to allow for more time.

Adjournments: the Rules

The guidelines concerning the grant of adjournments in asylum appeals are contained in rule 40 of the 2003 Procedure Rules:

> '(2) An adjudicator or the Tribunal must not adjourn a hearing on the application of a party, unless satisfied that the appeal or application cannot otherwise be justly determined.
>
> (3) Where a party applies for an adjournment of a hearing, he must –
>
> (a) if practicable, notify all other parties of the application
>
> (b) show good reason why an adjournment is necessary; and
>
> (c) produce evidence of any fact or matter relied upon in support of the application.
>
> (4) Where a hearing is adjourned, the appellate authority–
>
> (a) must fix a new date, time and place for the hearing; and
>
> (b) may give directions for the future conduct of the appeal or application.'

Rule 40 is subject to rule 13 which states that when an adjudicator adjourns an appeal he must give directions fixing a date by which the same or another adjudicator must hear the appeal or determine the appeal without a hearing (this does not apply where there is a fixed first and second hearing and the first is adjourned). This 'closure date' should be fixed according to the individual circumstances of the case but 'must not be more than six weeks after the date of the adjourned hearing'. This can be extended however by the adjudicator, either where all the parties consent, or in 'exceptional circumstances' where the appeal cannot be justly determined within six weeks, or by the closure date that has already been fixed, and there is an identifiable future date by which the appeal can be justly determined.

Adjournments: in practice

In practice the above provisions are not interpreted consistently and decisions often take into account a number of underlying factors such pressure on particular adjudicators or courts. As an application for more time to prepare a case can be made at the First Hearing or in writing prior to the appeal, it could be said that getting an adjournment on the day of the full hearing is where good advocacy shines through. If an important piece of evidence has not yet been obtained, there will have to be an application for an adjournment. An adjournment will not be granted unless the adjudicator is persuaded that the appeal cannot otherwise be justly determined. If the case is publicly funded the representative should try to have their application dealt with first, as this will avoid waiting at court and unnecessary expense to the public purse.

Sometimes there may not be a need for a formal application because the court has insufficient time to hear the case. For this reason it is useful before making such an application to discreetly check the effectiveness and time-estimates of the representatives for the other cases in the list. An adjudicator is more likely to grant an adjournment in a particular case if it is not going to be possible in any event to hear all the cases listed that day. If an adjournment request is not granted, the representative should have a full note of the reasons given for refusing it. The failure on the part of an adjudicator to grant an adjournment where justice demands it may well, in the event the case is dismissed, form a ground for leave to appeal to the Tribunal. Where for example the adjudicator does not adjourn to allow a medical report or translations of vital documents, these should be obtained in any event and submitted in the application to the Tribunal.

Absence of the appellant

A common preliminary issue is the absence of the appellant. Under rule 44 of the 2003 Procedure Rules an adjudicator *must* hear an appeal in the absence of a party or his representative, if satisfied that the party or his representative has been given notice of the date, time and place of the hearing, and has given no satisfactory explanation for his absence. However even if these conditions are not fulfilled, the adjudicator *may* still hear the appeal in the absence of a party if satisfied that any one of the following is applicable:

- a representative is present at the hearing;
- the party is outside the United Kingdom;
- the party is suffering from a communicable disease or there is a risk of him behaving in a violent or disorderly manner;
- the party is unable to attend the hearing because of illness, accident or some other good reason;
- the party is unrepresented and it is impracticable to give him notice of the hearing;
- the party has notified the appellate authority that he does not wish to attend the hearing.

An adjudicator may actually determine the appeal without a hearing if any of the following apply:

- the parties consent;
- the appellant is outside the United Kingdom; it is impracticable to give him notice of the hearing, and in both cases he is not represented;
- a party has failed to comply with a provision of the rules or a direction of the appellate authority and the adjudicator is satisfied that in all the circumstances, including the extent of the failure and any reasons for it, it is appropriate to determine the appeal without a hearing;
- the adjudicator is satisfied that having regard to the material before him and the nature of the issues raised, that the appeal

can be justly determined without a hearing. The adjudicator must not determine the appeal under this provision, however, without giving the parties notice of intention to do so, and the opportunity of making written representations as to whether there should be a hearing.

Dismissal without substantive consideration

Rule 33 of the old 2000 Procedure Rules has now gone in so far as an asylum applicant could, in the event of non-compliance by the Home Office, request that an adjudicator allow their appeal without consideration of the merits. However, under rule 45(1)(c) of the 2003 Procedure Rules, where there has been a failure on the part of the appellant to comply with the rules or a direction, the adjudicator may still *dismiss* the appeal without substantive consideration of the case. The Tribunal has held that for an adjudicator to dismiss an asylum appeal without considering whether the appellant would have a well-founded fear of persecution if returned, would rarely if ever be justified. However, it is worth bearing in mind that where the Home Office appeal to the Tribunal, then they will be the 'appellant' for the purposes of rule 45(1)(c) and non-compliance on their part could justify the Tribunal dismissing their appeal without looking at the merits.

Non-compliance

Where the Home Office have refused the application at first instance for non-compliance, such as the SEF not being submitted in time and the Refusal Letter has not dealt with the substantive merits of the case, the HOPO or the representative (or both) may wish to apply for an adjournment to allow the Home Office to consider the same. As stated in Chapter 4, it will always be desirable for the Home Office to have fully considered the merits of the case before the appeal is heard. However, representatives should also ensure that, should the adjudicator wish to press on and hear the whole case, they are prepared for this eventuality and have filed and served all the relevant and necessary evidence: *Ali Haddad* [2000] INLR 117. Of course, if the HOPO withdraws the original refusal of asylum, pursuant to a reconsideration and fresh decision, there is no longer an appeal before the adjudicator to hear.

Removal directions

If there is any dispute over the validity of the removal directions (see paragraph 8(1)(c), Schedule 2 of the Immigration Act 1971), this should also be discussed. The HOPO may agree that they are invalid, in which case there should sensibly be a joint application for an adjournment of the appeal to allow fresh removal directions to be drawn up and served. Although the Home Office can do this by faxing the removal directions to court on the day of hearing, adjudicators recognise that changing the destination country has an obvious impact on the basis of the appeal and that unfairness will result if there is no opportunity for the appellant to give further instructions and for objective evidence relating to the new country to be obtained.

Professional embarrassment

In some very limited circumstances, the representative cannot proceed with the hearing without being professionally embarrassed and consequently will have no choice but to withdraw from the case. It is difficult to state with any precision the situations in which this may arise as much depends on the nature and circumstances of the case. One example would be where the appellant insists on giving evidence to the adjudicator which the representative knows to be untrue. However, instances of professional embarrassment tend to be very rare. Given the fundamental nature of an asylum appeal, withdrawing from a case on the day of hearing and leaving the appellant unrepresented must be the very last option. Where the representative is in any doubt whatsoever, the Law Society or Bar Council should be contacted immediately.

Sensitive cases

Whilst all asylum appeals are invariably of a personal nature, there will be some which present particularly sensitive issues, for example where the appellant's experiences have been especially traumatic or are highly personal in nature. Such cases should always be held in private. Where the appellant is female the IAA Asylum Gender

Guidelines should be consulted and drawn to the attention of the adjudicator. Female appellants should of course be advised that their appeal can, if they wish, be heard by an all-female court (adjudicator, HOPO and interpreter). Given that unaccompanied minors are generally granted discretionary leave, it will be rare for them to proceed with an appeal until they have reached the age of 18. However, if such a situation does arise then a comprehensive witness statement will play a big part in lessening their ordeal. Where an appellant is particular young, adjudicators will rarely expect to see the appellant called to give evidence at all. Requests for special hearing arrangements should be made on the reply form and if a prior request has not been complied with on the day of the hearing, there will be an entitlement to an adjournment.

Exclusion clauses

It would only be appropriate to determine an exclusion point as a preliminary issue where the evidence strongly pointed to the appellant falling within Article 1(F) of the Refugee Convention. We have already set out in Chapter 1 the guidance given by the Tribunal in the case of *Gurung v Secretary of State for the Home Department* [2003] INLR 133, relating to exclusion clauses.

THE SUBSTANTIVE APPEAL

Nature and purpose

Generally speaking, the appeal hearing is adversarial in nature and this will mean that where the Home Office have not put facts raised by the appellant in issue, they should not be given the opportunity to do so unless the appellant is given a proper opportunity to respond. This makes even more sense given that the IAA has the power to set pre-hearing directions to identify and limit the issues in the appeal. Where the HOPO has agreed facts raised by the appellant or makes a concession, the adjudicator cannot go behind it: *R v Secretary of State for the Home Department, ex p Ganidagli* [2001] Imm AR 202.

The hearing therefore, is not designed to discover 'the truth' per se and nor is the role of an adjudicator one of investigator. However, while the adjudicator is required to hear both sides and make findings on the facts of the appellant's claim, the assessment of the objective evidence is more of an 'inquiry' into the state of affairs in the country in question. Moreover, the adjudicator must always approach the appeal on the basis that their decision should not put the United Kingdom in breach of the Refugee Convention and that, as a 'public authority' under s 6 of the Human Rights Act 1998, the IAA must not violate the ECHR. This approach may therefore require the adjudicator to ask questions and raise issues which have not been adequately dealt with by the parties.

Home Office unrepresented – implications

Where the Home Office are not represented, the representative's task changes, but does not necessarily become any easier. The first step will be to ascertain whether credibility has been challenged in the Refusal Letter. Where credibility is unchallenged then this should be made clear with the adjudicator from the outset. The next task will be to determine what evidence the adjudicator needs to hear and any specific additional evidence the appellant wishes to give. The case can then move to submissions on the appellant's evidence, the objective evidence and relevant case law. Different considerations apply however where credibility has been challenged

Home Office unrepresented – credibility challenged

Whether credibility is challenged in whole or in part, directly or indirectly, then without the HOPO the exercise will be to determine which if any of the particular challenges require evidence from the appellant. The importance of comprehensive preparation becomes apparent yet again, because ideally any challenges should have been dealt with in the appellant's witness statement. Examination-in-chief in this scenario is more relaxed given that there can be no challenge by way cross-examination, but it must be borne in mind that it is still for the appellant to prove their case to the requisite standard.

Home Office unrepresented – the guidelines

It is essential that representatives are fully aware of the Surendran guidelines (approved *MNM v Secretary of State for the Home Department* [2000] INLR 576) governing the conduct of asylum appeals where the Home Office are not represented (see appendix 5). Whilst an adjudicator does not have to accept an appellant's evidence as being true, that does not mean that they are entitled to 'descend into the arena' and cross-examine the appellant in place of the Home Office. Where the adjudicator requires evidence on an issue, he should whenever practicable ask questions of the appellant through the representative. Only then is the adjudicator to ask questions for clarification. Lengthy or hostile questioning would be grounds on which to appeal to the Tribunal. In *MNM v Secretary of State for the Home Department* [2000] INLR 576 it was further held that whilst asylum appeals are not covered by Article 6 of the ECHR, the same standards of fairness apply and that departures from them will be examined on appeal.

THE EVIDENCE

No strict rules of evidence

Rule 48 of the 2003 Procedure Rules permits an adjudicator to allow oral, documentary or other evidence to be given of any fact which appears to be relevant to an appeal, even where that evidence would be inadmissible in a court of law. In practical terms every advantage should be taken of this: for example, a question such as 'What did your friend tell you about the raid by the security forces?' would be sustainable, although of course the weight that will be given to such evidence may not be great. However, every piece of evidence to which *some* weight can be attached must be taken into account: *Karanakaran v Secretary of State for the Home Department* [2000] Imm AR 271.

Late service of evidence by the HOPO

Where the Home Office serve previously undisclosed, obscure or unfavourable evidence on the day of the hearing and the representative has had insufficient time to consider it or take instructions on it, rule 48 of the 2003 Procedure Rules regarding the late submission of evidence should be raised, and the admission of the evidence opposed.

CROSS-CHECKING THE EVIDENCE

The SEF

In the normal run of cases, a SEF having been duly completed by the appellant through his solicitor is the first and often crucial evidential document. The SEF should be checked for any errors and the statement checked against the interview and any subsequent statements for any discrepancies, inconsistencies or omissions, as well as for obvious mistakes and errors. More often than not, having checked and compared the documents against the SEF with the client present, there will be differences if for no other reason than the fact that often a good deal of time will have lapsed between the making of each document.

The record of interview (ROI)

The asylum interview is usually carried out after the SEF has been submitted. It is between these two documents that any differences usually arise. Checking these documents and questioning the appellant on any differences before the hearing is essential. Initially it is important to look at the written interview as a whole and to consider the following:

- Whether there was a representative present; whether the appellant confirmed that he was fit and well at the start and end of the interview; and whether there were any breaks due to the appellant feeling unwell or otherwise unable to continue.
- Whether the appellant signed the ROI at the end of the interview and whether the appellant or the representative made any additional comments.
- Whether there were any language problems in the interview – whether specifically noted by the appellant or representative, or apparent from reading the ROI.

- Whether the interviewing officer made a factual mistake and used that mistake as the basis for further questions which could have confused the appellant. For example, 'you were attacked for the first time in 1997, why did you not leave your country earlier?' whereas the appellant had in fact said he was first attacked in 1999.
- Whether the interview conformed to common law requirements of fairness. For example, have the questions been asked in a disparate and incongruous manner likely to confuse a reasonable client?
- Whether the questions have been asked without the appellant having had a proper opportunity to respond. A useful exercise is to consider the length of the interview against the actual number of questions asked. It is worth also considering the overall 'tone' of the interview – for example, whether the interviewing officer was discourteous or antagonistic.
- Whether there were any mistakes between the ROI and what the appellant states they actually said.

It is worth noting that a ROI mainly comprising long free-flowing answers and indicating that a client has required little prompting to disclose his account may be a positive indicator of credibility.

When checking the SEF against the ROI, the following should be considered:

- Has the client departed from the terms of the SEF?
- Did the interview actually test the SEF or did it assume the SEF as a basis for further questioning?
- Did the questions in the interview demand more detail than the SEF gave? In other words was there a natural expansion beyond the confines of the SEF?

Witness statements

Any additional statements made by the appellant may be approached by the adjudicator with greater reservation than the SEF or interview, because rightly or wrongly it is expected that an applicant should say all that is relevant at the very earliest opportunity. Great care should therefore have been taken in their preparation, especially as the statement will stand as the appellant's evidence-in-chief. Unfortunately many witness statements are prepared with insufficient care and attention. The representative should be highly conscious of whether the statement adds anything significantly new or changes anything, or whether it simply clarifies and expands on areas without departing from the basis of the claim.

The representative's own preparation of the case as well as the pre-hearing conference is crucial for comprehending and checking these documents. From a tactical perspective, any differences between the statement and the earlier documents must not come out in cross-examination, but should be dealt with in evidence-in-chief.

Other documents and reports

As already noted, the burden of showing that any document relied on by the appellant is genuine is on the appellant and the assessment is made by the adjudicator on the lower standard. This means that unless the HOPO has indicated that the documents are not challenged, the appellant must give evidence as to the provenance of each and every document relied on. If not already dealt with in a statement, the appellant must explain in examination-in-chief:

- what the document is and how it is relevant to the case;
- where the original is if not with the court or appellant;
- when and how they received the document and from whom;
- where available, any accompanying letter and envelope should be produced and the necessary explanations given.

If there is an allegation by the HOPO that a document is fraudulent, then the burden is on the HOPO to prove such an allegation beyond a reasonable doubt. However, such an allegation is rare and the HOPO is more likely to submit that 'little weight should be attached to the document'. It has to be said that careful judgement is required by representatives when faced with documents which appear to be inconsistent with the appellant's account or otherwise raise difficulties. The following may assist:

- Instructions must always be taken from the appellant and any difficulties pointed out.
- Although robust advice can be given, it is ultimately the appellant's case and therefore their choice as to whether they wish to rely on an unhelpful document.

- There is no duty to disclose unhelpful documents to the HOPO or adjudicator.
- If an unhelpful document is already in evidence and the HOPO or adjudicator are inclined to make it an issue then *Chiver* [1997] INLR 212 must of course be applied. In some cases it may need to be pointed out that often asylum applicants understandably want to strengthen their claim, but sometimes use improper means to do so.
- As already pointed out, representatives must be mindful of their professional duty not to mislead the court and not to proceed with an appeal in which they are professionally embarrassed.
- Although the latter scenario is fortunately rare, the blunt reality is that where documents are dubious, the adjudicator may weigh this against the appellant, regardless of the rest of the evidence.

WITNESSES

Any witnesses who are to give evidence should have a copy of their statements and have refreshed their memory prior to the hearing. The usual considerations applicable to any court hearing will apply and this will include whether or not to call a witness in the first place. This is usually dependent on whether their evidence is relevant and consistent. Witnesses ought to have made a statement which is comprehensive and can be adopted before they are tendered for any cross-examination. It is important to make sure that they are not present in court whilst the appellant is giving their evidence.

Where a witness was formerly an asylum applicant who now has leave to remain, their testimony could potentially have a bearing on their future status in the United Kingdom. Where it is found that they have lied to the court, the adjudicator can make a recommendation to the Secretary of State that their leave be revoked (s 76(2) of the 2002 Act). This will arise in very limited situations, one being that a witness gives evidence in court that contradicts what they previously said in their own claim for asylum, and it is clear that their status was obtained by deception.

Interpreters

Unless the client speaks very good English, it follows that they will be giving evidence through an interpreter. Adjudicators are well accustomed to ensuring that the interpreter and appellant understand one another, but difficulties can still arise during the course of the hearing. When they do, it is vital that they are immediately brought to the attention of the adjudicator. The appellant should have been forewarned that if they experience any difficulties with the interpreter, they should let the representative know immediately.

In the rare eventuality that the adjudicator insists on pressing on with the hearing despite serious problems, then the representative will have no option other than to continue with the hearing, taking full notes. In the event that the appeal is dismissed, this fact would no doubt form a strong basis for an appeal to the Tribunal.

Interpreters cannot make comment or express opinion on the evidence, but they are often encouraged to provide descriptive wording to place the answers given in their cultural context where necessary. There will be cases where the language, dialect or even accent of the appellant will be of particular importance to their credibility. The reply form should therefore be as specific as possible about the interpreter required. Failure to do so may not only lead to a lack of understanding and an unnecessary adjournment, but even where there is sufficient understanding to give evidence, an appellant may be left unable to demonstrate their ability to speak a particular language or dialect relevant to their claim.

Taking the oath

The representative should be aware that appellants originate from widely different cultural and religious backgrounds, and may have differing views on taking the oath. It is not compulsory, although some adjudicators consider it significant in assessing credibility. Rule 48(3) of the 2003 Procedure Rules states that an adjudicator '*may* require oral evidence of a witness to be given on oath or affirmation'. This is best discussed with the client prior to going into court and avoids any awkwardness later. One suggestion is asking the appellant in court that he understands the importance of telling the truth in such proceedings. This will often have the same beneficial impact as taking the oath.

Adopting the written evidence

There are usually going to be at least two documents that the appellant will need to adopt, whether in whole or with amendments having been made – namely the SEF and any further statement. Unless a preliminary challenge is made, the ROI automatically forms part of the evidence. Of course, the appellant may be asked whether any parts need clarification or addition, or to dispute the accuracy of some or all of the written record. It is fundamental however that the appellant is asked whether the interview was read back to him by his solicitors (or even a friend) given that it would not have been read back to him at the interview itself.

One common way of adopting the statements is:

> 'Do you remember completing a SEF with a statement attached which you signed and dated? (This is the first statement you made when you claimed asylum) Is the statement true to the best of your knowledge and belief? Are you content to adopt it as forming part of your evidence before the adjudicator? (As if you were saying the same in court today).'

EXAMINATION-IN-CHIEF

Knowing your witness

An initial task of the representative is to assess the appellant's ability as a witness and the likelihood of their giving relevant and cogent evidence. Caution must be exercised, however, given the differences in cultural and social backgrounds, not to mention language. Nevertheless, it may be that having spoken to the appellant, the representative forms the view that they will not be a good witness for one reason or another. Examples may be where it is anticipated that the appellant could potentially damage their credibility by giving too much or irrelevant evidence, or where they are overly emotional. However, a medical or psychiatric report will normally be required to support the position that the appellant should not give evidence at all.

Questions

Asking short simply-worded questions, rather than multiple questions is the key, given that they have to be translated first. A conference with the appellant before the hearing will hopefully have provided an insight into their ability as a witness. It is important to understand when control is needed and when the appellant can be left to speak on their own terms.

What evidence should be adduced

A significant challenge at the hearing is deciding what evidence to call. There is no definitive answer. The ultimate issue, however, namely the consequences of returning the appellant to their home country, should be kept at the forefront of the representative's mind. Put another way, what is the basis of the claim and what is needed to prove it? The answer in one sense therefore is to call as much evidence as is necessary to fulfil that obligation. This will depend in large part on the quality and extent of the written and documentary evidence – the more comprehensive and better presented it is, the less that will be required to be adduced in oral evidence. A well-prepared case on paper can work miracles with an adjudicator because it saves their time by defining and narrowing the issues.

Similarly, a proper approach to preparing and presenting an appeal will require assessing not only the strengths but also the weaknesses of the case. In considering the weaknesses of the case the representative is essentially taking the opposing viewpoint and that way can anticipate what challenges could be made in cross-examination. This is an extremely useful exercise because it allows for the representative to pre-empt challenges and adverse inferences by calling evidence from the appellant on their own terms.

Extent of oral evidence

Notwithstanding what has been said, we suggest that there will invariably be a need to call *some* evidence. Even if strictly unnecessary with the ultimate issue in mind, from a human perspective it will be desirable because it will bring the case to life by giving the appellant the opportunity of directly addressing the adjudicator on their fears of return. With the recent emphasis on cases being in written and submission form, it is sometimes easy, even for representatives, to lose sight of the human reality of these cases.

A pragmatic and balanced approach is called for. It is regrettably all too frequent that whatever matters are dealt with in evidence-in-chief, the appellant is again asked the very same questions in cross-examination which itself often adheres to a set list of open-ended questions. It must be advisable to deal with any major issues, which can be expected to be picked up on in cross-examination, recognising that there is always the opportunity of re-examination as a 'second bite'. Re-examination is particularly helpful where the adjudicator has been strict in the time allowed for examination-in-chief. It would be plainly unfair for an adjudicator to stop questioning on matters arising either from cross-examination or where they arise from his or her own questioning of the appellant.

The attitude and flexibility of the particular adjudicator therefore can make a big difference to the way the case is conducted. Similarly there must be a balance between reducing the time an appellant will spend giving oral evidence, which can be regarded as lessening their ordeal (albeit this could rarely be worse than what they have already endured), and allowing them their 'day in court'. If confronted with a particularly stringent adjudicator, the representative may need to be headstrong in persuading him or her that additional oral evidence is necessary for them to give the case the 'most anxious scrutiny.' In *R v Secretary of State for the Home Department, ex p Singh* [1998] INLR 608, the Court of Appeal recognised that although directions could require a witness statement to stand as evidence-in-chief, an adjudicator has a duty to ensure a fair hearing which could in appropriate cases require the exercise of discretion to permit supplementary oral evidence to be given.

Through all of these considerations it must be remembered that the burden of proof is on the appellant. There is nothing worse, in our view, than the HOPO being able to legitimately say in closing submissions 'we heard no evidence on (a disputed issue)'. The appellant's claim must be fully and comprehensively brought out prior to the submissions stage.

CROSS-EXAMINATION

Cross-examination can be defined as the questioning of a witness in such ways as to challenge, undermine, or qualify their evidence and thus the case of the party that called that witness. Effective cross-examination is typified by closed, leading questions. It is against this definition that cross-examination must be monitored by the appellant's representatives, and where it deviates objection can properly be made.

In reality 'cross-examination' at asylum hearings often takes the form of asking open-ended questions which are not faithful to the above formula. For example, questions will often be asked which repeat the questions already asked at the Home Office interview or in examination-in-chief. As cross-examination in asylum appeals is not simply a memory test, this can rarely be regarded as advancing the Home Office case. In such circumstances it would be appropriate for the appellant's representative to indicate to the adjudicator that the questioning is not serving any purpose. Adjudicators' reactions to any such objections differ: a few react quickly and even sternly, whilst the majority it seems are reluctant to interfere.

Why object?

The dangers of failing to object when appropriate are twofold. First, where cross-examination becomes inordinately lengthy, valuable hearing-time is wasted. Secondly, and more importantly, irrelevant questions could lead to the appellant becoming confused or agitated – giving evidence through an interpreter is difficult enough – and finding it harder to give evidence on important parts of the case. The representative's task is both to protect and promote the appellant's best interests, and the basis of any objection made must be to ensure they receive a fair hearing.

What has cross-examination achieved?

Representatives should be alert at all times to answers being given during cross-examination and whether or not they have damaged or weakened the case on the one hand or have served to strengthen it on the other. In the latter case, such answers need to be noted and highlighted in closing submissions.

The next consideration is the questions that were *not* asked. These can be significant and revealing and can be used to great effect in closing argument. There is nothing more satisfying than to be able to properly submit to the adjudicator that the 'appellant has been cross-examined at length and little or no progress has been made'; or 'the appellant's evidence has remained consistent and credible'; or even 'the appellant gave evidence about (a particular incident), that evidence was not challenged at all and I would therefore ask you to accept that evidence'.

Questioning by the adjudicator

The adjudicator of course has the right to ask questions for clarification at any stage during the proceedings, though most adjudicators will wait until cross-examination has been completed. Provided any direct questioning by the adjudicator is for clarification only there should be no objections made. It may often be the case where, for example, the representative has overlooked a point, that such questions can be useful to the case and indeed a necessary process leading to a fuller and more comprehensive understanding of it. It is vital however that a note of each question and answer is taken so that no misunderstanding occurs at a later stage.

RE-EXAMINATION

After cross-examination and any questions from the adjudicator, there may be a need for re-examination where other issues have been opened up and require further evidence. While there are no strict rules of evidence, any re-examination should normally be confined to the evidence already given. This is the final opportunity for the representative to put questions to the appellant to clarify and expand on their case. The criterion as to whether re-examination should be embarked upon must be whether it is *necessary*, bearing in mind the issues in the appeal. Representatives should also, of course, be aware of the danger of jeopardising a good case by asking too many questions.

CLOSING SUBMISSIONS

The following questions need to be asked by the representative of themselves throughout the hearing, with a view to formulating closing arguments:

- Does the written evidence contain the full reasons for the appeal to be allowed?
- Has oral evidence dealt with any omissions in the evidence?
- Has oral evidence dealt with any challenges to the appellant's credibility?
- Has the evidence been focused on the question of return?

The Refusal Letter and credibility

Refusal Letters are renowned for including formulaic paragraphs which lack legal force and are often irrelevant to the claim. One 'popular' example is the standard paragraph dealing with claiming asylum in the first safe country, whether the appellant was there for days or just passing through. Sometimes standard paragraphs are withdrawn by the HOPO. In any event, it is usually only certain parts of the Refusal Letter that raise relevant or substantial issues and need addressing in depth. A sensible approach for the representative will be to identify with the adjudicator which paragraphs in the Refusal Letter they consider germane to the case and to focus on those.

Where the Home Office are not represented at the hearing and the Refusal Letter challenges the credibility of only one aspect of the case, adjudicators invariably take the view that credibility as a whole is in issue and the representative must deal with this in submissions. Where the Refusal Letter does not challenge credibility and the Home Office are represented it will still be open to the HOPO to challenge it. It will be important to discuss this with the HOPO prior to the hearing, as the representative needs to be aware of what challenges will be made and whether they go to the heart of the claim. If an issue is not challenged, an adjudicator may be inclined to accept it without further ado. If the appellant's credibility has been weakened as a result of his oral evidence, the important thing to note is how damaging the inconsistency or omission really is. If it is not on a central aspect of the claim this should be made clear to the adjudicator. If it is on a vital aspect then this needs to be explained as best the representative can. In cases where the appellant appears to have been seriously discredited during evidence, the representative's duty still remains that of presenting the appellant's case in the best possible light.

Not just in closing

Whilst closing arguments are formally reserved to the end of the hearing, it is well worth bearing in mind that opportunities will arise throughout the course of the hearing for driving home important points. By way of illustration, one example might be where the adjudicator wishes to understand the relevance of a line of questioning or even part of a statement The representative might respond: 'This evidence is highly relevant because the Amnesty International report shows that even the families of party members are targeted by the security forces'. Interweaving and involving arguable points throughout the hearing is a useful tool to be used whenever reasonably possible.

The defining moment

It is at the stage of closing submissions that the representative has the critical role of persuading the adjudicator that the appellant should succeed in their appeal. This is the time for the representative to draw together and summarise the evidence, putting forward the strongest points, and the final chance to 'win over' the adjudicator. There is a balance to be struck however, between dealing with the relevant points and over-lengthy or protracted arguments. Wherever possible, shorter and punchier submissions are usually better.

Where the nature of the case demands longer closing submissions it is always a good tactic for the representative to indicate at the beginning that they are aware of the adjudicator's time constraints, but that certain arguments have to be heard in order to justly determine the appellant's case. If the representative has not wasted time so far, the adjudicator is likely to be understanding. In any event, the adjudicator should not place undue pressure on the representative and should be very sure of their reasons for any curtailment of submissions: *Katrinak v Secretary of State for the Home Department* [2001] INLR 499.

Tailoring submissions

The approach to making closing submissions may depend on whether a skeleton argument has already been submitted, and whether or not the emphasis or sometimes even the basis of the claim has been altered during course of the hearing. It is important to be flexible to the demands of the case as it unfolds, and to be alive to any indications the adjudicator may have given during the hearing. It can assist to invite the adjudicator to indicate before submissions what, if any, view he has as to the issues.

Be different

Adjudicators hear a large number of cases on a weekly basis, with determinations written up days or even weeks later. This highlights the need to make the case stand out in their mind as much as possible and to try and bring out the drama and the pathos of the case. Doing so in an appropriate way may make all the difference.

Recommendations

It is in the discretion of the adjudicator to make a recommendation that the appellant be granted discretionary leave based on the exceptional or compassionate circumstances of the case. The Home Office are not bound to accede to a recommendation and for this reason adjudicators now frequently decline to make them. There is now a significant overlap with the ECHR. For example, the balancing exercise under Article 8 will inevitably draw on compassionate factors which would previously have formed the basis for a recommendation. One approach may be that representatives should only seek a recommendation in cases where the most likely outcome is dismissal of both asylum and human rights appeals, as it may be considered that otherwise such a request will dilute the case.

The fact that an adjudicator makes a recommendation does not create a legitimate expectation that it will be followed by the Secretary of State, who can take into account all the material before him at the relevant time of making such a decision: *R v Secretary of State for the Home Department, ex p Alakesan* [1997] Imm AR 315. A refusal by an adjudicator to make an extra-statutory recommendation for leave to remain on compassionate grounds is not appealable to the Tribunal, nor susceptible to judicial review: *Khalib-Shahidi v Immigration Appeal Tribunal* [2001] Imm AR 124, CA.

However, it has been held that in considering whether to grant an applicant exceptional leave to remain, the Secretary of State was not entitled to reject an adjudicator's findings of fact relating to the circumstances of the individual, in the absence of fresh relevant evidence or showing that the adjudicator was misled: *R v Secretary of State for the Home Department, ex p Danaei* [1997] Imm AR 366.

'Determination reserved'

Only in the strongest (or weakest) cases do adjudicators announce their decision directly at the conclusion of the hearing. Generally an adjudicator will reserve their determination, which will be notified in written form at a later date, usually within 4–6 weeks.

Additional evidence/authorities

In exceptional circumstances, an adjudicator can agree to delay writing up their determination for a certain period of time, for example to allow further documents to be submitted. Equally, if a representative discovers a document or an authority that should have been submitted at the hearing but was not, they should fax and post it to the IAA hearing centre, marked for the urgent attention of that adjudicator. However, such documents may not be received by the adjudicator in time or at all, given the large volume of bundles now being sent to the IAA on a daily basis. This once again underlines the importance of ensuring the case is fully prepared in every respect prior to the day of the hearing.

CHAPTER 7

Appeals to the Immigration Appeal Tribunal

In this chapter we consider the scope and powers of the Immigration Appeal Tribunal (the Tribunal) as the second tier of the Immigration Appellate Authority, and the issues involved in drafting grounds for permission to appeal to the Tribunal. Three case studies then follow in which grounds of appeal have been prepared in respect of fictitious determinations. Finally, we deal with the substantive appeal hearing.

APPEALS

Appeals to the Tribunal are available to both asylum applicants and the Home Office from the decision of the adjudicator, but only with the permission of the Tribunal. The relevant provisions of the Nationality, Immigration and Asylum Act 2002 (the 2002 Act) are:

> **'101. Appeal to the Tribunal**
>
> (1) A party to an appeal to an Adjudicator under section 82 or 83 may, with the permission of the Immigration Appeal Tribunal, appeal to the Tribunal against the adjudicator's determination on a point of law.
>
> **102. Decision**
>
> (1) On an appeal under section 101 the Immigration Appeal Tribunal may –
>
> (a) affirm the adjudicator's decision;
>
> (b) make any decision which the adjudicator could have made;
>
> (c) remit the appeal to an adjudicator;
>
> (d) affirm a direction given by the adjudicator under section 87;
>
> (e) vary a direction given by an adjudicator under that section;

(f) give any direction which the adjudicator could have given under that section.

(2) In reaching their decision on an appeal under section 101 the Tribunal may consider evidence about any matter which they think relevant to the adjudicator's decision, including evidence which concerns a matter arising after the adjudicator's decision.'

BASES OF APPEAL

On the face of it, the 2002 Act purports to remove the power of the Tribunal to interfere with findings of fact made by an adjudicator. According to s 101(1) the Tribunal can only consider an appeal on a 'point of law'. Similarly, r 17(3) of thc Immigration and Asylum (Procedure) Rules 2003 (the 2003 Procedure Rules) stipulates that an 'error of law' must be identified. Whilst this change appears to narrow the scope on which appeals may be brought (under r 18(4)(c) of the old 2000 Procedure Rules grounds of appeal could challenge 'errors of fact or law'), in practice the potential bases for challenging an adjudicator's determination are unlikely to change very much, if at all. The Tribunal will doubtless continue to consider factual issues which are frequently and often inextricably linked to questions of law, for example: was the correct standard of proof applied ? It can also be expected that the Tribunal will maintain the requirement that an appeal hearing be fair.

It is significant that s 102(1)(c) the 2002 Act continues to provide for cases to be remitted back to an adjudicator for a re-hearing. Remittal was typically directed by the Tribunal where the adjudicator's findings on credibility and fact were insufficient or where it was accepted that an appellant had been deprived of a fair hearing. It must therefore be the case that remittals will continue to be used in the same way.

Furthermore, given that asylum and human rights cases demand 'the most anxious scrutiny', the Tribunal is bound to consider any matters that go to the level of scrutiny as well as the ultimate issue of whether returning the appellant to their home country will breach the United Kingdom's obligations under the Refugee Convention or the ECHR.

CONSIDERING THE DETERMINATION

Where the adjudicator has dismissed an appeal, the determination is first sent to the Home Office who in turn will serve it on the appellant and their representatives. Where the appeal has failed, a further appeal to the Tribunal must realistically be viewed as probably the last chance for the appellant to succeed. The representative's review of the adjudicator's determination must therefore be a careful and thorough process. Unfortunately, is not unknown for solicitors who had instructed counsel to represent the appellant at the appeal hearing, to not bother informing counsel that the appeal was dismissed and to review the determination and decide themselves whether or not there are grounds on which to appeal to the Tribunal.

This can never be regarded as being in the client's interests: not simply because they may lack the necessary expertise in drafting grounds (which can be complex in nature), but also because it will inevitably be the representative who represented the appellant at the hearing who is in the optimal position to consider properly whether there should be a further appeal. Usually there is vital information that can only be known or understood by the representative who was at the hearing on the day. Such details may well not appear on the face of the determination. An adjudicator will not always record all of the evidence or material considered in the appeal. For example, the adjudicator may not have recorded important documents or objective evidence submitted at the hearing itself. Credibility often turns on the nature of the oral evidence given at the hearing, particularly under cross-examination, and this testimony may not have been properly taken down by the adjudicator. Similarly, closing arguments made on behalf of the appellant are rarely fully recorded in determinations. Finally, issues often arise at hearings which are relevant to whether the appeal was determined fairly, such as whether the interpreter was performing competently or whether the adjudicator conducted the proceedings in a proper and judicial manner.

Underlining the above, we would draw an analogy with criminal proceedings in which it would be exceptional indeed for anyone other than defence counsel to draft grounds of appeal to the Court of Appeal against conviction or sentence. Of course, if counsel who represented the appellant at the appeal advises negatively, this should not prevent a second opinion being obtained or the solicitors themselves drafting grounds of appeal.

APPLYING FOR PERMISSION TO APPEAL

Appeals to the Tribunal are governed by Part 3 of the 2003 Procedure Rules. An application for permission to appeal is made by filing the application notice T1, stating the appellant's name and address, the representative's name and address, signed and dated, and including all the grounds of appeal and reasons in support. The application must also enclose the adjudicator's determination as well as a copy of any other material relied upon. The application must be lodged with the Tribunal within ten working days of the service of the determination, unless the applicant is in detention, in which case it is only five working days. The Tribunal may extend the relevant time limit retrospectively if by reason of 'special circumstances it would be unjust not to do so' (rule 16(2)). If an application is out of time, it will be necessary for the grounds to include a full explanation for this delay: *Galal Kamal Tofik* [2003] EWCA Civ 1138.

CRITERIA FOR GRANTING PERMISSION

Under rule 18(4) of the 2003 Procedure Rules the Tribunal may grant permission to appeal only if it is satisfied that:

(a) the appeal would have a real prospect of success; or
(b) there is some other compelling reason why the appeal should be heard.

The application for permission to appeal is determined by a single, legally qualified member of the Tribunal without a hearing. This determination must be in writing and give reasons, whether permission is granted or refused. The Tribunal may limit permission to one or more of the grounds of appeal. Where permission to appeal has been granted, grounds of appeal can only later be varied with the leave of the Tribunal hearing the case, and this will not be granted unless due to 'special circumstances, it would be unjust not to allow the variation' (rule 20(2)).

FORMULATING GROUNDS TO THE TRIBUNAL

Rule 17(3) of the 2003 Procedure Rules states that grounds of appeal must:

(a) identify the alleged errors of law in the adjudicator's determination and;

(b) *explain* why such errors made a *material difference* to the decision.

Rule 18(2) of the 2003 Procedure Rules states that the Tribunal is not required to consider grounds of appeal which have not been raised in the application. However, this must be read subject to *Robinson v Secretary of State for the Home Department* [1997] INLR 182 in which it was held by the Court of Appeal that the Tribunal, in considering an application for leave to appeal, should take any 'obvious point' in favour of the appellant even if it had not been specifically raised. The Court pointed out, however, that this did not mean that the Tribunal had to search for new points. It is only if a point has a 'strong prospect of success' that the Tribunal is required to take it.

DECIDING IF THERE ARE GROUNDS TO APPEAL

One approach to considering the determination would be to read it all the way through first and then to ask certain basic questions of it, as suggested below:

- Has the adjudicator correctly identified the appellant, their sex, their country of origin, and the country to which they are to be removed?
- Did the adjudicator set out the central issues in the appeal, i.e. the basis of the claim under the Refugee Convention and/or the Articles of the ECHR which were also relied on?
- Has the adjudicator properly directed himself on the law relating to the central issues? For example:
    - the burden and correct standard of proof;
    - the concept of persecution;
    - the appropriate standard of protection;
    - internal relocation;
    - any potential Convention reasons;
    - the risk of return as at the date of the hearing;
    - the application and scope of Article 3 of the ECHR;

  - the application and scope of Article 8 of the ECHR;
  - the balancing exercise and proportionality where Article 8 is in issue.
- Has the adjudicator gone behind any issues either specifically conceded or not challenged by the Home Office?
- What subjective evidence was relied on in this appeal? It may have been from several different sources: has it all been considered?
- Did the adjudicator find the appellant and/or any witnesses credible? If so, to what extent? Which parts of the account did the adjudicator accept?
- If the adjudicator did not find the appellant and/or the witnesses credible, has there been an undue delay ie in excess of 3 months, between the hearing and the determination ?
- Have sufficient reasons been given for adverse credibility findings ? If so, are they fair and justified?
- Has credibility been assessed with sufficient regard to the country background?
- Where both favourable and adverse credibility findings have been made, has the adjudicator properly considered the implications of the positive findings?
- Have the consequences of return been considered with proper regard to the country background: has all of the objective evidence been taken into account?
- Are the conclusions drawn by the adjudicator as to the consequences of return fair and reasonable on the totality of the evidence?
- Has further relevant evidence come to light since the date of the appeal, or has the country situation further deteriorated? If so, what effect does this have on the adjudicator's findings and conclusions?
- Is there any element of contradiction in the adjudicator's conclusions?
- Has the adjudicator made a recommendation for discretionary leave in terms that indicate he should have allowed the appeal outright?
- Did the adjudicator conduct the hearing fairly, particularly where the Home Office were unrepresented?
- Is there a complex question of law on which the appeal turned?

- Regardless of any of the above considerations, is there some feature of either the case or the determination that provides a 'compelling reason' why permission to appeal to the Tribunal should still be granted? For example did the adjudicator determine the appeal in the absence of the appellant and now evidence has come to light demonstrating that the appellant was not to blame for his non-attendance?

Sometimes there will be obvious answers to these questions from a simple perusal of the determination. In every case, however, checking through the written evidence and notes of the proceedings will at the very least be a salient reminder of the nature of the appeal and is an essential part of the exercise.

SPECIFIC CONSIDERATIONS

Although we have listed above in summary form a range of errors that commonly give rise to grounds for appeal, many of them are concerned with the nature and quality of reasoning in a determination. We deal with three inter-related aspects below.

Giving reasons

In *R v Immigration Appeal Tribunal, ex p Amin* [1992] Imm AR 367 the High Court considered an adjudicator's obligations to make and record conclusions on the evidence. The Court stated that the adjudicator should set out 'with some clarity' the evidence that was accepted, rejected, on which no conclusion could be reached, and which was irrelevant. The Court of Appeal approved this approach in *R (on the application of Muchai) v Secretary of State for the Home Department* [2001] EWCA Civ 932. In *R v Secretary of State for the Home Department, ex p Atputharajah* [2001] Imm AR 566 the Court held that there were two questions to be asked when determining the adequacy of reasons given by an adjudicator in his determination. Firstly, do the alleged defects in the reasons create a *genuine* as opposed to theoretical doubt whether a significant issue in dispute may not have been properly addressed or addressed at all? Secondly, if they do, is there any real doubt whether the decision would have been the same even if the reasons had been adequate?

Factual findings

In *Alam Bi v Immigration Appeal Tribunal* [1979–80] Imm AR 146 the Court of Appeal held that where the adjudicator's conclusions on the facts were 'unsustainable' the Tribunal could reverse the decision. In *Borissov v Secretary of State for the Home Department* [1996] Imm AR 524, the Court of Appeal stated that:

> 'The Immigration Appeal Tribunal will be most reluctant to interfere with a primary finding of fact by the special adjudicator which is dependent on his assessment of the reliability of credibility of a witness who has appeared before him.'

In *Ibrahim* (IAT) (17270) the Tribunal said that something more than the appellant disagreeing with the adjudicator's findings would be necessary and that there must be:

> '. . . an allegation that his (the adjudicator's) assessment of the evidence is flawed in that it discloses a fundamental error of approach.'

Significantly from an asylum applicant's point of view, in *Horvath v Secretary of State for the Home Department* [1999] INLR 7 the Tribunal held that although it had heard no oral evidence, it considered in the circumstances that it was not bound by the adjudicator's findings on credibility. In our experience the Tribunal is not infrequently willing to review factual findings of the adjudicator. Where the adjudicator has made wholly or partially favourable credibility findings it is helpful to summarise these, perhaps in bullet-points, before going on to demonstrate how these findings should have led the adjudicator to allow the appeal. An observation made by the Court of Appeal in *Arshad* [2001] EWCA Civ 587, in respect of an appeal to the Tribunal by the Home Office, applies equally to appeals by asylum applicants:

> 'It is, I think, fair to notice that the Secretary of State's grounds to the Tribunal while all very properly expressed in the language of legal challenge or *Wednesbury* irrationality, in some instances are at any rate close to being quarrels with the . . . (adjudicator's) findings of fact . . .'

Objective evidence

The proper assessment of the objective evidence relating to an asylum appeal is at least, if not more important, than an appellant's own fear. Consequently, where an adjudicator has not properly undertaken this crucial exercise the merits of an application for permission will have to be seriously considered.

Where the material before an adjudicator presents conflicting evidence as to the situation in an appellant's country of origin, the adjudicator will have to give reasons as to why certain items are preferred over others, the more so when favourable evidence is rejected as being unreliable.

Whilst the assessment of credibility must take place against the backcloth of the country background, a fair and full examination of the objective evidence serves a wider purpose, namely the issue of whether the appellant can be returned, irrespective of adverse credibility matters.

In almost every appeal the Home Office will rely on a CIPU report which draws on a number of sources. As already pointed out, not only does the quality of this document vary greatly, depending on the country in question, but the emphasis on human rights issues in particular tends to be more optimistic (sometimes positively rose-tinted) than reports of non-governmental organisations such as Amnesty International and Human Rights Watch. In any case, an adjudicator has to consider the various reports put before him and attach appropriate weight to them. What is appropriate will obviously depend on the issues in the case as well as the nature of the report submitted. We would suggest that relevant factors when considering different reports are:

- the date of report and the period of events it covers;
- the detail and depth of coverage;
- the nature of the organisation;
- the expertise and independence of the author/s;
- the sources relied on in the report.

Fresh evidence

Rule 21(1) of the 2003 Procedure Rules states that the Tribunal may consider any record or note made by the adjudicator of any hearing before him in connection with the appeal.

Where either party wishes the Tribunal to consider evidence not before the adjudicator r 21(2) requires that they file and serve written notice on the Tribunal and the other party stating both the nature of the evidence and an explanation as to why it was not submitted to the adjudicator, as soon as practicable after the parties have been notified that permission has been granted. The Tribunal may give directions as to the manner and time by which the evidence is to be given or filed.

In other jurisdictions the admission of fresh evidence on appeal tends to be more tightly controlled by the higher court, and such evidence less frequently submitted. However, the nature of asylum appeals and the rapidity with which country situations can change (sometimes literally overnight) mean that an appeal to the Tribunal is often more than simply a consideration of the adjudicator's determination and the grounds of appeal as raised by the applicant. The Tribunal's duty is to review the question of whether the individual concerned has a well-founded fear of persecution or is at risk of a breach of Article 3 ECHR. The Court of Appeal in *Robinson* stated:

> '. . . If it does not do so (consider whether there are obvious points which favour the appellant), there will be a danger that this country will be in breach of its obligations under the Convention. When we refer to an obvious point we mean a point which has a strong prospect of success if it is argued. Nothing less will do. It follows that leave to apply for judicial review of a refusal by the Tribunal to grant leave to appeal should be granted if the judge is of the opinion that it is properly arguable that a point not raised in the Grounds of Appeal to the Tribunal had a strong prospect of success if leave to appeal were to be granted.'

This overriding principle has a bearing on the approach to fresh evidence. In *R v Immigration Appeal Tribunal, ex p Aziz* [1999] INLR 355, it was decided that the civil test for the admission of new evidence was too restrictive for asylum appeals. Where evidence was credible and significantly cogent so that it would affect the decision, the Tribunal should be slow to refuse to allow it into evidence. In *R v Immigration Appeal Tribunal, ex p Chen Liu Guang* [2000] Imm AR 59 the High Court held that the Tribunal in considering whether to grant leave was entitled to take into account the fact that fresh evidence could have been put before the adjudicator as required by the directions. In *R (on the application of Azkhosravi) v Immigration Appeal Tribunal* [2001] EWCA Civ 977, the Court of Appeal approved the approach in *Aziz*. The Tribunal was entitled to look with scepticism at material which could have been adduced before the adjudicator and was entitled to an explanation as to why this was not done. However, it could not focus entirely on that aspect and pay no attention to the credibility of the fresh evidence, or its relevance to the issues in the case. To do otherwise could lead to injustice. A balancing exercise was required.

In order therefore to have the best chance of fresh evidence being admitted and given substantive consideration by the Tribunal, it should be accompanied by a witness statement establishing its provenance, content, relevance and the reason why it was not previously adduced. If the constraints of time do not permit this, at the very least these points should be covered within the body of the grounds of appeal.

Style and length of grounds

Grounds of appeal should not raise weak arguments, but equally should not understate strong ones. They should be clear and concise and deal with the issues in a logical and orderly manner. Although it is always tempting for lawyers to use elaborate language and lengthy or complex sentences, this should be avoided as much as possible. The grounds should be expressed in simple and straightforward language. By the same token, grounds of appeal to the Tribunal should not be overly long but 'cut to the chase'. There are currently somewhere in the region of 700 applications for permission every week. Of course, considering each application will also involve reading and cross-referencing with the determination and any other evidence referred to. It is very much worth bearing in mind these constraints when considering what points to take and how many sentences to devote to each.

Where there are no merits

If after a thorough examination of the adjudicator's determination, evidence and notes of hearing, the representative forms the view that there are no grounds which have a 'real prospect of success' and there is 'no other compelling reason' then grounds should not be drafted.

If counsel has conduct of the case, a prompt and appropriately detailed written advice should be faxed to the appellant's solicitors, explaining why there are no grounds for an appeal. Not only is this necessary as part of an ongoing duty towards the client, but it will inevitably assist the appellant's solicitor in advising the appellant, who will want to know why matters cannot be taken any further. A prompt negative advice will allow time for the solicitor to obtain a second opinion.

Lodging the grounds of appeal

If there are grounds they must be dealt with within the ten working day time limit. Counting from the second working day after the date of promulgation, midnight of the tenth working day is the deadline for faxing the application to the Tribunal support centre. However, representatives should bear in mind that faxing grounds close to the deadline may be risky, as the support centre's fax machines will be busy receiving grounds from other representatives. Given the current high volume of applications to the Tribunal, errors do occur: the fax transmission report should be kept and a wise precaution is to send a hard copy of the application in the post as well.

SAMPLE DETERMINATIONS AND GROUNDS OF APPEAL

While the constraints of space clearly prevent us from dealing with every possible scenario, below are three fictitious determinations which raise a number of material errors, both obvious and not so obvious. For illustrative purposes, these determinations contain more errors than would normally be expected (or at least we hope so). Each determination is followed by suggested grounds of appeal which are correspondingly longer than usual.

Below are the areas covered in the sample determinations and grounds of appeal:

- burden and standard of proof;
- credibility findings;

- failure to properly consider documentary, written and oral evidence;
- failure to properly consider objective evidence;
- weight given to evidence and approach to evidence as a whole;
- failure to give adequate reasons;
- illogical analysis and mistakes;
- refusal of adjournment;
- fresh evidence;
- fairness of hearing.

In the Immigration Appellate Authority Appeal Number: HX/999/2002

Heard at: York House **Promulgated:** 13 January 2003

THE IMMIGRATION ACTS

On: 6 December 2002

Dictated: 10 December 2002

Before:

Mrs U. N. Fayre

Adjudicator

Between:

MUSTAFA BETLAM

Appellant

and

THE SECRETARY OF STATE FOR THE HOME DEPARTMENT

Respondent

DETERMINATION AND REASONS

The Appeal

1. The Appellant, Mr Mustafa Betlam, (born 8.5.1965) is a citizen of Algeria who appeals under section 69(5) of the Immigration and Asylum Act 1999, against the decision of the Respondent on the 1st February 2002 to refuse leave to enter and to give directions for his removal to Algeria.

The Appellant's account

2. The Appellant's account, as taken from his SEF, interview and witness statement and his oral evidence before

me, can be summarised as follows. In January 1998 the Appellant moved from his birthplace of Constantine to Algiers, where he opened a restaurant in the tourist district. The restaurant did very well. In December 2000, four members of thc Group Islamique Armé (the GIA) came to the restaurant and demanded that the Appellant pay them money to support their struggle against the government. They gave him one week to raise 30,000 dinars failing which they would kill him. They subsequently returned a week later by which time the Appellant had managed to raise the money which he handed over to them. The following month the same four members of the GIA returned and demanded another 30,000 dinars. This time the Appellant said that he did not have the money and could not raise it. The GIA reacted by beating him severely with the butts of their rifles. They gave him just three days to raise the money and again threatened to kill him.

3. The Appellant contacted his father who told him that he must go to the police, and the appellant did just that. The police took a report and stated that when the GIA came again they would be watching from an observation post across the street. The GIA did come as the Appellant had been told and demanded their money. The police stormed into the restaurant and a gunfight ensued in which two policemen and two members of the GIA were fatally wounded, and the remaining two GIA members were captured. The Appellant managed to escape injury himself by hiding in the wine-cellar of the restaurant as soon as the shooting started.

4. The Appellant was warned by the police to close his restaurant and to stay away from the area for a while. The Appellant went to stay in hiding with his friend in another district of Algiers. When the Appellant returned to his restaurant after two weeks he found that it had been destroyed in an explosion. The Appellant was terrified and immediately returned to his friend's house whereupon he found that his friend had been killed by

having his throat cut. A threatening letter had been left by the GIA addressed to the Appellant, stating that he would be next.

5. The Appellant went back to the police station and reported what had happened. The police said that there was 'nothing further they could do' and they 'could not protect him 24 hours a day'. The Appellant went to his parents' home in Constantine where he hid for a week while his father arranged for an agent to take him to the United Kingdom. The Appellant travelled via France where he stayed for three days with an acquaintance of the agent before finally arriving in the UK. The Appellant stated that he did not claim asylum in France because the agent told him that if he did, his claim would not be accepted because he feared the GIA and that he would just be deported back to Algeria.

My Findings

6. In asylum and human rights cases it is for the appellant to prove his case. Whether an appellant has a well-founded fear of persecution has to be looked at in the round, taking all relevant circumstances into account and bearing in mind the situation as at the date of the hearing of the case (*Ravichandran v Secretary of State for the Home Department* [1996] Imm AR 97, CA). Moreover, the threshold for persecution is a high one.
7. The Appellant adopted his SEF, interview and statement at the hearing. I also heard evidence from him, which is set out in full in the Record of Proceedings. Viewed as a whole, the evidence is internally coherent and is capable of being believed. However, whilst I find that the Appellant is a credible witness that does not mean that I have to accept the whole of his account.
8. For example, I have before me a copy of the alleged letter from the GIA and a translation. The Appellant claims that the police would not send him the original. I find this explanation quite implausible and I therefore give the copy no weight at all.

9. Before proceeding to consider the substance of this claim, I must say that the Appellant's case is somewhat damaged because he had the opportunity to claim asylum in France but did not do so. I do not accept his explanation in this regard. Had he been in genuine need of protection he would have claimed in the first safe country and not waited until he reached the UK. That he has not done so seriously undermines the credibility of his claimed need of international protection.
10. Turning now to his account, I find that there must be many other restaurants in Algiers and I fail to see why the Appellant was approached rather than anyone else. The US State Department Report 2002 shows that the GIA have been active in Algeria for the best part of ten years now and in my view they would already have established their sources of income and assistance.
11. Notwithstanding my above concerns, I do not believe that the Appellant would now be of any further interest to the GIA. The GIA have apparently destroyed the Appellant's only source of income and I do not think that they would still hold it against him that two of their members were killed and two others captured. Nor am I convinced that the GIA would necessarily link the ambush by the police with the Appellant.
12. I find it highly implausible that it was at the very time that the Appellant had returned to his restaurant that the GIA should have found out where he had been hiding and killed his friend, despite the fact that the Appellant had already spent two weeks at his friend's house. Furthermore, just because the Appellant's friend was killed does not mean that the Appellant is at risk in the future. If the GIA were as deadly efficient as the Appellant makes them out to be, then they would have been able to track him down as well and would not have simply left him a threatening letter.
13. Neither has the Appellant proved to me that the authorities would be unable or unwilling to protect him. On his own account, the police were sympathetic and in my view he could have returned to them if there had been any further problems. Besides, *Horvath v Secretary of*

State for the Home Department [2000] Imm AR 552, HL, does not require a state to provide protection 24 hours a day and in my view the Appellant was being unrealistic in expecting this. There is no evidence from the Appellant that he took matters further or to a higher authority before seeking international protection, as required by *Horvath*. However, even if the Appellant would be of continuing interest to the GIA, I find that he could easily go to live with his parents in Constantine just as he did before leaving Algeria. The CIPU October 2002 report makes it clear that the larger cities are generally safe and therefore I do not accept that the GIA can be considered agents of persecution within the meaning of the Refugee Convention.

14. Although strictly my conclusions make this academic, I nevertheless note that the Refugee Convention requires any persecution faced by the Appellant to be for one of the five specific reasons of race, religion, nationality, social group or political opinion. At best, this case is simply one of criminal extortion and not political persecution and as I have already found above, there is nothing left to extort now.
15. So far as Article 3 is concerned I accept the Respondent's submission that it must stand or fall with the asylum claim and I accordingly dismiss the appeal on that basis.
16. Article 8 is not relied upon, but I dismiss it in any event.

Conclusion

17. I dismiss the asylum appeal and I dismiss the human rights appeal.

10.12.2002 U.N. Fayre

IN THE IMMIGRATION APPEAL TRIBUNAL
CASE NO. HX/999/2002

BETWEEN:

MUSTAFA BETLAM

Applicant

and

THE SECRETARY OF STATE FOR

THE HOME DEPARTMENT

Respondent

GROUNDS OF APPEAL

Introduction

1. Permission to appeal is sought in respect of the Determination of the Adjudicator Mrs U.N. Fayre notified on 13 January 2003, on the following grounds.

Standard of proof

2. The Adjudicator failed to direct herself on the correct standard of proof applicable to asylum and human rights claims, namely that of a 'real risk' of persecution and/or ill-treatment. This is always a fundamental error, but is particularly so in this case, where the Adjudicator has failed to make clear findings of fact.

Credibility

3. The Adjudicator stated that although the Applicant was a 'credible witness' that did not mean 'that I have to accept the whole of his account'. The rest of the determination stands in stark contrast to the Adjudicator's initial finding of credibility, as she does not appear to accept any of the following material parts of the Applicant's evidence:
    - the GIA letter;

- explanation for not claiming asylum in France;
- approach by the GIA;
- continuing adverse interest by the GIA;
- threat posed by GIA;
- lack of protection.

THE GIA LETTER

4. The Adjudicator had sight of an important piece of documentary evidence in the form of a copy of a threatening letter from the GIA addressed to the Applicant. The Adjudicator was clearly unreasonable in rejecting this document outright merely because the original was not in evidence. It is submitted that the Applicant in fact gave a very good explanation for the absence of the original – it was perfectly proper for the original to be given by him to the police and entirely predictable that they would not release back to him a piece of criminal evidence. The Applicant had a copy of the letter and was able to give clear evidence about its provenance. The standard of proof for documents is the same as for oral evidence: has the appellant shown that it is reasonably likely that the document is genuine? (*Tanveer Ahmed* [2002] INLR 345). In *Karanakaran v Secretary of State for the Home Department* [2000] Imm AR 271 the Court of Appeal stated: 'Everything capable of having a bearing has to be given the weight, great or little, due to it'. The Adjudicator was therefore wrong to give the GIA letter 'no weight at all'.

FAILURE TO CLAIM IN FRANCE

5. Contrary to the Adjudicator's view, the Applicant's case is not damaged by not claiming asylum in France. It was recognised in *R v Uxbridge Magistrates' Court, ex p Adimi* [2001] QB 667 that an asylum-seeker has an element of choice as to the country they claim asylum in. Moreover, the Applicant's explanation for not claiming there certainly has the ring of truth: in *R v Secretary of State for the Home Department, ex p Adan and*

Aitseguer [2001] 2 AC 477 it was noted that the French courts' interpretation of persecution under the Refugee Convention does not include acts of non-state agents (such as the GIA).

APPROACH BY THE GIA

6. The Adjudicator's opinion that the GIA would 'already have established' sources of support was a speculative and most unrealistic assessment of the way in which a terrorist group operates. The US State Department Report 2002 makes clear that the GIA continue to commit crimes of robbery and extortion. In any event, the Adjudicator failed to make a clear finding as to whether or not she accepted that the Applicant was in fact approached by the GIA as claimed.

CONTINUING ADVERSE INTEREST BY THE GIA

7. It was simplistic of the Adjudicator to suppose that the GIA would no longer have an interest in the Applicant because they had destroyed his restaurant. The Adjudicator has taken this evidence completely out of context. The GIA's interest in the Applicant is now no longer one of extortion, but clearly revenge for the police ambush. The GIA clearly do link the appellant with that ambush as they have gone to great lengths to take reprisals – by killing the Applicant's friend and leaving a death threat for him. Far from indicating a lack of interest, the destruction of the restaurant is in fact highly probative of a continuing adverse interest in the Applicant.

THREAT POSED BY GIA

8. In finding it 'implausible' that the GIA did not find the Applicant's hiding-place earlier, the Adjudicator was imposing too high a standard of proof, as the Applicant's account was perfectly possible. Given that the Adjudicator had accepted the Applicant as 'a credible

witness' she should have given him the benefit of the doubt: paragraph 25 of the UNHCR Handbook. If, as the Adjudicator appears to have accepted, the GIA were prepared to kill the Applicant's friend merely because the Applicant was hiding at his house, their leaving a letter for the Applicant at a time when he was clearly absent cannot be interpreted as having anything other than sinister implications for him.

Sufficiency of protection

9. It is irrelevant that the police were 'sympathetic.' Actions and not words are what are important. The Adjudicator failed to take into account that this case is not concerned with a generalised fear of random and isolated acts of terrorism, but a very personal and direct threat from the GIA. The Adjudicator further stated that the Applicant was unrealistic to 'expect' 24 hours a day protection. However, this was not the Applicant's evidence – he was merely repeating what he had been told by the police. It is further submitted that it was clear from the police's comments that they did not consider anything *less* than 24 hours a day protection to be practical or effective. Tellingly, they did not offer him anything less.

10. The Adjudicator was further of the view that the Applicant should return to the police if there were further problems or go to a higher authority. With respect, this was hardly the kind of case where this would be possible, given the actions of the GIA towards the Applicant thus far. It is submitted that on the particular facts of this case, the state was incapable of providing the appellant with the necessary level of protection. It was accepted by both the Court of Appeal and the Tribunal in *Noune v Secretary of State for the Home Department* [2001] INLR 526; 2001/TH/00744, that there will be circumstances in which Algeria cannot protect its citizens from Islamic extremists.

Internal relocation

11. In finding that the Applicant could 'easily go to live with his parents in Constantine' the Adjudicator failed to take into account that in the week prior to leaving Algeria the Applicant had merely been *hiding* at his parents' home. Furthermore, although the main cities are considered to be 'generally safe' the objective evidence shows that terrorist networks still exist in these cities. It is important to note that the Applicant's problems with the GIA were in Algiers, which being the capital is considered to be the safest part of Algeria. Given the serious human losses inflicted on the GIA by the Applicant, it is submitted that they will now always have an adverse interest in him and that on the particular facts of this case internal relocation is neither safe nor reasonable.

Convention reason

12. As has already been submitted, the GIA's interest in the Applicant had gone far beyond extortion. It must have been at least reasonably likely that the GIA would impute a political opinion to the Applicant by virtue of his non-cooperation with them and his full co-operation with the authorities: *Noune*.

Article 3 of the ECHR

13. In the alternative, the Adjudicator should clearly have allowed the appeal under Article 3 of the ECHR, which is engaged whenever there is a reasonable likelihood of torture or inhuman or degrading treatment and does not require there to be any particular reason or motivation behind the ill-treatment. The Adjudicator should have recognised that in this case Article 3 did not 'stand or fall' with the asylum appeal.

Conclusion

14. This Determination is both vague and confusingly laid out. The Adjudicator fails to make clear and reasoned findings or to undertake a proper assessment of the risk to this Applicant if returned to Algeria. Permission to appeal should properly be granted, as an appeal would have real prospects of success.

Date:

Name:

Address:

In the Immigration Appellate Authority Appeal Number: HX/000/2003

The Immigration Acts

Heard at: Taylor House **Determination promulgated:** 12 May 2003

On: 14 April 2003

Dictated: 28 April 2003

Before:

Mr L. Raymond

Adjudicator

Between:

ELENA TEDROS

Appellant

and

THE SECRETARY OF STATE FOR THE HOME DEPARTMENT

Respondent

DETERMINATION AND REASONS

Proceedings

1. The Appellant Elena Tedros is a female citizen of Eritrea who was born on 1st March 1977. Her father is Eritrean and her mother Ethiopian. She appeals against the decision of the Secretary of State refusing her leave to enter the United Kingdom. This appeal falls under section 69(1) of the Immigration and Asylum Act 1999 on the ground that her removal in consequence of such refusal would be contrary to the United Kingdom's obligations under the 1951 Convention relating to the Status of Refugees. The Appellant travelled directly to

the UK from Kenya. She arrived on the 4 February 1999 and claimed asylum on arrival.

Basis of asylum and human rights claims

2. The Appellant stated in her SEF that she had left Ethiopia when the government started deporting Eritreans. The Appellant was separated from her family when her father and brother were forcibly deported to Eritrea in July 1998. Her mother remains in Ethiopia but she has not had any contact with her since leaving Ethiopia. Although born in Eritrea, her family had all moved to Ethiopia when she was only two years old and she has not returned to Eritrea since. She could not return to Eritrea because of her mixed ethnicity and also because she would be liable to be sent for military service.
3. The Appellant confirmed all of this in her interview and also mentioned that she had been a supporter of the Eritrean Liberation Front Revolutionary Council (the ELF-RC). In her recent appeal statement she stated that she could not return because she has no friends or family there and life would be very difficult for her. At the hearing before me the Appellant also stated that she has formed a relationship with a Mr Abdul Khan, a British citizen.
4. The asylum and human rights claims were refused in a letter dated 8 January 2002.

The hearing

5. The Appellant gave oral evidence before me through an official interpreter using the Tigrinya language. The Appellant was also cross-examined following which I heard oral submissions from both parties. All of these matters are faithfully recorded in the Record of Proceedings.
6. In coming to my conclusions and for the avoidance of doubt I confirm that I have carefully considered all the documentary evidence before me, including the SEF, record of interview and the statement as well as the

Respondent's Refusal Letter. I have also taken into account the submissions and objective material from both sides. I have given very careful consideration to the oral evidence I heard from the Appellant.

7. The burden in asylum appeals is on the appellant to show that they have a well-founded fear of persecution for a Convention reason and that there is a 'serious risk' or 'reasonable degree of likelihood' of persecution if returned.

8. The assessment of whether an appellant's claim for asylum is made out has to be on the evidence as a whole going to past, present and future, and in accordance with the test of the reasonable degree of likelihood in *R v Secretary of State for the Home Department, ex p Sivakumaran* [1988] Imm AR 147, HL, and *Kaja v Secretary of State for the Home Department* [1995] Imm AR 1. This assessment must be made at the date of hearing.

Findings

9. For reasons which I will consider in further detail below, I am bound to find that the Appellant is not a credible witness and that her claim to asylum has been seriously undermined as a consequence.

10. When the Appellant originally applied for asylum the only reasons she gave for fearing return to Eritrea were her mixed ethnicity and military service. However, in her asylum interview she added a further strand to her claim, namely her support of the ELF-RC. In her statement which she adopted at the hearing, she now says that she was an active member of the ELF-RC. She further asks me to take into account her relationship with Mr Abdul Khan.

ELF-RC MEMBERSHIP

11. I find that it seriously detracts from the Appellant's credibility that she did not mention her membership of the ELF-RC at the first opportunity. Instead she left it

to the interview. That is not all. In her interview she described herself merely as a supporter. Since then, she has stated that she was in fact a fully-fledged member and told me in oral evidence that she has attended demonstrations in London against the Eritrean government. I find that had the Appellant been an active member whilst in Ethiopia, she would surely have mentioned this in interview if not earlier.

12. Nor do I accept that the Appellant's political beliefs have grown stronger since she has been in the UK. I find that this is an embellishment and that the Appellant is simply being opportunistic. She submitted a letter from the London branch of the ELF-RC stating that she had been an active member in the UK. Although not challenged by the Home Office Presenting Officer, I find this letter to be of little assistance. I note the letter is addressed to 'whom it may concern'. At the very highest I am prepared to accept that the Appellant *may* have been a supporter of the ELF-RC whilst in Ethiopia.

13. I note from the CIPU October 2003 report that it is only those persons who have a high level of involvement who are considered to be at risk. The Appellant certainly does not fall into this category. I do not consider therefore, that the Appellant would be at risk on return on this count.

MIXED ETHNICITY

14. The Appellant also bases her claim in part on the fact that she is of mixed ethnicity. The Appellant's evidence is that her brother and father were deported in 1998 to Eritrea as part of the mass expulsion of Eritreans. In oral evidence, the Appellant said that she remained with her mother in Ethiopia (she has no other siblings), but said that she went into hiding fearing that she would suffer the same fate. The Appellant left Ethiopia some seven months later. I have to consider the position as at the date of hearing in considering whether the Appellant's removal to Eritrea would place her at risk.

15. Although I find it difficult to understand why the Appellant stayed in Ethiopia for so long after her father and brother had been deported, it matters not. The objective evidence shows that the situation between the two countries has now improved significantly, in that there is now an end to the war. Deportees from Ethiopia to Eritrea have been assisted by the Eritrean government and I do not consider that mixed ethnicity is a real issue anymore. The objective evidence shows that there are thousands of persons of mixed ethnicity such as the Appellant who have been returned or have returned voluntarily to Eritrea in safety. I do not think that it can be realistically argued that the Appellant faces a risk of persecution by this reason alone. I am quite sure that she will receive sympathy and assistance from the Eritrean authorities and other agencies. Contrary to the submission made by the Appellant's representative, I do not imagine there will be any problems for the Appellant in being admitted to Eritrea – she was after all born there.

MILITARY SERVICE

16. The only issue remaining under the Refugee Convention is whether the Appellant would be liable to be called up and if so, whether the consequences would be such as to amount to persecution. I am prepared to accept on the basis of the Appellant's age that she could be liable for military service. I take into account also that the Eritrean authorities take an active role in finding deserters and draft evaders. However I note from the CIPU report that since 2001 women have increasingly been able to take on a non-combative role, and I find that the Appellant would not necessarily have to perform in a military capacity.
17. The Appellant's evidence throughout has been that she did not wish to fight in the army because she does not agree with the war with Ethiopia, but of course there is no longer a state of open hostilities between the two countries. The Appellant's objection to military service does not to my mind qualify her as a conscientious

objector, but even if it did the House of Lords decided in the case of *Sepet and Bulbul v Secretary of State for the Home Department* [2003] UKHL 15, [2003] 2 All ER 304, that there is no recognised right not to be required to perform military service against one's personal and moral convictions.

18. However, I still have to consider whether the conditions of military service and the likely punishment for avoidance thereof are likely to amount to persecution, as this was one of the exceptions acknowledged in *Sepet and Bulbul.*

19. The Peace Agreement between Eritrea and Ethiopia made in December 2000 brought an end to the war. I also note that there has been some degree of demobilisation since then. It is frankly far from certain that at this stage the Appellant would be punished for avoiding the draft, but I am forced to accept that this is a possibility. That being so I have considered the objective evidence, which states that the maximum penalty is three years' detention. It is doubtful in light of the changes I have just referred to, whether the Appellant would even be punished for her avoidance. But if she was the Tribunal have held in the case of *Jemila Ahiemed Yassin* [2002] UKIAT 04440 that a sentence of such length, given the conditions in Eritrean prisons, would not amount to persecution or a breach of the ECHR.

20. Given these findings I do not accept that the Appellant has a well-founded fear of persecution or that there would be a breach of Article 3 of the ECHR.

ARTICLE 8 ECHR

21. I now turn to consider the position relating to private and family life under Article 8 and whether there would be a breach of the Appellant's rights if she were to be returned. The Appellant has been in the UK for four years. Despite that there is no evidence before me that she has sought to make any contribution to our society either by paid or voluntary work. I have seen a letter

produced today by the Appellant from West Ham College which indicates that she has now completed a six month six-month course in computing and English. However, I can give that only little weight in the overall picture.

22. I note that despite the fact that the Appellant's immigration status was precarious she decided to form a relationship with a Mr Abdul Khan, from whom I had a witness statement but who did not attend the hearing. The statement confirmed what the Appellant told me at the hearing. Their evidence in summary was that they met in March 2000 and began cohabiting some six months later. Mr Abdul Khan is a 28-year-old British citizen who works as an estate agent in Swindon and earns enough money to pay a mortgage and support them both without recourse to public funds. Although I find it unsatisfactory that Mr Khan did not attend the hearing, I am prepared to accept on the lower standard of proof that the nature of the relationship is as they have stated. I also have taken into consideration that Mr Khan says in his statement that he could not just leave his life in this country.

23. Accordingly, I accept that the Appellant has established a private and family life in this country, and that removal as a consequence of the immigration decision would constitute an interference with that right. It was not disputed by the Appellant's representative that such a measure would be lawful and in pursuit of a legitimate aim, namely a fair and firm immigration control. However, I have to decide if such a measure would be disproportionate when weighed against the Secretary of State's need to enforce the UK's immigration policy.

24. I am fully aware that I have to undertake a balancing exercise between the competing needs of the individual and the state. I take into account that from the outset of this relationship the Appellant knew her immigration status to be uncertain and that there is no right for couples whether unmarried or even married, to choose their country of residence when there are alternatives. In this case the alternative is of course Eritrea. In light of

my consideration of the asylum and the Article 3 claim I do not consider that there are any insurmountable obstacles to the Appellant applying for entry clearance from Eritrea as Mr Khan's fiancé or even to this relationship continuing in Eritrea. I therefore dismiss the Article 8 claim as well.

Ruling

25. I dismiss this appeal on all grounds.

12 May 2003 L. Raymond

IN THE IMMIGRATION APPEAL TRIBUNAL
CASE NO. HX/000/2003

BETWEEN:

ELENA TEDROS

Applicant

and

THE SECRETARY OF STATE FOR

THE HOME DEPARTMENT

Respondent

GROUNDS OF APPEAL

Introduction

1. Leave to appeal is sought in respect of the Determination and Reasons of Adjudicator Mr L. Raymond notified on 6 June 2003, dismissing the Applicant's asylum and human rights appeals.

Risk on return

2. The Adjudicator erred in his assessment of risk to the appellant on return to Eritrea by failing to have any or any sufficient regard to the following factors.

ELF-RC MEMBERSHIP

3. The critical issue is not whether the Applicant is a member or supporter of the ELF-RC, but whether she would be likely to do anything that would bring her to the adverse attention of the Eritrean authorities: *Mekki El Nour Abdelbaqi* (IAT) (13980). The Eritrean government has recently instigated a crackdown on all forms of political dissent including politicians, students and journalists. The US State Department 2003 Report states:

'Arbitrary arrests and detentions continued to be problems; an unknown number of persons were detained without charge, some incommunicado, because of political opinion, suspected association with the Ethiopian Mengistu regime, radical Islamic elements, or terrorist organizations.'

4. It is at least reasonably likely that the Applicant's political activities in Ethiopia would bring her to the attention of the authorities in Eritrea. Furthermore, the Applicant's recent activities in London must be considered a relevant factor. The Adjudicator was wrong to dismiss out of hand the letter from the ELF-RC when it had not been challenged by the respondent: see *Oleed* [2003] INLR 179. The author of the letter would obviously not have known the name of the adjudicator who was going to hear the appeal.

MIXED RACE/CITIZENSHIP

5. By virtue of her father's Eritrean nationality, the Applicant would theoretically be eligible for Eritrean citizenship. The difficulty however would be in *proving* it. The relevant part of a letter from the Embassy of the State of Eritrea in London dated 29 August 2002 states:

   'A person who was born in Eritrea with an Eritrean father would be eligible for Eritrean nationality.

   The political views of 3 witnesses are not relevant to establishing eligibility for nationality and obtaining an Eritrean passport.'

6. In the case of *Tecle* [2002] EWCA Civ 1358, the Court of Appeal stated that 'what is required is the signature of 3 witnesses who know the applicant and can testify that she was in fact born in Eritrea with an Eritrean father.' On the facts of this case there is a serious likelihood that the Applicant will be unable to locate three witnesses of appropriate standing in the United Kingdom to attest to her birthplace and ethnicity.

MILITARY SERVICE

7. There is no challenge to the Adjudicator's finding that the Applicant has no claim under the Refugee Convention on the ground of military service alone. However, the Adjudicator failed to consider the actual treatment that the Applicant would be likely to receive. The US State Department report shows:

> 'The Government continued to deploy military police throughout the country using roadblocks, street sweeps, and house-to-house searches to find deserters and draft evaders . . . The Government continued to authorize the use of deadly force against anyone resisting or attempting to flee. There were reports of resistance, especially by parents of draft-age girls, which resulted in the deaths of both soldiers and civilians.
>
> . . .
>
> There were reports that women drafted to the national service were subjected to sexual harassment and abuse.'

8. The US State Department 2003 report continues:

> 'In some instances, authorities arrested and detained for several hours or even days individuals, including pregnant women, children under age 18, and citizens of other countries, who were not subject to national service obligations or had proper documentation showing they had completed or were exempt from national service.'

FAILED ASYLUM-SEEKERS

9. The Human Rights Watch 2003 report demonstrates that failed asylum-seekers are at risk on return to Eritrea:

> 'In October [2002], Malta deported over two hundred recent refugees. They were arrested upon arrival in Asmara, taken to a military camp, and held incommunicado. Eritreans caught attempting to flee the country were reportedly beaten and tortured.'

Overall risk

10. The Applicant would be returned to Eritrea as a young and single female who has no family there and has not set foot on Eritrean soil since the age of two, some 20 years ago. She would therefore be especially vulnerable. There is also a risk that on return the Applicant would be detained at a reception camp. Whilst a temporary identification document may be given to her, this would not grant her any formal status and would actually deem her to be of Ethiopian nationality. The US State Department Report states that:

> 'Government and army officials reportedly considered these Ethiopian deportees to be citizens who were trying to avoid national service. As a result, they were subjected to harassment and detention while the authorities checked their status.

Article 8 of the ECHR

11. The Adjudicator was unreasonable in concluding that the Applicant could seek entry clearance from Eritrea. Eritrea has no British Embassy and so no facilities for making such applications. Moreover, the US State Department Report states:

> 'Citizens were required to obtain an exit visa to travel outside the country. Citizens of national service age (18 to 40) . . . and others who had fallen out of favour with the Government routinely were denied exit visas . . . *In practice it was very difficult for anyone under the age of 40 to get an exit visa.* There were many instances in which the newly married spouse of a citizen living abroad was denied an exit visa to join the partner. Often the citizen in the country was denied an exit visa because the spouse could not prove payment of the 2-percent income tax, which was imposed on citizens who lived abroad or who had run afoul of the Government.'

(Emphasis added.)

12. As to the couple going to Eritrea together, it is submitted that even if (contrary to the above grounds) the

Applicant would not face a real risk of inhuman and degrading treatment on return, it is undeniable that her status in Eritrea will be utterly precarious. In contrast, the Applicant's partner is currently in well-paid employment and supports them both without any recourse to public funds. In these circumstances it strains proportionality beyond its proper limits to expect that the Applicant's partner should give up everything in the United Kingdom and go with the Applicant to Eritrea where they would face a wholly uncertain future. The burden is on the Secretary of State to show that any interference with this couple's private and family life is justified. There was no suggestion in the objective evidence before the Adjudicator that Mr Khan would even be admitted into Eritrea and as contended above there is no prospect of the Applicant seeking entry clearance from Eritrea.

Conclusion

13. For the reasons given this case has real prospects of success and permission to appeal should be granted.

Date:

Name:

Address:

In the Immigration Appellate Authority Appeal Number: HX/666/2003

The Immigration Acts

Heard at: Sessions House, Surbiton **Determination promul gated:** 19 June 2003

On: 27 May 2003

Dictated: 30 May 2003

Before:

Mr R. Herschmann

Adjudicator

Between:

MUJWILE PIERRE PATU

Appellant

and

THE SECRETARY OF STATE FOR THE HOME DEPARTMENT

Respondent

DETERMINATION AND REASONS

1. The Appellant was born on 13 October 1965 in what was then Zaire but is now the Democratic Republic of Congo (the DRC). He arrived in the United Kingdom on 5 May 2002 and claimed asylum by post on 10 May 2002. The Appellant has no dependants in the United Kingdom.
2. Pursuant to his application the Appellant was interviewed on 2 August 2002. The Secretary of State refused his application for asylum on 6 January 2003. In accordance with the refusal letter, the Secretary of State gave directions for the removal of the appellant to the DRC at a date and time to be notified.

3. On the 16 October 2002 the Appellant's representatives issued notice of appeal against the Secretary of State's refusal, contending that the decision was wrong in law and unreasonable and had given insufficient weight to the Appellant's evidence. In addition the Appellant's representatives raised Articles 2, 3, 5, 6, 8, 10 and 14 of the European Convention on Human Rights.
4. There was no Home Office Presenting Officer in attendance at the appeal hearing before me on 27 May 2003, only a standard letter asking me to dismiss the appeal and a copy of the CIPU March 2003 report on the DRC. I was satisfied that the Secretary of State had been served with the relevant notice as to the time and date of the hearing, and I proceeded to hear the case in accordance with rule 44 of the 2003 Procedure Rules.
5. When the case came before me for hearing at 11.00 a.m. the Appellant's representative made an application for an adjournment. The application was on the basis that the Appellant wished to procure a medical/psychiatric report. I noted from the file that at the date of the first hearing the Appellant's solicitors stated that they were in all respects ready to proceed. No application has been made in writing since that date.
6. The Appellant was represented by counsel who informed me that having had a conference with the Appellant that morning, she had grave concerns about the mental health of the Appellant who also had physical scarring which was 'indicative' of having been tortured. Counsel was also concerned about the Appellant's ability to give evidence and asked me to adjourn the case in the 'interests of justice'.
7. I ruled that there would be no adjournment. The Appellant and his representatives had had ample opportunity to obtain medical evidence if such was to be relied on. I pointed out that the Appellant seemed perfectly healthy to me and that if any problems arose during the hearing, I would deal with the situation accordingly. Mindful of the 'overriding objective' in rule 4 of the Procedure Rules, I decided that there would be no further delay and that this case would proceed today.

The Appellant's case for asylum

8. I heard oral evidence from the Appellant as well as submissions from counsel on his behalf, the relevant parts of which appear in this Determination. The Appellant adopted his screening interview, his SEF, and his substantive asylum interview. I was immediately struck by the fact that this Appellant had not bothered to make a further statement as was required by directions.

SCREENING INTERVIEW

9. The Appellant's case as stated at his screening interview is that he was a head teacher at a high school in Kinshasa, and that this brought him to the attention of the authorities. The Appellant claims that he was concerned by the injustices and cruelty of his own government as well as the various armed factions who are able to operate in his country and who he says have also committed numerous human rights abuses.

STATEMENT OF EVIDENCE FORM

10. In his SEF the Appellant went further and stated that he responded to the country's problems by teaching the students at his school about the history of the DRC and talking to them about human rights. He said that he would speak about the violence and rape that was destroying their country and that when they were older they would be able to do something about it. He further stated that the parents of his students would regularly invite him to chair local meetings. The Appellant had previously been arrested and detained by the authorities for having pamphlets at his school. This was in June 1997 and the Appellant was released after one day in detention. The Appellant stated that at the most recent of the meetings on 16 December 2001 the military attended and dispersed the participants. The Appellant said that he was not arrested on this occasion but that he later received a summons requiring him to attend the

police station for questioning. The Appellant did not respond to the summons and the security forces came to his home two days later. The Appellant was then dragged out of his home and in full view of his neighbours was accused of being an 'enemy of the government'. The soldiers then beat him outside his home and he says that he lost consciousness. When he woke up he was handcuffed in a prison cell. The Appellant says that he was detained for approximately four months during which he was regularly beaten and abused. Other prisoners were occasionally taken away and killed. He thought he could be 'killed at any moment'.

11. The Appellant claims that he came to be released when one of the pastors at the prison befriended him. He says that the pastor knew the governor of the prison and that one night his cell door was left open and he was allowed to escape from the back of the prison. The Appellant says that he then made his way to his home some three kilometres way, where he stayed the night before going to a friend's house, where he stayed in hiding for two weeks.

12. The Appellant says that after two weeks he felt able to return to the school. He resumed his activities. This time however he arranged a bigger meeting involving nearly 80 people who were all 'interested in abolishing cruelty and ill-treatment in the DRC'. The meeting was in progress when the security forces arrived en masse and proceeded to break up the meeting. Fearful that the security forces would arrest him and ill-treat him all over again, the Appellant made his escape from the back of the hall. The Appellant then travelled by boat to Congo-Brazzaville. A former student then put the Appellant in touch with an agent who arranged for his journey to the United Kingdom.

HOME OFFICE INTERVIEW

13. Unusually, the Home Office interview was short. Indeed the Appellant was asked only 16 questions and there is nothing in the interview which takes the case any further.

The issues

14. The Secretary of State does not accept the Appellant's account as to the reasons he gave for leaving the DRC. In summary the Secretary of State contends that the manner of the Appellant's escape from the final meeting was inherently implausible and that in any event he would be of no further interest to the authorities because he was not a high-level opponent of the government.

The hearing

15. I indicated to counsel that as there was no witness statement as required by the directions, I would not be permitting the Appellant to give lengthy oral evidence once his SEF and interviews had been adopted. However, as the Refusal Letter put credibility in issue, I informed counsel that she should put those matters to the Appellant, particularly the plausibility of his final escape and why he should be of any further interest to the authorities on return

The evidence

16. The Appellant adopted the above-mentioned evidence. Counsel then asked him for his response to paragraph 8 of the Refusal Letter concerning the escape from the last meeting. The Appellant said that he had been able to escape from the security forces who came to the school because they entered using the front entrance, whereas he had been chairing the meeting from the back of the hall and had been able to escape in the mêlée.
17. Counsel then asked him to confirm why he would have problems if he was to be returned. The Appellant stated that the authorities would kill him because of his activities and because he had escaped from them on the last occasion. The authorities are interested in anyone who opposes or criticises them. The Appellant insisted that no matter what would happen to him, he would continue

to speak out against 'the evil people destroying my mother country and her children, so long as there is still breath in this body'.

18. At that stage I noted that the Refusal Letter did not deal with the escape from the prison. I then proceeded to ask the Appellant why the pastor helped the Appellant. He said that it was because he believed in the same things as the Appellant. I then asked him why it should be that the governor of the prison would allow him to escape without even the payment of a bribe which I understand to be a common occurrence in the DRC. The Appellant simply insisted that this is what had happened. I pointed out that even if his cell door had been left open there must still have been difficulties in making good his escape. The Appellant stated that although all the cells would normally be locked, the other doors would often be left open to allow the guards to move around the prison quickly. I put it to the Appellant that this simply did not make sense and that he had better tell the truth. The Appellant had no answer. I then asked the Appellant how it was that he was able to evade being caught by a search-party. The Appellant replied that he was not aware that there was a search-party, although after I repeated the question he conceded that he must at some point have been noted as missing by the prison.

19. The Appellant then went on at length about the ill-treatment he said that he suffered. He told me that he was regularly beaten and that he was abused on several occasions. I asked him what he meant by the word 'abuse' and he told me through the interpreter that he had been raped by the prison guards. I asked him why he had not mentioned this before, and he said that he had not felt able to because he was 'embarrassed and ashamed'. The Appellant became visibly upset when he was recounting this event and I asked him if he needed a break, but he indicated that he was happy to proceed.

Submissions

20. I then indicated that I was ready to hear submissions. Counsel outlined the evidence that had already been

relied on by the Appellant. As far as the further evidence that the Appellant had given in response to my questioning, she submitted that it was credible and that I should accept it on the lower standard of proof. She further submitted that the Appellant had been arrested and detained twice already and had been fortunate to escape a third such arrest. He would be at risk from the authorities on account of his activities and his prominence in the local community. Moreover, there was a clear concern that even failed asylum-seekers were at risk on return to the DRC because they would be detained by the authorities on arrival in order to ascertain how they had been able to leave. She asked me to allow the asylum and human rights appeal under Article 3 of the ECHR.

My findings

21. In this case credibility is very much an issue. It is for the Appellant to persuade me that he is telling the truth or at least that a core part of his account is the truth. The Appellant's occupation was a head teacher in a school in the DRC. For reasons that I am about to explain, this is about the only piece of evidence in the case which I am prepared to accept.
22. It is noteworthy that in his screening interview the Appellant did not specify how his alleged concern for human rights brought him to the attention of the authorities, or what problems he had. I would have expected him to at least mention the date of his prior arrest as well as the precise dates of his most recent arrest and the occasion the security forces came to the Appellant's school, because if true, these would have been the central planks of his claim.
23. Furthermore, I find it quite unbelievable that the Appellant has today sought to introduce the allegation that he was raped by his captors. Had this been true he would have specifically mentioned that he was raped at the first opportunity, but he did not even mention this in his SEF or even in his interview, but chose instead to do so at this

hearing. Even at this stage, it was telling that the Appellant at first simply said that he suffered 'abuse'.

24. I found large parts of the rest of the Appellant's evidence to be implausible and vague. For example, it is very odd that a high school teacher would engage in this type of activity knowing that it could result in him losing his job. Nor do I understand why the parents of the students would regard him as a being a suitable or influential spokesman. The Appellant did not give any indication of political ambition or indeed any relevant experience in this area.
25. I find it most unsatisfactory and quite implausible that a regime that abuses human rights would, before detaining a person with a view to torturing them for making anti-government statements, issue courteous summonses to attend for questioning and simply wait for the Appellant to make himself available at his own leisure.
26. Also, I am in serious doubt as to why the soldiers would have punched and kicked the Appellant in the road outside his home in daylight and in full view of his neighbours. I would have thought that they would have either done this inside his home or later at the prison, or both. As it is, this part of the evidence is simply not credible.
27. The Appellant's account of his escape is nothing short of fanciful. He would have me believe that he befriended the pastor and that he helped the Appellant out of the goodness of his heart. I also find it difficult to believe that the prison governor would have placed himself in jeopardy of losing his post by assisting the appellant to escape. I am asked to accept that the Appellant casually made his way through gates which, conveniently, were left open. I find this to be utterly implausible. I should add that I also find the fact that the Appellant was allowed to escape given that he was under a sentence of death to be utterly implausible. However, even if I were prepared to believe such an account, I would still find it far-fetched that the Appellant, after being ill-treated as he described, would then have been able to run the 3 km to his home.

28. The Appellant stated in his evidence that having escaped from the prison he promptly returned to his school as if nothing had happened. If indeed the Appellant had been fearful of his life, it simply defies common sense that he would once again set himself up for further problems with the authorities. Furthermore, I should point out the Appellant's account of escape from the meeting before leaving the DRC is also incredible. It seems to me that if the authorities had indeed specifically wanted to capture him, they would surely have covered all of the hall's exits. I do not believe that this event took place in the manner described by the Appellant or at all.
29. Although I noted the Appellant was upset when talking about his treatment in prison this did not to me seem to be entirely probative. Although I cannot of course exclude the possibility that this individual has had some kind of distressing experience in the DRC, I have to look at the whole of his evidence and assess it in the round. In light of my other findings above I do not accept that he was ever detained as described. I find this embellishment to be very damaging to his credibility. Consequently, I do not consider that a medical report would have altered my view of the Appellant's credibility. I find that the Appellant's account is a complete fabrication designed solely to gain entry into the United Kingdom.

Conclusion

30. In light of my above comprehensive and adverse credibility findings, the Appellant has not made out his claim under the Refugee Convention. For the same reasons the appeal under Article 3 of the ECHR is also dismissed.

June 19 2003 R. Herschmann

IN THE IMMIGRATION APPEAL TRIBUNAL
CASE NO. HX/666/2003

BETWEEN:

MUJWILE PIERRE PATU

Applicant

and

THE SECRETARY OF STATE FOR

THE HOME DEPARTMENT

Respondent

GROUNDS OF APPEAL

Introduction

1. Permission to appeal against the Determination of the Adjudicator Mr R. Herschmann notified 19 June 2003, is sought on the following grounds.

Application for adjournment

2. It is submitted that the adjudicator was wrong to refuse an adjournment as the case could not proceed without a serious injustice to the applicant. Counsel at the hearing had 'grave concerns about the mental health of the appellant' and consequently there were serious doubts about his ability to give evidence. Where as here, an applicant's case involves an account of serious ill-treatment and visible scarring, the applicant must have a fair and proper opportunity to present it. The Adjudicator's reference at paragraph 7 to 'further delay' was misconceived. This was the first time the case had been listed for appeal and the Home Office, who were not even represented at the hearing, could hardly be said to be prejudiced by an adjournment.
3. The effect of the Adjudicator's refusal to adjourn is aptly summed up by the ambiguity of his own conclusion at paragraph 29:

> 'I cannot of course exclude the possibility that this individual has had some kind of distressing experience in the DRC.'

Fresh evidence – medical report

4. Since the hearing the Applicant has undergone a medical examination and the Tribunal has the benefit of the report of Dr. Siddiqui dated 6 June 2003 (enclosed with these grounds who is an expert in assessing the physical and psychological aspects of torture. The report starkly concludes:

   '. . . this patient has clearly been a victim of repeated beatings and rape . . . He is suffering from severe PTSD.'

5. This evidence, which was not available at the hearing and for which an adjournment was sought, substantially undermines the Adjudicator's adverse credibility findings. The Tribunal is invited to admit the report into evidence pursuant to Rule 21 of the 2003 Procedure Rules.

Failure to apply correct standard of proof

6. The Adjudicator fails to direct himself on the lower standard of proof. At paragraph 21 he merely states:

   'It is for the Appellant to persuade me that he is telling the truth or at least that a core part of his account is the truth.'

Adverse credibility findings

7. The determination rejects the claim in its entirety solely by reference to alleged implausibilities and without any reasoning in support. Not only is the route through the alleged implausibilities itself speculative, but the Adjudicator is unable to point to any real inconsistency in the Applicant's evidence.

INTEREST BY THE AUTHORITIES

8. The Adjudicator thought it 'noteworthy' at paragraph 22 that the Applicant was not specific in the screening interview about 'how' his human rights beliefs had brought him to the attention of the authorities. This adverse inference was entirely unfair. The Applicant laid out the essential basis of his claim and has not subsequently deviated from it. The Applicant could not be expected to go into any further detail at the screening interview which is by definition limited in scope. In *Jeevaponkalan* (IAT) (17742) the Tribunal held that where an appellant is invited to give only succinct answers to the questions he was asked, it would be an injustice to then go behind that invitation.

RAPE

9. As to paragraph 23, it is not at all 'unbelievable' that the Applicant did not mention that he was raped in his SEF or in his interview; because he was 'embarrassed and ashamed' is perfectly consistent with the behaviour of many victims of rape. The Adjudicator is also of the view that it is 'telling' that the Applicant initially used the word 'abuse' in his oral evidence. It certainly is, but not in an adverse way – the fact that the Applicant addressed the issue euphemistically is consistent with his reluctance to mention it at any stage previously. In any event, the Tribunal is now asked to consider the medical report as corroboration of the Applicant's account.

APPLICANT'S ACTIVITIES

10. Contrary to the Adjudicator's view at paragraph 24, there is nothing 'odd' about an individual having such strong beliefs that they are prepared to risk their employment. It was precisely the combination of the Applicant's responsible occupation as a headteacher and his willingness to speak about his beliefs that made him a 'suitable' spokesman for his students' parents as well. As the Applicant was speaking out about the human

rights situation in the DRC rather than politics in general, the Adjudicator's reference to 'ambition' and 'experience' is irrelevant.

SUMMONS

11. At paragraph 25 the Adjudicator stated that it was 'quite implausible' that:

> '. . . a regime that abuses human rights would, before detaining a person with a view to torturing them for making anti-government statements, issue *courteous* summonses to attend for questioning and simply wait for the Appellant to *make himself available at his own leisure*.'
>
> (Emphasis added.)

Not only is this statement highly speculative, but the words 'courteous' and 'make himself available at his own leisure' are an inappropriate gloss on the Applicant's original evidence and give the impression that the Adjudicator was not considering this case with an open mind.

ILL-TREATMENT BY SOLDIERS

12. The Adjudicator's 'doubt' at paragraph 26 about the Applicant being punched and kicked outside his home is misplaced. The objective evidence shows that the DRC security forces frequently commit far worse abuses in public and with impunity. In any event the use of the word 'doubt' suggests a misapplication of the low standard of proof.

ESCAPE FROM PRISON

13. The Adjudicator finds the account of the escape from prison to be 'fanciful' and 'utterly implausible' (paragraph 27). On the contrary, the Applicant's account is coherent and by no means implausible. The Adjudicator has also factually erred in his assessment: the Applicant

did not befriend the pastor; it was the pastor who befriended the Applicant because 'they believed in the same things'. Again, the Adjudicator's use of language speaks volumes about his approach:

'I am asked to accept that the Appellant *casually* made his way through gates *conveniently* left open.'

(Emphasis added.)

The Applicant did not say 'casually' or 'conveniently' in his evidence.

14. The Adjudicator also refers in the same paragraph to the fact that the Applicant was under a 'sentence of death'. This is another factual error. The Applicant's evidence was that people in the prison were being killed and that he thought he could become one of them. The Adjudicator should have appreciated that a 'sentence of death' would only arise where there had been a charge, trial and sentence, none of which the Applicant had experienced.

RETURN TO SCHOOL

15. As to paragraph 28, it was *not* the Applicant's evidence that he '. . . *promptly* returned to his school as *if nothing had happened*' (emphasis added). In any event, there was no reason for the Applicant to assume that he would encounter further problems with the authorities by simply returning to his employment.

FINAL ESCAPE

16. The Adjudicator also found the Applicant's escape from the final meeting at his school to be 'incredible' (paragraph 28 of the determination). This comment is speculative and there is no indication that the Adjudicator has applied the low standard of proof by asking himself whether it was possible that the Applicant escaped as described.

Failure to consider objective evidence

17. The Adjudicator has failed to assess the Applicant's credibility in the context of the objective evidence, which shows that the DRC is a country in which serious human rights violations by both state and non-state agents occur with frequency and impunity: see for example Human Rights Watch Report 2003. It was of course the Applicant's case that it was such occurrences that forced him to speak out against the authorities and led to their persecution of him.

Conduct of the hearing

18. The Adjudicator's conduct of the hearing was unfair and did not comply with the guidance out in the case of *MNM v Secretary of State for the Home Department* [2000] INLR 576 and the *Surendran* guidelines. As demonstrated at paragraph 18 of the determination, the Adjudicator questioned the Applicant on issues in the case, when this should have been done through the Applicant's counsel at first instance. Moreover, the manner of the questioning was akin to cross-examination. For example:

    '. . . *I put it* to the Appellant that this simply did not make sense and that he had *better tell the truth.* The Appellant had no answer.'

    (Emphasis added.)

19. The determination only records six questions asked of the Applicant by the Adjudicator. What the determination does *not* record is that the Adjudicator in fact asked the Applicant a total of 32 direct questions on just five points. Despite counsel's timely objection that this was contrary to the *Surendran* guidelines, the manner of the Adjudicator throughout the questioning remained disbelieving and hostile (enclosed is a copy of the relevant pages of counsel's notes of the hearing). Consequently, it is submitted that the Applicant was deprived of a fair hearing.

Conclusion

20. For all the reasons given, it is respectfully submitted that leave to appeal should properly be granted. The hearing of this case was unfair, the assessment of the evidence is flawed and the overall conclusion is unsustainable.

Date:

Name:

Address:

DEFENDING APPEALS

Even-handedness

In the case of *Oleed* [2003] INLR 179, the Court of Appeal expressed concern that there is a perception that the Tribunal approach appeals by an appellant and the Home Office in different ways – particularly in respect of the adjudicator's findings of fact. The Court referred to *Arshad* [2001] EWCA Civ 587 in which it was stated:

> 'I am somewhat anxious that this case portrays a (no doubt unconscious) lack of even-handedness on the part of the IAT as between an immigrant's appeal and a Home Office appeal. In the former class of case experience shows that the IAT will not generally go behind findings of fact made by an Adjudicator who has heard the witness (notably the appellant).'

In *Oleed* itself the Court concluded:

> 'Before us it was accepted on behalf of the Secretary of State that the Tribunal should act even-handedly and should only set aside a decision of an Adjudicator who has heard the evidence if it is plainly wrong or unsustainable.'

As matters currently stand, when the Home Office appeal to the Tribunal against the determination of an adjudicator allowing an asylum or human rights claim, they rarely if ever go to the lengths of putting before the Tribunal the evidence that was actually before the adjudicator at the original hearing, or even their own Respondent's bundle. It sometimes seems that all the Home Office have to do to succeed in their own appeals is to draw the Tribunal's attention to parts of the determination which on the face of it may appear to be problematic, but which if assessed in the context of all the evidence in the appeal below, may well be entirely proper and reasonable.

There should be a Practice Direction requiring the Home Office, when it is their appeal, to put before the Tribunal *all* the evidence submitted by both sides to the adjudicator. It is unfair that this burden currently lies on the asylum applicant who has already succeeded in having their appeal allowed: the Tribunal should not be looking, in the first place, to the representative of the asylum applicant to justify the adjudicator's findings and conclusions. However, unless and until such a Direction is made, representatives must recognise that in order to give the client the very best opportunity of preserving a successful claim, they must serve on the Tribunal all the evidence that was relied on before the adjudicator, so that the Tribunal do not assess the determination in isolation from the evidence.

Changes in the country situation

A further important point raised in *Oleed* [2003] INLR 179, is whether a successful claim before an adjudicator should be re-evaluated by the Tribunal against objective evidence arising since the date of the original hearing, where the adjudicator's determination was otherwise reasonable. The Court of Appeal stated:

'Mr Wilken submitted . . . that even if we were to allow the appeal and quash the decision of the Immigration Appeal Tribunal the effect of that would be to revive the appeal before the Tribunal. He submitted that the situation was changing in Sri Lanka and that it would be useful for the Immigration Appeal Tribunal to consider the position in the light of the present day situation.

It might well be useful but I do not consider that it would be a proper use of this court's powers now to send the case back to the Tribunal. The powers of this court are set out in CPR Part 52.10. We have all the powers of the lower court. We may set aside or vary any order made by the lower court. Those provisions give us the power to allow the appeal from the Immigration Appeal Tribunal, set aside its determination, substitute a determination dismissing the appeal from the Adjudicator and thus restore his determination. The present is in my judgement an appropriate case in which to exercise that power. I accept that the Tribunal examines the situation in the country from which the refugee is fleeing as at the date of its determination. However, in the present case in my judgement there was nothing wrong with the Adjudicator's determination, there was therefore no reason to appeal it and it would be wrong for the Home Secretary, on the back of an appeal which has been dismissed, to seek to re-examine the threat to the refugee with reference to a date later than the adjudicator's determination. To permit this would merely encourage appeals by a party who has no ground for appeal but hopes that the situation would change sufficiently to enable him to advance different arguments on different facts on appeal. Such procedures would not be in anyone's interest.'

CROSS-APPEALS

A cross-appeal is where the respondent, in an appeal against a determination allowing some but not all of their claims, wishes to argue that their other claims should have succeeded as well, or that their claim should have succeeded for different reasons to that found by the adjudicator. The most obvious examples are:

- The adjudicator accepted there was a well-founded fear of persecution, but not that a Convention reason was engaged and therefore dismissed the appeal under the Refugee Convention, but allowed the appeal under Article 3 of the ECHR.
- The adjudicator did not allow the appeal under the Refugee Convention or under Article 3 of the ECHR, but allowed it under Article 8.

Strictly speaking of course, a client in either position would be entitled to apply for permission to appeal to the Tribunal against the unfavourable decisions as of right. In reality, such a course would have to be weighed-up very carefully indeed. An application for permission to appeal to the Tribunal would, if granted, give the Home Office an opportunity to cross-appeal against the favourable decisions of the adjudicator, which they might not otherwise have considered doing. This is a risk which must always be balanced against the potential benefits of trying to appeal, given that the safest option in many cases would be to not take things any further.

Equally, when a client has succeeded on at least one claim and that is appealed by the Home Office, the representative should think carefully before making a cross-appeal in respect of the claims that did not succeed. It is obvious that if the Tribunal is confronted by a determination which for various reasons both sides are dissatisfied with, they may be tempted to remit it to be re-heard all over again and in so doing the successful claim will evaporate. If however it is properly thought that a cross-appeal is appropriate, the procedural requirements in rule 19 of the 2003 Procedure Rules must be followed.

THE SUBSTANTIVE APPEAL HEARING

The Tribunal consists of a legally-qualified chairperson and usually two (though sometimes only one) lay member. The Home Office are always represented at the appeal hearing. The appellant makes their argument first, followed by submissions from the respondent and a brief reply from the appellant.

Much of what we have said regarding drafting grounds of appeal will be beneficial in terms of the preparation of arguments for the substantive hearing. It is primarily the grounds identified in the application for permission that should form the basis of the substantive hearing in the Tribunal. Indeed, it is common practice for the grounds to act as a skeleton argument for the hearing. Well-drafted and detailed grounds may need little by way of amplification and will concentrate the mind of the Tribunal on the issues. Therefore, it will often not be necessary for there to be a separate skeleton argument for the full hearing. There will be cases, however, which require more detail than is contained in the grounds of appeal or where there is a difficult question of law requiring significant research and citation of authorities. Similarly, a skeleton argument can be crucial where it is the Home Office's appeal: the Tribunal will be greatly assisted by knowing in advance the arguments that will be put forward on behalf of the respondent.

The Tribunal hearing is primarily, though not exclusively, a review of the decision made below. The starting-point of that review will be the adjudicator's determination and the grounds of appeal. The Tribunal will also have sight of the adjudicator's Record of Proceedings and any bundles lodged by either side. Where appropriate the Tribunal may consider objective evidence in the same way as an adjudicator and reach its own conclusions on the risk of return.

The hearing will sometimes, however, require oral evidence, particularly if the appellant did not attend the hearing before the adjudicator or there is a witness who has not given evidence before. As already stated, rule 21 of the 2003 Procedure Rules must be complied with and the Tribunal will expect that any application to adduce oral evidence, either with or without an interpreter, is made well in advance of the hearing itself. On a tactical note, the representative should consider whether it would in fact be better to request the Tribunal to remit the case for the evidence to be heard by an adjudicator rather than hear it themselves. It might be thought that it will be easier to persuade a single adjudicator that the witness is credible than a Tribunal constitution of two or three.

Remittal

Rule 22(1) of the 2003 Procedure Rules empowers the Tribunal to remit an appeal with directions as to how the appeal must be determined. A legally-qualified member of the Tribunal can also remit the case without the need for a hearing if there are no objections. Remittal may be to the same adjudicator where there have been positive findings on credibility, but not where, for example, there has been a fundemental misdirection on the law. However, remittal to the same adjudicator will be rare as the Tribunal are usually just as well placed to determine the appeal. Remittal will more often be to a different adjudicator where there are serious errors or omissions and there is a need for the evidence to be heard afresh.

No merit certificates

A 'no-merit certificate' must be issued where either the Tribunal considers that the appeal or application to the Tribunal is 'vexatious or unreasonable'. The Tribunal will then serve a copy of the certificate on the parties and the representatives as well as the Legal Services Commission who will also receive a copy of the Tribunal's determination. A certificate of no merit is likely to have implications in terms of the representatives' payment for conducting such an appeal. Doubtless too, the meaning of 'vexatious or unreasonable' in this context will be the subject of a 'starred' Tribunal decision, if not a decision by the Court of Appeal. It is to be hoped that the definition will recognise the particular humanitarian considerations involved in asylum and human rights cases, and will not place undue pressure on representatives not to make applications for leave to the Tribunal.

Tribunal determinations

If the Tribunal remit a case to be re-heard by a different adjudicator, this is usually announced at the hearing. Where the Tribunal are likely to dismiss or allow the appeal outright, then it will normally reserve its decision. In all cases however, there will be a written determination sent to both parties.

CHAPTER 8

Judicial Review and Statutory Review

INTRODUCTION

This chapter is concerned with how to challenge asylum or human rights decisions where there is no statutory right of appeal. The most common examples of such decisions are:

- an asylum claim that has been certified by the Secretary of State as a 'third country' case, preventing any substantive consideration of the claim at all;
- an asylum or human rights claim that has been refused by the Secretary of State at first instance and has been certified as 'clearly unfounded', preventing an in-country right of appeal;
- an application for permission to appeal to the Tribunal against an adjudicator's determination that has been refused;
- an appeal to the Tribunal has been remitted for re-hearing;
- the Secretary of State has refused to entertain a fresh claim;
- unexpected removals.

REVIEW NOT RE-HEARING

We are concerned here with two different procedures:

- Judicial review.
- Statutory review.

In both procedures it is important to recognise that what is being invoked is a review and not a re-hearing. This means that the merits of the decision will not be in issue, or at least not directly: rather it will be the process by which the decision came to be made. The process of reviewing a decision presupposes that the court which originally made the decision was best-placed to assess the evidential substance of the case and that such decisions should generally not be interfered with unless it can be demonstrated that the decision-making process itself was flawed in some way.

PRINCIPLES OF JUDICIAL REVIEW

Judicial review is the procedure by which the High Court exercises a supervisory jurisdiction over the decisions of inferior courts and tribunals and the acts of public bodies. Traditionally, the High Court was not concerned with reassessing the merits of the decision or act, but reviewing the procedure by which it had been reached and whether this was contrary to public law principles. In the famous case of *Associated Provincial Picture Houses Ltd v Wednesbury Corpn* [1948] 1 KB 223, CA, it was held that the following were grounds for interfering with the decision:

(i) unlawfulness;
(ii) procedural unfairness;
(iii) unreasonableness.

In the asylum and human rights context

It has to be acknowledged that even prior to the Human Rights Act 1998, applications for judicial review of asylum decisions were accorded a closer degree of examination than other applications, giving rise to the concept of 'anxious scrutiny' previously discussed in this book.

The Court of Appeal stated in *R v Coventry City Council, ex p Phoenix Aviation* [1995] 3 All ER 37 that: 'when fundamental human rights are in play, the courts will adopt a more interventionist role'. In the leading case of *R v Ministry of Defence, ex p Smith* [1996] QB 517, the Court of Appeal approved the following description of the High Court's task when considering a judicial review turning on human rights issues:

> 'The court may not interfere with the exercise of an administrative discretion on substantial grounds save where the court is satisfied that the decision is unreasonable in the sense that it is beyond the range of responses open to a reasonable decision-maker. But in judging whether the decision-maker has exceeded this margin of appreciation the human rights context is important. The more substantial the interference with human rights, the more the court will require by way of justification before it is satisfied that the decision is reasonable in the sense outlined above.'

The above approach has been termed 'super-*Wednesbury*' review. In *Turgut v Secretary of State for the Home Department* [2000] INLR 292 the Court of Appeal was concerned with the allegation that the Secretary of State's decision to return a failed asylum-seeker to Turkey would breach Article 3 ECHR, in so far as there was objective evidence suggesting that such individuals were ill-treated by the authorities. This was one of the first cases in which the Court was asked to consider the proper approach to judicial review decisions concerning Article 3. The Court concluded that:

(i) It had an obligation in an Article 3 challenge to subject the Secretary of State's decision to 'rigorous examination' and would do that by considering the underlying factual material on which the decision was based. However, the High Court's role remained of a supervisory nature. The critical date for the Court's assessment of risk was the date of the Court's consideration of the case: see *Chahal v United Kingdom* (1996) 23 EHRR 413.

(ii) The Court then had to consider whether there were substantial grounds for believing that the returnee would face a real risk of being subjected to treatment contrary to Article 3.

(iii) The right not to be exposed to a real risk of Article 3 ill-treatment is both absolute and fundamental; it is not a qualified right requiring a balance to be struck with some competing social need.

Post-Human Rights Act 1998

With the coming into force of the Human Rights Act 1998, the High Court has become particularly concerned with ensuring that judicial review is an effective remedy where human rights are engaged. The most significant development in judicial review in this regard has been the use of 'proportionality', not only as a principle that informs and tightens the 'super-*Wednesbury*' approach, but now as a free-standing ground of review in its own right. The most obvious context for proportionality in immigration judicial reviews is in the balancing exercise to be conducted under Article 8 of the ECHR. There have been a number of decisions by the High Court itself, the Court of Appeal and the House of Lords, some of which have already been referred to in Chapter 2.

The current position is that where qualified rights are in issue, any restriction must be strictly proportionate. In *R (on the application of Daly) v Secretary of State for the Home Department* [2001] UKHL 26, [2001] 2 AC 532, the House of Lords stated:

> '. . . There is a material difference between the *Wednesbury* and *Smith* grounds of review and the approach of proportionality applicable in respect of review where Convention rights are at stake.
>
> . . . The contours of the principle of proportionality are familiar. In *de Freitas v Permanent Secretary of Ministry of Agriculture, Fisheries, Lands and Housing* [1999] 1 AC 69, the Privy Council adopted a three-stage test. Lord Clyde observed, at 80, that in determining whether a limitation (by an act, rule or decision) is arbitrary or excessive the court should ask itself:
>
>> "whether: (i) the legislative objective is sufficiently important to justify limiting a fundamental right; (ii) the measures designed to meet the legislative objective are rationally connected to it; and (iii) the means used to impair the right or freedom are no more than is necessary to accomplish the objective."
>
> . . . The starting point is that there is an overlap between the traditional grounds of review and the approach of proportionality. Most cases would be decided in the same way whichever approach is adopted. But the intensity of review is somewhat greater under the proportionality approach.'

The House of Lords went on to explain three critical differences between traditional judicial review and proportionality:

(i) The doctrine of proportionality may require the reviewing court to assess the balance which the decision-maker has struck, not merely whether it is within the range of rational or reasonable decisions.
(ii) The proportionality test may go further than traditional grounds of review in that it may require attention to be directed to the relative weight to be accorded to interests and considerations.
(iii) Even the heightened scrutiny test developed in *R v Ministry of Defence, ex p Smith* [1996] QB 517 at 554 is not necessarily

appropriate to the protection of human rights. When the case of *Smith* itself was eventually heard by the European Court of Human Rights, the Court concluded:

> '. . . the threshold at which the High Court and the Court of Appeal could find the Ministry of Defence policy irrational was placed so high that it effectively excluded any consideration by the domestic courts of the question of whether the interference with the applicants' rights answered a *pressing social need* or was proportionate to the national security and public order aims pursued, principles which lie at the heart of the court's analysis of complaints under Article 8 of the Convention.'
>
> (Emphasis added.)

Although the House of Lords pointed out that the above principles did not mean a shift to merits review, there is an increasing recognition that the Human Rights Act and the concept of proportionality require the process of fact-finding and decision-making to be examined with 'greater amplitude': *Q* [2003] 3 WLR 365.

JUDICIAL REVIEW PROCEDURE

This part of the chapter will outline judicial review procedure and practice in general, before giving guidance on judicially reviewing particular kinds of decisions.

Judicial review cases were formerly heard in the High Court, Queen's Bench Division, Crown Office List, now called the Administrative Court. The procedure has also been modernised and is contained in Part 54 of the Civil Procedure Rules. In the cases we are concerned with, the defendant in an application for judicial review will usually either be the Secretary of State or the Immigration Appeal Tribunal. It must be noted that where the judicial review application is concerned with either the determination of an adjudicator who heard the appeal in Scotland, or the decision of the Tribunal in an appeal against such a determination, the application must be made to the Court of Session in Scotland, unless there is an emergency: *R (on the application of Majead) v Immigration Appeal Tribunal* [2003] EWCA Civ 615, [2003] All ER (D) 11 (Apr).

The claim form

A judicial review commences as an application for permission, which is initially dealt with by a single High Court judge on paper. The application for permission must be made using Form N461 (the claim form). The claim form and notes for guidance are available in hard copy from the Administrative Court Office at the Royal Courts of Justice. They are also on the Court Service website (www.courtservice.gov.uk) and can be downloaded in PDF format and completed on a PC using Acrobat Reader. The claim form must be lodged promptly after the decision challenged and in any event within three months.

The claim form has the following sections that must be completed with details of:

1. The claimant and defendant.
2. Other interested parties.
3. The decision to be judicially reviewed.
4. Public funding/ exceptional urgency/compliance with pre-action protocol/ issues under Human Rights act 1998.
5. Grounds for judicial review.
6. Remedies sought.
7. Other applications.
8. Facts relied on.
9. Supporting documents (in the form of an indexed paginated bundle).

With the growth in scope of judicial review, the Administrative Court has had to consider an ever-increasing number of applications for permission to proceed with judicial review. That in turn means that in practice a single High Court judge will not have a great deal of time to consider a typical application on paper. It is therefore important to make the judge's task as easy as possible, so that precious time is not wasted on making sense of the papers but rather spent on considering the merits of the application.

The detailed statement of grounds

Rather like the preparation of the statement in the SEF in Chapter 3, we suggest that a separate document titled 'detailed statement of grounds' be drafted. The grounds should deal with each of the following in turn:

- the claimant and defendant;
- the facts relied upon;
- the decision(s) to be judicially reviewed;
- the grounds for judicial review, including any issues under Human Rights Act 1998;
- the remedies sought.

The claim form can then be completed, but the main sections 3, 5, 6 and 8 can simply state 'see attached'. The detailed statement of grounds should be separate from both the claim form and the bundle, enabling quick cross-referencing by the judge to the supporting evidence.

Much of what we have already said regarding skeleton arguments and drafting grounds of appeal to the Tribunal is of equal relevance here. The detailed statement of grounds should of course be clear and concise. The relevant history of the case should be set out in chronological order. This may entail summarising the original basis of the claim, the evidence in support and the arguments put forward on appeal to the adjudicator or the Tribunal. The information should be sufficiently detailed to put the grounds for judicial review in their proper context, but no more. Quotations from the supporting documents are helpful if relevant and kept short, but should always refer to the bundle by page and paragraph number. The decision or decisions to be challenged should then be identified and the arguments for challenge dealt with in order of importance or strength.

If, as is likely, there are human rights as well as asylum issues, these must be dealt with by reference to the appropriate Article of the ECHR. Where the claimant is raising an issue or seeking a remedy under the Human Rights Act 1998, the claim form must include the information required by paragraph 16 of the Practice Direction supplementing Part 16 of the Civil Procedure Rules. All authorities referred to in the grounds must be given their full citation and the relevant sections quoted. The Practice Direction requires copies of all statutory materials and authorities to be supplied with the claim form, grounds and bundle.

If the application is out of time (ie outside the three month time limit) the reasons for this should be fully explained. The longer the delay, the more careful the explanation will need to be.

Finally, the grounds should conclude with a paragraph setting out the remedies sought. Typically, these will be:

- a Quashing Order – quashing the decision or determination;
- a Mandatory Order – requiring the defendant to re-consider the case;
- a Prohibitory Order – this will usually be required to prevent the Secretary of State from taking any steps to remove the claimant while the application for judicial review is being considered. The Home Office's policy is not to remove an individual who can demonstrate that they have made an application for judicial review e.g. by informing them of the 'CO number' for the claim.

In accordance with the concept of 'front-loading', the detailed statement of grounds should as far as possible be capable of standing as the entirety of the claimant's case. Inevitably there will be occasions where the constraints of time will press representatives to simply ask themselves 'will these grounds do?' In emergency cases and/or where information is incomplete, that will be an adequate standard. However, in all other cases it is as well to bear in mind that it is now becoming increasingly difficult to obtain public funding for renewed applications for permission to seek judicial review, and that the new statutory review procedure (dealt with below) does not even permit an oral hearing. There is thus now very good reason to do the utmost to put in the written grounds before the single judge every point that is properly intended to be relied on by the claimant and to ensure that rather than simply being raised, each point is explained sufficiently to convey in plain terms its significance to the case.

SAMPLE DETAILED STATEMENT OF GROUNDS

IN THE HIGH COURT OF JUSTICE CASE No: CO/

QUEEN'S BENCH DIVISION

ADMINISTRATIVE COURT

In the matter of an application for Judicial Review

BETWEEN:

THE QUEEN ON THE APPLICATION OF

ION LUKSHU

Claimant

and

THE IMMIGRATION APPEAL TRIBUNAL

Defendant

DETAILED STATEMENT OF GROUNDS

Background

1. The Claimant is a male citizen of Romania (d.o.b 10.9.1975) who fled his country on 2 February 2002 to the United Kingdom via France, arriving on 4 February 2002 and claiming asylum promptly the very next day.
2. Pursuant to his asylum application, the Claimant completed an SEF and attached statement dated 14 February 2002 (see pages 24–44 of bundle). The Claimant was subsequently interviewed by the Home Office on 3 May 2002 (see pages 45–55 of bundle).
3. The Secretary of State refused the asylum application on 17 May 2002 (see pages 21–23 of bundle). A Notice of Appeal and Statement of Additional Grounds raising Article 3 of the ECHR was lodged on 27 May 2002 (see pages 11–20 of bundle).
4. In due course the appeal came before Adjudicator Mr G. Morgan for hearing at York House on 26 August 2002. The Adjudicator heard the appeal and reserved his decision.

5. The Adjudicator dismissed both the asylum and Article 3 claims in a Determination notified on 17 September 2002 (see pages 6–10 of bundle).
6. An application for permission to appeal to the Immigration Appeal Tribunal was made on 4 October 2002 (see pages 3–5 of bundle).
7. The Tribunal refused to grant permission to appeal in a Decision notified on 11 November 2002 (see pages 1–2 of bundle).

Decision challenged

8. The Claimant challenges the Tribunal's refusal to grant permission to appeal as being unlawful and/or unreasonable.

TRIBUNAL'S REASONS

9. The Tribunal refused leave because:

> 'The Adjudicator was entitled to find that the police had not imputed a political opinion to the Appellant and that there was no real likelihood of persecution or ill-treatment on return.'
>
> (see paragraph 3 of Decision, page 2 of bundle)

ADJUDICATOR'S CONCLUSIONS – CHARGES AGAINST CLAIMANT

10. The Adjudicator accepted the Claimant's overall account as credible, but decided that:

> '. . . the problems he encountered with the Police in Romania are examples of prosecution not persecution. If there are charges outstanding against him there is nothing to suggest that he would not get a fair trial in Romania according to the country information before me, or that the punishment would be disproportionate. The judiciary is independent and properly constituted in Romania.'
>
> (See paragraph 11 of Determination, page 8 of bundle)

11. With the respect to the Tribunal and to the Adjudicator, the Claimant's case was far from being this simple. On his account, the charges of fraud against him were concocted by the Police in retaliation for his refusal to provide them with information concerning Mr Igor Vladin, the Leader of the newly-formed National Democratic Party. The Claimant was Mr Vladin's personal bodyguard. The Claimant feared that any such information would be used to undermine the credibility of Mr Vladin, as he was at that time involved in a high-profile dispute with various high-ranking members of the ruling Social Democratic Party of Romania, against whom Mr Vladin had made accusations of corruption.
12. The Adjudicator was surely wrong in law to label 'prosecution' what was in reality a politically-motivated vendetta. In *Noune v Secretary of State for the Home Department* [2001] INLR 526 the Court of Appeal observed that a refusal to co-operate with the demands of Islamic extremists was perfectly capable of amounting to imputed political opinion and thus engaging the Refugee Convention. It is submitted that the Adjudicator did not consider whether, as a consequence of refusing to give incriminating information about a leading opposition politician, the Police had imputed a political opinion to the Claimant.
13. Moreover, the Adjudicator's view that the charges against the Claimant would result in a 'fair trial' gave insufficient weight to the above political dimension of his case and assumed that the Claimant would in fact be brought to Court, when being false charges, this was not necessarily so.
14. Further or alternatively, the Adjudicator's assessment of the Romanian judiciary did not take proper account of all the objective evidence:

    'The ruling Party of Social Democracy of Romania . . . showed little respect for the rule of law. *It instructed judges how to rule in certain cases* and made partisan dismissals from and appointments to the judiciary.

Corruption continued to be widespread and to undermine the legal system, the economy and public confidence in government . . .'

(Emphasis added.)

(Amnesty International Report 2002, page 59 of bundle)

'Under the law, the judicial branch is independent of other government branches; *however, it remains subject to influence by the executive branch*. Although members of the Senior Council of Magistrates, which controls the selection, promotion, transfer, and sanctioning of judges, are appointed by Parliament from a list provided by the courts and prosecutorial offices represented on the council, the Justice Minister may avoid the appointment of unwanted members by simply keeping them off the agenda. *The judicial system is widely regarded as weak, inefficient, and suffering from systemic corruption*, although the Ministry of Justice is investigating and bringing prosecutions against corrupt judges and officers.'

(Emphasis added.)

(US State Department 2002 report, page 63 of bundle)

15. It is submitted that these concerns about the independence of the judiciary were of particular significance to the Claimant's case, given that it would be a politically-motivated prosecution.

ADJUDICATOR'S CONCLUSIONS – ATTACKS ON THE CLAIMANT

16. The Adjudicator went on to state:

'The other incidents involving the attacks on the street and assaults whilst detained are matters of a criminal nature and as such do not engage the Refugee Convention.'

(See paragraph 12 of Determination, page 9 of bundle.)

17. However, that conclusion ignored the Claimant's evidence that these 'other incidents' were all part of the same pattern:
    - At the end of November 2001 the Claimant attended the Police Station and was requested to tell the Police all he knew about Mr Vladin's affairs. The Claimant refused. He was threatened and given a week to reconsider.
    - A week later the Claimant received a threatening phone-call from the Police.
    - Three days after that the Claimant was arrested and charged with fraud, although he was not shown any evidence on which the charges were based. Significantly, directly after being charged he was again asked to provide information about Mr Vladin and again he refused.
    - He was detained at the Police Station for 4 days, during which time he was beaten by the Police with truncheons.
    - On two separate occasions in December 2001 he was attacked by balaclava-wearing men, who told him to co-operate with the Police. The Claimant required medical treatment for numerous cuts and bruises on both occasions.
    - On 7 January 2002 the Claimant was yet again summoned to the Police Station. He did not attend, but went into hiding until he left Romania on 2 February 2002. During his time in hiding his parents informed him that the Police were still looking for him.
    - Since the Claimant's departure from Romania, his parents informed him that the Police visited their home about once a month looking for him, and that strangers dressed in 'plainclothes' and posing as his friends have also asked about his whereabouts.
18. It is respectfully submitted that the Adjudicator erred in viewing the 'other incidents' as disparate criminal acts which did not engage the Refugee Convention. The Police were directly or indirectly responsible for *all* of

the above occurrences which were designed to force the Claimant to give evidence against Mr Vladin for political purposes and which therefore, it is submitted, amounted to persecution for a Convention reason.

ADJUDICATOR'S CONCLUSIONS – SUFFICIENCY OF PROTECTION

19. The Adjudicator decided:

> 'There is no suggestion in the objective material that there is not a general sufficiency of protection in Romania. It was incumbent upon Mr Lukshu to report his problems to the police and exhaust his domestic remedies before claiming international protection. This is what the Convention requires.'
>
> (See paragraph 12 of Determination, page 9 of bundle.)

20. It is submitted that in considering the question of what protection was *in reality* available to the Claimant, the Adjudicator took no account of his asylum interview:

Q31: 'Did you try to tell Mr Vladin about your problems?'

A: 'I wasn't able to see him because he was out of the country on business.'

Q32: 'Did you report these problems to the Police authorities?'

A: 'No, because the Police told me that the Police Commissioner himself had authorised them to deal with me.'

Q33: 'Did you make attempts to go to any other authorities?'

A: 'If you lived in Romania you would know that there is no point in doing such a thing, because they are all linked with one another. My problems would only get worse.'

(See pages 50–51 of bundle.)

21. Nor did the Adjudicator take into account the Claimant's witness statement dated 19 August 2002, in which he responded to paragraph 4 of the Refusal Letter as follows:

> 'I disagree with paragraph 4, as the Police act on the orders of the Government. The Commissioner of the Police has connections with many ministers. The Police are not independent, they work for the Government and are well-known for doing its "dirty work".'
>
> (See page 57 of bundle.)

22. Thus, the Adjudicator's finding on protection was fundamentally flawed by a failure to take account of relevant considerations.

ADJUDICATOR'S CONCLUSIONS – THE HUMAN RIGHTS APPEAL

23. The Adjudicator dealt with this appeal in just one sentence:

> 'As these matters were criminal in nature I do not consider that any Articles of the European Convention are engaged.'
>
> (See paragraph 14 of Determination, page 10 of bundle.)

24. It is submitted that this conclusion was also flawed. As the Adjudicator had found that there was no Refugee Convention reason, it was clearly incumbent on him to give separate and careful consideration to the human rights appeal, particularly as Article 3 of the ECHR is absolute and does not require torture or inhuman or degrading treatment to be carried out for any particular reason.

Conclusion

25. It is submitted that the Adjudicator's Determination ignores the most critical aspects of the Claimant's account and fails to properly consider the objective evidence.
26. For these reasons, an appeal to the Tribunal would have reasonable prospects of success. It follows that the Tribunal's decision to refuse permission to appeal was unlawful and/or unreasonable.

Relief sought

27. The Claimant therefore respectfully seeks:
    (1) a Quashing Order in respect of the Tribunal's decision;
    (2) a Mandatory Order requiring the Tribunal to grant leave to appeal;
    (3) an Interim Prohibitory Order preventing the Secretary of State from taking any steps to remove the Claimant from the United Kingdom until such time as these proceedings have concluded.

Date:

Name:

Address:

FURTHER PROCEDURAL MATTERS

The bundle

The Administrative Court Practice Direction requires the bundle to be paginated and indexed. We suggest that it be compiled in three sections:

A. *Previous proceedings and decisions* – this should include copies of the previous Home Office decisions, grounds of appeal and determinations etc.
B. *Evidence specific to case* – SEFs, interview records, representations, witness statements, documentary evidence, medical reports, expert evidence etc.
C. *Objective evidence* – for example, country reports, generic reports, newspaper articles etc.

Each section should be in chronological order, with the earliest item first. Original documents should *never* go into the bundle or, as we have previously indicated, be hole-punched, stapled or damaged in any way.

There should be a 'master bundle' containing the clearest copies of all the documents, which should be paginated. The sections of the documents which have been cross-referenced from the detailed statement of grounds should then be highlighted by side-lining in black (not underlining which tends to obscure the text). The additional copies can then be made from the paginated highlighted version. An index should then be made.

The Practice Direction also requires a list of essential reading. Rather than draft another separate document, this requirement is quickly and easily complied with by marking each essential document with an asterisk on the index and a sub-heading 'Essential Reading' at the foot of the index, indicating that this is the asterixed or highlighted documents. Finally, a good tip for presentation is to put the claim form, grounds and bundle in a ring binder. If time or resources do not permit this, then it is advisable to insert a piece of card at the end of the bundle, as the last page always seems to get torn or lost.

Lodging and service

There should be two copies of the claim form, grounds and bundle for the Court and an additional copy for each defendant or interested party. Lodging must be done at the Administrative Court Office. The Court Office opens at 10.00 a.m. and normally shuts at 4.30 p.m. and at 2.30 p.m. during the summer vacation.

A fee of £30.00 payable by cash or cheque to 'Her Majesty's Paymaster General' is required to be paid to the Court Fees Office first.

The Clerk at the Administrative Court Office will then check the documents before accepting them and opening a new Court file. It is at this stage that the Court Office issues a standard letter confirming that the claim has been lodged, and this will give the all-important Crown Office reference number. If removal of the client is imminent this 'CO number' must be immediately communicated to the Immigration Service so that the removal directions can be stayed. Service of the claim form, grounds and bundle on the defendant and interested party must be effected within seven days and confirmation of service sent to the Court Office.

The acknowledgement of service

The defendant or interested party has 21 days from the date of service to complete Form N462 (the acknowledgement of service) and lodge it with the Court Office, and a further seven days to serve it on the claimant.

The most important part of the acknowledgement of service is section C, namely the summary of grounds for contesting the claim. This will set out the arguments why that party does not consider there to be any grounds for judicial review or, exceptionally, why relief should not be granted in any event.

Response to acknowledgement of service?

Although there is no specific provision for the claimant to make a response to the defendant's acknowledgement of service, such a document may sometimes be merited if the acknowledgement of service has raised issues that have not been dealt with in the detailed statement of grounds and it is likely that the single judge will refuse permission on the basis of wrong or incomplete information. This is particularly so given the increasing difficulty of obtaining public funding for renewal of applications. Any response should be sent to the Administrative Court Office and served on the Defendant as soon as possible.

Decision on permission on paper

It will usually be four to six weeks before a decision is reached by the single judge. This will be sent to all the parties. If permission is refused a claimant has only seven days to notify the Administrative Court Office of an intention to renew the application. This now requires *further* written grounds to explain why, in the light of the single judge's observations on the refusal of permission, the application is being pursued. The grounds for renewal should also be served on the defendant.

In other cases, the single judge may list the application for permission for an oral hearing, without making a decision on paper. This will be where the judge considers that the case is not clear-cut enough to grant or refuse permission without further information or submissions from the parties, or where the issues of law at stake are particularly novel or complex.

If permission is granted, the application will proceed to a full hearing. Where the merits of the case are strong, but do not involve any important question of law or principle, the defendant may offer to compromise the application by way of a Consent Order. A Consent Order is a written agreement made between the parties informing the Court that the parties wish to settle the claim and requesting the Court's formal endorsement of the settlement and any necessary relief.

JUDICIAL REVIEW HEARINGS

Permission hearings

The permission hearing will usually be listed with a number of other such applications before a High Court judge other than the judge who refused permission on paper. A High Court judge, with very few exceptions, will have previously been a Queen's Counsel in private practice. He or she can be fairly regarded as being a more demanding tribunal than either adjudicators or indeed most compositions of the Immigration Appeal Tribunal. That said, High Court judges vary in background and outlook far more than they are given credit for.

As in any court, it is often beneficial to gauge the judge's approach (or even mood) before making submissions. For this reason, representatives who have not appeared in front of a particular judge before are often content to have their application heard later in the morning. When the case is called on, it is customary to begin submissions by saying 'My Lord, I represent the claimant, my learned friend Ms Smith represents the Secretary of State, who is the defendant/interested party in this application'. The representative should then proceed to ask the judge if he has had an opportunity to read the papers. As we have said, the Administrative Court deals with an ever-increasing volume of work and it should not be taken for granted that the judge has read everything that will be relied on. However it will generally be the case that the judge will have seen the detailed statement of grounds, any documents referred to in it, and the acknowledgement of service.

Unless a prior request has been made for more time, the permission hearing will have been given a time estimate of about 20 minutes. It is therefore critical to make the best possible use of time. It is at this stage that the effort of drafting coherent grounds, and a well-presented bundle should at least get the representative off on the right foot: there is nothing worse than a judge stating that although he has read the papers 'ground X does not make any sense' or that 'document Y is incomplete'. Any opening comments made by the judge will tend to be important for two related reasons:

- he may indicate that he will grant permission if he can be satisfied about a particular point;
- even if it is not a favourable indication, it will still allow the representative to focus on what the judge sees as the important issues.

The representative should consider moulding their submissions to the judge's opening indications. However, there will always be applications where the representative is of the view that the judge has not grasped what the case is really about. This may require lengthy reference to the original decision or to parts of the evidence. Even so, any further indications from the judge must be heeded.

If the representative has time to pre-empt points made in the acknowledgement of service or to distinguish an authority that will be relied on by counsel for the Secretary of State, so much the better. But it should be borne in mind that if their opponent is called on to make submissions the representative will have the opportunity to briefly reply. The representative should conclude their arguments with 'My Lord, unless I can assist you further, those are my submissions'.

The judge will then invite counsel for the Secretary of State to make submissions in response. The representative may then reply, although this should be kept short.

Decisions to grant or refuse permission at an oral hearing are with very few exceptions made directly after submissions. If permission is granted on all or some of the grounds, the matter will be listed for a full hearing on a later date. If it is refused that will generally be the end of the case. In some cases there may be merit in renewing the application to the Court of Appeal (see Chapter 9), but that does not require the representative to make any additional submission to the judge at this stage. Counsel for the Secretary of State may at this point apply for costs. It will be rare that such an application can or should be resisted by the representative. In practical terms, such a costs order may mean very little: the Secretary of State will be far more concerned to enforce removal directions against the claimant than costs orders. If the application was publicly funded, the representative should make an application for a detailed assessment of the claimant's costs. Unless the judge was of the view that the application for judicial review was completely hopeless, such an assessment will normally be granted.

Full hearings

A skeleton argument must be submitted 21 days in advance of the hearing. In order to make the judge's task as simple as possible, the skeleton argument should subsume and replace the detailed statement of grounds, so that the judge does not have to constantly switch between two written arguments. If both sides are going to be relying on more than a few authorities, it will be helpful to lodge an agreed bundle of authorities in advance of the hearing.

Much of what has already been said regarding permission hearings is of course applicable here too. However, a full judicial review hearing will often be listed for two or more hours, depending on the complexity of the issues. While in a permission hearing the representative has to focus very much on conveying the points in their simplest form; the full hearing provides more time for elaboration of the written arguments. As such hearings will often involve more detailed reference to evidence and case law, a useful part of preparation is carefully pre-reading the extracts which are going to be relied on, so that when they are recited in Court, this is done with the appropriate emphasis rather than in a monotonous way – particularly with long passages.

JUDICIAL REVIEW OF PARTICULAR DECISIONS

Third country cases

These are cases in which the Secretary of State refuses to give substantive consideration to an asylum claim, on the basis that the applicant can be removed to a 'safe third country'. In practice, the Secretary of State will do this where the applicant has already made an asylum claim in another European Union state. All Member States are signatories to the Dublin Convention, which is a Treaty intended to prevent asylum-seekers making multiple claims, by laying down a system for deciding which Member State should be responsible for considering a claim.

The main provision is s 80 of the Nationality, Immigration and Asylum Act 2002 (the 2002 Act), which substitutes s 11 of the Immigration and Asylum Act 1999 (the 1999 Act) as follows:

> **'11. Removal of asylum claimant under standing arrangement with member States**
>
> (1) In determining whether a person in relation to whom a certificate has been issued under subsection (2) may be removed from the United Kingdom, a member State is to be regarded as-

(a) a place where a person's life and liberty is not threatened by reason of his race, religion, nationality, membership of a particular social group, or political opinion; and

(b) a place from which a person will not be sent to another country otherwise than in accordance with the Refugee Convention.

(2) Nothing in section 77 of the Nationality, Immigration and Asylum Act 2002 prevents a person who has made a claim for asylum ("the claimant") from being removed from the United Kingdom to a member State if the Secretary of State has certified that-

(a) the member State has accepted that, under standing arrangements, it is the responsible State in relation to the claimant's claim for asylum; and

(b) in his opinion, the claimant is not a national or citizen of the member State to which he is to be sent.

(3) Subsection (4) applies where a person who is the subject of a certificate under subsection (2)-

(a) has instituted or could institute an appeal under section 82(1) of the Nationality, Immigration and Asylum Act 2002 (immigration appeal), and

(b) has made a human rights claim (within the meaning of section 113 of that Act).

(4) The person may not be removed from the United Kingdom in reliance upon this section unless-

(a) the appeal is finally determined, withdrawn or abandoned (within the meaning of section 104 of that Act) or can no longer be brought (ignoring any possibility of an appeal out of time with permission), or

(b) the Secretary of State has issued a certificate in relation to the human rights claim under section 93(2)(b) of that Act (clearly unfounded claim).

(5) In this section "standing arrangements" means arrangements in force between two or more member States for determining which State is responsible for considering applications for asylum.'

The less-often used section 12 of the 1999 Act (as amended by statutory instrument 2003 No. 1016) states:

> **'12. Removal of asylum claimants in other circumstances**
>
> (1) Subsection (2) applies if the Secretary of State intends to remove a person who has made a claim for asylum ("the claimant") from the United Kingdom to-
>
> (a) a member State, or a territory which forms part of a member State, otherwise than under standing arrangements; or
>
> (b) a country other than a member State which is designated by order made by the Secretary of State for the purposes of this section.
>
> (2) Nothing in section 77 of the Nationality, Immigration and Asylum Act 2002 prevents the claimant's removal if the Secretary of State has certified that, in his opinion, the conditions set out in subsection (7) are fulfilled;
>
> . . .
>
> (4) Subsection (5) applies if the Secretary of State intends to remove a person who has made a claim for asylum ('the claimant') from the United Kingdom to a country which is not-
>
> (a) a member State; or
>
> (b) a country designated under subsection (1)(b)
>
> (5) Nothing in section 77 of the Nationality, Immigration and Asylum Act 2002 prevents the claimant's removal if the Secretary of State has certified that, in his opinion, the conditions set out in subsection (7) are fulfilled;
>
> . . .
>
> (7) The conditions are that-
>
> (a) he is not a national or citizen of the country to which he is to be sent;
>
> (b) his life and liberty would not be threatened there by reason of his race, religion, nationality, membership of a particular social group, or political opinion; and
>
> (c) the government of that country would not send him to another country otherwise than in accordance with the Refigee Convention.

(7A) Subsection (7B) applies where a person who is the subject of a certificate under subsection (2) or (5)-
  (a) has instituted or could institute an appeal under section 82(1) of the Nationality, Immigration and Asylum Act 2002 (immigration appeal), and
  (b) has made a human rights claim (within the meaning of section 113 of that Act).

(7B) The person may not be removed from the United Kingdom in reliance upon this section unless -
  (a) the appeal is finally determined, withdrawn or abandoned (within the meaning of section 104 of that Act) or can no longer be brought (ignoring any possibility of an appeal out of time with permission), or
  (b) the Secretary of State has issued a certificate in relation to the human rights claim under section 93(2)(b) of that Act (clearly unfounded claim).

(8) "Standing arrangements" has the same meaning as in section 11.'

The above provisions give the Secretary of State power to:

- certify a claim as a third country case (s 11(2) of the 1999 Act (as substituted) or s 12(2) of the 1999 Act (as amended);
- certify a subsequent claim, that removal pursuant to the third country certificate would breach the applicant's human rights, as 'clearly unfounded' thus preventing a right of appeal to an adjudicator prior to removal itself (s 11(4)(b) of the 1999 Act (as substituted) or s 12(7B)(b) of the 1999 Act (as amended) with s 93(2)(b) of the 2002 Act.

Third country certificates

Challenges to such certificates are likely to involve complex considerations of the third country's legal procedures for dealing with asylum applications. In the leading case of *R (Yogathas and Thangarasa) v Secretary of State for the Home Department* [2002] UKHL 36, [2003] 1 AC 920, the House of Lords held as follows:

(i) The Secretary of State and the courts 'should not readily infer that a friendly sovereign state which is party to the Geneva Convention will not perform the obligations it has solemnly undertaken'.

(ii) Although there were differences between the tests applied in Germany and the United Kingdom regarding internal relocation, the differences were not so great as to compel the conclusion that removal of Tamil asylum applicants to Germany would give rise to a real risk that they would be sent back to Sri Lanka or elsewhere otherwise than in accordance with the Refugee Convention.

(iii) 'Legal niceties and refinements' in respect of comparative asylum procedures should not be allowed to obstruct the very simple and practical objective of the Refugee Convention, namely preventing the return of applicants to places where they will or may suffer persecution.

(iv) Although Germany took a different view of persecution by non-state agents, this 'protection gap' was more apparent than real. Germany had other provisions under which an applicant could seek protection and in the case of *TI v United Kingdom* [2000] INLR 211 the European Court of Human Rights concluded that there was no real likelihood that a Tamil asylum applicant would be returned from Germany to Sri Lanka to face treatment contrary to Article 3 of the ECHR.

(v) Before certifying as 'manifestly unfounded' an allegation in a third-country case that removal would breach the applicant's human rights, the Secretary of State was required to consider the allegation and any evidence in support carefully. But no matter what the sophistication of argument or the volume of material submitted, this was still only a 'screening process' and not a 'full-blown merits review'.

(vi) The Secretary of State was entitled to certify the claim as 'manifestly unfounded' if after reviewing the evidence, he was 'reasonably and conscientiously satisfied that the allegation must clearly fail'.

Representatives must be aware that third country cases tend to be very complicated indeed and will inevitably require reference to more specialised textbooks.

'Clearly unfounded' certificates

Section 93(2)(b) of the 2002 Act is the successor to s 72(2)(a) of the 1999 Act, which gave the Secretary of State the power to certify a human rights claim as 'manifestly unfounded' and deny a right of appeal to an adjudicator prior to removal. In *ZL and VL v Secretary of State for the Home Department* [2003] EWCA Civ 25, [2003] INLR 224 (discussed further below) it was held that 'clearly unfounded' is equivalent to 'manifestly unfounded' and so the case law on s 72(2)(a) of the 1999 Act will still be relevant.

In *Ahmadi* [2002] EWHC 1897 (Admin) the High Court considered a challenge to a 'manifestly unfounded' certificate, issued in respect of an allegation that the return of an Afghani family to Germany would result in a deterioration of their psychiatric health and breach their rights under Article 8 ECHR. The Court concluded that:

(i) The expression 'manifestly unfounded' was equivalent to the term 'unarguable'.

(ii) The Secretary of State could properly issue a certificate if he was satisfied that there was 'plainly nothing of substance in the case' and was not required to conduct a 'deep or exhaustive examination of the merits'.

(iii) Where the Secretary of State was faced with conflicting expert evidence and there was no obvious reason to prefer one report to the other, any decision to certify the human rights claim as manifestly unfounded must proceed on the report most favourable to the claimant.

Ahmadi was followed in *R (on the application of Razgar) v Secretary of State for the Home Department* [2002] EWHC 2554 (QB), [2003] Imm AR 269, in which the High Court further noted:

(i) Where there were factual disputes, the Secretary of State before certifying a human rights allegation as manifestly unfounded, had to consider not his own view of the facts, but whether the claimant might prevail on that point before an adjudicator.

(ii) If there were 'obvious reasons' to reject the claimant's material it was open to the Secretary of State to conclude that the claim was 'clearly bound to fail'. If there was no reason why the Secretary of State should reject the claimant's material and there was an arguable case, it could not be certified.

In *Razgar, Soumahoro and Nadarajah* [2003] EWCA Civ 840, the Court of Appeal heard linked appeals on the issue of 'manifestly unfounded' certificates and held:

(i) There was no need to gloss or amplify the very clear statements in *Yogathas and Thangarasa* as to the meaning of 'manifestly unfounded', albeit the High Court's comments in *Razgar* were not inconsistent with them.

(ii) Although judicial review of a certificate was not a merits review, but a supervisory review, the Secretary of State's decision would nevertheless receive 'rigorous examination' and where the issues were ones of fact, there would be 'little scope for deference' by the Court to the Secretary of State's view.

(iii) In relation to the balancing exercise under Article 8 of the ECHR and following *Edore v Secretary of State for the Home Department* [2003] EWCA Civ 716, [2003] 27 LS Gaz R 36:

  (a) Where there were no disputes of fact, the certificate had to be approached on the basis that an adjudicator would have to decide whether the Secretary of State's decision was within the range of reasonable responses.

  (b) When the facts were in dispute, the certificate had to be examined on the basis that an adjudicator would be making a fresh decision on proportionality, albeit paying deference to the Secretary of State's view on the weight to be given to the importance of maintaining an effective immigration policy.

(iv) Where Article 8(2) was not considered by the Secretary of State prior to issuing the certificate, the Court should be 'especially reluctant' to permit the Secretary of State to advance arguments under Article 8(2) at the judicial review stage.

(v) Although the Secretary of State was entitled in appropriate cases to reject an applicant's account as incredible and to conclude that the account would be bound to be rejected by an adjudicator on appeal, in view of the high threshold of the 'manifestly unfounded' test, the Secretary of State should be 'very cautious' before doing so.

(vi) Parliament had set a 'very high threshold' for the issue of a 'manifestly unfounded' certificate and as such, the Secretary of State could not lawfully issue such a certificate unless the claim was 'bound to fail before an adjudicator', as opposed to there merely being a 'very real possibility' that it would fail.

No in-country right of appeal

'Clearly unfounded' asylum and human rights claims

The 2002 Act has also given the Secretary of State power to certify as 'clearly unfounded' asylum and human rights claims made by applicants from certain designated states, who have claimed only in the United Kingdom and would therefore be removed directly back to their home countries. The relevant provision is section 94:

> **'94. Appeal from within United Kingdom: unfounded human rights or asylum claim**
>
> (1) This section applies to an appeal under section 82(1) where the appellant has made an asylum claim or a human rights claim (or both).
>
> (2) A person may not bring an appeal to which this section applies in reliance on section 92(4) if the Secretary of State certifies that the claim or claims mentioned in subsection (1) is or are clearly unfounded.
>
> (3) If the Secretary of State is satisfied that an asylum claimant or human rights claimant is entitled to reside in a State listed in subsection (4) he shall certify the claim under subsection (2) unless satisfied that it is not clearly unfounded.
>
> (4) Those States are-
>
> (a) the Republic of Cyprus,
> (b) the Czech Republic,
> (c) the Republic of Estonia,
> (d) the Republic of Hungary,
> (e) the Republic of Latvia,
> (f) the Republic of Lithuania,
> (g) the Republic of Malta,
> (h) the Republic of Poland,
> (i) the Slovak Republic, and

(j) the Republic of Slovenia.

(5) The Secretary of State may by order add a State, or part of a State, to the list in subsection (4) if satisfied that-

(a) there is in general in that State or part no serious risk of persecution of persons entitled to reside in that State or part, and

(b) removal to that State or part of persons entitled to reside there will not in general contravene the United Kingdom's obligations under the Human Rights Convention.'

Section 94(3) requires the Secretary of State to certify all claims by applicants from the designated states, unless satisfied that the claim is not "clearly unfounded". A certificate issued under s 94(2) prevents an in-country right of appeal to an adjudicator.

Section 115 of the 2002 Act is a transitional provision in very similar terms to s 94 which was designed to allow the new 'clearly unfounded' certificate to be issued in respect of claims by applicants from the designated states where there would otherwise have been a right of appeal to an adjudicator under the 1999 Act.

In *ZL and VL v Secretary of State for the Home Department* [2003] INLR 224, the Court of Appeal considered the implications of these provisions and held that:

(i) The fast-track procedure for claims made by individuals from the designated states was itself fair and reasonable. However, it was recognised by the Court of Appeal that where evidence became available that could not be put before the Secretary of State prior to the initial decision, due to the tight constraints of that procedure (a target of seven days) such evidence should be considered by the High Court in judicial review proceedings.

(ii) The Court laid down the test for 'clearly unfounded':
'If on at least one legitimate view of the facts or the law the claim may succeed, the claim will not be clearly unfounded.'

(iii) Where the decision turned on credibility alone, it would only be appropriate for the Secretary of State to certify if satisfied that 'nobody could believe the applicant's story'.

(iv) Although many asylum claims from Czech nationals were likely to be 'clearly unfounded', some will nevertheless raise specific issues which would not be susceptible to fast-track determination. The 'clearly unfounded' certificate was not to be used as a 'rubber stamp'.

It is submitted that the latter point is of particular importance, given that subsequent statutory instruments (2003 No. 249; 2003 No. 1919) have added the following states to the list in section 94(4):
(k) The Republic of Albania
(l) Bulgaria
(m) Serbia and Montenegro (including Kosovo)
(n) Jamaica
(o) Macedonia
(p) The Republic of Moldova
(q) Romania
(r) Bangladesh
(s) Bolivia
(t) Brazil
(u) Ecuador
(v) Sri Lanka
(w) South Africa
(x) Ukraine
Judicial review of s 94 certificates will therefore require representatives to research the objective evidence for these countries, as well as Tribunal decisions on issues such as the protection available in them, and to put all relevant materials in the bundle before the High Court. Generic expert reports, or if there is time, a specifically-prepared report, are also likely to be valuable.

Refusal of leave to appeal to Tribunal

The old procedure – judicial review

Prior to statutory review, an application for judicial review could be made where the Tribunal had wrongly refused permission to appeal. The case law relating to such applications will still be relevant. In *Deldadeh* (CO/69/2000) the High Court held that when the Tribunal had refused permission to appeal on a factually erroneous basis, the burden switched to the Secretary of State to show that if the application had been considered properly, no reasonable Tribunal could have granted permission to appeal.

As we have emphasised, the application for permission to appeal to the Tribunal should include *all* material grounds of appeal. However, if for some reason this was not done then a new ground can still be raised in judicial review. The Court of Appeal held in *Robinson v Secretary of State for the Home Department* [1997] INLR 182 that permission to apply for judicial review should be granted if a point not raised in the grounds to the Tribunal would have a 'strong prospect of success' if permission to appeal had been granted. *Robinson* was followed in the recent case of *Naing and Eyaz* [2003] EWHC 771 (Admin), in which the High Court emphasised that the point had to be both readily discernible *and* have a strong prospect of success.

The Court of Appeal in *Galal Kamal Tofik* [2003] EWCA Civ 1138 held that where an application for permission to appeal to the Tribunal included an explanation for it being outside the time limit, the Tribunal had both a statutory and common law duty to give reasons for a refusal to extend time.

In *R v Secretary of State for the Home Department, ex p Demiroglu* [2002] Imm AR 78 the High Court held that permission to apply for judicial review should *not* be granted where the underlying appeal to the Tribunal had 'no conceivable prospect of success'.

The new procedure – statutory review

With the coming into force of s 101 of the 2002 Act, judicial review of the Tribunal's decision to refuse leave to appeal was replaced by a new High Court procedure called 'statutory review'. Statutory review can be applied for on the ground that the Tribunal 'made an error of law'. It is to be hoped that this is interpreted widely to include unfairness and unreasonable factual assessments, as otherwise there will be a risk that unsuccessful applicants will be returned to their country of origin in breach of the United Kingdom's obligations under the Refugee Convention and the ECHR.

Section 101 of the 2002 Act states:

> '. . .
>
> (2) A party to an application to the Tribunal for permission to appeal under subsection (1) may apply to the High

Court or, in Scotland, to the Court of Session for a review of the Tribunal's decision on the ground that the Tribunal made an error of law.

(3) Where an application is made under subsection (2)–
 (a) it shall be determined by a single judge by reference only to written submissions,
 (b) the judge may affirm or reverse the Tribunal's decision,
 (c) the judge's decision shall be final, and
 (d) if, in an application to the High Court, the judge thinks the application had no merit he shall issue a certificate under this paragraph (which shall be dealt with in accordance with Civil Procedure Rules).'

The Civil Procedure (Amendment) Rules 2003, amending Part 54 of the Civil Procedure Rules, make clear that statutory review will be a quicker process than judicial review:

- The application must be lodged not later than 14 days after the applicant is deemed to have received notice of the Tribunal's decision.
- The application will be determined by a single judge without a hearing.
- The decision of the judge will be final: there will not be a renewal or an appeal.

This much shorter timescale and the absence of any further appeal will of course put representatives under greater pressure than ever before. Much of what has been said above, regarding the preparation of the detailed statement of grounds and bundle for judicial review will apply here too. The sample detailed statement of grounds was itself for a judicial review of a refusal of leave by the Tribunal and would only need slight changes to serve as written grounds for statutory review.

Statutory review – the test

Although the actual procedure of statutory review can be regarded as being far less forgiving than that of judicial review, the test itself does not appear to be a particularly high one. Part 54.25 of the Civil Procedure Rules now states:

'. . .

(4) Where the Tribunal refused permission to appeal, the court will reverse the Tribunal's decision only if it is satisfied that–
   (a) the Tribunal *may* have made an error of law; and
   (b) either–
      (i) the appeal would have a real prospect of success; or
      (ii) there is some other compelling reason why the appeal should be heard.'

Remittal of appeal by Tribunal

Where the Tribunal have heard an appeal and have decided that the adjudicator's findings are flawed or insufficient, it will usually decide to remit the case to be re-heard by a different adjudicator. In the majority of cases, this can be regarded as the fairest outcome for the client. However, there will be some cases, for example where the adjudicator found the appellant credible and allowed the appeal and the Secretary of State has appealed, where a remittal to a different adjudicator for the appeal to be re-heard, will be to the client's distinct disadvantage. The representative should consider whether any of the following apply:

- The adjudicator made all the positive factual findings that were necessary for the appeal to be allowed.
- The Tribunal have not given the adjudicator the proper deference as the primary finder of fact.
- It would be oppressive for the client to be required to give evidence again, before another adjudicator.

If one or more of these features are present and from a tactical perspective there is a concern that the client would not necessarily be found credible by another adjudicator, judicial review of the remittal should be contemplated. In practice however, this could prove an uphill struggle, as the High Court may not view remittal as the end of the road for the claimant.

Refusal by Secretary of State to treat application as fresh claim

Fresh claims are governed by rule 346 of the Immigration Rules (HC 395), which states:

> 'Where an asylum applicant has previously been refused asylum during his stay in the United Kingdom, the Secretary of State will determine whether any further representations should be treated as a fresh application for asylum. The Secretary of State will treat representations as a fresh application for asylum if the claim advanced in the representations is sufficiently different from the earlier claim that there is a realistic prospect that the conditions set out in paragraph 334 will be satisfied. In considering whether to treat the representations as a fresh claim, the Secretary of State will disregard any material which:
> (i) is not significant; or
> (ii) is not credible; or
> (iii) was available to the applicant at the time when the previous application was refused or when any appeal was determined.'

There are two stages: first, whether the Home office will actually treat the new evidence as amounting to a fresh claim; and secondly, whether or not that evidence is accepted. Where the Home Office do not accept that the evidence can in itself amount to a fresh application, the only remedy is judicial review.

In *Secretary of State for the Home Department v Boybeyi* [1997] INLR 130, the Court of Appeal held that the Secretary of State had to determine the following questions:

(i) Does the claim relate to substantially the same circumstances as before?
(ii) Even if it does is there fresh evidence in support of it?
(iii) If the answer is yes, is the evidence credible?
(iv) Is there any good reason why it was not advanced before?

In the earlier case of *R v Secretary of State for the Home Department, ex p Onibiyo* [1996] QB 768, it was held that where there is evidence of a relevant and substantial change in circumstances, or where new evidence is advanced which could not reasonably have been advanced earlier, an obligation arises to entertain the newly made claim whatever the grounds for rejection of the previous one, unless:

(i) the new evidence is not intrinsically credible (or credible on the face of it);

(ii) it is not capable, even if accepted, of producing a different outcome: is there in other words a real issue to be determined?

Onibiyo formulated the 'acid test', namely whether, comparing the new claim with one previously rejected and excluding material on which the claimant could reasonably be expected to rely in the earlier claim, the new claim was sufficiently different from the earlier claim to admit a realistic prospect that a favourable view could be taken of the new claim. This test was refined in *Ravichandran v Secretary of State for the Home Department* [1996] Imm AR 97, CA, to the extent that a later claim may be a fresh claim if it is supported by convincing fresh evidence of the same persecution said to be feared in the earlier claim. An intensification of the degree of persecution from the same source is capable of giving rise to a fresh claim. The words 'realistic prospect' have been interpreted as meaning that a favourable view could be taken of the new claim, and that it would probably have an important influence on the result of the case, though need not be incontrovertible.

The Rules and case law are equally applicable to human rights claims. In the recent case of *R (on the application of Ratnam) v Secretary of State for the Home Department* [2003] EWHC 398 (Admin) it was held that where a fresh human rights claim was made based on material new to that previously put forward, the general procedure in respect of fresh claims for asylum contained in rule 346 of the Immigration Rules applied.

Ancillary decisions

In addition to substantive decisions, judicial review can also be used to challenge decisions which are ancillary to the asylum or human rights claim itself, for example a failure to conduct an asylum interview in accordance with the Home Office Protocol leading to prejudice, see for example: *R (on the application of Yaseetharan) v Secretary of State for the Home Department* [2003] Imm AR 62. Also potentially open to judicial review would be the decision of the Secretary of State to set removal directions to a country other than that of which the appellant is a national or habitual resident. In *Zeqaj* [2003] INLR 109, the Court of Appeal reversed the starred decision of the Tribunal and held that a challenge to removal directions other than on the basis that removal would be a breach of the Refugee Convention or the ECHR would have to be by way of judicial review.

Detention and habeas corpus

Judicial review can be used to challenge the Secretary of State's decision to detain an individual where there is no right to apply for bail, or where bail applications have been unsuccessful. As well as judicial review of decisions to detain or to refuse bail, the High Court also has the jurisdiction to grant a 'writ of habeas corpus'. The two remedies are legally distinct:

- Habeas corpus is applied for on the ground that there is no power to detain.
- Judicial review is directed towards the lawfulness, fairness, reasonableness or proportionality of the decision to detain.

The above distinction may not matter greatly in practical terms, as both applications can and should be made in the same High Court proceedings: *Abdul Raheen Sheikh* (CA) (C/2000/2847).

Failure to apply policy consistently

In *R v Secretary of State for the Home Department, ex p Abdi* [1996] 1 WLR 298, HL, it was stated in relation to a Somali family reunion case that the Secretary of State must have regard to, properly take into account and give effect to its own policy. If this is not done, the case will have to go back to the Secretary of State for reconsideration in light of the relevant policy.

Unexpected removals and injunctions

While the Secretary of State is entitled to remove failed asylum applicants who have no rights of appeal left in the United Kingdom, the terms of enforcing removal are often random and sudden. There are two situations that could give rise to a potential claim for judicial review of a decision to effect removal without prior notice:

- The Secretary of State has acted too hastily in seeking to remove, in that the individual concerned still has an outstanding application or appeal.
- Such delay has elapsed between the dismissal of the original claim or appeal and the removal itself that there has been a change of circumstances entitling the individual to make a fresh asylum or human rights claim or other application, but due to the lack of notice of removal this could not be done.

Unfortunately, in such cases there is often very little time for representatives to take proper instructions and to draft a fully argued claim for judicial review before the claimant is removed from the United Kingdom altogether. However, if the representative is of the opinion that it is arguable that removal would be unlawful on one or more of the judicial review grounds (including proportionality) then the representative should make urgent representations to the Immigration Service. In the first instance there should be a request for the removal directions to be stayed for a minimum period of three working days in order to lodge a judicial review application, which often tends to be granted.

If the Home Office refuses to stay the removal directions, the representative will have to apply to the High Court for a Prohibitory injunction preventing removal. In an emergency such applications can be made out of hours to the Duty High Court judge by telephoning the Royal Courts of Justice at any time.

Even if the Secretary of State has removed the claimant, this does not in principle prevent an application for judicial review if there are grounds to show that the removal was unlawful.

CHAPTER 9

The Court of Appeal, House of Lords and the European Court

In this chapter we shall consider in outline only, appeals to:

- The Court of Appeal
- The House of Lords
- The European Court of Human Rights.

THE COURT OF APPEAL (CIVIL DIVISION)

Jurisdiction

There is a right of appeal to the Court of Appeal (Civil Division) from:

(i) a final decision (as opposed to a remittal) of the Tribunal, unless the appeal before an adjudicator was heard in Scotland, in which case the application for leave should be made to the Court of Session (*Gardi v Secretary of State for the Home Department (No.2)* [2002] EWCA Civ 1560, [2002] All ER (D) 306 (Oct));

(ii) a decision of the High Court on a full judicial review;

(iii) a refusal by the High Court to grant permission to apply for judicial review.

It should be noted that in the first two situations above, there is a requirement to first seek the permission of the court below.

Procedure

The relevant provisions are contained in Part 52 of the Civil Procedure Rules and its accompanying Practice Direction. An application to appeal to the Court of Appeal must be made within 14 days of deemed notification of the Tribunal's decision to refuse leave to appeal; within 14 days of the High Court's decision on full judicial review; within 7 days of a refusal of permission to apply for judicial review.

The application must be made on form N161 (the appellant's notice). The form and notes for guidance are available in hard copy from the Civil Appeals Office at the Royal Courts of Justice. They are also on the Court Service website (www.courtservice.gov.uk) and can be downloaded in PDF format and completed on a PC using Acrobat Reader.

As well as the appellant's notice and attached grounds of appeal, a bundle of supporting documentation should be included in the application. We suggest that it should be compiled using similar sections as for a Tribunal or judicial review bundle:

A. *Previous proceedings and decisions* – this should include copies of the previous Home Office decisions, grounds of appeal and determinations etc. It should now also include a copy of either the decision of the Tribunal to refuse permission to appeal to the Court of Appeal or the decision of the High Court. In the case of a refusal of permission to apply for judicial review after an oral hearing, the transcript will usually have to be specifically ordered from Smith Bernal. It will also be helpful to include the skeleton arguments relied on before the Tribunal or the High Court.

B. *Evidence specific to case* – SEFs, interview records, representations, witness statements, documentary evidence, medical reports, expert evidence etc.

C. *Objective evidence* – for example country reports, generic reports, newspaper articles etc.

Two copies of the notice, grounds of appeal and bundle must be lodged with the Civil Appeals Office and one copy for each defendant or interested party. Where the decision under appeal is that of the Tribunal, they should also be served with a copy.

The application will be considered in the first instance on paper by a single Lord Justice. If permission is granted, the case will be listed for a full hearing usually before three Lords Justices. If permission is refused, it can be renewed at an oral hearing before one or two Lords Justices.

Role of the Court of Appeal

The Court of Appeal is *generally* concerned with questions of law rather than evidence. The Court has held that where an expert tribunal, such as the Immigration Appeal Tribunal, has considered an appeal and has produced a careful, structured and reasonable decision, there will rarely be grounds for a further appeal: *Tecle* [2002] EWCA Civ 1358.

That said, in asylum and human rights cases the line between law and fact can often be very blurred. The Court of Appeal has shown itself to be willing in certain cases to examine allegations that: expert evidence was not properly considered by the Tribunal (*S* [2002] INLR 416); positive credibility findings should not have been overturned by the Tribunal (*Oleed* [2003] INLR 179); or that the conclusion of an adjudicator that torture was not for a Convention reason was flawed (*R (on the application of Sivakumar) v Immigration Appeal Tribunal* [2001] EWCA Civ 1196, [2001] All ER (D) 322).

Consideration of fresh evidence

The Court of Appeal will generally not admit fresh evidence without good explanation. However, it has also recognised that it would be difficult to give claims involving fundamental rights the anxious scrutiny they require if relevant evidence is shut out on a purely technical basis. For example, the Court in *Haile v Immigration Appeal Tribunal* [2001] EWCA Civ 663, [2001] All ER (D) 54 (May), decided that although the evidence in question could and should have been adduced in the court below, the wider interests of justice required the fresh evidence to be admitted. In *A* [2003] EWCA Civ 175 the Court took the view that the fresh evidence was in fact so compelling that the appeal should be allowed under Article 3 of the ECHR without it being remitted back to the Tribunal for reconsideration.

In *Habibullah Khan* [2003] EWCA Civ 530 the Court was faced with clearly relevant and apparently credible fresh evidence and in the particular circumstances of the case stated:

> 'In my judgment this court must take account of this material. I am personally untroubled as to the precise jurisprudential

basis upon which we should do so. It is *plainly just* that this information should be considered . . .

. . .

Whatever the precise limits of this court's power to admit new evidence in such cases as this, I have no doubt that we should do so where there is material which appears to show that the factual basis on which the Tribunal proceeded was, through no fault of its own, simply wrong.'

(Emphasis added.)

Representation by Queen's Counsel

Where a case involves particularly complex issues, or ones that will affect many other cases, the representative should seriously consider instructing a Queen's Counsel. Examples would be where the decision of the Tribunal under appeal is starred or the High Court judge himself granted permission to appeal.

Powers of Court

The Court of Appeal possesses all the powers of the lower court and can uphold, vary or set aside and replace the decision being appealed. In rare cases the Court of Appeal will grant permission to appeal its judgement to the House of Lords.

THE HOUSE OF LORDS

The Judicial Committee of the House of Lords is the highest court in the United Kingdom. It only adjudicates on questions of law of general public importance. Permission to appeal is required from the Court of Appeal. If this is not granted, a petition has to be drafted and lodged with the House of Lords.

The petition is referred to an Appeals Committee of three Law Lords, who will then make a provisional decision as to whether to grant leave. If minded to grant leave, the Appeals Committee will then invite written objections from the other parties, before making a final decision to grant or refuse leave. Where the Appeals Committee is unable to make a unanimous decision on whether to grant leave, it can order that there be an oral hearing. Where leave is refused, there is no further right of appeal and no requirement to give reasons.

If leave to appeal is granted, the case is set down for hearing before an Appellate Committee of five Law Lords.

Further information on procedure is contained in the Practice Directions and Standing Orders Applicable to Civil Appeals (November 2002), which are available from the Judicial Office of the House of Lords.

THE EUROPEAN COURT OF HUMAN RIGHTS

With the advent of the Human Rights Act 1998, it was thought that there would be less need for individuals in the United Kingdom to make applications to the European Court of Human Rights in Strasbourg. The purpose of the Act was after all to 'better protect' human rights in the United Kingdom by ensuring that the Convention rights could be expressly raised before the domestic courts.

However, there will still be cases where a representative is firmly of the view that a particular decision of the Secretary of State or a decision of the Tribunal or Court of Appeal does not recognise the human rights consequences to their client of removal or deportation. Such cases may justify an application to the European Court itself.

An application is made in the first instance in the form of a letter of introduction addressed to the Registrar of the European Court in Strasbourg, France. The letter must:

- identify the applicant;
- summarise the facts pertaining to the complaint(s);
- outline any domestic proceedings which have been brought and the decision(s);
- set out the Articles which are said to have been breached.

As there is a strict six-month time limit (from the date of the final event or decision giving rise to the complaint) for making an application to the European Court, the representative should draft the letter in wide terms so as to ensure that all arguable issues are raised within time. The initial letter of introduction will generally be taken to 'stop the clock' for the purposes of the time limit. The Registrar will reply to the letter and enclose the formal application form, which should be completed as carefully and comprehensively as possible and without delay.

The above should be taken as a starting-point and no more. Representatives who think they may have a case suitable for the European Court of Human Rights must consult one of the many practitioner texts that are now available before embarking on 'the road to Strasbourg'!

Appendices

Nationality, Immigration and Asylum Act 2002

2002 CHAPTER 41

An Act to make provision about nationality, immigration and asylum; to create offences in connection with international traffic in prostitution; to make provision about international projects connected with migration; and for connected purposes.

[7th November 2002]

BE IT ENACTED by the Queen's most Excellent Majesty, by and with the advice and consent of the Lords Spiritual and Temporal, and Commons, in this present Parliament assembled, and by the authority of the same, as follows:—

Part 1
Nationality

1 Naturalisation: knowledge of language and society

(1) The following shall be inserted after the word "and" after paragraph 1(1)(c) of Schedule 1 to the British Nationality Act 1981 (c 61) (requirements for naturalisation)—

"(ca) that he has sufficient knowledge about life in the United Kingdom; and".

(2) In paragraph 2(e) of that Schedule (waiver)—

(a) for "the requirement specified in paragraph 1(1)(c)" there shall be substituted "either or both of the requirements specified in paragraph 1(1)(c) and (ca)", and

(b) for "expect him to fulfil it" there shall be substituted "expect him to fulfil that requirement or those requirements".

(3) The following shall be inserted after section 41(1)(b) of that Act (regulations)—

"(ba) for determining whether a person has sufficient knowledge of a language for the purpose of an application for naturalisation;

(bb) for determining whether a person has sufficient knowledge about life in the United Kingdom for the purpose of an application for naturalisation;".

(4) The following shall be inserted after section 41(1) of that Act—

"(1A) Regulations under subsection (1)(ba) or (bb) may, in particular—

(a) make provision by reference to possession of a specified qualification;

(b) make provision by reference to possession of a qualification of a specified kind;

(c) make provision by reference to attendance on a specified course;

(d) make provision by reference to attendance on a course of a specified kind;

(e) make provision by reference to a specified level of achievement;

(f) enable a person designated by the Secretary of State to determine sufficiency of knowledge in specified circumstances;

(g) enable the Secretary of State to accept a qualification of a specified kind as evidence of sufficient knowledge of a language."

2 Naturalisation: spouse of citizen

(1) Paragraphs 3 and 4 of Schedule 1 to the British Nationality Act 1981 (c 61) (requirements for naturalisation as British citizen: spouse of citizen) shall be amended as follows—

(a) in paragraph 3(e) for "requirement specified in paragraph 1(1)(b)" substitute "requirements specified in paragraph 1(1)(b), (c) and (ca)", and

(b) in paragraph 4(c) omit "and (e)".

(2) Paragraphs 7 and 8 of that Schedule (requirements for naturalisation as British overseas territories citizen: spouse of citizen) shall be amended as follows—

(a) in paragraph 7(e) for "requirement specified in paragraph 5(1)(b)" substitute "requirements specified in paragraph 5(1)(b) and (c)", and

(b) in paragraph 8(c) omit "and (e)".

3 Citizenship ceremony, oath and pledge

Schedule 1 (which makes provision about citizenship ceremonies, oaths and pledges) shall have effect.

4 Deprivation of citizenship

(1) The following shall be substituted for section 40 of the British Nationality Act 1981 (deprivation of citizenship)—

"40 Deprivation of citizenship

(1) In this section a reference to a person's "citizenship status" is a reference to his status as—

(a) a British citizen,

(b) a British overseas territories citizen,

(c) a British Overseas citizen,

(d) a British National (Overseas),

(e) a British protected person, or

(f) a British subject.

(2) The Secretary of State may by order deprive a person of a citizenship status if the Secretary of State is satisfied that the person has done anything seriously prejudicial to the vital interests of—

(a) the United Kingdom, or

(b) a British overseas territory.

(3) The Secretary of State may by order deprive a person of a citizenship status which results from his registration or naturalisation if the Secretary of State is satisfied that the registration or naturalisation was obtained by means of—

(a) fraud,

(b) false representation, or

(c) concealment of a material fact.

(4) The Secretary of State may not make an order under subsection (2) if he is satisfied that the order would make a person stateless.

(5) Before making an order under this section in respect of a person the Secretary of State must give the person written notice specifying—

(a) that the Secretary of State has decided to make an order,

(b) the reasons for the order, and

(c) the person's right of appeal under section 40A(1) or under section 2B of the Special Immigration Appeals Commission Act 1997 (c 68).

(6) Where a person acquired a citizenship status by the operation of a law which applied to him because of his registration or naturalisation under an enactment having effect before commencement, the Secretary of State may by order deprive the person of the citizenship status if the Secretary of State is satisfied that the registration or naturalisation was obtained by means of—

(a) fraud,

(b) false representation, or

(c) concealment of a material fact.

40A Deprivation of citizenship: appeal

(1) A person who is given notice under section 40(5) of a decision to make an order in respect of him under section 40 may appeal against the decision to an adjudicator appointed under section 81 of the Nationality, Immigration and Asylum Act 2002 (immigration appeal).

(2) Subsection (1) shall not apply to a decision if the Secretary of State certifies that it was taken wholly or partly in reliance on information which in his opinion should not be made public—

(a) in the interests of national security,

(b) in the interests of the relationship between the United Kingdom and another country, or

(c) otherwise in the public interest.

(3) A party to an appeal to an adjudicator under subsection (1) may, with the permission of the Immigration Appeal Tribunal, appeal to the Tribunal against the adjudicator's determination on a point of law.

(4) A party to an appeal to the Immigration Appeal Tribunal under subsection (3) may bring a further appeal on a point of law—

(a) where the decision of the adjudicator was made in Scotland, to the Court of Session, or
(b) in any other case, to the Court of Appeal.

(5) An appeal under subsection (4) may be brought only with the permission of—
(a) the Tribunal, or
(b) if the Tribunal refuses permission, the court referred to in subsection (4)(a) or (b).

(6) An order under section 40 may not be made in respect of a person while an appeal under this section or section 2B of the Special Immigration Appeals Commission Act 1997 (c 68)—
(a) has been instituted and has not yet been finally determined, withdrawn or abandoned, or
(b) could be brought (ignoring any possibility of an appeal out of time with permission).

(7) Rules under section 106 of the Nationality, Immigration and Asylum Act 2002 (immigration appeal: rules) may make provision about an appeal under this section.

(8) Directions under section 107 of that Act (practice directions) may make provision about an appeal under this section."

(2) The following shall be inserted before section 3 of the Special Immigration Appeals Commission Act 1997 (jurisdiction: bail)—

"2B A person may appeal to the Special Immigration Appeals Commission against a decision to make an order under section 40 of the British Nationality Act 1981 (c 61) (deprivation of citizenship) if he is not entitled to appeal under section 40A(1) of that Act because of a certificate under section 40A(2)."

(3) In section 5(1)(a) and (b) and (2) of that Act (procedure) after "section 2" there shall be inserted "or 2B".

(4) In exercising a power under section 40 of the British Nationality Act 1981 after the commencement of subsection (1) above the Secretary of State may have regard to anything which—
(a) occurred before commencement, and
(b) he could have relied on (whether on its own or with other matters) in making an order under section 40 before commencement.

5 Resumption of citizenship

In the following provisions of the British Nationality Act 1981 (c 61) the words ", if a woman," shall cease to have effect—
(a) section 10(1) and (2) (registration as British citizen following renunciation of citizenship), and
(b) section 22(1) and (2) (registration as British overseas territories citizen following renunciation of citizenship).

6 Nationality decision: discrimination

(1) Section 19D of the Race Relations Act 1976 (c 74) (discrimination by public authority: permitted cases) shall be amended as follows.

(2) In subsection (1) for "immigration and nationality functions" substitute "immigration functions".
(3) For subsections (4) and (5) substitute—
"(4) In subsection (1) "immigration functions" means functions exercisable by virtue of any of the enactments mentioned in subsection (5).
(5) Those enactments are—
- (a) the Immigration Acts (within the meaning of section 158 of the Nationality, Immigration and Asylum Act 2002) excluding sections 28A to 28K of the Immigration Act 1971 (c 77) so far as they relate to offences under Part III of that Act;
- (b) the Special Immigration Appeals Commission Act 1997 (c 68);
- (c) provision made under section 2(2) of the European Communities Act 1972 (c 68) which relates to immigration or asylum; and
- (d) any provision of Community law which relates to immigration or asylum."

(4) Section 19E of the Race Relations Act 1976 (monitoring of use of section 19D) shall be amended as follows—
- (a) in subsection (3)(a) for "immigration and nationality functions" substitute "immigration functions", and
- (b) omit subsection (7).

(5) In section 71A of that Act (general statutory duty: special cases)—
- (a) in subsection (1) the words "(within the meaning of section 19D(1))" shall be omitted, and
- (b) the following shall be inserted after subsection (1)—

"(1A) In subsection (1) "immigration and nationality functions" means functions exercisable by virtue of—
- (a) the Immigration Acts (within the meaning of section 158 of the Nationality, Immigration and Asylum Act 2002) excluding sections 28A to 28K of the Immigration Act 1971 so far as they relate to offences under Part III of that Act;
- (b) the British Nationality Act 1981;
- (c) the British Nationality (Falkland Islands) Act 1983 (c 6);
- (d) the British Nationality (Hong Kong) Act 1990 (c 34);
- (e) the Hong Kong (War Wives and Widows) Act 1996 (c 41);
- (f) the British Nationality (Hong Kong) Act 1997 (c 20);
- (g) the Special Immigration Appeals Commission Act 1997 (c 68);
- (h) provision made under section 2(2) of the European Communities Act 1972 (c 68) which relates to the subject matter of an enactment within any of paragraphs (a) to (g); or
- (i) any provision of Community law which relates to the subject matter of an enactment within any of those paragraphs."

7 Nationality decision: reasons and review

(1) Section 44(2) and (3) of the British Nationality Act 1981 (c 61) (no requirement to give reasons for discretionary decision, and no right of appeal) shall cease to have effect.

(2) Section 1(5) of the British Nationality (Hong Kong) Act 1990 (c 34) (no requirement to give reasons for discretionary decision, and no right of appeal) shall cease to have effect.

8 Citizenship: registration

In paragraph 3(1)(b) of Schedule 2 to the British Nationality Act 1981 (application by person born in United Kingdom or overseas territory for registration as citizen: age requirement) the words "had attained the age of ten but" shall cease to have effect.

9 Legitimacy of child

(1) The following shall be substituted for section 50(9) of the British Nationality Act 1981 (interpretation: child)—

"(9) For the purposes of this Act a child's mother is the woman who gives birth to the child.

(9A) For the purposes of this Act a child's father is—

(a) the husband, at the time of the child's birth, of the woman who gives birth to the child, or

(b) where a person is treated as the father of the child under section 28 of the Human Fertilisation and Embryology Act 1990 (c 37) (father), that person, or

(c) where neither paragraph (a) nor paragraph (b) applies, any person who satisfies prescribed requirements as to proof of paternity.

(9B) In subsection (9A)(c) "prescribed" means prescribed by regulations of the Secretary of State; and the regulations—

(a) may confer a function (which may be a discretionary function) on the Secretary of State or another person,

(b) may make provision which applies generally or only in specified circumstances,

(c) may make different provision for different circumstances,

(d) must be made by statutory instrument, and

(e) shall be subject to annulment in pursuance of a resolution of either House of Parliament.

(9C) The expressions "parent", "child" and "descended" shall be construed in accordance with subsections (9) and (9A)."

(2) In section 3(6) of that Act (registration of minor as British citizen)—

(a) after paragraph (a) insert "and",

(b) the word "and" after paragraph (b) shall cease to have effect, and

(c) paragraph (c) (illegitimate child) shall cease to have effect.

(3) In section 17(6) of that Act (registration of minor as British overseas territories citizen)—

(a) after paragraph (a) insert "and",

(b) the word "and" after paragraph (b) shall cease to have effect, and

(c) paragraph (c) (illegitimate child) shall cease to have effect.

(4) Section 47 of that Act (legitimated children) shall cease to have effect.

(5) In Schedule 2 to that Act (persons otherwise stateless)—

(a) in paragraph 1(1)(b) (person born in United Kingdom), the words "he is born legitimate and" shall cease to have effect, and

(b) in paragraph 2(1)(b) (person born in British overseas territory), the words "he is born legitimate and" shall cease to have effect.

10 Right of abode: certificate of entitlement

(1) The Secretary of State may by regulations make provision for the issue to a person of a certificate that he has the right of abode in the United Kingdom.

(2) The regulations may, in particular—

(a) specify to whom an application must be made;

(b) specify the place (which may be outside the United Kingdom) to which an application must be sent;

(c) provide that an application must be made in a specified form;

(d) provide that an application must be accompanied by specified documents;

(e) require the payment of a fee on the making of an application;

(f) specify the consequences of failure to comply with a requirement under any of paragraphs (a) to (e) above;

(g) provide for a certificate to cease to have effect after a period of time specified in or determined in accordance with the regulations;

(h) make provision about the revocation of a certificate.

(3) The regulations may—

(a) make provision which applies generally or only in specified cases or circumstances;

(b) make different provision for different purposes;

(c) include consequential, incidental or transitional provision.

(4) The regulations—

(a) must be made by statutory instrument, and

(b) shall be subject to annulment in pursuance of a resolution of either House of Parliament.

(5) The Immigration Act 1971 (c 77) shall be amended as follows—

(a) in section 3(9)(b) (proof of entitlement to right of abode) the words "issued by or on behalf of the Government of the United Kingdom certifying that he has such a right of abode" shall cease to have effect, and

(b) in section 33(1) for the definition of "certificate of entitlement" substitute—

""certificate of entitlement" means a certificate under section 10 of the Nationality, Immigration and Asylum Act 2002 that a person has the right of abode in the United Kingdom;".

(6) Regulations under this section may, in particular, include provision saving, with or without modification, the effect of a certificate which—

(a) is issued before the regulations come into force, and

(b) is a certificate of entitlement for the purposes of sections 3(9) and 33(1) of the Immigration Act 1971 as those sections have effect before the commencement of subsection (5) above.

11 Unlawful presence in United Kingdom

(1) This section applies for the construction of a reference to being in the United Kingdom "in breach of the immigration laws" in section 4(2) or (4) or 50(5) of, or Schedule 1 to, the British Nationality Act 1981 (c 61).

(2) A person is in the United Kingdom in breach of the immigration laws if (and only if) he—

- (a) is in the United Kingdom,
- (b) does not have the right of abode in the United Kingdom within the meaning of section 2 of the Immigration Act 1971,
- (c) does not have leave to enter or remain in the United Kingdom (whether or not he previously had leave),
- (d) is not a qualified person within the meaning of the Immigration (European Economic Area) Regulations 2000 (SI 2000/2326) (person entitled to reside in United Kingdom without leave) (whether or not he was previously a qualified person),
- (e) is not a family member of a qualified person within the meaning of those regulations (whether or not he was previously a family member of a qualified person),
- (f) is not entitled to enter and remain in the United Kingdom by virtue of section 8(1) of the Immigration Act 1971 (crew) (whether or not he was previously entitled), and
- (g) does not have the benefit of an exemption under section 8(2) to (4) of that Act (diplomats, soldiers and other special cases) (whether or not he previously had the benefit of an exemption).

(3) Section 11(1) of the Immigration Act 1971 (person deemed not to be in United Kingdom before disembarkation, while in controlled area or while under immigration control) shall apply for the purposes of this section as it applies for the purposes of that Act.

(4) This section shall be treated as always having had effect except in relation to a person who on the commencement of this section is, or has been at any time since he last entered the United Kingdom—

- (a) a qualified person within the meaning of the regulations referred to in subsection (2)(d), or
- (b) a family member of a qualified person within the meaning of those regulations.

(5) This section is without prejudice to the generality of—

- (a) a reference to being in a place outside the United Kingdom in breach of immigration laws, and
- (b) a reference in a provision other than one specified in subsection (1) to being in the United Kingdom in breach of immigration laws.

12 British citizenship: registration of certain persons without other citizenship

(1) The following shall be inserted after section 4A of the British Nationality Act 1981 (c 61) (registration as British citizen)—

"4B Acquisition by registration: certain persons without other citizenship

(1) This section applies to a person who has the status of—

(a) British Overseas citizen,

(b) British subject under this Act, or

(c) British protected person.

(2) A person to whom this section applies shall be entitled to be registered as a British citizen if—

(a) he applies for registration under this section,

(b) the Secretary of State is satisfied that the person does not have, apart from the status mentioned in subsection (1), any citizenship or nationality, and

(c) the Secretary of State is satisfied that the person has not after 4th July 2002 renounced, voluntarily relinquished or lost through action or inaction any citizenship or nationality."

(2) In section 14(1) of that Act (meaning of British citizen "by descent"), in paragraph (d) for "section 5" there shall be substituted "section 4B or 5".

13 British citizenship: registration of certain persons born between 1961 and 1983

(1) The following shall be inserted after section 4B of the British Nationality Act 1981 (registration as British citizen)—

"4C Acquisition by registration: certain persons born between 1961 and 1983

(1) A person is entitled to be registered as a British citizen if—

(a) he applies for registration under this section, and

(b) he satisfies each of the following conditions.

(2) The first condition is that the applicant was born after 7th February 1961 and before 1st January 1983.

(3) The second condition is that the applicant would at some time before 1st January 1983 have become a citizen of the United Kingdom and Colonies by virtue of section 5 of the British Nationality Act 1948 (c 56) if that section had provided for citizenship by descent from a mother in the same terms as it provided for citizenship by descent from a father.

(4) The third condition is that immediately before 1st January 1983 the applicant would have had the right of abode in the United Kingdom by virtue of section 2 of the Immigration Act 1971 (c 77) had he become a citizen of the United Kingdom and Colonies as described in subsection (3) above."

(2) In section 14(1) of that Act (meaning of British citizen "by descent"), in paragraph (d) after the words "section 4B" (as substituted by section 12(2) of this Act) there shall be inserted ", 4C".

14 Hong Kong

A person may not be registered as a British overseas territories citizen under a provision of the British Nationality Act 1981 (c 61) by virtue of a connection with Hong Kong.

15 Repeal of spent provisions
Schedule 2 (which repeals spent provisions) shall have effect.

Part 2
Accommodation Centres

Establishment

16 Establishment of centres

(1) The Secretary of State may arrange for the provision of premises for the accommodation of persons in accordance with this Part.

(2) A set of premises provided under this section is referred to in this Act as an "accommodation centre".

(3) The Secretary of State may arrange for—

- (a) the provision of facilities at or near an accommodation centre for sittings of adjudicators appointed for the purpose of Part 5 in accordance with a determination of the Lord Chancellor under paragraph 2 of Schedule 4;
- (b) the provision of facilities at an accommodation centre for the taking of steps in connection with the determination of claims for asylum (within the meaning of section 18(3)).

Use of centres

17 Support for destitute asylum-seeker

(1) The Secretary of State may arrange for the provision of accommodation for a person in an accommodation centre if—

- (a) the person is an asylum-seeker or the dependant of an asylum-seeker, and
- (b) the Secretary of State thinks that the person is destitute or is likely to become destitute within a prescribed period.

(2) The Secretary of State may make regulations about procedure to be followed in respect of the provision of accommodation under this section.

(3) The regulations may, in particular, make provision—

- (a) specifying procedure to be followed in applying for accommodation in an accommodation centre;
- (b) providing for an application to be combined with an application under or in respect of another enactment;
- (c) requiring an applicant to provide information;
- (d) specifying circumstances in which an application may not be considered (which provision may, in particular, provide for an application not to be considered where the Secretary of State is not satisfied that the information provided is complete or accurate or that the applicant is co-operating with enquiries under paragraph (e));
- (e) about the making of enquiries by the Secretary of State;
- (f) requiring a person to notify the Secretary of State of a change in circumstances.

(4) Sections 18 to 20 define the following expressions for the purpose of this Part—

(a) asylum-seeker,
(b) dependant, and
(c) destitute.

18 Asylum-seeker: definition

(1) For the purposes of this Part a person is an "asylum-seeker" if—

(a) he is at least 18 years old,
(b) he is in the United Kingdom,
(c) a claim for asylum has been made by him at a place designated by the Secretary of State,
(d) the Secretary of State has recorded the claim, and
(e) the claim has not been determined.

(2) A person shall continue to be treated as an asylum-seeker despite subsection (1)(e) while—

(a) his household includes a dependent child who is under 18, and
(b) he does not have leave to enter or remain in the United Kingdom.

(3) A claim for asylum is a claim by a person that to remove him from or require him to leave the United Kingdom would be contrary to the United Kingdom's obligations under—

(a) the Convention relating to the Status of Refugees done at Geneva on 28th July 1951 and its Protocol, or
(b) Article 3 of the Convention for the Protection of Human Rights and Fundamental Freedoms agreed by the Council of Europe at Rome on 4th November 1950.

19 Destitution: definition

(1) Where a person has dependants, he and his dependants are destitute for the purpose of this Part if they do not have and cannot obtain both—

(a) adequate accommodation, and
(b) food and other essential items.

(2) Where a person does not have dependants, he is destitute for the purpose of this Part if he does not have and cannot obtain both—

(a) adequate accommodation, and
(b) food and other essential items.

(3) In determining whether accommodation is adequate for the purposes of subsection (1) or (2) the Secretary of State must have regard to any matter prescribed for the purposes of this subsection.

(4) In determining whether accommodation is adequate for the purposes of subsection (1) or (2) the Secretary of State may not have regard to—

(a) whether a person has an enforceable right to occupy accommodation,
(b) whether a person shares all or part of accommodation,
(c) whether accommodation is temporary or permanent,
(d) the location of accommodation, or
(e) any other matter prescribed for the purposes of this subsection.

(5) The Secretary of State may by regulations specify items which are or are not to be treated as essential items for the purposes of subsections (1) and (2).

(6) The Secretary of State may by regulations—

(a) provide that a person is not to be treated as destitute for the purposes of this Part in specified circumstances;

(b) enable or require the Secretary of State in deciding whether a person is destitute to have regard to income which he or a dependant of his might reasonably be expected to have;

(c) enable or require the Secretary of State in deciding whether a person is destitute to have regard to support which is or might reasonably be expected to be available to the person or a dependant of his;

(d) enable or require the Secretary of State in deciding whether a person is destitute to have regard to assets of a prescribed kind which he or a dependant of his has or might reasonably be expected to have;

(e) make provision as to the valuation of assets.

20 Dependant: definition

For the purposes of this Part a person is a "dependant" of an asylum-seeker if (and only if) that person—

(a) is in the United Kingdom, and

(b) is within a prescribed class.

21 Sections 17 to 20: supplementary

(1) This section applies for the purposes of sections 17 to 20.

(2) The Secretary of State may inquire into and decide a person's age.

(3) A claim for asylum shall be treated as determined at the end of such period as may be prescribed beginning with—

(a) the date on which the Secretary of State notifies the claimant of his decision on the claim, or

(b) if the claimant appeals against the Secretary of State's decision, the date on which the appeal is disposed of.

(4) A notice under subsection (3)(a)—

(a) must be in writing, and

(b) if sent by first class post to the claimant's last known address or to the claimant's representative, shall be treated as being received by the claimant on the second day after the day of posting.

(5) An appeal is disposed of when it is no longer pending for the purpose of—

(a) Part 5 of this Act, or

(b) the Special Immigration Appeals Commission Act 1997 (c 68).

22 Immigration and Asylum Act 1999, s 95

The Secretary of State may provide support under section 95 of the Immigration and Asylum Act 1999 (c 33) (destitute asylum-seeker) by arranging for the provision of accommodation in an accommodation centre.

23 Person subject to United Kingdom entrance control

(1) A residence restriction may include a requirement to reside at an accommodation centre.

(2) In subsection (1) "residence restriction" means a restriction imposed under—

(a) paragraph 21 of Schedule 2 to the Immigration Act 1971 (c 77) (temporary admission or release from detention), or

(b) paragraph 2(5) of Schedule 3 to that Act (control pending deportation).

(3) Where a person is required to reside in an accommodation centre by virtue of subsection (1) the Secretary of State must arrange for the provision of accommodation for the person in an accommodation centre.

(4) But if the person is required to leave an accommodation centre by virtue of section 26 or 30 he shall be treated as having broken the residence restriction referred to in subsection (1).

(5) The Secretary of State may provide support under section 4 of the Immigration and Asylum Act 1999 (persons subject to entrance control) (including that section as amended by section 49 of this Act) by arranging for the provision of accommodation in an accommodation centre.

24 Provisional assistance

(1) If the Secretary of State thinks that a person may be eligible for the provision of accommodation in an accommodation centre under section 17, he may arrange for the provision for the person, pending a decision about eligibility, of—

(a) accommodation in an accommodation centre, or

(b) other support or assistance (of any kind).

(2) Section 99 of the Immigration and Asylum Act 1999 (c 33) (provision of support by local authority) shall have effect in relation to the provision of support for persons under subsection (1) above as it has effect in relation to the provision of support for asylum-seekers under sections 95 and 98 of that Act.

25 Length of stay

(1) The Secretary of State may not arrange for the provision of accommodation for a person in an accommodation centre if he has been a resident of an accommodation centre for a continuous period of six months.

(2) But—

(a) subsection (1) may be disapplied in respect of a person, generally or to a specified extent, by agreement between the Secretary of State and the person, and

(b) if the Secretary of State thinks it appropriate in relation to a person because of the circumstances of his case, the Secretary of State may direct that subsection (1) shall have effect in relation to the person as if the period specified in that subsection were the period of nine months.

(3) Section 51 is subject to this section.

(4) The Secretary of State may by order amend subsection (1) or (2)(b) so as to substitute a shorter period for a period specified.

26 Withdrawal of support

(1) The Secretary of State may stop providing support for a person under section 17 or 24 if—

(a) the Secretary of State suspects that the person or a dependant of his has committed an offence by virtue of section 35, or

(b) the person or a dependant of his has failed to comply with directions of the Secretary of State as to the time or manner of travel to accommodation provided under section 17 or 24.

(2) The Secretary of State may by regulations specify other circumstances in which he may stop providing support for a person under section 17 or 24.

(3) In determining whether or not to provide a person with support or assistance under section 17 or 24 of this Act or section 4, 95 or 98 of the Immigration and Asylum Act 1999 (asylum-seeker) the Secretary of State may take into account the fact that—

(a) he has withdrawn support from the person by virtue of this section or section 30(4) or (5), or

(b) circumstances exist which would have enabled the Secretary of State to withdraw support from the person by virtue of this section had he been receiving support.

(4) This section is without prejudice to section 103 of the Immigration and Asylum Act 1999 (c 33) (appeal against refusal to support).

Operation of centres

27 Resident of centre

A reference in this Part to a resident of an accommodation centre is a reference to a person for whom accommodation in the centre is provided—

(a) under section 17,

(b) by virtue of section 22,

(c) by virtue of section 23, or

(d) under section 24.

28 Manager of centre

A reference in this Part to the manager of an accommodation centre is a reference to a person who agrees with the Secretary of State to be wholly or partly responsible for the management of the centre.

29 Facilities

(1) The Secretary of State may arrange for the following to be provided to a resident of an accommodation centre—

(a) food and other essential items;

(b) money;

(c) assistance with transport for the purpose of proceedings under the Immigration Acts or in connection with a claim for asylum;

(d) transport to and from the centre;

(e) assistance with expenses incurred in connection with carrying out voluntary work or other activities;
(f) education and training;
(g) facilities relating to health;
(h) facilities for religious observance;
(i) anything which the Secretary of State thinks ought to be provided for the purpose of providing a resident with proper occupation and for the purpose of maintaining good order;
(j) anything which the Secretary of State thinks ought to be provided for a person because of his exceptional circumstances.

(2) The Secretary of State may make regulations specifying the amount or maximum amount of money to be provided under subsection (1)(b).

(3) The Secretary of State may arrange for the provision of facilities in an accommodation centre for the use of a person in providing legal advice to a resident of the centre.

(4) The Secretary of State shall take reasonable steps to ensure that a resident of an accommodation centre has an opportunity to obtain legal advice before any appointment made by an immigration officer or an official of the Secretary of State for the purpose of obtaining information from the resident to be used in determining his claim for asylum.

(5) The Secretary of State may by order amend subsection (1) so as to add a reference to facilities which may be provided.

30 Conditions of residence

(1) The Secretary of State may make regulations about conditions to be observed by residents of an accommodation centre.

(2) Regulations under subsection (1) may, in particular, enable a condition to be imposed in accordance with the regulations by—
(a) the Secretary of State, or
(b) the manager of an accommodation centre.

(3) A condition imposed by virtue of this section may, in particular—
(a) require a person not to be absent from the centre during specified hours without the permission of the Secretary of State or the manager;
(b) require a person to report to an immigration officer or the Secretary of State.

(4) If a resident of an accommodation centre breaches a condition imposed by virtue of this section, the Secretary of State may—
(a) require the resident and any dependant of his to leave the centre;
(b) authorise the manager of the centre to require the resident and any dependant of his to leave the centre.

(5) If a dependant of a resident of an accommodation centre breaches a condition imposed by virtue of this section, the Secretary of State may—
(a) require the resident and any dependant of his to leave the centre;
(b) authorise the manager of the centre to require the resident and any dependant of his to leave the centre.

(6) Regulations under this section must include provision for ensuring that a person subject to a condition is notified of the condition in writing.

(7) A condition imposed by virtue of this section is in addition to any restriction imposed under paragraph 21 of Schedule 2 to the Immigration Act 1971 (c 77) (control of entry to United Kingdom) or under paragraph 2(5) of Schedule 3 to that Act (control pending deportation).
(8) A reference in this Part to a condition of residence is a reference to a condition imposed by virtue of this section.

31 Financial contribution by resident

(1) A condition of residence may, in particular, require a resident of an accommodation centre to make payments to—
- (a) the Secretary of State, or
- (b) the manager of the centre.

(2) The Secretary of State may make regulations enabling him to recover sums representing the whole or part of the value of accommodation and other facilities provided to a resident of an accommodation centre if—
- (a) accommodation is provided for the resident in response to an application by him for support,
- (b) when the application was made the applicant had assets which were not capable of being realised, and
- (c) the assets have become realisable.

(3) In subsection (2) "assets" includes assets outside the United Kingdom.
(4) An amount recoverable by virtue of regulations made under subsection (2) may be recovered—
- (a) as a debt due to the Secretary of State;
- (b) by another prescribed method (which may include the imposition or variation of a residence condition).

32 Tenure

(1) A resident of an accommodation centre shall not be treated as acquiring a tenancy of or other interest in any part of the centre (whether by virtue of an agreement between the resident and another person or otherwise).
(2) Subsection (3) applies where—
- (a) the Secretary of State decides to stop arranging for the provision of accommodation in an accommodation centre for a resident of the centre, or
- (b) a resident of an accommodation centre is required to leave the centre in accordance with section 30.

(3) Where this subsection applies—
- (a) the Secretary of State or the manager of the centre may recover possession of the premises occupied by the resident, and
- (b) the right under paragraph (a) shall be enforceable in accordance with procedure prescribed by regulations made by the Secretary of State.

(4) Any licence which a resident of an accommodation centre has to occupy premises in the centre shall be an excluded licence for the purposes of the Protection from Eviction Act 1977 (c 43).

(5) The following shall be inserted after section 3A(7A) of the Protection from Eviction Act 1977 (disapplication of section 3: Part VI of Immigration and Asylum Act 1999 (c 33))—

"(7B) Section 32 of the Nationality, Immigration and Asylum Act 2002 (accommodation centre: tenure) provides for a resident's licence to occupy an accommodation centre to be an excluded licence."

(6) The following shall be inserted after section 23A(5A) of the Rent (Scotland) Act 1984 (c 58) (excluded tenancies and occupancy rights)—

"(5B) Nothing in section 23 of this Act applies to a resident's occupancy of an accommodation centre provided under section 16 or 24(1)(b) of the Nationality, Immigration and Asylum Act 2002 ("resident" being construed in accordance with section 27 of that Act)."

(7) In this section a reference to an accommodation centre includes a reference to premises in which accommodation is provided under section 24(1)(b).

33 Advisory Groups

(1) The Secretary of State shall appoint a group (to be known as an Accommodation Centre Advisory Group) for each accommodation centre.

(2) The Secretary of State may by regulations—

- (a) confer functions on Advisory Groups;
- (b) make provision about the constitution and proceedings of Advisory Groups.

(3) Regulations under subsection (2)(a) must, in particular, provide for members of an accommodation centre's Advisory Group—

- (a) to visit the centre;
- (b) to hear complaints made by residents of the centre;
- (c) to report to the Secretary of State.

(4) The manager of an accommodation centre must permit a member of the centre's Advisory Group on request—

- (a) to visit the centre at any time;
- (b) to visit any resident of the centre at any time, provided that the resident consents.

(5) A member of an Advisory Group shall hold and vacate office in accordance with the terms of his appointment (which may include provision about retirement, resignation or dismissal).

(6) The Secretary of State may—

- (a) defray expenses of members of an Advisory Group;
- (b) make facilities available to members of an Advisory Group.

General

34 The Monitor of Accommodation Centres

(1) The Secretary of State shall appoint a person as Monitor of Accommodation Centres.

(2) The Monitor shall monitor the operation of this Part of this Act and shall, in particular, consider—

- (a) the quality and effectiveness of accommodation and other facilities provided in accommodation centres,

(b) the nature and enforcement of conditions of residence,
(c) the treatment of residents, and
(d) whether, in the case of any accommodation centre, its location prevents a need of its residents from being met.

(3) In exercising his functions the Monitor shall consult—
(a) the Secretary of State, and
(b) such other persons as he considers appropriate.

(4) The Monitor shall report to the Secretary of State about the matters considered by the Monitor in the course of the exercise of his functions—
(a) at least once in each calendar year, and
(b) on such occasions as the Secretary of State may request.

(5) Where the Secretary of State receives a report under subsection (4)(a) he shall lay a copy before Parliament as soon as is reasonably practicable.

(6) The Monitor shall hold and vacate office in accordance with the terms of his appointment (which may include provision about retirement, resignation or dismissal).

(7) The Secretary of State may—
(a) pay fees and allowances to the Monitor;
(b) defray expenses of the Monitor;
(c) make staff and other facilities available to the Monitor.

(8) The Secretary of State may appoint more than one person to act jointly as Monitor (in which case they shall divide or share functions in accordance with the terms of their appointment and, subject to that, by agreement between them).

(9) A person who is employed within a government department may not be appointed as Monitor of Accommodation Centres.

35 Ancillary provisions

(1) The following provisions of the Immigration and Asylum Act 1999 (c 33) shall apply for the purposes of this Part as they apply for the purposes of Part VI of that Act (support for asylum-seeker)—
(a) section 105 (false representation),
(b) section 106 (dishonest representation),
(c) section 107 (delay or obstruction),
(d) section 108 (failure of sponsor to maintain),
(e) section 109 (offence committed by body),
(f) section 112 (recovery of expenditure),
(g) section 113 (recovery of expenditure from sponsor),
(h) section 124 (corporation sole), and
(i) section 127 (redirection of post).

(2) In the application of section 112 a reference to something done under section 95 or 98 of that Act shall be treated as a reference to something done under section 17 or 24 of this Act.

(3) In the application of section 113 a reference to section 95 of that Act shall be treated as a reference to section 17 of this Act.

36 Education: general

(1) For the purposes of section 13 of the Education Act 1996 (c 56) (general responsibility of local education authority) a resident of an accommodation centre shall not be treated as part of the population of a local education authority's area.

(2) A child who is a resident of an accommodation centre may not be admitted to a maintained school or a maintained nursery (subject to section 37).

(3) But subsection (2) does not prevent a child's admission to a school which is—

- (a) a community special school or a foundation special school, and
- (b) named in a statement in respect of the child under section 324 of the Education Act 1996 (c 56) (special educational needs).

(4) In subsections (2) and (3)—

- (a) "maintained school" means a maintained school within the meaning of section 20(7) of the School Standards and Framework Act 1998 (c 31) (definition), and
- (b) "maintained nursery" means a facility for nursery education, within the meaning of section 117 of that Act, provided by a local education authority.

(5) The following shall not apply in relation to a child who is a resident of an accommodation centre (subject to section 37)—

- (a) section 86(1) and (2) of the School Standards and Framework Act 1998 (parental preference),
- (b) section 94 of that Act (appeal),
- (c) section 19 of the Education Act 1996 (education out of school),
- (d) section 316(2) and (3) of that Act (child with special educational needs to be educated in mainstream school), and
- (e) paragraphs 3 and 8 of Schedule 27 to that Act (special education needs: making of statement: parental preference).

(6) The power of the Special Educational Needs Tribunal under section 326(3) of the Education Act 1996 (appeal against content of statement) is subject to subsection (2) above.

(7) A person exercising a function under this Act or the Education Act 1996 shall (subject to section 37) secure that a child who is a resident of an accommodation centre and who has special educational needs shall be educated by way of facilities provided under section 29(1)(f) of this Act unless that is incompatible with—

- (a) his receiving the special educational provision which his learning difficulty calls for,
- (b) the provision of efficient education for other children who are residents of the centre, or
- (c) the efficient use of resources.

(8) A person may rely on subsection (7)(b) only where there is no action—

- (a) which could reasonably be taken by that person or by another person who exercises functions, or could exercise functions, in respect of the accommodation centre concerned, and
- (b) as a result of which subsection (7)(b) would not apply.

(9) An accommodation centre is not a school within the meaning of section 4 of the Education Act 1996 (definition); but—

(a) the School Inspections Act 1996 (c 57) shall apply to educational facilities provided at an accommodation centre as if the centre were a school (for which purpose a reference to the appropriate authority shall be taken as a reference to the person (or persons) responsible for the provision of education at the accommodation centre),

(b) section 329A of the Education Act 1996 (review or assessment of educational needs at request of responsible body) shall have effect as if—

(i) an accommodation centre were a relevant school for the purposes of that section,

(ii) a child for whom education is provided at an accommodation centre under section 29(1)(f) were a registered pupil at the centre, and

(iii) a reference in section 329A to the responsible body in relation to an accommodation centre were a reference to any person providing education at the centre under section 29(1)(f), and

(c) section 140 of the Learning and Skills Act 2000 (c 21) (learning difficulties: assessment of post-16 needs) shall have effect as if an accommodation centre were a school.

(10) Subsections (1), (2) and (5) shall not apply in relation to an accommodation centre if education is not provided for children who are residents of the centre under section 29(1)(f).

(11) An expression used in this section and in the Education Act 1996 (c 56) shall have the same meaning in this section as in that Act.

37 Education: special cases

(1) This section applies to a child if a person who provides education to residents of an accommodation centre recommends in writing to the local education authority for the area in which the centre is that this section should apply to the child on the grounds that his special circumstances call for provision that can only or best be arranged by the authority.

(2) A local education authority may—

(a) arrange for the provision of education for a child to whom this section applies;

(b) disapply a provision of section 36 in respect of a child to whom this section applies.

(3) In determining whether to exercise a power under subsection (2) in respect of a child a local education authority shall have regard to any relevant guidance issued by the Secretary of State.

(4) The governing body of a maintained school shall comply with a requirement of the local education authority to admit to the school a child to whom this section applies.

(5) Subsection (4) shall not apply where compliance with a requirement would prejudice measures taken for the purpose of complying with a duty

arising under section 1(6) of the School Standards and Framework Act 1998 (c 31) (limit on infant class size).

(6) A local education authority may not impose a requirement under subsection (4) in respect of a school unless the authority has consulted the school in accordance with regulations made by the Secretary of State.

(7) In the case of a maintained school for which the local education authority are the admission authority, the authority may not arrange for the admission of a child to whom this section applies unless the authority has notified the school in accordance with regulations made by the Secretary of State.

(8) In this section—

(a) "maintained school" means a maintained school within the meaning of section 20(7) of the School Standards and Framework Act 1998 (definition), and

(b) an expression which is also used in the Education Act 1996 (c 56) shall have the same meaning as it has in that Act.

38 Local authority

(1) A local authority may in accordance with arrangements made by the Secretary of State—

(a) assist in arranging for the provision of an accommodation centre;

(b) make premises available for an accommodation centre;

(c) provide services in connection with an accommodation centre.

(2) In particular, a local authority may—

(a) incur reasonable expenditure;

(b) provide services outside its area;

(c) provide services jointly with another body;

(d) form a company;

(e) tender for or enter into a contract;

(f) do anything (including anything listed in paragraphs (a) to (e)) for a preparatory purpose.

(3) In this section "local authority" means—

(a) a local authority within the meaning of section 94 of the Immigration and Asylum Act 1999 (c 33), and

(b) a Northern Ireland authority within the meaning of section 110 of that Act and an Education and Library Board established under Article 3 of the Education and Libraries (Northern Ireland) Order 1986 (SI 1986/ 594 (NI 3)).

39 "Prescribed": orders and regulations

(1) In this Part "prescribed" means prescribed by the Secretary of State by order or regulations.

(2) An order or regulations under this Part may—

(a) make provision which applies generally or only in specified cases or circumstances (which may be determined wholly or partly by reference to location);

(b) make different provision for different cases or circumstances;

(c) include consequential, transitional or incidental provision.

(3) An order or regulations under this Part must be made by statutory instrument.

(4) An order or regulations under any of the following provisions of this Part shall be subject to annulment in pursuance of a resolution of either House of Parliament—

(a) section 17,
(b) section 19,
(c) section 20,
(d) section 21,
(e) section 26,
(f) section 29,
(g) section 31,
(h) section 32,
(i) section 33,
(j) section 37,
(k) section 40, and
(l) section 41.

(5) An order under section 25 or regulations under section 30 may not be made unless a draft has been laid before and approved by resolution of each House of Parliament.

40 Scotland

(1) The Secretary of State may not make arrangements under section 16 for the provision of premises in Scotland unless he has consulted the Scottish Ministers.

(2) The Secretary of State may by order make provision in relation to the education of residents of accommodation centres in Scotland.

(3) An order under subsection (2) may, in particular—

(a) apply, disapply or modify the effect of an enactment (which may include a provision made by or under an Act of the Scottish Parliament);
(b) make provision having an effect similar to the effect of a provision of section 36 or 37.

41 Northern Ireland

(1) The Secretary of State may not make arrangements under section 16 for the provision of premises in Northern Ireland unless he has consulted the First Minister and the deputy First Minister.

(2) The Secretary of State may by order make provision in relation to the education of residents of accommodation centres in Northern Ireland.

(3) An order under subsection (2) may, in particular—

(a) apply, disapply or modify the effect of an enactment (which may include a provision made by or under Northern Ireland legislation);
(b) make provision having an effect similar to the effect of a provision of section 36 or 37.

42 Wales

The Secretary of State may not make arrangements under section 16 for the provision of premises in Wales unless he has consulted the National Assembly for Wales.

Part 3
Other Support and Assistance

43 Asylum-seeker: form of support

(1) The Secretary of State may make an order restricting the application of section 96(1)(b) of the Immigration and Asylum Act 1999 (c 33) (support for asylum-seeker: essential living needs)—

(a) in all circumstances, to cases in which support is being provided under section 96(1)(a) (accommodation), or

(b) in specified circumstances only, to cases in which support is being provided under section 96(1)(a).

(2) An order under subsection (1)(b) may, in particular, make provision by reference to—

(a) location;

(b) the date of an application.

(3) An order under subsection (1) may include transitional provision.

(4) An order under subsection (1)—

(a) must be made by statutory instrument, and

(b) may not be made unless a draft has been laid before and approved by resolution of each House of Parliament.

44 Destitute asylum-seeker

(1) Section 94 of the Immigration and Asylum Act 1999 (c 33) (support for destitute asylum-seeker) shall be amended as follows.

(2) In subsection (1) for the definition of "asylum-seeker" substitute—

"“asylum-seeker” means a person—

(a) who is at least 18 years old,

(b) who is in the United Kingdom,

(c) who has made a claim for asylum at a place designated by the Secretary of State,

(d) whose claim has been recorded by the Secretary of State, and

(e) whose claim has not been determined;".

(3) In subsection (1) for the definition of "dependant" substitute—

"“dependant” in relation to an asylum-seeker or a supported person means a person who—

(a) is in the United Kingdom, and

(b) is within a prescribed class;".

(4) For subsection (3) substitute—

"(3) A claim for asylum shall be treated as determined for the purposes of subsection (1) at the end of such period as may be prescribed beginning with—

(a) the date on which the Secretary of State notifies the claimant of his decision on the claim, or

(b) if the claimant appeals against the Secretary of State's decision, the date on which the appeal is disposed of.

(3A) A person shall continue to be treated as an asylum-seeker despite paragraph (e) of the definition of "asylum-seeker" in subsection (1) while—

(a) his household includes a dependant child who is under 18, and

(b) he does not have leave to enter or remain in the United Kingdom."

(5) Omit subsections (5) and (6).

(6) The following shall be substituted for section 95(2) to (8) of the Immigration and Asylum Act 1999 (c 33) (support for destitute asylum-seeker: interpretation)—

"(2) Where a person has dependants, he and his dependants are destitute for the purpose of this section if they do not have and cannot obtain both—

(a) adequate accommodation, and

(b) food and other essential items.

(3) Where a person does not have dependants, he is destitute for the purpose of this section if he does not have and cannot obtain both—

(a) adequate accommodation, and

(b) food and other essential items.

(4) In determining whether accommodation is adequate for the purposes of subsection (2) or (3) the Secretary of State must have regard to any matter prescribed for the purposes of this subsection.

(5) In determining whether accommodation is adequate for the purposes of subsection (2) or (3) the Secretary of State may not have regard to—

(a) whether a person has an enforceable right to occupy accommodation,

(b) whether a person shares all or part of accommodation,

(c) whether accommodation is temporary or permanent,

(d) the location of accommodation, or

(e) any other matter prescribed for the purposes of this subsection.

(6) The Secretary of State may by regulations specify items which are or are not to be treated as essential items for the purposes of subsections (2) and (3).

(7) The Secretary of State may by regulations—

(a) provide that a person is not to be treated as destitute for the purposes of this Part in specified circumstances;

(b) enable or require the Secretary of State in deciding whether a person is destitute to have regard to income which he or a dependant of his might reasonably be expected to have;

(c) enable or require the Secretary of State in deciding whether a person is destitute to have regard to support which is or might reasonably be expected to be available to the person or a dependant of his;

(d) enable or require the Secretary of State in deciding whether a person is destitute to have regard to assets of a prescribed kind which he or a dependant of his has or might reasonably be expected to have;

(e) make provision as to the valuation of assets."

45 Section 44: supplemental

(1) The following shall be substituted for section 96(1)(b) of the Immigration and Asylum Act 1999 (ways of providing support)—

"(b) by providing the supported person and his dependants (if any) with food and other essential items;".

(2) In section 97 of the Immigration and Asylum Act 1999 (c 33) (support: supplemental)—

(a) in subsection (4) for "essential living needs" there shall be substituted "food and other essential items",

(b) in subsection (5) for "essential living needs" there shall be substituted "food and other essential items", and

(c) in subsection (6) for "living needs" there shall be substituted "items".

(3) Paragraphs 2 and 6 of Schedule 8 to the Immigration and Asylum Act 1999 (support: regulations) shall cease to have effect.

(4) In paragraph 3 of Schedule 9 to the Immigration and Asylum Act 1999 (support: interim provision)—

(a) for "Subsections (3) to (8) of section 95" substitute "Subsections (2) to (6) of section 95", and

(b) for "subsections (5) and (7)" substitute "subsections (4) and (5)".

(5) The following shall be substituted for section 21(1B) of the National Assistance Act 1948 (c 29) (duty of local authority to provide accommodation: exclusion of destitute asylum-seeker: interpretation)—

"(1B) Section 95(2) to (7) of that Act shall apply for the purposes of subsection (1A) above; and for that purpose a reference to the Secretary of State in section 95(4) or (5) shall be treated as a reference to a local authority."

(6) The following shall be substituted for section 45(4B) of the Health Services and Public Health Act 1968 (c 46) (local authority promotion of welfare of elderly: exclusion of destitute asylum-seeker: interpretation)—

"(4B) Section 95(2) to (7) of that Act shall apply for the purposes of subsection (4A) above; and for that purpose a reference to the Secretary of State in section 95(4) or (5) shall be treated as a reference to a local authority."

(7) The following shall be substituted for paragraph 2(2B) of Schedule 8 to the National Health Service Act 1977 (c 49) (local authority arrangements for prevention and care: exclusion of asylum-seeker: interpretation)—

"(2B) Section 95(2) to (7) of that Act shall apply for the purposes of sub-paragraph (2A) above; and for that purpose a reference to the Secretary of State in section 95(4) or (5) shall be treated as a reference to a local social services authority."

46 Section 44: supplemental: Scotland and Northern Ireland

(1) The following shall be substituted for section 12(2B) of the Social Work (Scotland) Act 1968 (c 49)(general social welfare services of local authorities – exclusion of destitute asylum seeker: interpretation)—

"(2B) Section 95(2) to (7) of that Act shall apply for the purposes of subsection (2A) of this section; and for that purpose a reference to the Secretary of State in section 95(4) or (5) shall be treated as a reference to a local authority."

(2) The following shall be substituted for section 13A(5) of that Act (provision of residential accommodation with nursing – exclusion of destitute asylum seeker: interpretation)—

"(5) Section 95(2) to (7) of that Act shall apply for the purposes of subsection (4) of this section; and for that purpose a reference to the Secretary of State in section 95(4) or (5) shall be treated as a reference to a local authority."

(3) The following shall be substituted for section 13B(4) of that Act (provision of care and after-care – exclusion of destitute asylum seeker: interpretation)—

"(4) Section 95(2) to (7) of that Act shall apply for the purposes of subsection (3) of this section; and for that purpose a reference to the Secretary of State in section 95(4) or (5) shall be treated as a reference to a local authority."

(4) The following shall be substituted for section 7(4) of the Mental Health (Scotland) Act 1984 (c 36)(functions of local authorities – exclusion of destitute asylum seeker: interpretation)—

"(4) Section 95(2) to (7) of that Act shall apply for the purposes of subsection (3) of this section; and for that purpose a reference to the Secretary of State in section 95(4) or (5) shall be treated as a reference to a local authority."

(5) The following shall be substituted for section 8(5) of that Act (provision of after-care services – exclusion of destitute asylum seeker: interpretation)—

"(5) Section 95(2) to (7) of that Act shall apply for the purposes of subsection (4) of this section; and for that purpose a reference to the Secretary of State in section 95(4) or (5) shall be treated as a reference to a local authority."

(6) The following shall be substituted for Article 7(3A) of the Health and Personal Social Services (Northern Ireland) Order 1972 (SI 1972/1265 (NI 14)) (prevention of illness, care and after-care: exclusion of asylum-seeker: interpretation)—

"(3A) Section 95(2) to (7) of that Act shall apply for the purpose of paragraph (3); and for that purpose a reference to the Secretary of State in section 95(4) or (5) shall be treated as a reference to the Department."

(7) The following shall be substituted for Article 15(7) of that Order (general social welfare: exclusion of destitute asylum-seeker: interpretation)—

"(7) Section 95(2) to (7) of that Act shall apply for the purpose of paragraph (6); and for that purpose a reference to the Secretary of State in section 95(4) or (5) shall be treated as a reference to the Department."

47 Asylum-seeker: family with children

The following shall be substituted for section 122 of the Immigration and Asylum Act 1999 (c 33) (destitute asylum-seeker with child: duty to support)—

"122 Family with children

(1) This section applies where a person ("the asylum-seeker") applies for support under section 95 of this Act or section 17 of the Nationality, Immigration and Asylum Act 2002 (accommodation centres) if—

(a) the Secretary of State thinks that the asylum-seeker is eligible for support under either or both of those sections, and

(b) the asylum-seeker's household includes a dependant child who is under 18.

(2) The Secretary of State must offer the provision of support for the child, as part of the asylum-seeker's household, under one of the sections mentioned in subsection (1).

(3) A local authority (or, in Northern Ireland, an authority) may not provide assistance for a child if—

(a) the Secretary of State is providing support for the child in accordance with an offer under subsection (2),

(b) an offer by the Secretary of State under subsection (2) remains open in respect of the child, or

(c) the Secretary of State has agreed that he would make an offer in respect of the child under subsection (2) if an application were made as described in subsection (1).

(4) In subsection (3) "assistance" means assistance under—

(a) section 17 of the Children Act 1989 (c 41) (local authority support),

(b) section 22 of the Children (Scotland) Act 1995 (c 36) (similar provision for Scotland), or

(c) Article 18 of the Children (Northern Ireland) Order 1995 (SI 1995/755 (NI 2)) (similar provision for Northern Ireland).

(5) The Secretary of State may by order disapply subsection (3) in specified circumstances.

(6) Where subsection (3) ceases to apply to a child because the Secretary of State stops providing support, no local authority may provide assistance for the child except the authority for the area within which the support was provided."

48 Young asylum-seeker

The following provisions of the Immigration and Asylum Act 1999 (c 33) shall have effect as if the definition of asylum-seeker in section 94(1) of that Act did not exclude persons who are under 18—

(a) section 110 (local authority expenditure on asylum-seekers), and

(b) section 111 (grants to voluntary organisations).

49 Failed asylum-seeker

(1) The following shall be added at the end of section 4 of the Immigration and Asylum Act 1999 (accommodation for person on temporary admission or release)—

"(2) The Secretary of State may provide, or arrange for the provision of, facilities for the accommodation of a person if—

(a) he was (but is no longer) an asylum-seeker, and
(b) his claim for asylum was rejected.

(3) The Secretary of State may provide, or arrange for the provision of, facilities for the accommodation of a dependant of a person for whom facilities may be provided under subsection (2).

(4) The following expressions have the same meaning in this section as in Part VI of this Act (as defined in section 94)—

(a) asylum-seeker,
(b) claim for asylum, and
(c) dependant."

(2) The present section 4 of the Immigration and Asylum Act 1999 (c 33) becomes subsection (1) (and its heading becomes "Accommodation").

50 Conditions of support

(1) The following shall be inserted after section 95(9) of the Immigration and Asylum Act 1999 (support for asylum-seeker: condition)—

"(9A) A condition imposed under subsection (9) may, in particular, relate to—

(a) any matter relating to the use of the support provided, or
(b) compliance with a restriction imposed under paragraph 21 of Schedule 2 to the 1971 Act (temporary admission or release from detention) or paragraph 2 or 5 of Schedule 3 to that Act (restriction pending deportation)."

(2) The following shall be inserted after paragraph 6 of Schedule 9 to that Act (asylum-seeker: interim support)—

"6A The regulations may, in particular, require support to be provided subject to a condition of compliance with any restriction imposed under paragraph 21 of Schedule 2 to the 1971 Act (temporary admission or release from detention) or paragraph 2 or 5 of Schedule 3 to that Act (restriction pending deportation)."

51 Choice of form of support

(1) The Secretary of State may refuse to provide support for a person under a provision specified in subsection (2) on the grounds that an offer has been made to the person of support under another provision specified in that subsection.

(2) The provisions are—

(a) sections 17 and 24 of this Act,

(b) section 4 of the Immigration and Asylum Act 1999 (accommodation for person temporarily admitted or released from detention), and

(c) sections 95 and 98 of that Act (support for destitute asylum-seeker).

(3) In deciding under which of the provisions listed in subsection (2) to offer support to a person the Secretary of State may—

(a) have regard to administrative or other matters which do not concern the person's personal circumstances;

(b) regard one of those matters as conclusive;

(c) apply different criteria to different persons for administrative reasons (which may include the importance of testing the operation of a particular provision).

52 Back-dating of benefit for refugee

In section 123(7) of the Immigration and Asylum Act 1999 (c 33) (back-dating of benefit for refugee: deduction for support received) after "under this Part" there shall be inserted "or Part 2 of the Nationality, Immigration and Asylum Act 2002 (accommodation centres)".

53 Asylum-seeker: appeal against refusal to support

The following shall be substituted for section 103 of the Immigration and Asylum Act 1999 (asylum support appeal)—

"103 Appeals: general

(1) This section applies where a person has applied for support under—

(a) section 95,

(b) section 17 of the Nationality, Immigration and Asylum Act 2002, or

(c) both.

(2) The person may appeal to an adjudicator against a decision that the person is not qualified to receive the support for which he has applied.

(3) The person may also appeal to an adjudicator against a decision to stop providing support under a provision mentioned in subsection (1).

(4) But subsection (3) does not apply—

(a) to a decision to stop providing support under one of the provisions mentioned in subsection (1) if it is to be replaced immediately by support under the other provision, or

(b) to a decision taken on the ground that the person is no longer an asylum-seeker or the dependant of an asylum-seeker.

(5) On an appeal under this section an adjudicator may—

(a) require the Secretary of State to reconsider a matter;

(b) substitute his decision for the decision against which the appeal is brought;

(c) dismiss the appeal.

(6) An adjudicator must give his reasons in writing.

(7) If an appeal under this section is dismissed the Secretary of State shall not consider any further application by the appellant for support under a

provision mentioned in subsection (1)(a) or (b) unless the Secretary of State thinks there has been a material change in circumstances.
(8) An appeal under this section may not be brought or continued by a person who is outside the United Kingdom.

103A Appeals: location of support under section 95
(1) The Secretary of State may by regulations provide for a decision as to where support provided under section 95 is to be provided to be appealable to an adjudicator under this Part.
(2) Regulations under this section may provide for a provision of section 103 to have effect in relation to an appeal under the regulations with specified modifications.

103B Appeals: travelling expenses
The Secretary of State may pay reasonable travelling expenses incurred by an appellant in connection with attendance for the purposes of an appeal under or by virtue of section 103 or 103A."

54 Withholding and withdrawal of support
Schedule 3 (which makes provision for support to be withheld or withdrawn in certain circumstances) shall have effect.

55 Late claim for asylum: refusal of support
(1) The Secretary of State may not provide or arrange for the provision of support to a person under a provision mentioned in subsection (2) if—
- (a) the person makes a claim for asylum which is recorded by the Secretary of State, and
- (b) the Secretary of State is not satisfied that the claim was made as soon as reasonably practicable after the person's arrival in the United Kingdom.

(2) The provisions are—
- (a) sections 4, 95 and 98 of the Immigration and Asylum Act 1999 (c 33) (support for asylum-seeker, &c), and
- (b) sections 17 and 24 of this Act (accommodation centre).

(3) An authority may not provide or arrange for the provision of support to a person under a provision mentioned in subsection (4) if—
- (a) the person has made a claim for asylum, and
- (b) the Secretary of State is not satisfied that the claim was made as soon as reasonably practicable after the person's arrival in the United Kingdom.

(4) The provisions are—
- (a) section 29(1)(b) of the Housing (Scotland) Act 1987 (c 26) (accommodation pending review),
- (b) section 188(3) or 204(4) of the Housing Act 1996 (c 52) (accommodation pending review or appeal), and
- (c) section 2 of the Local Government Act 2000 (c 22) (promotion of well-being).

(5) This section shall not prevent—

(a) the exercise of a power by the Secretary of State to the extent necessary for the purpose of avoiding a breach of a person's Convention rights (within the meaning of the Human Rights Act 1998 (c 42)),

(b) the provision of support under section 95 of the Immigration and Asylum Act 1999 (c 33) or section 17 of this Act in accordance with section 122 of that Act (children), or

(c) the provision of support under section 98 of the Immigration and Asylum Act 1999 or section 24 of this Act (provisional support) to a person under the age of 18 and the household of which he forms part.

(6) An authority which proposes to provide or arrange for the provision of support to a person under a provision mentioned in subsection (4)—

(a) must inform the Secretary of State if the authority believes that the person has made a claim for asylum,

(b) must act in accordance with any guidance issued by the Secretary of State to determine whether subsection (3) applies, and

(c) shall not be prohibited from providing or arranging for the provision of support if the authority has complied with paragraph (a) and (b) and concluded that subsection (3) does not apply.

(7) The Secretary of State may by order—

(a) add, remove or amend an entry in the list in subsection (4);

(b) provide for subsection (3) not to have effect in specified cases or circumstances.

(8) An order under subsection (7)—

(a) may include transitional, consequential or incidental provision,

(b) must be made by statutory instrument, and

(c) may not be made unless a draft has been laid before and approved by resolution of each House of Parliament.

(9) For the purposes of this section "claim for asylum" has the same meaning as in section 18.

(10) A decision of the Secretary of State that this section prevents him from providing or arranging for the provision of support to a person is not a decision that the person does not qualify for support for the purpose of section 103 of the Immigration and Asylum Act 1999 (appeals).

(11) This section does not prevent a person's compliance with a residence restriction imposed in reliance on section 70 (induction).

56 Provision of support by local authority

(1) Section 99 of the Immigration and Asylum Act 1999 (provision of support by local authority) shall be amended as follows.

(2) In subsection (1)—

(a) after "local authority" insert "or Northern Ireland authority", and

(b) at the end add "or 98".

(3) For subsections (2) and (3) substitute—

"(2) Support may be provided by an authority in accordance with arrangements made with the authority or with another person.
(3) Support may be provided by an authority in accordance with arrangements made under section 95 only in one or more of the ways mentioned in section 96(1) and (2)."
(4) In subsection (4)—
(a) for "A local authority" substitute "An authority", and
(b) at the end add "or 98".
(5) In subsection (5)—
(a) for "a local authority" substitute "an authority", and
(b) in paragraph (b) for "bodies who are not local authorities" substitute "other bodies".

57 Application for support: false or incomplete information
At the end of paragraph 12(c) of Schedule 8 to the Immigration and Asylum Act 1999 (c 33) (asylum-seeker support: procedure: disregarding of application) there shall be inserted "(which may, in particular, provide for an application not to be entertained where the Secretary of State is not satisfied that the information provided is complete or accurate or that the applicant is co-operating with enquiries under paragraph (d))".

58 Voluntary departure from United Kingdom
(1) A person is a "voluntary leaver" for the purposes of this section if—
(a) he is not a British citizen or an EEA national,
(b) he leaves the United Kingdom for a place where he hopes to take up permanent residence (his "new place of residence"), and
(c) the Secretary of State thinks that it is in the person's interest to leave the United Kingdom and that the person wishes to leave.
(2) The Secretary of State may make arrangements to—
(a) assist voluntary leavers;
(b) assist individuals to decide whether to become voluntary leavers.
(3) The Secretary of State may, in particular, make payments (whether to voluntary leavers or to organisations providing services for them) which relate to—
(a) travelling and other expenses incurred by or on behalf of a voluntary leaver, or a member of his family or household, in leaving the United Kingdom;
(b) expenses incurred by or on behalf of a voluntary leaver, or a member of his family or household, on or shortly after arrival in his new place of residence;
(c) the provision of services designed to assist a voluntary leaver, or a member of his family or household, to settle in his new place of residence;
(d) expenses in connection with a journey undertaken by a person (with or without his family or household) to prepare for, or to assess the possibility of, his becoming a voluntary leaver.

(4) In subsection (1)(a) "EEA national" means a national of a State which is a contracting party to the Agreement on the European Economic Area signed at Oporto on 2nd May 1992 (as it has effect from time to time).

(5) The following provisions of the Immigration Act 1971 (c 77) shall cease to have effect—

(a) section 29 (contributions to expenses of persons returning abroad), and

(b) section 31(d) (expenses).

59 International projects

(1) The Secretary of State may participate in a project which is designed to—

(a) reduce migration,

(b) assist or ensure the return of migrants,

(c) facilitate co-operation between States in matters relating to migration,

(d) conduct or consider research about migration, or

(e) arrange or assist the settlement of migrants (whether in the United Kingdom or elsewhere).

(2) In particular, the Secretary of State may—

(a) provide financial support to an international organisation which arranges or participates in a project of a kind described in subsection (1);

(b) provide financial support to an organisation in the United Kingdom or another country which arranges or participates in a project of that kind;

(c) provide or arrange for the provision of financial or other assistance to a migrant who participates in a project of that kind;

(d) participate in financial or other arrangements which are agreed between Her Majesty's Government and the government of one or more other countries and which are or form part of a project of that kind.

(3) In this section—

(a) "migrant" means a person who leaves the country where he lives hoping to settle in another country (whether or not he is a refugee within the meaning of any international Convention), and

(b) "migration" shall be construed accordingly.

(4) Subsection (1) does not—

(a) confer a power to remove a person from the United Kingdom, or

(b) affect a person's right to enter or remain in the United Kingdom.

60 Northern Ireland authorities

(1) In section 110(9) of the Immigration and Asylum Act 1999 (c 33) (support: payment to local authority: Northern Ireland authority) after paragraph (b) there shall be added

"; or

(c) a Health and Social Services trust established under the Health and Personal Social Services (Northern Ireland) Order 1991 (SI 1991/194 (NI 1).”

(2) In section 94(1) of that Act (support: interpretation) after the definition of “local authority” there shall be inserted—

““Northern Ireland authority” has the meaning given by section 110(9).”

61 Repeal of spent provisions

The following provisions of the Immigration and Asylum Act 1999 shall cease to have effect—

(a) section 96(4) to (6) (which relate to a provision about support for asylum-seekers which has been repealed by order), and

(b) section 166(4)(e) (order under section 96(5): procedure).

Part 4
Detention and Removal

Detention

62 Detention by Secretary of State

(1) A person may be detained under the authority of the Secretary of State pending—

(a) a decision by the Secretary of State whether to give directions in respect of the person under paragraph 10, 10A or 14 of Schedule 2 to the Immigration Act 1971 (c 77) (control of entry: removal), or

(b) removal of the person from the United Kingdom in pursuance of directions given by the Secretary of State under any of those paragraphs.

(2) Where the Secretary of State is empowered under section 3A of that Act (powers of Secretary of State) to examine a person or to give or refuse a person leave to enter the United Kingdom, the person may be detained under the authority of the Secretary of State pending—

(a) the person’s examination by the Secretary of State,

(b) the Secretary of State’s decision to give or refuse the person leave to enter,

(c) a decision by the Secretary of State whether to give directions in respect of the person under paragraph 8 or 9 of Schedule 2 to that Act (removal), or

(d) removal of the person in pursuance of directions given by the Secretary of State under either of those paragraphs.

(3) A provision of Schedule 2 to that Act about a person who is detained or liable to detention under that Schedule shall apply to a person who is detained or liable to detention under this section: and for that purpose—

(a) a reference to paragraph 16 of that Schedule shall be taken to include a reference to this section,

(b) a reference in paragraph 21 of that Schedule to an immigration officer shall be taken to include a reference to the Secretary of State, and

(c) a reference to detention under that Schedule or under a provision or Part of that Schedule shall be taken to include a reference to detention under this section.

(4) In the case of a restriction imposed under paragraph 21 of that Schedule by virtue of this section—

(a) a restriction imposed by an immigration officer may be varied by the Secretary of State, and

(b) a restriction imposed by the Secretary of State may be varied by an immigration officer.

(5) In subsection (1) the reference to paragraph 10 of that Schedule includes a reference to that paragraph as applied by virtue of section 10 of the Immigration and Asylum Act 1999 (c 33) (persons unlawfully in United Kingdom: removal).

(6) Subsection (5) is without prejudice to the generality of section 159.

(7) A power under this section which is exercisable pending a decision of a particular kind by the Secretary of State is exercisable where the Secretary of State has reasonable grounds to suspect that he may make a decision of that kind.

(8) At the end of section 11(1) of the Immigration Act 1971 (c 77) (person not deemed to have entered United Kingdom while detained, &c) there shall be inserted "or section 62 of the Nationality, Immigration and Asylum Act 2002".

(9) In section 24(1)(e) of the Immigration Act 1971 (offence: failure to comply with restriction) for "or to an immigration officer" there shall be substituted ", to an immigration officer or to the Secretary of State".

(10) In the Mental Health Act 1983 (c 20)—

(a) at the end of section 48(2)(d) (detained persons susceptible to transfer for mental treatment: immigration) there shall be added "or under section 62 of the Nationality, Immigration and Asylum Act 2002 (detention by Secretary of State)", and

(b) in the heading of section 53 (supplemental provision) the reference to the Immigration Act 1971 becomes a reference to the Immigration Acts.

(11) In the Mental Health (Scotland) Act 1984 (c 36)—

(a) at the end of section 71(2)(c) (detained persons who may be transferred to hospital for mental treatment) there shall be added "or under section 62 of the Nationality, Immigration and Asylum Act 2002 (detention by the Secretary of State)", and

(b) at the end of section 74(1)(b) (further provision about such persons) there shall be added "or under section 62 of the Nationality, Immigration and Asylum Act 2002 (detention by the Secretary of State)".

(12) In the Mental Health (Northern Ireland) Order 1986 (SI 1986/595 (NI 4))—

(a) at the end of Article 54(2)(d) (detained persons susceptible to transfer for mental treatment: immigration) there shall be added "or under section 62 of the Nationality, Immigration and Asylum Act 2002 (detention by Secretary of State)", and

(b) in the heading of Article 59 (supplemental provision) the reference to the Immigration Act 1971 becomes a reference to the Immigration Acts.

(13) Section 53 of the Immigration and Asylum Act 1999 (c 33) (bail) shall be amended as follows—

(a) at the end of subsection (1) add "or under section 62 of the Nationality, Immigration and Asylum Act 2002", and

(b) at the end of subsection (3)(a) add "or under section 62 of the Nationality, Immigration and Asylum Act 2002".

(14) In section 147 of that Act (detention centres: interpretation) at the end of the definition of "detained persons" there shall be inserted "or under section 62 of the Nationality, Immigration and Asylum Act 2002 (detention by Secretary of State);".

(15) Section 23(2) of the Anti-terrorism, Crime and Security Act 2001 (c 24) (detention of suspected international terrorist) shall be amended as follows—

(a) omit "and" after paragraph (a), and

(b) after paragraph (b) add—

", and

(c) section 62 of the Nationality, Immigration and Asylum Act 2002 (detention by Secretary of State)."

(16) In section 24(1) of that Act (bail) after "the Immigration Act 1971" insert ", or under section 62 of the Nationality, Immigration and Asylum Act 2002,".

63 Control of entry to United Kingdom, &c: use of force

In paragraph 17(2) of Schedule 2 to the Immigration Act 1971 (c 77) (control of entry, &c: person liable to detention: use of force) for "if need be by force" there shall be substituted "if need be by reasonable force".

64 Escorts

The following shall be added after paragraph 17(2) of Schedule 2 to the Immigration Act 1971 (detention for examination or removal: right to enter premises)—

"(3) Sub-paragraph (4) applies where an immigration officer or constable—

(a) enters premises in reliance on a warrant under sub-paragraph (2), and

(b) detains a person on the premises.

(4) A detainee custody officer may enter the premises, if need be by reasonable force, for the purpose of carrying out a search.

(5) In sub-paragraph (4)—

"detainee custody officer" means a person in respect of whom a certificate of authorisation is in force under section 154 of the Immigration and Asylum Act 1999 (c 33) (detained persons: escort and custody), and

"search" means a search under paragraph 2(1)(a) of Schedule 13 to that Act (escort arrangements: power to search detained person)."

65 Detention centres: custodial functions

(1) The following shall be substituted for section 154(5) of the Immigration and Asylum Act 1999 (power to confer functions of detainee custody officers on prison officers and prisoner custody officers)—

"(5) The Secretary of State may confer functions of detainee custody officers on prison officers or prisoner custody officers."

(2) The following shall be added at the end of Schedule 11 to that Act (detainee custody officers)—

"8 Prison officers and prisoner custody officers

A reference in this Schedule to a detainee custody officer includes a reference to a prison officer or prisoner custody officer exercising custodial functions."

(3) The following shall be added at the end of Schedule 12 to that Act (discipline at detention centre)—

"9 Prison officers and prisoner custody officers

A reference in this Schedule to a detainee custody officer includes a reference to a prison officer or prisoner custody officer exercising custodial functions."

66 Detention centres: change of name

(1) In section 147 of the Immigration and Asylum Act 1999 (c 33) (Part VIII: interpretation)—

(a) the definition of "detention centre" shall cease to have effect, and

(b) the following shall be inserted after the definition of "prisoner custody officer"—

""removal centre" means a place which is used solely for the detention of detained persons but which is not a short-term holding facility, a prison or part of a prison;".

(2) In the provisions listed in subsection (3) (and any relevant headings)—

(a) for the words "detention centre" there shall be substituted the words "removal centre", and

(b) for the words "detention centres" there shall be substituted the words "removal centres".

(3) The provisions are—

(a) in section 147 of the Immigration and Asylum Act 1999 (Part VIII: interpretation), the definitions of "contracted out detention centre", "contractor", "custodial functions", "detention centre contract", "detention centre rules", and "directly managed detention centre",

(b) section 148 of that Act (management of centre),
(c) sections 149 and 150 of that Act (contracting out),
(d) section 151 of that Act (intervention by Secretary of State),
(e) section 152 of that Act (visiting committee),
(f) section 153 of that Act (rules),
(g) section 155 of that Act (custodial functions),
(h) section 157 of that Act (short-term holding facility),
(i) section 158 of that Act (disclosure of information),
(j) section 159 of that Act (power of constable),
(k) Schedule 11 to that Act (detainee custody officer),
(l) Schedule 12 to that Act (procedure at detention centre),
(m) Schedule 13 to that Act (escort),
(n) section 141(5)(e) and (6) of that Act (fingerprinting),
(o) section 5A(5A) of the Prison Act 1952 (c 52) (Chief Inspector of Prisons), and
(p) paragraph 13 of Schedule 4A to the Water Industry Act 1991 (c 56) (disconnection).

(4) A reference in an enactment or instrument to a detention centre within the meaning of Part VIII of the Immigration and Asylum Act 1999 (c 33) shall be construed as a reference to a removal centre within the meaning of that Part.

67 Construction of reference to person liable to detention

(1) This section applies to the construction of a provision which—
(a) does not confer power to detain a person, but
(b) refers (in any terms) to a person who is liable to detention under a provision of the Immigration Acts.

(2) The reference shall be taken to include a person if the only reason why he cannot be detained under the provision is that—
(a) he cannot presently be removed from the United Kingdom, because of a legal impediment connected with the United Kingdom's obligations under an international agreement,
(b) practical difficulties are impeding or delaying the making of arrangements for his removal from the United Kingdom, or
(c) practical difficulties, or demands on administrative resources, are impeding or delaying the taking of a decision in respect of him.

(3) This section shall be treated as always having had effect.

Temporary release

68 Bail

(1) This section applies in a case where an immigration officer not below the rank of chief immigration officer has sole or shared power to release a person on bail in accordance with—
(a) a provision of Schedule 2 to the Immigration Act 1971 (c 77) (control of entry) (including a provision of that Schedule applied by a provision of that Act or by another enactment), or
(b) section 9A of the Asylum and Immigration Appeals Act 1993 (c 23) (pending appeal from Immigration Appeal Tribunal).

(2) In respect of an application for release on bail which is instituted after the expiry of the period of eight days beginning with the day on which detention commences, the power to release on bail—

(a) shall be exercisable by the Secretary of State (as well as by any person with whom the immigration officer's power is shared under the provision referred to in subsection (1)), and

(b) shall not be exercisable by an immigration officer (except where he acts on behalf of the Secretary of State).

(3) In relation to the exercise by the Secretary of State of a power to release a person on bail by virtue of subsection (2), a reference to an immigration officer shall be construed as a reference to the Secretary of State.

(4) The Secretary of State may by order amend or replace subsection (2) so as to make different provision for the circumstances in which the power to release on bail may be exercised by the Secretary of State and not by an immigration officer.

(5) An order under subsection (4)—

(a) may include consequential or transitional provision,

(b) must be made by statutory instrument, and

(c) may not be made unless a draft has been laid before and approved by resolution of each House of Parliament.

(6) The following provisions of Part III of the Immigration and Asylum Act 1999 (c 33) (Bail) shall cease to have effect—

(a) sections 44 to 52 (routine bail hearings),

(b) section 53(5) (bail under regulations to match bail under Part III), and

(c) section 55 (grants to advisory organisations).

69 Reporting restriction: travel expenses

(1) The Secretary of State may make a payment to a person in respect of travelling expenses which the person has incurred or will incur for the purpose of complying with a reporting restriction.

(2) In subsection (1) "reporting restriction" means a restriction which—

(a) requires a person to report to the police, an immigration officer or the Secretary of State, and

(b) is imposed under a provision listed in subsection (3).

(3) Those provisions are—

(a) paragraph 21 of Schedule 2 to the Immigration Act 1971 (c 77) (temporary admission or release from detention),

(b) paragraph 29 of that Schedule (bail), and

(c) paragraph 2 or 5 of Schedule 3 to that Act (pending deportation).

70 Induction

(1) A residence restriction may be imposed on an asylum-seeker or a dependant of an asylum-seeker without regard to his personal circumstances if—

(a) it requires him to reside at a specified location for a period not exceeding 14 days, and

(b) the person imposing the residence restriction believes that a programme of induction will be made available to the asylum-seeker at or near the specified location.

(2) In subsection (1) "residence restriction" means a restriction imposed under—

(a) paragraph 21 of Schedule 2 to the Immigration Act 1971 (temporary admission or release from detention), or

(b) paragraph 2(5) of Schedule 3 to that Act (control pending deportation).

(3) In this section—

"asylum-seeker" has the meaning given by section 18 of this Act but disregarding section 18(1)(a),

"dependant of an asylum-seeker" means a person who appears to the Secretary of State to be making a claim or application in respect of residence in the United Kingdom by virtue of being a dependant of an asylum-seeker, and

"programme of induction" means education about the nature of the asylum process.

(4) Regulations under subsection (3)—

(a) may make different provision for different circumstances,

(b) must be made by statutory instrument, and

(c) shall be subject to annulment in pursuance of a resolution of either House of Parliament.

(5) Subsection (6) applies where the Secretary of State arranges for the provision of a programme of induction (whether or not he also provides other facilities to persons attending the programme and whether or not all the persons attending the programme are subject to residence restrictions).

(6) A local authority may arrange for or participate in the provision of the programme or other facilities.

(7) In particular, a local authority may—

(a) incur reasonable expenditure;

(b) provide services outside its area;

(c) provide services jointly with another body;

(d) form a company;

(e) tender for or enter into a contract;

(f) do anything (including anything listed in paragraphs (a) to (e)) for a preparatory purpose.

(8) In this section "local authority" means—

(a) a local authority within the meaning of section 94 of the Immigration and Asylum Act 1999 (c 33), and

(b) a Northern Ireland authority within the meaning of section 110 of that Act.

71 Asylum-seeker: residence, &c restriction

(1) This section applies to—

(a) a person who makes a claim for asylum at a time when he has leave to enter or remain in the United Kingdom, and

(b) a dependant of a person within paragraph (a).

(2) The Secretary of State or an immigration officer may impose on a person to whom this section applies any restriction which may be imposed under paragraph 21 of Schedule 2 to the Immigration Act 1971 (c 77) (control of entry: residence, reporting and occupation restrictions) on a person liable to detention under paragraph 16 of that Schedule.

(3) Where a restriction is imposed on a person under subsection (2)—

(a) the restriction shall be treated for all purposes as a restriction imposed under paragraph 21 of that Schedule, and

(b) if the person fails to comply with the restriction he shall be liable to detention under paragraph 16 of that Schedule.

(4) A restriction imposed on a person under this section shall cease to have effect if he ceases to be an asylum-seeker or the dependant of an asylum-seeker.

(5) In this section—

"asylum-seeker" has the same meaning as in section 70,

"claim for asylum" has the same meaning as in section 18, and

"dependant" means a person who appears to the Secretary of State to be making a claim or application in respect of residence in the United Kingdom by virtue of being a dependant of another person.

(6) Regulations under subsection (5)—

(a) may make different provision for different circumstances,

(b) must be made by statutory instrument, and

(c) shall be subject to annulment in pursuance of a resolution of either House of Parliament.

Removal

72 Serious criminal

(1) This section applies for the purpose of the construction and application of Article 33(2) of the Refugee Convention (exclusion from protection).

(2) A person shall be presumed to have been convicted by a final judgment of a particularly serious crime and to constitute a danger to the community of the United Kingdom if he is—

(a) convicted in the United Kingdom of an offence, and

(b) sentenced to a period of imprisonment of at least two years.

(3) A person shall be presumed to have been convicted by a final judgment of a particularly serious crime and to constitute a danger to the community of the United Kingdom if—

(a) he is convicted outside the United Kingdom of an offence,

(b) he is sentenced to a period of imprisonment of at least two years, and

(c) he could have been sentenced to a period of imprisonment of at least two years had his conviction been a conviction in the United Kingdom of a similar offence.

(4) A person shall be presumed to have been convicted by a final judgment of a particularly serious crime and to constitute a danger to the community of the United Kingdom if—

(a) he is convicted of an offence specified by order of the Secretary of State, or
(b) he is convicted outside the United Kingdom of an offence and the Secretary of State certifies that in his opinion the offence is similar to an offence specified by order under paragraph (a).

(5) An order under subsection (4)—
(a) must be made by statutory instrument, and
(b) shall be subject to annulment in pursuance of a resolution of either House of Parliament.

(6) A presumption under subsection (2), (3) or (4) that a person constitutes a danger to the community is rebuttable by that person.

(7) A presumption under subsection (2), (3) or (4) does not apply while an appeal against conviction or sentence—
(a) is pending, or
(b) could be brought (disregarding the possibility of appeal out of time with leave).

(8) Section 34(1) of the Anti-terrorism, Crime and Security Act 2001 (c 24) (no need to consider gravity of fear or threat of persecution) applies for the purpose of considering whether a presumption mentioned in subsection (6) has been rebutted as it applies for the purpose of considering whether Article 33(2) of the Refugee Convention applies.

(9) Subsection (10) applies where—
(a) a person appeals under section 82, 83 or 101 of this Act or under section 2 of the Special Immigration Appeals Commission Act 1997 (c 68) wholly or partly on the ground that to remove him from or to require him to leave the United Kingdom would breach the United Kingdom's obligations under the Refugee Convention, and
(b) the Secretary of State issues a certificate that presumptions under subsection (2), (3) or (4) apply to the person (subject to rebuttal).

(10) The adjudicator, Tribunal or Commission hearing the appeal—
(a) must begin substantive deliberation on the appeal by considering the certificate, and
(b) if in agreement that presumptions under subsection (2), (3) or (4) apply (having given the appellant an opportunity for rebuttal) must dismiss the appeal in so far as it relies on the ground specified in subsection (9)(a).

(11) For the purposes of this section—
(a) "the Refugee Convention" means the Convention relating to the Status of Refugees done at Geneva on 28th July 1951 and its Protocol, and
(b) a reference to a person who is sentenced to a period of imprisonment of at least two years—
(i) does not include a reference to a person who receives a suspended sentence (unless at least two years of the sentence are not suspended),
(ii) includes a reference to a person who is sentenced to detention, or ordered or directed to be detained, in an institution

other than a prison (including, in particular, a hospital or an institution for young offenders), and

(iii) includes a reference to a person who is sentenced to imprisonment or detention, or ordered or directed to be detained, for an indeterminate period (provided that it may last for two years).

73 Family

(1) The following shall be inserted after paragraph 10 of Schedule 2 to the Immigration Act 1971 (c 77) (control of entry: removal)—

"**10A** Where directions are given in respect of a person under any of paragraphs 8 to 10 above, directions to the same effect may be given under that paragraph in respect of a member of the person's family."

(2) Section 10 of the Immigration and Asylum Act 1999 (c 33) (removal of person unlawfully in United Kingdom) shall be amended as follows.

(3) In subsection (1)(c) omit—

(a) "("the first directions")", and

(b) "("the other person")".

(4) The following shall be substituted for subsections (3) to (5) (removal of family)—

"(3) Directions for the removal of a person may not be given under subsection (1)(c) unless the Secretary of State has given the person written notice of the intention to remove him.

(4) A notice under subsection (3) may not be given if—

(a) the person whose removal under subsection (1)(a) or (b) is the cause of the proposed directions under subsection (1)(c) has left the United Kingdom, and

(b) more than eight weeks have elapsed since that person's departure.

(5) If a notice under subsection (3) is sent by first class post to a person's last known address, that subsection shall be taken to be satisfied at the end of the second day after the day of posting.

(5A) Directions for the removal of a person under subsection (1)(c) cease to have effect if he ceases to belong to the family of the person whose removal under subsection (1)(a) or (b) is the cause of the directions under subsection (1)(c)."

(5) In paragraph 16(2) of Schedule 2 to the Immigration Act 1971 (c 77) (control of entry, &c: detention) for the words "8 to 10" there shall be substituted "8 to 10A".

74 Deception

In section 10(1) of the Immigration and Asylum Act 1999 (c 33) (removal) the following shall be substituted for paragraph (b)—

"(b) he uses deception in seeking (whether successfully or not) leave to remain;".

75 Exemption from deportation

(1) Section 7 of the Immigration Act 1971 (existing residents exempt from deportation) shall be amended as follows.

(2) Subsection (1)(a) (which is redundant) shall cease to have effect.

(3) The following shall be substituted for subsection (1)(b)—

"(b) shall not be liable to deportation under section 3(5) if at the time of the Secretary of State's decision he had for the last five years been ordinarily resident in the United Kingdom and Islands;".

(4) The following shall be added at the end of section 10 of the Immigration and Asylum Act 1999 (removal)—

"(10) A person shall not be liable to removal from the United Kingdom under this section at a time when section 7(1)(b) of the Immigration Act 1971 (Commonwealth and Irish citizens ordinarily resident in United Kingdom) would prevent a decision to deport him."

76 Revocation of leave to enter or remain

(1) The Secretary of State may revoke a person's indefinite leave to enter or remain in the United Kingdom if the person—

(a) is liable to deportation, but

(b) cannot be deported for legal reasons.

(2) The Secretary of State may revoke a person's indefinite leave to enter or remain in the United Kingdom if—

(a) the leave was obtained by deception,

(b) the person would be liable to removal because of the deception, but

(c) the person cannot be removed for legal or practical reasons.

(3) The Secretary of State may revoke a person's indefinite leave to enter or remain in the United Kingdom if the person, or someone of whom he is a dependant, ceases to be a refugee as a result of—

(a) voluntarily availing himself of the protection of his country of nationality,

(b) voluntarily re-acquiring a lost nationality,

(c) acquiring the nationality of a country other than the United Kingdom and availing himself of its protection, or

(d) voluntarily establishing himself in a country in respect of which he was a refugee.

(4) In this section—

"indefinite leave" has the meaning given by section 33(1) of the Immigration Act 1971 (c 77) (interpretation),

"liable to deportation" has the meaning given by section 3(5) and (6) of that Act (deportation),

"refugee" has the meaning given by the Convention relating to the Status of Refugees done at Geneva on 28th July 1951 and its Protocol, and

"removed" means removed from the United Kingdom under—

(a) paragraph 9 or 10 of Schedule 2 to the Immigration Act 1971 (control of entry: directions for removal), or

(b) section 10(1)(b) of the Immigration and Asylum Act 1999 (c 33) (removal of persons unlawfully in United Kingdom: deception).

(5) A power under subsection (1) or (2) to revoke leave may be exercised—

(a) in respect of leave granted before this section comes into force;

(b) in reliance on anything done before this section comes into force.

(6) A power under subsection (3) to revoke leave may be exercised—

(a) in respect of leave granted before this section comes into force, but

(b) only in reliance on action taken after this section comes into force.

(7) In section 10(1) of the Immigration and Asylum Act 1999 (removal of persons unlawfully in United Kingdom) after paragraph (b) (and before the word "or") there shall be inserted—

"(ba) his indefinite leave to enter or remain has been revoked under section 76(3) of the Nationality, Immigration and Asylum Act 2002 (person ceasing to be refugee);".

77 No removal while claim for asylum pending

(1) While a person's claim for asylum is pending he may not be—

(a) removed from the United Kingdom in accordance with a provision of the Immigration Acts, or

(b) required to leave the United Kingdom in accordance with a provision of the Immigration Acts.

(2) In this section—

(a) "claim for asylum" means a claim by a person that it would be contrary to the United Kingdom's obligations under the Refugee Convention to remove him from or require him to leave the United Kingdom, and

(b) a person's claim is pending until he is given notice of the Secretary of State's decision on it.

(3) In subsection (2) "the Refugee Convention" means the Convention relating to the Status of Refugees done at Geneva on 28th July 1951 and its Protocol.

(4) Nothing in this section shall prevent any of the following while a claim for asylum is pending—

(a) the giving of a direction for the claimant's removal from the United Kingdom,

(b) the making of a deportation order in respect of the claimant, or

(c) the taking of any other interim or preparatory action.

(5) Section 15 of the Immigration and Asylum Act 1999 (c 33) (protection from removal or deportation) shall cease to have effect.

78 No removal while appeal pending

(1) While a person's appeal under section 82(1) is pending he may not be—

(a) removed from the United Kingdom in accordance with a provision of the Immigration Acts, or

(b) required to leave the United Kingdom in accordance with a provision of the Immigration Acts.

(2) In this section "pending" has the meaning given by section 104.

(3) Nothing in this section shall prevent any of the following while an appeal is pending—

(a) the giving of a direction for the appellant's removal from the United Kingdom,

(b) the making of a deportation order in respect of the appellant (subject to section 79), or

(c) the taking of any other interim or preparatory action.

(4) This section applies only to an appeal brought while the appellant is in the United Kingdom in accordance with section 92.

79 Deportation order: appeal

(1) A deportation order may not be made in respect of a person while an appeal under section 82(1) against the decision to make the order—

(a) could be brought (ignoring any possibility of an appeal out of time with permission), or

(b) is pending.

(2) In this section "pending" has the meaning given by section 104.

80 Removal of asylum-seeker to third country

The following shall be substituted for section 11 of the Immigration and Asylum Act 1999 (c 33) (removal of asylum claimant under standing arrangements with member States)—

"11 Removal of asylum claimant under standing arrangement with member States

(1) In determining whether a person in relation to whom a certificate has been issued under subsection (2) may be removed from the United Kingdom, a member State is to be regarded as—

(a) a place where a person's life and liberty is not threatened by reason of his race, religion, nationality, membership of a particular social group, or political opinion; and

(b) a place from which a person will not be sent to another country otherwise than in accordance with the Refugee Convention.

(2) Nothing in section 77 of the Nationality, Immigration and Asylum Act 2002 prevents a person who has made a claim for asylum ("the claimant") from being removed from the United Kingdom to a member State if the Secretary of State has certified that—

(a) the member State has accepted that, under standing arrangements, it is the responsible State in relation to the claimant's claim for asylum; and

(b) in his opinion, the claimant is not a national or citizen of the member State to which he is to be sent.

(3) Subsection (4) applies where a person who is the subject of a certificate under subsection (2)—

(a) has instituted or could institute an appeal under section 82(1) of the Nationality, Immigration and Asylum Act 2002 (immigration appeal), and
(b) has made a human rights claim (within the meaning of section 113 of that Act).

(4) The person may not be removed from the United Kingdom in reliance upon this section unless—
(a) the appeal is finally determined, withdrawn or abandoned (within the meaning of section 104 of that Act) or can no longer be brought (ignoring any possibility of an appeal out of time with permission), or
(b) the Secretary of State has issued a certificate in relation to the human rights claim under section 93(2)(b) of that Act (clearly unfounded claim).

(5) In this section "standing arrangements" means arrangements in force between two or more member States for determining which State is responsible for considering applications for asylum."

Part 5
Immigration and Asylum Appeals

Appeal to adjudicator

81 Adjudicators

(1) The Lord Chancellor shall appoint adjudicators for the purposes of this Part.

(2) A person is eligible for appointment as an adjudicator only if he—
(a) has a seven year general qualification within the meaning of section 71 of the Courts and Legal Services Act 1990 (c 41),
(b) is an advocate or solicitor in Scotland of at least seven years' standing,
(c) is a member of the Bar of Northern Ireland, or a solicitor of the Supreme Court of Northern Ireland, of at least seven years' standing, or
(d) has legal or other experience which in the Lord Chancellor's opinion makes him suitable for appointment.

(3) The Lord Chancellor—
(a) shall appoint one of the adjudicators as Chief Adjudicator,
(b) may appoint one of the adjudicators as Deputy Chief Adjudicator,
(c) may appoint one or more adjudicators as Regional Adjudicator, and
(d) may appoint one or more adjudicators as Deputy Regional Adjudicator.

(4) The Chief Adjudicator shall perform such functions as the Lord Chancellor may assign to him.

(5) The Deputy Chief Adjudicator—
(a) may act for the Chief Adjudicator if he is unable to act or unavailable, and

(b) shall perform such other functions as the Chief Adjudicator may delegate or assign to him.

(6) A Regional Adjudicator shall perform such functions as the Chief Adjudicator may assign to him.

(7) A Deputy Regional Adjudicator—

(a) may act for the Regional Adjudicator whose deputy he is if the Regional Adjudicator is unable to act or unavailable, and

(b) shall perform such other functions as may be delegated or assigned to him by the Regional Adjudicator whose deputy he is or assigned to him by the Chief Adjudicator.

(8) Schedule 4 (which makes further provision about adjudicators) shall have effect.

82 Right of appeal: general

(1) Where an immigration decision is made in respect of a person he may appeal to an adjudicator.

(2) In this Part "immigration decision" means—

(a) refusal of leave to enter the United Kingdom,

(b) refusal of entry clearance,

(c) refusal of a certificate of entitlement under section 10 of this Act,

(d) refusal to vary a person's leave to enter or remain in the United Kingdom if the result of the refusal is that the person has no leave to enter or remain,

(e) variation of a person's leave to enter or remain in the United Kingdom if when the variation takes effect the person has no leave to enter or remain,

(f) revocation under section 76 of this Act of indefinite leave to enter or remain in the United Kingdom,

(g) a decision that a person is to be removed from the United Kingdom by way of directions under section 10(1)(a), (b) or (c) of the Immigration and Asylum Act 1999 (c 33) (removal of person unlawfully in United Kingdom),

(h) a decision that an illegal entrant is to be removed from the United Kingdom by way of directions under paragraphs 8 to 10 of Schedule 2 to the Immigration Act 1971 (c 77) (control of entry: removal),

(i) a decision that a person is to be removed from the United Kingdom by way of directions given by virtue of paragraph 10A of that Schedule (family),

(j) a decision to make a deportation order under section 5(1) of that Act, and

(k) refusal to revoke a deportation order under section 5(2) of that Act.

(3) A variation or revocation of the kind referred to in subsection (2)(e) or (f) shall not have effect while an appeal under subsection (1) against that variation or revocation—

(a) could be brought (ignoring any possibility of an appeal out of time with permission), or

(b) is pending.

(4) The right of appeal under subsection (1) is subject to the exceptions and limitations specified in this Part.

83 Appeal: asylum claim

(1) This section applies where a person has made an asylum claim and—

(a) his claim has been rejected by the Secretary of State, but

(b) he has been granted leave to enter or remain in the United Kingdom for a period exceeding one year (or for periods exceeding one year in aggregate).

(2) The person may appeal to an adjudicator against the rejection of his asylum claim.

84 Grounds of appeal

(1) An appeal under section 82(1) against an immigration decision must be brought on one or more of the following grounds—

(a) that the decision is not in accordance with immigration rules;

(b) that the decision is unlawful by virtue of section 19B of the Race Relations Act 1976 (c 74) (discrimination by public authorities);

(c) that the decision is unlawful under section 6 of the Human Rights Act 1998 (c 42) (public authority not to act contrary to Human Rights Convention) as being incompatible with the appellant's Convention rights;

(d) that the appellant is an EEA national or a member of the family of an EEA national and the decision breaches the appellant's rights under the Community Treaties in respect of entry to or residence in the United Kingdom;

(e) that the decision is otherwise not in accordance with the law;

(f) that the person taking the decision should have exercised differently a discretion conferred by immigration rules;

(g) that removal of the appellant from the United Kingdom in consequence of the immigration decision would breach the United Kingdom's obligations under the Refugee Convention or would be unlawful under section 6 of the Human Rights Act 1998 as being incompatible with the appellant's Convention rights.

(2) In subsection (1)(d) "EEA national" means a national of a State which is a contracting party to the Agreement on the European Economic Area signed at Oporto on 2nd May 1992 (as it has effect from time to time).

(3) An appeal under section 83 must be brought on the grounds that removal of the appellant from the United Kingdom would breach the United Kingdom's obligations under the Refugee Convention.

85 Matters to be considered

(1) An appeal under section 82(1) against a decision shall be treated by the adjudicator as including an appeal against any decision in respect of which the appellant has a right of appeal under section 82(1).

(2) If an appellant under section 82(1) makes a statement under section 120, the adjudicator shall consider any matter raised in the statement which constitutes a ground of appeal of a kind listed in section 84(1) against the decision appealed against.
(3) Subsection (2) applies to a statement made under section 120 whether the statement was made before or after the appeal was commenced.
(4) On an appeal under section 82(1) or 83(2) against a decision an adjudicator may consider evidence about any matter which he thinks relevant to the substance of the decision, including evidence which concerns a matter arising after the date of the decision.
(5) But in relation to an appeal under section 82(1) against refusal of entry clearance or refusal of a certificate of entitlement under section 10—
(a) subsection (4) shall not apply, and
(b) the adjudicator may consider only the circumstances appertaining at the time of the decision to refuse.

86 Determination of appeal
(1) This section applies on an appeal under section 82(1) or 83.
(2) The adjudicator must determine—
(a) any matter raised as a ground of appeal (whether or not by virtue of section 85(1)), and
(b) any matter which section 85 requires him to consider.
(3) The adjudicator must allow the appeal in so far as he thinks that—
(a) a decision against which the appeal is brought or is treated as being brought was not in accordance with the law (including immigration rules), or
(b) a discretion exercised in making a decision against which the appeal is brought or is treated as being brought should have been exercised differently.
(4) For the purposes of subsection (3) a decision that a person should be removed from the United Kingdom under a provision shall not be regarded as unlawful if it could have been lawfully made by reference to removal under another provision.
(5) In so far as subsection (3) does not apply, the adjudicator shall dismiss the appeal.
(6) Refusal to depart from or to authorise departure from immigration rules is not the exercise of a discretion for the purposes of subsection (3)(b).

87 Successful appeal: direction
(1) If an adjudicator allows an appeal under section 82 or 83 he may give a direction for the purpose of giving effect to his decision.
(2) A person responsible for making an immigration decision shall act in accordance with any relevant direction under subsection (1).
(3) But a direction under this section shall not have effect while an appeal under section 101 or a further appeal—
(a) could be brought (ignoring any possibility of an appeal out of time with permission), or
(b) has been brought and has not been finally determined.

(4) A direction under subsection (1) shall be treated as part of the determination of the appeal for the purposes of section 101.

Exceptions and limitations

88 Ineligibility

(1) This section applies to an immigration decision of a kind referred to in section 82(2)(a), (b), (d) or (e).

(2) A person may not appeal under section 82(1) against an immigration decision which is taken on the grounds that he or a person of whom he is a dependant—

- (a) does not satisfy a requirement as to age, nationality or citizenship specified in immigration rules,
- (b) does not have an immigration document of a particular kind (or any immigration document),
- (c) is seeking to be in the United Kingdom for a period greater than that permitted in his case by immigration rules, or
- (d) is seeking to enter or remain in the United Kingdom for a purpose other than one for which entry or remaining is permitted in accordance with immigration rules.

(3) In subsection (2)(b) "immigration document" means—

- (a) entry clearance,
- (b) a passport,
- (c) a work permit or other immigration employment document within the meaning of section 122, and
- (d) a document which relates to a national of a country other than the United Kingdom and which is designed to serve the same purpose as a passport.

(4) Subsection (2) does not prevent the bringing of an appeal on any or all of the grounds referred to in section 84(1)(b), (c) and (g).

89 Visitor or student without entry clearance

(1) This section applies to a person who applies for leave to enter the United Kingdom—

- (a) as a visitor,
- (b) in order to follow a course of study for which he has been accepted and which will not last more than six months,
- (c) in order to study but without having been accepted for a course, or
- (d) as the dependant of a person who applies for leave to enter as a visitor or for a purpose described in paragraph (b) or (c).

(2) A person may not appeal under section 82(1) against refusal of leave to enter the United Kingdom if at the time of the refusal he does not have entry clearance.

(3) Subsection (2) does not prevent the bringing of an appeal on any or all of the grounds referred to in section 84(1)(b), (c) and (g).

90 Non-family visitor

(1) A person who applies for entry clearance for the purpose of entering the United Kingdom as a visitor may appeal under section 82(1) against refusal of entry clearance only if the application was made for the purpose of visiting a member of the applicant's family.

(2) In subsection (1) the reference to a member of the applicant's family shall be construed in accordance with regulations.

(3) Regulations under subsection (2) may, in particular, make provision wholly or partly by reference to the duration of two individuals' residence together.

(4) Subsection (1) does not prevent the bringing of an appeal on either or both of the grounds referred to in section 84(1)(b) and (c).

91 Student

(1) A person may not appeal under section 82(1) against refusal of entry clearance if he seeks it—

- (a) in order to follow a course of study for which he has been accepted and which will not last more than six months,
- (b) in order to study but without having been accepted for a course, or
- (c) as the dependant of a person seeking entry clearance for a purpose described in paragraph (a) or (b).

(2) Subsection (1) does not prevent the bringing of an appeal on either or both of the grounds referred to in section 84(1)(b) and (c).

92 Appeal from within United Kingdom: general

(1) A person may not appeal under section 82(1) while he is in the United Kingdom unless his appeal is of a kind to which this section applies.

(2) This section applies to an appeal against an immigration decision of a kind specified in section 82(2)(c), (d), (e), (f) and (j).

(3) This section also applies to an appeal against refusal of leave to enter the United Kingdom where at the time of the refusal the appellant is in the United Kingdom and has—

- (a) entry clearance, or
- (b) a work permit.

(4) This section also applies to an appeal against an immigration decision if the appellant—

- (a) has made an asylum claim, or a human rights claim, while in the United Kingdom, or
- (b) is an EEA national or a member of the family of an EEA national and makes a claim to the Secretary of State that the decision breaches the appellant's rights under the Community Treaties in respect of entry to or residence in the United Kingdom.

93 Appeal from within United Kingdom: "third country" removal

(1) A person may not appeal under section 82(1) while he is in the United Kingdom if a certificate has been issued in relation to him under section

11(2) or 12(2) of the Immigration and Asylum Act 1999 (c 33) (removal of asylum claimants to "third country").

(2) But subsection (1) does not apply to an appeal if—

(a) the appellant has made a human rights claim, and

(b) the Secretary of State has not certified that in his opinion the human rights claim is clearly unfounded.

94 Appeal from within United Kingdom: unfounded human rights or asylum claim

(1) This section applies to an appeal under section 82(1) where the appellant has made an asylum claim or a human rights claim (or both).

(2) A person may not bring an appeal to which this section applies in reliance on section 92(4) if the Secretary of State certifies that the claim or claims mentioned in subsection (1) is or are clearly unfounded.

(3) If the Secretary of State is satisfied that an asylum claimant or human rights claimant is entitled to reside in a State listed in subsection (4) he shall certify the claim under subsection (2) unless satisfied that it is not clearly unfounded.

(4) Those States are—

(a) the Republic of Cyprus,

(b) the Czech Republic,

(c) the Republic of Estonia,

(d) the Republic of Hungary,

(e) the Republic of Latvia,

(f) the Republic of Lithuania,

(g) the Republic of Malta,

(h) the Republic of Poland,

(i) the Slovak Republic,

(j) the Republic of Slovenia,

[(k) the Republic of Albania,

(l) Bulgaria,

(m) Serbia and Montenegro,

(n) Jamaica,

(o) Macedonia,

(p) the Republic of Moldova, and

(q) Romania].

(5) The Secretary of State may by order add a State, or part of a State, to the list in subsection (4) if satisfied that—

(a) there is in general in that State or part no serious risk of persecution of persons entitled to reside in that State or part, and

(b) removal to that State or part of persons entitled to reside there will not in general contravene the United Kingdom's obligations under the Human Rights Convention.

(6) The Secretary of State may by order remove from the list in subsection (4) a State or part added under subsection (5).

(7) A person may not bring an appeal to which this section applies in reliance on section 92(4) if the Secretary of State certifies that—

(a) it is proposed to remove the person to a country of which he is not a national or citizen, and
(b) there is no reason to believe that the person's rights under the Human Rights Convention will be breached in that country.

(8) In determining whether a person in relation to whom a certificate has been issued under subsection (7) may be removed from the United Kingdom, the country specified in the certificate is to be regarded as—
(a) a place where a person's life and liberty is not threatened by reason of his race, religion, nationality, membership of a particular social group, or political opinion, and
(b) a place from which a person will not be sent to another country otherwise than in accordance with the Refugee Convention.

(9) Where a person in relation to whom a certificate is issued under this section subsequently brings an appeal under section 82(1) while outside the United Kingdom, the appeal shall be considered as if he had not been removed from the United Kingdom.

95 Appeal from outside United Kingdom: removal

A person who is outside the United Kingdom may not appeal under section 82(1) on the ground specified in section 84(1)(g) (except in a case to which section 94(9) applies).

96 Earlier right of appeal

(1) An appeal under section 82(1) against an immigration decision ("the new decision") in respect of a person may not be brought or continued if the Secretary of State or an immigration officer certifies—
(a) that the person was notified of a right to appeal under that section against another immigration decision (whether or not an appeal was brought and whether or not any appeal brought has been determined),
(b) that in the opinion of the Secretary of State or the immigration officer the new decision responds to a claim or application which the person made in order to delay his removal from the United Kingdom or the removal of a member of his family, and
(c) that in the opinion of the Secretary of State or the immigration officer the person had no other legitimate purpose for making the claim or application.

(2) An appeal under section 82(1) against an immigration decision in respect of a person may not be brought or continued if the Secretary of State or an immigration officer certifies that the immigration decision relates to an application or claim which relies on a ground which the person—
(a) raised on an appeal under that section against another immigration decision,
(b) should have included in a statement which he was required to make under section 120 in relation to another immigration decision or application, or
(c) would have been permitted or required to raise on an appeal

against another immigration decision in respect of which he chose not to exercise a right of appeal.

(3) A person may not rely on any ground in an appeal under section 82(1) if the Secretary of State or an immigration officer certifies that the ground was considered in another appeal under that section brought by that person.

(4) In subsection (1) "notified" means notified in accordance with regulations under section 105.

(5) Subsections (1) to (3) apply to prevent or restrict a person's right of appeal whether or not he has been outside the United Kingdom since an earlier right of appeal arose or since a requirement under section 120 was imposed.

(6) In this section a reference to an appeal under section 82(1) includes a reference to an appeal under section 2 of the Special Immigration Appeals Commission Act 1997 (c 68) which is or could be brought by reference to an appeal under section 82(1).

97 National security, &c

(1) An appeal under section 82(1) or 83(2) against a decision in respect of a person may not be brought or continued if the Secretary of State certifies that the decision is or was taken—

(a) by the Secretary of State wholly or partly on a ground listed in subsection (2), or

(b) in accordance with a direction of the Secretary of State which identifies the person to whom the decision relates and which is given wholly or partly on a ground listed in subsection (2).

(2) The grounds mentioned in subsection (1) are that the person's exclusion or removal from the United Kingdom is—

(a) in the interests of national security, or

(b) in the interests of the relationship between the United Kingdom and another country.

(3) An appeal under section 82(1) or 83(2) against a decision may not be brought or continued if the Secretary of State certifies that the decision is or was taken wholly or partly in reliance on information which in his opinion should not be made public—

(a) in the interests of national security,

(b) in the interests of the relationship between the United Kingdom and another country, or

(c) otherwise in the public interest.

(4) In subsections (1)(a) and (b) and (3) a reference to the Secretary of State is to the Secretary of State acting in person.

98 Other grounds of public good

(1) This section applies to an immigration decision of a kind referred to in section 82(2)(a) or (b).

(2) An appeal under section 82(1) against an immigration decision may not be brought or continued if the Secretary of State certifies that the decision is or was taken—

(a) by the Secretary of State wholly or partly on the ground that the exclusion or removal from the United Kingdom of the person to whom the decision relates is conducive to the public good, or

(b) in accordance with a direction of the Secretary of State which identifies the person to whom the decision relates and which is given wholly or partly on that ground.

(3) In subsection (2)(a) and (b) a reference to the Secretary of State is to the Secretary of State acting in person.

(4) Subsection (2) does not prevent the bringing of an appeal on either or both of the grounds referred to in section 84(1)(b) and (c).

(5) Subsection (2) does not prevent the bringing of an appeal against an immigration decision of the kind referred to in section 82(2)(a) on the grounds referred to in section 84(1)(g).

99 Sections 96 to 98: appeal in progress

(1) This section applies where a certificate is issued under section 96(1) or (2), 97 or 98 in respect of a pending appeal.

(2) The appeal shall lapse.

Appeal from adjudicator

100 Immigration Appeal Tribunal

(1) There shall continue to be an Immigration Appeal Tribunal.

(2) Schedule 5 (which makes provision about the Tribunal) shall have effect.

101 Appeal to Tribunal

(1) A party to an appeal to an adjudicator under section 82 or 83 may, with the permission of the Immigration Appeal Tribunal, appeal to the Tribunal against the adjudicator's determination on a point of law.

(2) A party to an application to the Tribunal for permission to appeal under subsection (1) may apply to the High Court or, in Scotland, to the Court of Session for a review of the Tribunal's decision on the ground that the Tribunal made an error of law.

(3) Where an application is made under subsection (2)—

(a) it shall be determined by a single judge by reference only to written submissions,

(b) the judge may affirm or reverse the Tribunal's decision,

(c) the judge's decision shall be final, and

(d) if, in an application to the High Court, the judge thinks the application had no merit he shall issue a certificate under this paragraph (which shall be dealt with in accordance with Civil Procedure Rules).

(4) The Lord Chancellor may by order repeal subsections (2) and (3).

102 Decision

(1) On an appeal under section 101 the Immigration Appeal Tribunal may—

(a) affirm the adjudicator's decision;

(b) make any decision which the adjudicator could have made;
(c) remit the appeal to an adjudicator;
(d) affirm a direction given by the adjudicator under section 87;
(e) vary a direction given by the adjudicator under that section;
(f) give any direction which the adjudicator could have given under that section.

(2) In reaching their decision on an appeal under section 101 the Tribunal may consider evidence about any matter which they think relevant to the adjudicator's decision, including evidence which concerns a matter arising after the adjudicator's decision.

(3) But where the appeal under section 82 was against refusal of entry clearance or refusal of a certificate of entitlement—
(a) subsection (2) shall not apply, and
(b) the Tribunal may consider only the circumstances appertaining at the time of the decision to refuse.

(4) In remitting an appeal to an adjudicator under subsection (1)(c) the Tribunal may, in particular—
(a) require the adjudicator to determine the appeal in accordance with directions of the Tribunal;
(b) require the adjudicator to take additional evidence with a view to the appeal being determined by the Tribunal.

103 Appeal from Tribunal

(1) Where the Immigration Appeal Tribunal determines an appeal under section 101 a party to the appeal may bring a further appeal on a point of law—
(a) where the original decision of the adjudicator was made in Scotland, to the Court of Session, or
(b) in any other case, to the Court of Appeal.

(2) An appeal under this section may be brought only with the permission of—
(a) the Tribunal, or
(b) if the Tribunal refuses permission, the court referred to in subsection (1)(a) or (b).

(3) The remittal of an appeal to an adjudicator under section 102(1)(c) is not a determination of the appeal for the purposes of subsection (1) above.

Procedure

104 Pending appeal

(1) An appeal under section 82(1) is pending during the period—
(a) beginning when it is instituted, and
(b) ending when it is finally determined, withdrawn or abandoned (or when it lapses under section 99).

(2) An appeal under section 82(1) is not finally determined for the purposes of subsection (1)(b) while a further appeal or an application under section 101(2)—
(a) has been instituted and is not yet finally determined, withdrawn or abandoned, or

(b) may be brought (ignoring the possibility of an appeal out of time with permission).

(3) The remittal of an appeal to an adjudicator under section 102(1)(c) is not a final determination for the purposes of subsection (2) above.

(4) An appeal under section 82(1) shall be treated as abandoned if the appellant—

(a) is granted leave to enter or remain in the United Kingdom, or

(b) leaves the United Kingdom.

(5) An appeal under section 82(2)(a), (c), (d), (e) or (f) shall be treated as finally determined if a deportation order is made against the appellant.

105 Notice of immigration decision

(1) The Secretary of State may make regulations requiring a person to be given written notice where an immigration decision is taken in respect of him.

(2) The regulations may, in particular, provide that a notice under subsection (1) of a decision against which the person is entitled to appeal under section 82(1) must state—

(a) that there is a right of appeal under that section, and

(b) how and when that right may be exercised.

(3) The regulations may make provision (which may include presumptions) about service.

106 Rules

(1) The Lord Chancellor may make rules—

(a) regulating the exercise of the right of appeal under section 82, 83 or 101;

(b) prescribing procedure to be followed in connection with proceedings under section 82, 83, 101(1) or 103.

(2) In particular, rules under subsection (1)—

(a) must entitle an appellant to be legally represented at any hearing of his appeal;

(b) may enable or require an appeal to be determined without a hearing;

(c) may enable or require an appeal to be dismissed without substantive consideration where practice or procedure has not been complied with;

(d) may enable or require an adjudicator or the Immigration Appeal Tribunal to treat an appeal as abandoned in specified circumstances;

(e) may enable or require an adjudicator or the Tribunal to determine an appeal in the absence of parties in specified circumstances;

(f) may enable or require an adjudicator or the Tribunal to determine an appeal by reference only to written submissions in specified circumstances;

(g) may make provision about the adjournment of an appeal by an adjudicator (which may include provision prohibiting an adjudicator from adjourning except in specified circumstances);

(h) may make provision about the treatment of adjourned appeals by an adjudicator (which may include provision requiring an adjudicator to determine an appeal within a specified period);
(i) may make provision about the use of electronic communication in the course of or in connection with a hearing;
(j) may make provision about the remittal of an appeal by the Tribunal to an adjudicator under section 102;
(k) may enable an adjudicator to set aside a decision of himself or another adjudicator;
(l) may enable the Tribunal to set aside a decision of the Tribunal;
(m) must make provision about the consolidation of appeals (which may, in particular, include provision for the adjournment or remission of a further appeal under section 101);
(n) may make provision (which may include presumptions) about service;
(o) may confer ancillary powers on an adjudicator or the Tribunal;
(p) may confer a discretion on an adjudicator or the Tribunal;
(q) may require an adjudicator or the Tribunal to give notice of a determination to a specified person;
(r) may require or enable notice of a determination to be given on behalf of an adjudicator or the Tribunal;
(s) may make provision about the grant of bail by an adjudicator or the Tribunal (which may, in particular, include provision which applies or is similar to any enactment).

(3) Rules under subsection (1)—
(a) may enable an adjudicator or the Tribunal to make an award of costs or expenses,
(b) may make provision (which may include provision conferring discretion on a court) for the taxation or assessment of costs or expenses,
(c) may make provision about interest on an award of costs or expenses (which may include provision conferring a discretion or providing for interest to be calculated in accordance with provision made by the rules),
(d) may enable an adjudicator or the Tribunal to disallow all or part of a representative's costs or expenses,
(e) may enable an adjudicator or the Tribunal to require a representative to pay specified costs or expenses, and
(f) shall make provision in respect of proceedings before an adjudicator or the Tribunal which has an effect similar to that of section 101(3)(d) and the Civil Procedure Rules referred to there.

(4) A person commits an offence if without reasonable excuse he fails to comply with a requirement imposed in accordance with rules under subsection (1) to attend before an adjudicator or the Tribunal—
(a) to give evidence, or
(b) to produce a document.

(5) A person who is guilty of an offence under subsection (4) shall be liable on summary conviction to a fine not exceeding level 3 on the standard scale.

107 Practice directions

(1) The President of the Immigration Appeal Tribunal may give directions as to the practice to be followed by the Tribunal.
(2) The Chief Adjudicator may give directions as to the practice to be followed by adjudicators.

108 Forged document: proceedings in private

(1) This section applies where it is alleged—
(a) that a document relied on by a party to an appeal under section 82, 83 or 101 is a forgery, and
(b) that disclosure to that party of a matter relating to the detection of the forgery would be contrary to the public interest.
(2) The adjudicator or the Immigration Appeal Tribunal—
(a) must investigate the allegation in private, and
(b) may proceed in private so far as necessary to prevent disclosure of the matter referred to in subsection (1)(b).

General

109 European Union and European Economic Area

(1) Regulations may provide for, or make provision about, an appeal against an immigration decision taken in respect of a person who has or claims to have a right under any of the Community Treaties.
(2) The regulations may—
(a) apply a provision of this Act or the Special Immigration Appeals Commission Act 1997 (c 68) with or without modification;
(b) make provision similar to a provision made by or under this Act or that Act;
(c) disapply or modify the effect of a provision of this Act or that Act.
(3) In subsection (1) "immigration decision" means a decision about—
(a) a person's entitlement to enter or remain in the United Kingdom, or
(b) removal of a person from the United Kingdom.

110 Grants

(1) The Secretary of State may make a grant to a voluntary organisation which provides—
(a) advice or assistance to persons who have a right of appeal under this Part;
(b) other services for the welfare of those persons.
(2) A grant under this section may be subject to terms or conditions (which may include conditions as to repayment).

111 Monitor of certification of claims as unfounded

(1) The Secretary of State shall appoint a person to monitor the use of the powers under sections 94(2) and 115(1).

(2) The person appointed under this section shall make a report to the Secretary of State—

(a) once in each calendar year, and

(b) on such occasions as the Secretary of State may request.

(3) Where the Secretary of State receives a report under subsection (2)(a) he shall lay a copy before Parliament as soon as is reasonably practicable.

(4) The person appointed under this section shall hold and vacate office in accordance with the terms of his appointment (which may include provision about retirement, resignation or dismissal).

(5) The Secretary of State may—

(a) pay fees and allowances to the person appointed under this section;

(b) defray expenses of the person appointed under this section.

(6) A person who is employed within a government department may not be appointed under this section.

112 Regulations, &c

(1) Regulations under this Part shall be made by the Secretary of State.

(2) Regulations and rules under this Part—

(a) must be made by statutory instrument, and

(b) shall be subject to annulment in pursuance of a resolution of either House of Parliament.

(3) Regulations and rules under this Part—

(a) may make provision which applies generally or only in a specified case or in specified circumstances,

(b) may make different provision for different cases or circumstances,

(c) may include consequential, transitional or incidental provision, and

(d) may include savings.

(4) An order under section 94(5) or 115(8)—

(a) must be made by statutory instrument,

(b) may not be made unless a draft has been laid before and approved by resolution of each House of Parliament, and

(c) may include transitional provision.

(5) An order under section 94(6) or 115(9)—

(a) must be made by statutory instrument,

(b) shall be subject to annulment in pursuance of a resolution of either House of Parliament, and

(c) may include transitional provision.

(6) An order under section 101(4)—

(a) must be made by statutory instrument,

(b) may not be made unless a draft has been laid before and approved by resolution of each House of Parliament,

(c) may include consequential or transitional provision, and

(d) may include savings.

113 Interpretation

(1) In this Part, unless a contrary intention appears—

"asylum claim" means a claim made by a person to the Secretary of State at a place designated by the Secretary of State that to remove the person from or require him to leave the United Kingdom would breach the United Kingdom's obligations under the Refugee Convention,

"entry clearance" has the meaning given by section 33(1) of the Immigration Act 1971 (c 77) (interpretation),

"human rights claim" means a claim made by a person to the Secretary of State at a place designated by the Secretary of State that to remove the person from or require him to leave the United Kingdom would be unlawful under section 6 of the Human Rights Act 1998 (c 42) (public authority not to act contrary to Convention) as being incompatible with his Convention rights,

"the Human Rights Convention" has the same meaning as "the Convention" in the Human Rights Act 1998 and "Convention rights" shall be construed in accordance with section 1 of that Act,

"illegal entrant" has the meaning given by section 33(1) of the Immigration Act 1971,

"immigration rules" means rules under section 1(4) of that Act (general immigration rules),

"prescribed" means prescribed by regulations,

"the Refugee Convention" means the Convention relating to the Status of Refugees done at Geneva on 28th July 1951 and its Protocol,

"visitor" means a visitor in accordance with immigration rules, and

"work permit" has the meaning given by section 33(1) of the Immigration Act 1971 (c 77) (interpretation).

(2) A reference to varying leave to enter or remain in the United Kingdom does not include a reference to adding, varying or revoking a condition of leave.

114 Repeal

(1) Part IV of the Immigration and Asylum Act 1999 (c 33) (appeals) shall cease to have effect.

(2) Schedule 6 (which makes transitional provision in connection with the repeal of Part IV of that Act and its replacement by this Part) shall have effect.

(3) Schedule 7 (consequential amendments) shall have effect.

115 Appeal from within United Kingdom: unfounded human rights or asylum claim: transitional provision

(1) A person may not bring an appeal under section 65 or 69 of the Immigration and Asylum Act 1999 (human rights and asylum) while in the United Kingdom if—

(a) the Secretary of State certifies that the appeal relates to a human rights claim or an asylum claim which is clearly unfounded, and

(b) the person does not have another right of appeal while in the United Kingdom under Part IV of that Act.

(2) A person while in the United Kingdom may not bring an appeal under section 69 of that Act, or raise a question which relates to the Human Rights Convention under section 77 of that Act, if the Secretary of State certifies that—

(a) it is proposed to remove the person to a country of which he is not a national or citizen, and

(b) there is no reason to believe that the person's rights under the Human Rights Convention will be breached in that country.

(3) A person while in the United Kingdom may not bring an appeal under section 65 of that Act (human rights) if the Secretary of State certifies that—

(a) it is proposed to remove the person to a country of which he is not a national or citizen, and

(b) there is no reason to believe that the person's rights under the Human Rights Convention will be breached in that country.

(4) In determining whether a person in relation to whom a certificate has been issued under subsection (2) or (3) may be removed from the United Kingdom, the country specified in the certificate is to be regarded as—

(a) a place where a person's life and liberty is not threatened by reason of his race, religion, nationality, membership of a particular social group, or political opinion, and

(b) a place from which a person will not be sent to another country otherwise than in accordance with the Refugee Convention.

(5) Where a person in relation to whom a certificate is issued under this section subsequently brings an appeal or raises a question under section 65, 69 or 77 of that Act while outside the United Kingdom, the appeal or question shall be considered as if he had not been removed from the United Kingdom.

(6) If the Secretary of State is satisfied that a person who makes a human rights claim or an asylum claim is entitled to reside in a State listed in subsection (7), he shall issue a certificate under subsection (1) unless satisfied that the claim is not clearly unfounded.

(7) Those States are—

(a) the Republic of Cyprus,
(b) the Czech Republic,
(c) the Republic of Estonia,
(d) the Republic of Hungary,
(e) the Republic of Latvia,
(f) the Republic of Lithuania,
(g) the Republic of Malta,
(h) the Republic of Poland,
(i) the Slovak Republic,
(j) the Republic of Slovenia,
[(k) the Republic of Albania,
(l) Bulgaria,
(m) Serbia and Montenegro,
(n) Jamaica,
(o) Macedonia,

(p) the Republic of Moldova, and
(q) Romania].

(8) The Secretary of State may by order add a State, or part of a State, to the list in subsection (7) if satisfied that—

(a) there is in general in that State or part no serious risk of persecution of persons entitled to reside in that State or part, and
(b) removal to that State or part of persons entitled to reside there will not in general contravene the United Kingdom's obligations under the Human Rights Convention.

(9) The Secretary of State may by order remove from the list in subsection (7) a State or part added under subsection (8).

(10) In this section "asylum claim" and "human rights claim" have the meanings given by section 113 but—

(a) a reference to a claim in that section shall be treated as including a reference to an allegation, and
(b) a reference in that section to making a claim at a place designated by the Secretary of State shall be ignored.

116 Special Immigration Appeals Commission: Community Legal Service

In paragraph 2(1) of Schedule 2 to the Access to Justice Act 1999 (c 22) (Community Legal Service: courts and tribunals in which advocacy may be funded) the following shall be inserted after paragraph (h) (and before the word "or" which appears immediately after that paragraph)—

"(ha) the Special Immigration Appeals Commission,".

117 Northern Ireland appeals: legal aid

(1) In Part 1 of Schedule 1 to the Legal Aid, Advice and Assistance (Northern Ireland) Order 1981 (SI 1981/228 (NI 8)) (proceedings for which legal aid may be given under Part II of that Order) the following shall be inserted after paragraph 6—

"6A Proceedings before an adjudicator appointed for the purposes of Part 5 of the Nationality, Immigration and Asylum Act 2002, the Immigration Appeal Tribunal or the Special Immigration Appeals Commission."

(2) The amendment made by subsection (1) is without prejudice to the power to make regulations under Article 10(2) of the Legal Aid, Advice and Assistance (Northern Ireland) Order 1981 amending or revoking the provision inserted by that subsection.

Part 6
Immigration Procedure

Applications

118 Leave pending decision on variation application

The following shall be substituted for section 3C of the Immigration Act 1971 (c 77) (continuation of leave to enter or remain pending decision on application for variation)—

"3C Continuation of leave pending variation decision

(1) This section applies if—

(a) a person who has limited leave to enter or remain in the United Kingdom applies to the Secretary of State for variation of the leave,

(b) the application for variation is made before the leave expires, and

(c) the leave expires without the application for variation having been decided.

(2) The leave is extended by virtue of this section during any period when—

(a) the application for variation is neither decided nor withdrawn,

(b) an appeal under section 82(1) of the Nationality, Asylum and Immigration Act 2002 could be brought against the decision on the application for variation (ignoring any possibility of an appeal out of time with permission), or

(c) an appeal under that section against that decision is pending (within the meaning of section 104 of that Act).

(3) Leave extended by virtue of this section shall lapse if the applicant leaves the United Kingdom.

(4) A person may not make an application for variation of his leave to enter or remain in the United Kingdom while that leave is extended by virtue of this section.

(5) But subsection (4) does not prevent the variation of the application mentioned in subsection (1)(a).

(6) In this section a reference to an application being decided is a reference to notice of the decision being given in accordance with regulations under section 105 of that Act (notice of immigration decision)."

119 Deemed leave on cancellation of notice

In paragraph 6(3) of Schedule 2 to the Immigration Act 1971 (c 77) (deemed leave on cancellation of notice of refusal) after "and the immigration officer does not at the same time give him indefinite or limited leave to enter" there shall be inserted "or require him to submit to further examination".

120 Requirement to state additional grounds for application

(1) This section applies to a person if—

(a) he has made an application to enter or remain in the United Kingdom, or

(b) an immigration decision within the meaning of section 82 has been taken or may be taken in respect of him.

(2) The Secretary of State or an immigration officer may by notice in writing require the person to state—

(a) his reasons for wishing to enter or remain in the United Kingdom,

(b) any grounds on which he should be permitted to enter or remain in the United Kingdom, and

(c) any grounds on which he should not be removed from or required to leave the United Kingdom.

(3) A statement under subsection (2) need not repeat reasons or grounds set out in—
(a) the application mentioned in subsection (1)(a), or
(b) an application to which the immigration decision mentioned in subsection (1)(b) relates.

121 Compliance with procedure

The following shall be inserted after section 31A(3) of the Immigration Act 1971 (procedural requirements for application)—

"(3A) Regulations under this section may provide that a failure to comply with a specified requirement of the regulations—
(a) invalidates an application,
(b) does not invalidate an application, or
(c) invalidates an application in specified circumstances (which may be described wholly or partly by reference to action by the applicant, the Secretary of State, an immigration officer or another person)."

Work permit

122 Fee for work permit, &c

(1) The Secretary of State may by regulations require an application for an immigration employment document to be accompanied by a fee prescribed in the regulations.

(2) In subsection (1) "immigration employment document" means—
(a) a work permit, and
(b) any other document which relates to employment and is issued for a purpose of immigration rules or in connection with leave to enter or remain in the United Kingdom.

(3) Regulations under subsection (1)—
(a) may make provision which applies generally or only in specified cases or circumstances (or except in specified cases or circumstances), and
(b) may make different provision for different cases or circumstances.

(4) In particular, regulations by virtue of subsection (3)(a) which create an exception may make provision by reference to an arrangement with the Secretary of State under which a payment is made in respect of—
(a) a specified number or class of applications, or
(b) a specified period of time.

(5) Regulations under subsection (1)—
(a) must be made by statutory instrument, and
(b) shall be subject to annulment in pursuance of a resolution of either House of Parliament.

(6) In this section—
"immigration rules" has the meaning given by section 33(1) of the Immigration Act 1971 (c 77) (interpretation), and
"work permit" has the meaning given by that section.

123 Advice about work permit, &c

(1) Section 82 of the Immigration and Asylum Act 1999 (c 33) (immigration advice and services: interpretation) shall be amended as follows.

(2) In the definition of "relevant matters" in subsection (1), after paragraph (b) there shall be inserted—

"(ba) an application for an immigration employment document;".

(3) At the end of the section add—

"(3) In the definition of "relevant matters" in subsection (1) "immigration employment document" means—

(a) a work permit (within the meaning of section 33(1) of the Immigration Act 1971 (interpretation)), and

(b) any other document which relates to employment and is issued for a purpose of immigration rules or in connection with leave to enter or remain in the United Kingdom."

Authority-to-carry scheme

124 Authority to carry

(1) Regulations made by the Secretary of State may authorise him to require a person (a "carrier") to pay a penalty if the carrier brings a passenger to the United Kingdom and—

(a) the carrier was required by an authority-to-carry scheme to seek authority under the scheme to carry the passenger, and

(b) the carrier did not seek authority before the journey to the United Kingdom commenced or was refused authority under the scheme.

(2) An "authority-to-carry scheme" is a scheme operated by the Secretary of State which requires carriers to seek authority to bring passengers to the United Kingdom.

(3) An authority-to-carry scheme must specify—

(a) the class of carrier to which it applies (which may be defined by reference to a method of transport or otherwise), and

(b) the class of passenger to which it applies (which may be defined by reference to nationality, the possession of specified documents or otherwise).

(4) The Secretary of State may operate different authority-to-carry schemes for different purposes.

(5) Where the Secretary of State makes regulations under subsection (1) he must—

(a) identify in the regulations the authority-to-carry scheme to which they refer, and

(b) lay the authority-to-carry scheme before Parliament.

(6) Regulations under subsection (1) may, in particular—

(a) apply or make provision similar to a provision of sections 40 to 43 of and Schedule 1 to the Immigration and Asylum Act 1999 (c 33) (charge for passenger without document);

(b) do anything which may be done under a provision of any of those sections;

(c) amend any of those sections.

(7) Regulations by virtue of subsection (6)(a) may, in particular—

(a) apply a provision with modification;
(b) apply a provision which confers power to make legislation.

(8) The grant or refusal of authority under an authority-to-carry scheme shall not be taken to determine whether a person is entitled or permitted to enter the United Kingdom.

(9) Regulations under this section—
(a) must be made by statutory instrument, and
(b) may not be made unless a draft has been laid before and approved by resolution of each House of Parliament.

Evasion of procedure

125 Carriers' liability

Schedule 8 (which amends Part II of the Immigration and Asylum Act 1999 (carriers' liability)) shall have effect.

Provision of information by traveller

126 Physical data: compulsory provision

(1) The Secretary of State may by regulations—
(a) require an immigration application to be accompanied by specified information about external physical characteristics of the applicant;
(b) enable an authorised person to require an individual who makes an immigration application to provide information about his external physical characteristics;
(c) enable an authorised person to require an entrant to provide information about his external physical characteristics.

(2) In subsection (1) "immigration application" means an application for—
(a) entry clearance,
(b) leave to enter or remain in the United Kingdom, or
(c) variation of leave to enter or remain in the United Kingdom.

(3) Regulations under subsection (1) may not—
(a) impose a requirement in respect of a person to whom section 141 of the Immigration and Asylum Act 1999 (c 33) (fingerprinting) applies, during the relevant period within the meaning of that section, or
(b) enable a requirement to be imposed in respect of a person to whom that section applies, during the relevant period within the meaning of that section.

(4) Regulations under subsection (1) may, in particular—
(a) require, or enable an authorised person to require, the provision of information in a specified form;
(b) require an individual to submit, or enable an authorised person to require an individual to submit, to a specified process by means of which information is obtained or recorded;
(c) make provision about the effect of failure to provide information

or to submit to a process (which may, in particular, include provision for an application to be disregarded or dismissed if a requirement is not satisfied);

(d) confer a function (which may include the exercise of a discretion) on an authorised person;

(e) require an authorised person to have regard to a code (with or without modification);

(f) require an authorised person to have regard to such provisions of a code (with or without modification) as may be specified by direction of the Secretary of State;

(g) make provision about the use and retention of information provided (which may include provision permitting the use of information for specified purposes which do not relate to immigration);

(h) make provision which applies generally or only in specified cases or circumstances;

(i) make different provision for different cases or circumstances.

(5) Regulations under subsection (1) must—

(a) include provision about the destruction of information obtained or recorded by virtue of the regulations,

(b) require the destruction of information at the end of the period of ten years beginning with the day on which it is obtained or recorded in a case for which destruction at the end of another period is not required by or in accordance with the regulations, and

(c) include provision similar to section 143(2) and (10) to (13) of the Immigration and Asylum Act 1999 (c 33) (fingerprints: destruction of copies and electronic data).

(6) In so far as regulations under subsection (1) require an individual under the age of 16 to submit to a process, the regulations must make provision similar to section 141(3) to (5) and (13) of the Immigration and Asylum Act 1999 (fingerprints: children).

(7) In so far as regulations under subsection (1) enable an authorised person to require an individual under the age of 16 to submit to a process, the regulations must make provision similar to section 141(3) to (5), (12) and (13) of that Act (fingerprints: children).

(8) Regulations under subsection (1)—

(a) must be made by statutory instrument, and

(b) shall not be made unless a draft of the regulations has been laid before and approved by resolution of each House of Parliament.

(9) In this section—

"authorised person" has the meaning given by section 141(5) of the Immigration and Asylum Act 1999 (authority to take fingerprints),

"code" has the meaning given by section 145(6) of that Act (code of practice),

"entrant" has the meaning given by section 33(1) of the Immigration Act 1971 (c 77) (interpretation),

"entry clearance" has the meaning given by section 33(1) of that Act, and
"external physical characteristics" includes, in particular, features of the iris or any other part of the eye.

127 Physical data: voluntary provision

(1) The Secretary of State may operate a scheme under which an individual may supply, or submit to the obtaining or recording of, information about his external physical characteristics to be used (wholly or partly) in connection with entry to the United Kingdom.

(2) In particular, the Secretary of State may—

(a) require an authorised person to use information supplied under a scheme;

(b) make provision about the collection, use and retention of information supplied under a scheme (which may include provision requiring an authorised person to have regard to a code);

(c) charge for participation in a scheme.

(3) In this section the following expressions have the same meaning as in section 126—

(a) "authorised person",

(b) "code", and

(c) "external physical characteristics".

128 Data collection under Immigration and Asylum Act 1999

(1) The following shall be added at the end of section 144 of the Immigration and Asylum Act 1999 (c 33) (collection of data about external physical characteristics) (which becomes subsection (1))—

"(2) In subsection (1) "external physical characteristics" includes, in particular, features of the iris or any other part of the eye."

(2) The following shall be inserted after section 145(2) of that Act (codes of practice)—

"(2A) A person exercising a power under regulations made by virtue of section 144 must have regard to such provisions of a code as may be specified."

Disclosure of information by public authority

129 Local authority

(1) The Secretary of State may require a local authority to supply information for the purpose of establishing where a person is if the Secretary of State reasonably suspects that—

(a) the person has committed an offence under section 24(1)(a), (b), (c), (e) or (f), 24A(1) or 26(1)(c) or (d) of the Immigration Act 1971 (c 77) (illegal entry, deception, &c), and

(b) the person is or has been resident in the local authority's area.

(2) A local authority shall comply with a requirement under this section.

(3) In the application of this section to England and Wales "local authority" means—

(a) a county council,

(b) a county borough council,
(c) a district council,
(d) a London borough council,
(e) the Common Council of the City of London, and
(f) the Council of the Isles of Scilly.

(4) In the application of this section to Scotland "local authority" means a council constituted under section 2 of the Local Government etc (Scotland) Act 1994 (c 39).

(5) In the application of this section to Northern Ireland—
(a) a reference to a local authority shall be taken as a reference to the Northern Ireland Housing Executive, and
(b) the reference to a local authority's area shall be taken as a reference to Northern Ireland.

130 Inland Revenue

(1) The Commissioners of Inland Revenue may supply the Secretary of State with information for the purpose of establishing where a person is if the Secretary of State reasonably suspects—
(a) that the person does not have leave to enter or remain in the United Kingdom, and
(b) that the person does not have permission to work in accordance with section 1(2) of the Immigration Act 1971 (c 77) (general principles).

(2) The Commissioners of Inland Revenue may supply the Secretary of State with information for the purpose of establishing where a person is if the Secretary of State reasonably suspects that the person has undertaken employment in the United Kingdom in breach of—
(a) a condition attached to leave to enter or remain in the United Kingdom,
(b) a restriction imposed under paragraph 21 of Schedule 2 to the Immigration Act 1971 (control of entry), or
(c) a restriction imposed under paragraph 2 of Schedule 3 to that Act (deportation).

(3) The Commissioners of Inland Revenue may supply the Secretary of State with information for the purpose of determining whether an applicant for naturalisation under the British Nationality Act 1981 (c 61) is of good character.

(4) The Commissioners of Inland Revenue may supply the Secretary of State with information for the purpose of applying, in the case of an applicant for entry clearance within the meaning of section 33 of the Immigration Act 1971, a provision of rules under section 3 of that Act relating to maintenance or accommodation.

(5) Information supplied to the Secretary of State under any of subsections (1) to (4) may be supplied by him to another person only—
(a) for a purpose specified in any of those subsections,
(b) for the purpose of legal proceedings, or

(c) with consent (which may be general or specific) of the Commissioners of Inland Revenue, for a purpose for which the Commissioners could supply the information.

(6) A power of the Commissioners of Inland Revenue under this section—

(a) may be exercised on their behalf only by a person authorised (generally or specifically) for the purpose, and

(b) may be exercised despite any statutory or other requirement of confidentiality.

131 Police, &c

Information may be supplied under section 20 of the Immigration and Asylum Act 1999 (c 33) (supply of information to Secretary of State) for use for the purpose of determining whether an applicant for naturalisation under the British Nationality Act 1981 is of good character.

132 Supply of document, &c to Secretary of State

(1) Section 20 of the Immigration and Asylum Act 1999 (supply of information to Secretary of State) shall be amended as follows.

(2) After subsection (1) insert—

"(1A) This section also applies to a document or article which—

(a) comes into the possession of a person listed in subsection (1) or someone acting on his behalf, or

(b) is discovered by a person listed in subsection (1) or someone acting on his behalf."

(3) In subsection (2) after "information" insert ", document or article".

(4) After subsection (2) insert—

"(2A) The Secretary of State may—

(a) retain for immigration purposes a document or article supplied to him under subsection (2), and

(b) dispose of a document or article supplied to him under subsection (2) in such manner as he thinks appropriate (and the reference to use in subsection (2) includes a reference to disposal)."

(5) In subsection (6) after "information" insert ", documents or articles".

133 Medical inspectors

(1) This section applies to a person if an immigration officer acting under Schedule 2 to the Immigration Act 1971 (c 77) (control on entry, &c) has brought the person to the attention of—

(a) a medical inspector appointed under paragraph 1(2) of that Schedule, or

(b) a person working under the direction of a medical inspector appointed under that paragraph.

(2) A medical inspector may disclose to a health service body—

(a) the name of a person to whom this section applies,

(b) his place of residence in the United Kingdom,

(c) his age,

(d) the language which he speaks,

(e) the nature of any disease with which the inspector thinks the person may be infected,
(f) relevant details of the person's medical history,
(g) the grounds for an opinion mentioned in paragraph (e) (including the result of any test or examination which has been carried out), and
(h) the inspector's opinion about action which the health service body should take.

(3) A disclosure may be made under subsection (2) only if the medical inspector thinks it necessary for the purpose of—
(a) preventative medicine,
(b) medical diagnosis,
(c) the provision of care or treatment, or
(d) the management of health care services.

(4) For the purposes of this section "health service body" in relation to a person means a body which carries out functions in an area which includes his place of residence and which is—
(a) in relation to England—
(i) a Primary Care Trust established under section 16A of the National Health Service Act 1977 (c 49),
(ii) a National Health Service Trust established under section 5 of the National Health Service and Community Care Act 1990 (c 19),
(iii) a Strategic Health Authority established under section 8 of the National Health Service Act 1977,
(iv) a Special Health Authority established under section 11 of that Act, or
(v) the Public Health Laboratory Service Board,
(b) in relation to Wales—
(i) a Health Authority or Local Health Board established under section 8 or 16BA of that Act,
(ii) a National Health Service Trust established under section 5 of the National Health Service and Community Care Act 1990, or
(iii) the Public Health Laboratory Service Board,
(c) in relation to Scotland—
(i) a Health Board, Special Health Board or National Health Service Trust established under section 2 or 12A of the National Health Service (Scotland) Act 1978 (c 29), or
(ii) the Common Services Agency for the Scottish Health Service established under section 10 of that Act, or
(d) in relation to Northern Ireland—
(i) a Health and Social Services Board established under the Health and Personal Social Services (Northern Ireland) Order 1972 (SI 1972/1265 (NI 14)),
(ii) a Health and Social Services trust established under the Health and Personal Social Services (Northern Ireland) Order 1991 (SI 1991/194 (NI 1)), or

(iii) the Department of Health, Social Services and Public Safety.

Disclosure of information by private person

134 Employer

(1) The Secretary of State may require an employer to supply information about an employee whom the Secretary of State reasonably suspects of having committed an offence under—

(a) section 24(1)(a), (b), (c), (e) or (f), 24A(1) or 26(1)(c) or (d) of the Immigration Act 1971 (c 77) (illegal entry, deception, &c),

(b) section 105(1)(a), (b) or (c) of the Immigration and Asylum Act 1999 (c 33) (support for asylum-seeker: fraud), or

(c) section 106(1)(a), (b) or (c) of that Act (support for asylum-seeker: fraud).

(2) The power under subsection (1) may be exercised to require information about an employee only if the information—

(a) is required for the purpose of establishing where the employee is, or

(b) relates to the employee's earnings or to the history of his employment.

(3) In this section a reference to an employer or employee—

(a) includes a reference to a former employer or employee, and

(b) shall be construed in accordance with section 8(8) of the Asylum and Immigration Act 1996 (c 49) (restrictions on employment).

(4) Where—

(a) a business (the "employment agency") arranges for one person (the "worker") to provide services to another (the "client"), and

(b) the worker is not employed by the employment agency or the client,

this section shall apply as if the employment agency were the worker's employer while he provides services to the client.

135 Financial institution

(1) The Secretary of State may require a financial institution to supply information about a person if the Secretary of State reasonably suspects that—

(a) the person has committed an offence under section 105(1)(a), (b) or (c) or 106(1)(a), (b) or (c) of the Immigration and Asylum Act 1999 (c 33) (support for asylum-seeker: fraud),

(b) the information is relevant to the offence, and

(c) the institution has the information.

(2) In this section "financial institution" means—

(a) a person who has permission under Part 4 of the Financial Services and Markets Act 2000 (c 8) to accept deposits, and

(b) a building society (within the meaning given by the Building Societies Act 1986 (c 53)).

136 Notice

(1) A requirement to provide information under section 134 or 135 must be imposed by notice in writing specifying—

(a) the information,
(b) the manner in which it is to be provided, and
(c) the period of time within which it is to be provided.

(2) A period of time specified in a notice under subsection (1)(c)—

(a) must begin with the date of receipt of the notice, and
(b) must not be less than ten working days.

(3) A person on whom a notice is served under subsection (1) must provide the Secretary of State with the information specified in the notice.

(4) Information provided under subsection (3) must be provided—

(a) in the manner specified under subsection (1)(b), and
(b) within the time specified under subsection (1)(c).

(5) In this section "working day" means a day which is not—

(a) Saturday,
(b) Sunday,
(c) Christmas Day,
(d) Good Friday, or
(e) a day which is a bank holiday under the Banking and Financial Dealings Act 1971 (c 80) in any part of the United Kingdom.

137 Disclosure of information: offences

(1) A person commits an offence if without reasonable excuse he fails to comply with section 136(3).

(2) A person who is guilty of an offence under subsection (1) shall be liable on summary conviction to—

(a) imprisonment for a term not exceeding three months,
(b) a fine not exceeding level 5 on the standard scale, or
(c) both.

138 Offence by body

(1) Subsection (2) applies where an offence under section 137 is committed by a body corporate and it is proved that the offence—

(a) was committed with the consent or connivance of an officer of the body, or
(b) was attributable to neglect on the part of an officer of the body.

(2) The officer, as well as the body, shall be guilty of the offence.

(3) In this section a reference to an officer of a body corporate includes a reference to—

(a) a director, manager or secretary,
(b) a person purporting to act as a director, manager or secretary, and
(c) if the affairs of the body are managed by its members, a member.

(4) Where an offence under section 137 is committed by a partnership (other than a limited partnership), each partner shall be guilty of the offence.

(5) Subsection (1) shall have effect in relation to a limited partnership as if—

(a) a reference to a body corporate were a reference to a limited partnership, and
(b) a reference to an officer of the body were a reference to a partner.

139 Privilege against self-incrimination
(1) Information provided by a person pursuant to a requirement under section 134 or 135 shall not be admissible in evidence in criminal proceedings against that person.
(2) This section shall not apply to proceedings for an offence under section 137.

Immigration services

140 Immigration Services Commissioner
(1) The following shall be inserted after paragraph 7(1) of Schedule 5 to the Immigration and Asylum Act 1999 (c 33) (investigation by Commissioner: power of entry)—
"(1A) This paragraph also applies if the Commissioner is investigating a matter under paragraph 5(5) and—
(a) the matter is of a kind described in paragraph 5(3)(a), (b) or (d) (for which purpose a reference to an allegation shall be treated as a reference to a suspicion of the Commissioner), and
(b) there are reasonable grounds for believing that particular premises are being used in connection with the provision of immigration advice or immigration services by a registered person."
(2) The following shall be inserted after paragraph 3 of Schedule 6 to the Immigration and Asylum Act 1999 (c 33) (registration by Commissioner)—

"3A Variation of registration
The Commissioner may vary a person's registration—
(a) so as to make it have limited effect in any of the ways mentioned in paragraph 2(2); or
(b) so as to make it have full effect."
(3) The following shall be inserted after section 87(3)(e) of the Immigration and Asylum Act 1999 (Immigration Services Tribunal: jurisdiction) (before the word "or")—
"(ea) to vary a registration under paragraph 3A of that Schedule;".

Immigration control

141 EEA ports: juxtaposed controls
(1) The Secretary of State may by order make provision for the purpose of giving effect to an international agreement which concerns immigration control at an EEA port (whether or not it also concerns other aspects of frontier control at the port).
(2) An order under this section may make any provision which appears to the Secretary of State—
(a) likely to facilitate implementation of the international agreement (including those aspects of the agreement which relate to frontier control other than immigration control), or

(b) appropriate as a consequence of provision made for the purpose of facilitating implementation of the agreement.

(3) In particular, an order under this section may—

(a) provide for a law of England and Wales to have effect, with or without modification, in relation to a person in a specified area or anything done in a specified area;

(b) provide for a law of England and Wales not to have effect in relation to a person in a specified area or anything done in a specified area;

(c) provide for a law of England and Wales to be modified in its effect in relation to a person in a specified area or anything done in a specified area;

(d) disapply or modify an enactment in relation to a person who has undergone a process in a specified area;

(e) disapply or modify an enactment otherwise than under paragraph (b), (c) or (d);

(f) make provision conferring a function (which may include—

(i) provision conferring a discretionary function;

(ii) provision conferring a function on a servant or agent of the government of a State other than the United Kingdom);

(g) create or extend the application of an offence;

(h) impose or permit the imposition of a penalty;

(i) require the payment of, or enable a person to require the payment of, a charge or fee;

(j) make provision about enforcement (which may include—

(i) provision conferring a power of arrest, detention or removal from or to any place;

(ii) provision for the purpose of enforcing the law of a State other than the United Kingdom);

(k) confer jurisdiction on a court or tribunal;

(l) confer immunity or provide for indemnity;

(m) make provision about compensation;

(n) impose a requirement, or enable a requirement to be imposed, for a person to co-operate with or to provide facilities for the use of another person who is performing a function under the order or under the international agreement (which may include a requirement to provide facilities without charge);

(o) make provision about the disclosure of information.

(4) An order under this section may—

(a) make provision which applies generally or only in specified circumstances;

(b) make different provision for different circumstances;

(c) amend an enactment.

(5) An order under this section—

(a) must be made by statutory instrument,

(b) may not be made unless the Secretary of State has consulted with such persons as appear to him to be appropriate, and

(c) may not be made unless a draft has been laid before and approved by resolution of each House of Parliament.

(6) In this section—

"EEA port" means a port in an EEA State from which passengers are commonly carried by sea to or from the United Kingdom,

"EEA State" means a State which is a contracting party to the Agreement on the European Economic Area signed at Oporto on 2nd May 1992 (as it has effect from time to time),

"frontier control" means the enforcement of law which relates to, or in so far as it relates to, the movement of persons or goods into or out of the United Kingdom or another State,

"immigration control" means arrangements made in connection with the movement of persons into or out of the United Kingdom or another State,

"international agreement" means an agreement made between Her Majesty's Government and the government of another State, and

"specified area" means an area (whether of the United Kingdom or of another State) specified in an international agreement.

Country information

142 Advisory Panel on Country Information

(1) The Secretary of State shall appoint a group of not fewer than ten nor more than 20 individuals (to be known as the Advisory Panel on Country Information).

(2) The Secretary of State shall appoint one member of the Advisory Panel as its Chairman.

(3) The function of the Advisory Panel shall be to consider and make recommendations to the Secretary of State about the content of country information.

(4) In this section "country information" means information about conditions in countries outside the United Kingdom which the Secretary of State compiles and makes available, for purposes connected with immigration, to—

(a) immigration officers, and

(b) other officers of the Secretary of State.

(5) The function of the Advisory Panel shall be shared among its members in accordance with arrangements made by the Chairman.

(6) A member of the Advisory Panel shall hold and vacate office in accordance with the terms of his appointment (which may include provision about retirement, resignation or dismissal).

(7) The Secretary of State may—

(a) pay fees and allowances to members of the Advisory Panel;

(b) defray expenses of members of the Advisory Panel;

(c) make staff and other facilities available to the Advisory Panel.

Part 7
Offences

Substance

143 Assisting unlawful immigration, &c

The following shall be substituted for section 25 of the Immigration Act 1971 (c 77) (assisting illegal entry)—

"25 Assisting unlawful immigration to member State

(1) A person commits an offence if he—

(a) does an act which facilitates the commission of a breach of immigration law by an individual who is not a citizen of the European Union,

(b) knows or has reasonable cause for believing that the act facilitates the commission of a breach of immigration law by the individual, and

(c) knows or has reasonable cause for believing that the individual is not a citizen of the European Union.

(2) In subsection (1) "immigration law" means a law which has effect in a member State and which controls, in respect of some or all persons who are not nationals of the State, entitlement to—

(a) enter the State,

(b) transit across the State, or

(c) be in the State.

(3) A document issued by the government of a member State certifying a matter of law in that State—

(a) shall be admissible in proceedings for an offence under this section, and

(b) shall be conclusive as to the matter certified.

(4) Subsection (1) applies to anything done—

(a) in the United Kingdom,

(b) outside the United Kingdom by an individual to whom subsection (5) applies, or

(c) outside the United Kingdom by a body incorporated under the law of a part of the United Kingdom.

(5) This subsection applies to—

(a) a British citizen,

(b) a British overseas territories citizen,

(c) a British National (Overseas),

(d) a British Overseas citizen,

(e) a person who is a British subject under the British Nationality Act 1981 (c 61), and

(f) a British protected person within the meaning of that Act.

(6) A person guilty of an offence under this section shall be liable—

(a) on conviction on indictment, to imprisonment for a term not exceeding 14 years, to a fine or to both, or

(b) on summary conviction, to imprisonment for a term not exceeding six months, to a fine not exceeding the statutory maximum or to both.

25A Helping asylum-seeker to enter United Kingdom

(1) A person commits an offence if—

(a) he knowingly and for gain facilitates the arrival in the United Kingdom of an individual, and

(b) he knows or has reasonable cause to believe that the individual is an asylum-seeker.

(2) In this section "asylum-seeker" means a person who intends to claim that to remove him from or require him to leave the United Kingdom would be contrary to the United Kingdom's obligations under—

(a) the Refugee Convention (within the meaning given by section 167(1) of the Immigration and Asylum Act 1999 (c 33) (interpretation)), or

(b) the Human Rights Convention (within the meaning given by that section).

(3) Subsection (1) does not apply to anything done by a person acting on behalf of an organisation which—

(a) aims to assist asylum-seekers, and

(b) does not charge for its services.

(4) Subsections (4) to (6) of section 25 apply for the purpose of the offence in subsection (1) of this section as they apply for the purpose of the offence in subsection (1) of that section.

25B Assisting entry to United Kingdom in breach of deportation or exclusion order

(1) A person commits an offence if he—

(a) does an act which facilitates a breach of a deportation order in force against an individual who is a citizen of the European Union, and

(b) knows or has reasonable cause for believing that the act facilitates a breach of the deportation order.

(2) Subsection (3) applies where the Secretary of State personally directs that the exclusion from the United Kingdom of an individual who is a citizen of the European Union is conducive to the public good.

(3) A person commits an offence if he—

(a) does an act which assists the individual to arrive in, enter or remain in the United Kingdom,

(b) knows or has reasonable cause for believing that the act assists the individual to arrive in, enter or remain in the United Kingdom, and

(c) knows or has reasonable cause for believing that the Secretary of State has personally directed that the individual's exclusion from the United Kingdom is conducive to the public good.

(4) Subsections (4) to (6) of section 25 apply for the purpose of an offence under this section as they apply for the purpose of an offence under that section.

25C Forfeiture of vehicle, ship or aircraft

(1) This section applies where a person is convicted on indictment of an offence under section 25, 25A or 25B.

(2) The court may order the forfeiture of a vehicle used or intended to be used in connection with the offence if the convicted person—

(a) owned the vehicle at the time the offence was committed,

(b) was at that time a director, secretary or manager of a company which owned the vehicle,

(c) was at that time in possession of the vehicle under a hire-purchase agreement,

(d) was at that time a director, secretary or manager of a company which was in possession of the vehicle under a hire-purchase agreement, or

(e) was driving the vehicle in the course of the commission of the offence.

(3) The court may order the forfeiture of a ship or aircraft used or intended to be used in connection with the offence if the convicted person—

(a) owned the ship or aircraft at the time the offence was committed,

(b) was at that time a director, secretary or manager of a company which owned the ship or aircraft,

(c) was at that time in possession of the ship or aircraft under a hire-purchase agreement,

(d) was at that time a director, secretary or manager of a company which was in possession of the ship or aircraft under a hire-purchase agreement,

(e) was at that time a charterer of the ship or aircraft, or

(f) committed the offence while acting as captain of the ship or aircraft.

(4) But in a case to which subsection (3)(a) or (b) does not apply, forfeiture may be ordered only—

(a) in the case of a ship, if subsection (5) or (6) applies;

(b) in the case of an aircraft, if subsection (5) or (7) applies.

(5) This subsection applies where—

(a) in the course of the commission of the offence, the ship or aircraft carried more than 20 illegal entrants, and

(b) a person who, at the time the offence was committed, owned the ship or aircraft or was a director, secretary or manager of a company which owned it, knew or ought to have known of the intention to use it in the course of the commission of an offence under section 25, 25A or 25B.

(6) This subsection applies where a ship's gross tonnage is less than 500 tons.

(7) This subsection applies where the maximum weight at which an aircraft (which is not a hovercraft) may take off in accordance with its certificate of airworthiness is less than 5,700 kilogrammes.
(8) Where a person who claims to have an interest in a vehicle, ship or aircraft applies to a court to make representations on the question of forfeiture, the court may not make an order under this section in respect of the ship, aircraft or vehicle unless the person has been given an opportunity to make representations.
(9) In the case of an offence under section 25, the reference in subsection (5)(a) to an illegal entrant shall be taken to include a reference to—
- (a) an individual who seeks to enter a member State in breach of immigration law (within the meaning of section 25), and
- (b) an individual who is a passenger for the purpose of section 145 of the Nationality, Immigration and Asylum Act 2002 (traffic in prostitution).

(10) In the case of an offence under section 25A, the reference in subsection (5)(a) to an illegal entrant shall be taken to include a reference to—
- (a) an asylum-seeker (within the meaning of that section), and
- (b) an individual who is a passenger for the purpose of section 145(1) of the Nationality, Immigration and Asylum Act 2002.

(11) In the case of an offence under section 25B, the reference in subsection (5)(a) to an illegal entrant shall be taken to include a reference to an individual who is a passenger for the purpose of section 145(1) of the Nationality, Immigration and Asylum Act 2002."

144 Section 143: consequential amendments
(1) The Immigration Act 1971 (c 77) shall be amended as follows.
(2) Section 25A (detention of ship, aircraft or vehicle) shall be renumbered as section 25D (and its title becomes "Detention of ship, aircraft or vehicle") and—
- (a) in subsection (1) for "section 25(1)(a) or (b)" substitute "section 25, 25A or 25B",
- (b) in subsections (2) and (4) for "section 25(6)" substitute "section 25C",
- (c) for subsection (3) substitute—

"(3) A person (other than the arrested person) may apply to the court for the release of a ship, aircraft or vehicle on the grounds that—
- (a) he owns the ship, aircraft or vehicle,
- (b) he was, immediately before the detention of the ship, aircraft or vehicle, in possession of it under a hire-purchase agreement, or
- (c) he is a charterer of the ship or aircraft.", and
- (d) omit subsection (7).

(3) In section 28A (arrest without warrant)—
- (a) in subsection (3)(a) for "section 25(1)" substitute "section 25, 25A or 25B",
- (b) omit subsection (4),
- (c) in subsection (10) omit ", (4)(b)", and

(d) in subsection (11) omit ", (4)".

(4) In section 28B(5) (search and arrest by warrant) for ", section 24A or section 25(2)" substitute ", 24A".

(5) In section 28C(1) (search and arrest without warrant) for "section 25(1)" substitute "section 25, 25A or 25B".

(6) In section 28D(4) (entry and search of premises) for "section 24A or section 25" substitute "24A, 25, 25A, 25B".

(7) In section 28F (the title to which becomes "Entry and search of premises following arrest under section 25, 25A or 25B") in subsection (1) for "section 25(1)" substitute "section 25, 25A, 25B".

(8) After section 33(1) (interpretation) insert—

"(1A) A reference to being an owner of a vehicle, ship or aircraft includes a reference to being any of a number of persons who jointly own it."

145 Traffic in prostitution

(1) A person commits an offence if he arranges or facilitates the arrival in the United Kingdom of an individual (the "passenger") and—

(a) he intends to exercise control over prostitution by the passenger in the United Kingdom or elsewhere, or

(b) he believes that another person is likely to exercise control over prostitution by the passenger in the United Kingdom or elsewhere.

(2) A person commits an offence if he arranges or facilitates travel within the United Kingdom by an individual (the "passenger") in respect of whom he believes that an offence under subsection (1) may have been committed and—

(a) he intends to exercise control over prostitution by the passenger in the United Kingdom or elsewhere, or

(b) he believes that another person is likely to exercise control over prostitution by the passenger in the United Kingdom or elsewhere.

(3) A person commits an offence if he arranges or facilitates the departure from the United Kingdom of an individual (the "passenger") and—

(a) he intends to exercise control over prostitution by the passenger outside the United Kingdom, or

(b) he believes that another person is likely to exercise control over prostitution by the passenger outside the United Kingdom.

(4) For the purposes of subsections (1) to (3) a person exercises control over prostitution by another if for purposes of gain he exercises control, direction or influence over the prostitute's movements in a way which shows that he is aiding, abetting or compelling the prostitution.

(5) A person guilty of an offence under this section shall be liable—

(a) on conviction on indictment, to imprisonment for a term not exceeding 14 years, to a fine or to both, or

(b) on summary conviction, to imprisonment for a term not exceeding six months, to a fine not exceeding the statutory maximum or to both.

146 Section 145: supplementary

(1) Subsections (1) to (3) of section 145 apply to anything done—

(a) in the United Kingdom,

(b) outside the United Kingdom by an individual to whom subsection (2) applies, or

(c) outside the United Kingdom by a body incorporated under the law of a part of the United Kingdom.

(2) This subsection applies to—

(a) a British citizen,

(b) a British overseas territories citizen,

(c) a British National (Overseas),

(d) a British Overseas citizen,

(e) a person who is a British subject under the British Nationality Act 1981 (c 61), and

(f) a British protected person within the meaning of that Act.

(3) Sections 25C and 25D of the Immigration Act 1971 (c 77) (forfeiture or detention of vehicle, &c) shall apply in relation to an offence under section 145 of this Act as they apply in relation to an offence under section 25 of that Act.

(4) The following shall be inserted after paragraph 2(m) of Schedule 4 to the Criminal Justice and Court Services Act 2000 (c 43) (offence against child)—

"(n) an offence under section 145 of the Nationality, Immigration and Asylum Act 2002 (traffic in prostitution)."

147 Employment

(1) Section 8 of the Asylum and Immigration Act 1996 (c 49) (employment: offence) shall be amended as follows.

(2) For subsection (2) (defence) substitute—

"(2) It is a defence for a person charged with an offence under this section to prove that before the employment began any relevant requirement of an order of the Secretary of State under subsection (2A) was complied with.

(2A) An order under this subsection may—

(a) require the production to an employer of a document of a specified description;

(b) require the production to an employer of one document of each of a number of specified descriptions;

(c) require an employer to take specified steps to retain, copy or record the content of a document produced to him in accordance with the order;

(d) make provision which applies generally or only in specified circumstances;

(e) make different provision for different circumstances."

(3) After subsection (6) insert—

"(6A) Where an offence under this section is committed by a partnership (other than a limited partnership) each partner shall be guilty of the offence and shall be liable to be proceeded against and punished accordingly.

(6B) Subsection (5) shall have effect in relation to a limited partnership as if—

(a) a reference to a body corporate were a reference to a limited partnership, and

(b) a reference to an officer of the body were a reference to a partner."

(4) At the end of the section add—

"(9) Section 28(1) of the Immigration Act 1971 (c 77) (extended time limit for prosecution) shall apply in relation to an offence under this section.

(10) An offence under this section shall be treated as—

(a) a relevant offence for the purpose of sections 28B and 28D of that Act (search, entry and arrest), and

(b) an offence under Part III of that Act (criminal proceedings) for the purposes of sections 28E, 28G and 28H (search after arrest)."

148 Registration card

The following shall be inserted after section 26 of the Immigration Act 1971 (general offences)—

"26A Registration card

(1) In this section "registration card" means a document which—

(a) carries information about a person (whether or not wholly or partly electronically), and

(b) is issued by the Secretary of State to the person wholly or partly in connection with a claim for asylum (whether or not made by that person).

(2) In subsection (1) "claim for asylum" has the meaning given by section 18 of the Nationality, Immigration and Asylum Act 2002.

(3) A person commits an offence if he—

(a) makes a false registration card,

(b) alters a registration card with intent to deceive or to enable another to deceive,

(c) has a false or altered registration card in his possession without reasonable excuse,

(d) uses or attempts to use a false registration card for a purpose for which a registration card is issued,

(e) uses or attempts to use an altered registration card with intent to deceive,

(f) makes an article designed to be used in making a false registration card,

(g) makes an article designed to be used in altering a registration card with intent to deceive or to enable another to deceive, or

(h) has an article within paragraph (f) or (g) in his possession without reasonable excuse.

(4) In subsection (3) "false registration card" means a document which is designed to appear to be a registration card.

(5) A person who is guilty of an offence under subsection (3)(a), (b), (d), (e), (f) or (g) shall be liable—

(a) on conviction on indictment, to imprisonment for a term not exceeding ten years, to a fine or to both, or
(b) on summary conviction, to imprisonment for a term not exceeding six months, to a fine not exceeding the statutory maximum or to both.

(6) A person who is guilty of an offence under subsection (3)(c) or (h) shall be liable—
(a) on conviction on indictment, to imprisonment for a term not exceeding two years, to a fine or to both, or
(b) on summary conviction, to imprisonment for a term not exceeding six months, to a fine not exceeding the statutory maximum or to both.

(7) The Secretary of State may by order—
(a) amend the definition of "registration card" in subsection (1);
(b) make consequential amendment of this section.

(8) An order under subsection (7)—
(a) must be made by statutory instrument, and
(b) may not be made unless a draft has been laid before and approved by resolution of each House of Parliament."

149 Immigration stamp

The following shall be inserted after section 26A of the Immigration Act 1971 (c 77) (registration card: falsification, &c) (inserted by section 148 above)—

"26B Possession of immigration stamp

(1) A person commits an offence if he has an immigration stamp in his possession without reasonable excuse.

(2) A person commits an offence if he has a replica immigration stamp in his possession without reasonable excuse.

(3) In this section—
(a) "immigration stamp" means a device which is designed for the purpose of stamping documents in the exercise of an immigration function,
(b) "replica immigration stamp" means a device which is designed for the purpose of stamping a document so that it appears to have been stamped in the exercise of an immigration function, and
(c) "immigration function" means a function of an immigration officer or the Secretary of State under the Immigration Acts.

(4) A person who is guilty of an offence under this section shall be liable—
(a) on conviction on indictment, to imprisonment for a term not exceeding two years, to a fine or to both, or
(b) on summary conviction, to imprisonment for a term not exceeding six months, to a fine not exceeding the statutory maximum or to both."

150 Sections 148 and 149: consequential amendments

(1) The following shall be inserted after section 28A(9) of the Immigration Act 1971 (arrest without warrant)—

"(9A) A constable or immigration officer may arrest without warrant a person—

(a) who has committed an offence under section 26A or 26B; or

(b) whom he has reasonable grounds for suspecting has committed an offence under section 26A or 26B."

(2) In section 28B(5) of that Act (search and arrest by warrant) after ", 24A" there shall be inserted ", 26A or 26B.".

(3) In section 28D(4) of that Act (search of premises) after ", 25B" there shall be inserted ", 26A or 26B".

151 False information

In section 26(3) of the Immigration Act 1971 (general offences: "relevant enactment")—

(a) the word "or" after paragraph (c) shall cease to have effect, and

(b) after paragraph (d) there shall be inserted—

"; or

(e) the Nationality, Immigration and Asylum Act 2002 (apart from Part 5)."

Procedure

152 Arrest by immigration officer

The following shall be inserted after section 28A of the Immigration Act 1971 (c 77) (arrest without warrant)—

"28AA Arrest with warrant

(1) This section applies if on an application by an immigration officer a justice of the peace is satisfied that there are reasonable grounds for suspecting that a person has committed an offence under—

(a) section 24(1)(d), or

(b) section 8 of the Asylum and Immigration Act 1996 (c 49) (employment: offence).

(2) The justice of the peace may grant a warrant authorising any immigration officer to arrest the person.

(3) In the application of this section to Scotland a reference to a justice of the peace shall be treated as a reference to the sheriff or a justice of the peace."

153 Power of entry

(1) The following shall be inserted after section 28C of the Immigration Act 1971 (search and arrest without warrant)—

"28CA Business premises: entry to arrest

(1) A constable or immigration officer may enter and search any business premises for the purpose of arresting a person—

(a) for an offence under section 24,

(b) for an offence under section 24A, or
(c) under paragraph 17 of Schedule 2.

(2) The power under subsection (1) may be exercised only—
(a) to the extent that it is reasonably required for a purpose specified in subsection (1),
(b) if the constable or immigration officer has reasonable grounds for believing that the person whom he is seeking is on the premises,
(c) with the authority of the Secretary of State (in the case of an immigration officer) or a Chief Superintendent (in the case of a constable), and
(d) if the constable or immigration officer produces identification showing his status.

(3) Authority for the purposes of subsection (2)(c)—
(a) may be given on behalf of the Secretary of State only by a civil servant of the rank of at least Assistant Director, and
(b) shall expire at the end of the period of seven days beginning with the day on which it is given.

(4) Subsection (2)(d) applies—
(a) whether or not a constable or immigration officer is asked to produce identification, but
(b) only where premises are occupied.

(5) Subsection (6) applies where a constable or immigration officer—
(a) enters premises in reliance on this section, and
(b) detains a person on the premises.

(6) A detainee custody officer may enter the premises for the purpose of carrying out a search.

(7) In subsection (6)—

"detainee custody officer" means a person in respect of whom a certificate of authorisation is in force under section 154 of the Immigration and Asylum Act 1999 (c 33) (detained persons: escort and custody), and

"search" means a search under paragraph 2(1)(a) of Schedule 13 to that Act (escort arrangements: power to search detained person)."

(2) The following shall be substituted for section 146(2) of the Immigration and Asylum Act 1999 (use of force)—

"(2) A person exercising a power under any of the following may if necessary use reasonable force—
(a) section 28CA, 28FA or 28FB of the 1971 Act (business premises: entry to arrest or search),
(b) section 141 or 142 of this Act, and
(c) regulations under section 144 of this Act."

154 Power to search for evidence

The following shall be inserted after section 28F of the Immigration Act 1971 (c 77) (entry and search)—

"28FA Search for personnel records: warrant unnecessary

(1) This section applies where—

(a) a person has been arrested for an offence under section 24(1) or 24A(1),
(b) a person has been arrested under paragraph 17 of Schedule 2,
(c) a constable or immigration officer reasonably believes that a person is liable to arrest for an offence under section 24(1) or 24A(1), or
(d) a constable or immigration officer reasonably believes that a person is liable to arrest under paragraph 17 of Schedule 2.

(2) A constable or immigration officer may search business premises where the arrest was made or where the person liable to arrest is if the constable or immigration officer reasonably believes—
(a) that a person has committed an immigration employment offence in relation to the person arrested or liable to arrest, and
(b) that employee records, other than items subject to legal privilege, will be found on the premises and will be of substantial value (whether on their own or together with other material) in the investigation of the immigration employment offence.

(3) A constable or officer searching premises under subsection (2) may seize and retain employee records, other than items subject to legal privilege, which he reasonably suspects will be of substantial value (whether on their own or together with other material) in the investigation of—
(a) an immigration employment offence, or
(b) an offence under section 105 or 106 of the Immigration and Asylum Act 1999 (c 33) (support for asylum-seeker: fraud).

(4) The power under subsection (2) may be exercised only—
(a) to the extent that it is reasonably required for the purpose of discovering employee records other than items subject to legal privilege,
(b) if the constable or immigration officer produces identification showing his status, and
(c) if the constable or immigration officer reasonably believes that at least one of the conditions in subsection (5) applies.

(5) Those conditions are—
(a) that it is not practicable to communicate with a person entitled to grant access to the records,
(b) that permission to search has been refused,
(c) that permission to search would be refused if requested, and
(d) that the purpose of a search may be frustrated or seriously prejudiced if it is not carried out in reliance on subsection (2).

(6) Subsection (4)(b) applies—
(a) whether or not a constable or immigration officer is asked to produce identification, but
(b) only where premises are occupied.

(7) In this section "immigration employment offence" means an offence under section 8 of the Asylum and Immigration Act 1996 (c 49) (employment).

28FB Search for personnel records: with warrant

(1) This section applies where on an application made by an immigration officer in respect of business premises a justice of the peace is satisfied that there are reasonable grounds for believing—

- (a) that an employer has provided inaccurate or incomplete information under section 134 of the Nationality, Immigration and Asylum Act 2002 (compulsory disclosure by employer),
- (b) that employee records, other than items subject to legal privilege, will be found on the premises and will enable deduction of some or all of the information which the employer was required to provide, and
- (c) that at least one of the conditions in subsection (2) is satisfied.

(2) Those conditions are—

- (a) that it is not practicable to communicate with a person entitled to grant access to the premises,
- (b) that it is not practicable to communicate with a person entitled to grant access to the records,
- (c) that entry to the premises or access to the records will not be granted unless a warrant is produced, and
- (d) that the purpose of a search may be frustrated or seriously prejudiced unless an immigration officer arriving at the premises can secure immediate entry.

(3) The justice of the peace may issue a warrant authorising an immigration officer to enter and search the premises.

(4) Subsection (7)(a) of section 28D shall have effect for the purposes of this section as it has effect for the purposes of that section.

(5) An immigration officer searching premises under a warrant issued under this section may seize and retain employee records, other than items subject to legal privilege, which he reasonably suspects will be of substantial value (whether on their own or together with other material) in the investigation of—

- (a) an offence under section 137 of the Nationality, Immigration and Asylum Act 2002 (disclosure of information: offences) in respect of a requirement under section 134 of that Act, or
- (b) an offence under section 105 or 106 of the Immigration and Asylum Act 1999 (c 33) (support for asylum-seeker: fraud)."

155 Sections 153 and 154: supplemental

The following shall be added at the end of section 28L of the Immigration Act 1971 (c 77) (interpretation) (which becomes subsection (1))—

"(2) In this Part "business premises" means premises (or any part of premises) not used as a dwelling.

(3) In this Part "employee records" means records which show an employee's—

- (a) name,
- (b) date of birth,
- (c) address,
- (d) length of service,

(e) rate of pay, or
(f) nationality or citizenship.

(4) The Secretary of State may by order amend section 28CA(3)(a) to reflect a change in nomenclature.

(5) An order under subsection (4)—
(a) must be made by statutory instrument, and
(b) shall be subject to annulment in pursuance of a resolution of either House of Parliament."

156 Time limit on prosecution

(1) In section 28(1) of the Immigration Act 1971 (c 77) (extended time limit for prosecution) the words ", 24A, 25" shall cease to have effect.

(2) Section 24A(4) of that Act (deception: application of extended time limit) shall cease to have effect.

Part 8
General

157 Consequential and incidental provision

(1) The Secretary of State may by order make consequential or incidental provision in connection with a provision of this Act.

(2) An order under this section may, in particular—
(a) amend an enactment;
(b) modify the effect of an enactment.

(3) An order under this section must be made by statutory instrument.

(4) An order under this section which amends an enactment shall not be made unless a draft has been laid before and approved by resolution of each House of Parliament.

(5) Any other order under this section shall be subject to annulment pursuant to a resolution of either House of Parliament.

158 Interpretation: "the Immigration Acts"

(1) A reference to "the Immigration Acts" is to—
(a) the Immigration Act 1971,
(b) the Immigration Act 1988 (c 14),
(c) the Asylum and Immigration Appeals Act 1993 (c 23),
(d) the Asylum and Immigration Act 1996 (c 49),
(e) the Immigration and Asylum Act 1999 (c 33), and
(f) this Act.

(2) This section has effect in relation to a reference in this Act or any other enactment (including an enactment passed or made before this Act).

(3) The following shall be substituted for section 32(5) of the Immigration Act 1971—

"(5) In subsection (4) "the Immigration Acts" has the meaning given by section 158 of the Nationality, Immigration and Asylum Act 2002."

(4) The following shall be substituted for the definition of "the Immigration Acts" in section 167(1) of the Immigration and Asylum Act 1999—

""the Immigration Acts" has the meaning given by section 158 of the Nationality, Immigration and Asylum Act 2002."

159 Applied provision

(1) Subsection (2) applies where this Act amends or refers to a provision which is applied by, under or for purposes of—

(a) another provision of the Act which contains the provision, or

(b) another Act.

(2) The amendment or reference shall have effect in relation to the provision as applied.

(3) Where this Act applies a provision of another Act, a reference to that provision in any enactment includes a reference to the provision as applied by this Act.

160 Money

(1) Expenditure of the Secretary of State or the Lord Chancellor in connection with a provision of this Act shall be paid out of money provided by Parliament.

(2) An increase attributable to this Act in the amount payable out of money provided by Parliament under another enactment shall be paid out of money provided by Parliament.

(3) A sum received by the Secretary of State or the Lord Chancellor in connection with a provision of this Act shall be paid into the Consolidated Fund.

161 Repeals

The provisions listed in Schedule 9 are hereby repealed to the extent specified.

162 Commencement

(1) Subject to subsections (2) to (5), the preceding provisions of this Act shall come into force in accordance with provision made by the Secretary of State by order.

(2) The following provisions shall come into force on the passing of this Act—

(a) section 6,

(b) section 7,

(c) section 10(1) to (4) and (6),

(d) section 11,

(e) section 15 (and Schedule 2),

(f) section 16,

(g) section 35(1)(h),

(h) section 38,

(i) section 40(1),

(j) section 41(1),

(k) section 42,

(l) section 43,

(m) section 48,

(n) section 49,
(o) section 50,
(p) section 56,
(q) section 58,
(r) section 59,
(s) section 61,
(t) section 67,
(u) section 69,
(v) section 70,
(w) section 115 and paragraph 29 of Schedule 7 (and the relevant entry in Schedule 9),
(x) section 157, and
(y) section 160.

(3) Section 5 shall have effect in relation to—
(a) an application made after the passing of this Act, and
(b) an application made, but not determined, before the passing of this Act.

(4) Section 8 shall have effect in relation to—
(a) an application made on or after a date appointed by the Secretary of State by order, and
(b) an application made, but not determined, before that date.

(5) Section 9 shall have effect in relation to a child born on or after a date appointed by the Secretary of State by order.

(6) An order under subsection (1) may—
(a) make provision generally or for a specified purpose only (which may include the purpose of the application of a provision to or in relation to a particular place or area);
(b) make different provision for different purposes;
(c) include transitional provision;
(d) include savings;
(e) include consequential provision;
(f) include incidental provision.

(7) An order under this section must be made by statutory instrument.

163 Extent

(1) A provision of this Act which amends or repeals a provision of another Act or inserts a provision into another Act has the same extent as the provision amended or repealed or as the Act into which the insertion is made (ignoring, in any case, extent by virtue of an Order in Council).

(2) Sections 145 and 146 extend only to—
(a) England and Wales, and
(b) Northern Ireland.

(3) A provision of this Act to which neither subsection (1) nor subsection (2) applies extends to—
(a) England and Wales,
(b) Scotland, and
(c) Northern Ireland.

(4) Her Majesty may by Order in Council direct that a provision of this Act is to extend, with or without modification or adaptation, to—
  (a) any of the Channel Islands;
  (b) the Isle of Man.
(5) Subsection (4) does not apply in relation to the extension to a place of a provision which extends there by virtue of subsection (1).

164 Short title
This Act may be cited as the Nationality, Immigration and Asylum Act 2002.

SCHEDULE 1
Citizenship Ceremony, Oath and Pledge

Section 3

1 The following shall be substituted for section 42 of the British Nationality Act 1981 (c 61) (registration and naturalisation: fee and oath)—

"42 Registration and naturalisation: citizenship ceremony, oath and pledge
(1) A person of full age shall not be registered under this Act as a British citizen unless he has made the relevant citizenship oath and pledge specified in Schedule 5 at a citizenship ceremony.
(2) A certificate of naturalisation as a British citizen shall not be granted under this Act to a person of full age unless he has made the relevant citizenship oath and pledge specified in Schedule 5 at a citizenship ceremony.
(3) A person of full age shall not be registered under this Act as a British overseas territories citizen unless he has made the relevant citizenship oath and pledge specified in Schedule 5.
(4) A certificate of naturalisation as a British overseas territories citizen shall not be granted under this Act to a person of full age unless he has made the relevant citizenship oath and pledge specified in Schedule 5.
(5) A person of full age shall not be registered under this Act as a British Overseas citizen or a British subject unless he has made the relevant citizenship oath specified in Schedule 5.
(6) Where the Secretary of State thinks it appropriate because of the special circumstances of a case he may—
  (a) disapply any of subsections (1) to (5), or
  (b) modify the effect of any of those subsections.
(7) Sections 5 and 6 of the Oaths Act 1978 (c 19) (affirmation) apply to a citizenship oath; and a reference in this Act to a citizenship oath includes a reference to a citizenship affirmation.

42A Registration and naturalisation: fee
(1) A person shall not be registered under a provision of this Act as a citizen of any description or as a British subject unless any fee payable by virtue of this Act in connection with the registration has been paid.

(2) A certificate of naturalisation shall not be granted to a person under a provision of this Act unless any fee payable by virtue of this Act in connection with the grant of the certificate has been paid.

42B Registration and naturalisation: timing

(1) A person who is registered under this Act as a citizen of any description or as a British subject shall be treated as having become a citizen or subject—

(a) immediately on making the required citizenship oath and pledge in accordance with section 42, or

(b) where the requirement for an oath and pledge is disapplied, immediately on registration.

(2) A person granted a certificate of naturalisation under this Act as a citizen of any description shall be treated as having become a citizen—

(a) immediately on making the required citizenship oath and pledge in accordance with section 42, or

(b) where the requirement for an oath and pledge is disapplied, immediately on the grant of the certificate.

(3) In the application of subsection (1) to registration as a British Overseas citizen or as a British subject the reference to the citizenship oath and pledge shall be taken as a reference to the citizenship oath."

2 The following shall be substituted for Schedule 5 to the British Nationality Act 1981 (c 61)—

"SCHEDULE 5

Citizenship Oath and Pledge

1 The form of citizenship oath and pledge is as follows for registration of or naturalisation as a British citizen—

Oath

"I, *[name]*, swear by Almighty God that, on becoming a British citizen, I will be faithful and bear true allegiance to Her Majesty Queen Elizabeth the Second, Her Heirs and Successors according to law."

Pledge

"I will give my loyalty to the United Kingdom and respect its rights and freedoms. I will uphold its democratic values. I will observe its laws faithfully and fulfil my duties and obligations as a British citizen."

2 The form of citizenship oath and pledge is as follows for registration of or naturalisation as a British overseas territories citizen—

Oath

"I, *[name]*, swear by Almighty God that, on becoming a British overseas territories citizen, I will be faithful and bear true allegiance to Her Majesty Queen Elizabeth the Second, Her Heirs and Successors according to law."

Pledge

"I will give my loyalty to *[name of territory]* and respect its rights and freedoms. I will uphold its democratic values. I will observe its laws faithfully and fulfil my duties and obligations as a British overseas territories citizen."

3 The form of citizenship oath is as follows for registration of a British Overseas citizen—
I, *[name]*, swear by Almighty God that, on becoming a British Overseas citizen, I will be faithful and bear true allegiance to Her Majesty Queen Elizabeth the Second, Her Heirs and Successors according to law."

4 The form of citizenship oath is as follows for registration of a British subject—
"I, *[name]*, swear by Almighty God that, on becoming a British subject, I will be faithful and bear true allegiance to Her Majesty Queen Elizabeth the Second, Her Heirs and Successors according to law."."

3 Section 41 of the British Nationality Act 1981 (c 61) (regulations) shall be amended as follows.

4 For subsection (1)(d) substitute—
"(d) for the time within which an obligation to make a citizenship oath and pledge at a citizenship ceremony must be satisfied;
(da) for the time within which an obligation to make a citizenship oath or pledge must be satisfied;
(db) for the content and conduct of a citizenship ceremony;
(dc) for the administration and making of a citizenship oath or pledge;
(dd) for the registration and certification of the making of a citizenship oath or pledge;
(de) for the completion and grant of a certificate of registration or naturalisation;".

5 In subsection (2)(c)—
(a) for "the taking there of any oath of allegiance" substitute "the making there of a citizenship oath or pledge", and
(b) for "granted or taken" substitute "or granted".

6 In subsection (3)(a) for "taking of oaths of allegiance" substitute "making of oaths and pledges of citizenship".

7 After subsection (3) insert—
"(3A) Regulations under subsection (1)(d) to (de) may, in particular—
(a) enable the Secretary of State to designate or authorise a person to exercise a function (which may include a discretion) in connection with a citizenship ceremony or a citizenship oath or pledge;
(b) require, or enable the Secretary of State to require, a local authority to provide specified facilities and to make specified arrangements in connection with citizenship ceremonies;

(c) impose, or enable the Secretary of State to impose, a function (which may include a discretion) on a local authority or on a registrar.

(3B) In subsection (3A)—

"local authority" means—

(a) in relation to England and Wales, a county council, a county borough council, a metropolitan district council, a London Borough Council and the Common Council of the City of London, and

(b) in relation to Scotland, a council constituted under section 2 of the Local Government etc (Scotland) Act 1994 (c 39), and

"registrar" means—

(a) in relation to England and Wales, a superintendent registrar of births, deaths and marriages (or, in accordance with section 8 of the Registration Service Act 1953 (c 37), a deputy superintendent registrar), and

(b) in relation to Scotland, a district registrar within the meaning of section 7(12) of the Registration of Births, Deaths and Marriages (Scotland) Act 1965 (c 49)."

8 The Secretary of State may make a payment to a local authority in respect of anything done by the authority in accordance with regulations made by virtue of section 41(3A) of the British Nationality Act 1981 (c 61).

9 (1) A local authority must—

(a) comply with a requirement imposed on it by regulations made by virtue of that section, and

(b) carry out a function imposed on it by regulations made by virtue of that section.

(2) A local authority on which a requirement or function is imposed by regulations made by virtue of that section—

(a) may provide facilities or make arrangements in addition to those which it is required to provide or make, and

(b) may make a charge for the provision of facilities or the making of arrangements under paragraph (a) which does not exceed the cost of providing the facilities or making the arrangements.

SCHEDULE 2
Nationality: Repeal of Spent Provisions

Section 15

1 The following provisions of the British Nationality Act 1981 (c 61) shall cease to have effect—

(a) section 7 (registration as British citizen by virtue of residence or employment),

(b) section 8 (registration as British citizen by virtue of marriage),
(c) section 9 (registration as British citizen by virtue of father's status),
(d) section 19 (registration as British Dependent Territories citizen by virtue of residence),
(e) section 20 (registration as British Dependent Territories citizen by virtue of marriage),
(f) section 21 (registration as British Dependent Territories citizen by virtue of father's status),
(g) section 27(2) (entitlement of minor to registration as British Overseas citizen),
(h) section 28 (registration as British Overseas citizen by virtue of marriage), and
(i) section 33 (registration as British subject of certain women by virtue of earlier entitlement).

2 Nothing in this Schedule has any effect in relation to a registration made under a provision before its repeal.

SCHEDULE 3
Withholding and Withdrawal of Support

Section 54

Ineligibility for support

1 (1) A person to whom this paragraph applies shall not be eligible for support or assistance under—
(a) section 21 or 29 of the National Assistance Act 1948 (c 29) (local authority: accommodation and welfare),
(b) section 45 of the Health Services and Public Health Act 1968 (c 46) (local authority: welfare of elderly),
(c) section 12 or 13A of the Social Work (Scotland) Act 1968 (c 49) (social welfare services),
(d) Article 7 or 15 of the Health and Personal Social Services (Northern Ireland) Order 1972 (SI 1972/1265 (NI 14)) (prevention of illness, social welfare, &c),
(e) section 21 of and Schedule 8 to the National Health Service Act 1977 (c 49) (social services),
(f) section 29(1)(b) of the Housing (Scotland) Act 1987 (c 26) (interim duty to accommodate in case of apparent priority need where review of a local authority decision has been requested),
(g) section 17, 23C, 24A or 24B of the Children Act 1989 (c 41) (welfare and other powers which can be exercised in relation to adults),
(h) Article 18, 35 or 36 of the Children (Northern Ireland) Order 1995 (SI 1995/755 (NI 2)) (welfare and other powers which can be exercised in relation to adults),

(i) sections 22, 29 and 30 of the Children (Scotland) Act 1995 (c 36) (provisions analogous to those mentioned in paragraph (g)),
(j) section 188(3) or 204(4) of the Housing Act 1996 (c 52) (accommodation pending review or appeal),
(k) section 2 of the Local Government Act 2000 (c 22) (promotion of well-being),
(l) a provision of the Immigration and Asylum Act 1999 (c 33), or
(m) a provision of this Act.

(2) A power or duty under a provision referred to in sub-paragraph (1) may not be exercised or performed in respect of a person to whom this paragraph applies (whether or not the person has previously been in receipt of support or assistance under the provision).

(3) An approval or directions given under or in relation to a provision referred to in sub-paragraph (1) shall be taken to be subject to sub-paragraph (2).

Exceptions

2 (1) Paragraph 1 does not prevent the provision of support or assistance—
(a) to a British citizen, or
(b) to a child, or
(c) under or by virtue of regulations made under paragraph 8, 9 or 10 below, or
(d) in a case in respect of which, and to the extent to which, regulations made by the Secretary of State disapply paragraph 1, or
(e) in circumstances in respect of which, and to the extent to which, regulations made by the Secretary of State disapply paragraph 1.

(2) Regulations under sub-paragraph (1)(d) may confer a discretion on the Secretary of State.

(3) Regulations under sub-paragraph (1)(e) may, in particular, disapply paragraph 1 to the provision of support or assistance by a local authority to a person where the authority—
(a) has taken steps in accordance with guidance issued by the Secretary of State to determine whether paragraph 1 would (but for the regulations) apply to the person, and
(b) has concluded on the basis of those steps that there is no reason to believe that paragraph 1 would apply.

(4) Regulations under sub-paragraph (1)(d) or (e) may confer a discretion on an authority.

(5) A local authority which is considering whether to give support or assistance to a person under a provision listed in paragraph 1(1) shall act in accordance with any relevant guidance issued by the Secretary of State under sub-paragraph (3)(a).

(6) A reference in this Schedule to a person to whom paragraph 1 applies includes a reference to a person in respect of whom that paragraph is disapplied to a limited extent by regulations under sub-paragraph (1)(d) or (e), except in a case for which the regulations provide otherwise.

3 Paragraph 1 does not prevent the exercise of a power or the performance of a duty if, and to the extent that, its exercise or performance is necessary for the purpose of avoiding a breach of—

(a) a person's Convention rights, or
(b) a person's rights under the Community Treaties.

First class of ineligible person: refugee status abroad

4 (1) Paragraph 1 applies to a person if he—

(a) has refugee status abroad, or
(b) is the dependant of a person who is in the United Kingdom and who has refugee status abroad.

(2) For the purposes of this paragraph a person has refugee status abroad if—

(a) he does not have the nationality of an EEA State, and
(b) the government of an EEA State other than the United Kingdom has determined that he is entitled to protection as a refugee under the Refugee Convention.

Second class of ineligible person: citizen of other EEA State

5 Paragraph 1 applies to a person if he—

(a) has the nationality of an EEA State other than the United Kingdom, or
(b) is the dependant of a person who has the nationality of an EEA State other than the United Kingdom.

Third class of ineligible person: failed asylum-seeker

6 (1) Paragraph 1 applies to a person if—

(a) he was (but is no longer) an asylum-seeker, and
(b) he fails to cooperate with removal directions issued in respect of him.

(2) Paragraph 1 also applies to a dependant of a person to whom that paragraph applies by virtue of sub-paragraph (1).

Fourth class of ineligible person: person unlawfully in United Kingdom

7 Paragraph 1 applies to a person if—

(a) he is in the United Kingdom in breach of the immigration laws within the meaning of section 11, and
(b) he is not an asylum-seeker.

Travel assistance

8 The Secretary of State may make regulations providing for arrangements to be made enabling a person to whom paragraph 1 applies by virtue of paragraph 4 or 5 to leave the United Kingdom.

Temporary accommodation

9 (1) The Secretary of State may make regulations providing for arrangements to be made for the accommodation of a person to whom paragraph 1 applies pending the implementation of arrangements made by virtue of paragraph 8.

(2) Arrangements for a person by virtue of this paragraph—

(a) may be made only if the person has with him a dependent child, and

(b) may include arrangements for a dependent child.

10 (1) The Secretary of State may make regulations providing for arrangements to be made for the accommodation of a person if—

(a) paragraph 1 applies to him by virtue of paragraph 7, and

(b) he has not failed to cooperate with removal directions issued in respect of him.

(2) Arrangements for a person by virtue of this paragraph—

(a) may be made only if the person has with him a dependent child, and

(b) may include arrangements for a dependent child.

Assistance and accommodation: general

11 Regulations under paragraph 8, 9 or 10 may—

(a) provide for the making of arrangements under a provision referred to in paragraph 1(1) or otherwise;

(b) confer a function (which may include the exercise of a discretion) on the Secretary of State, a local authority or another person;

(c) provide that arrangements must be made in a specified manner or in accordance with specified principles;

(d) provide that arrangements may not be made in a specified manner;

(e) require a local authority or another person to have regard to guidance issued by the Secretary of State in making arrangements;

(f) require a local authority or another person to comply with a direction of the Secretary of State in making arrangements.

12 (1) Regulations may, in particular, provide that if a person refuses an offer of arrangements under paragraph 8 or fails to implement or cooperate with arrangements made for him under that paragraph—

(a) new arrangements may be made for him under paragraph 8, but

(b) new arrangements may not be made for him under paragraph 9.

(2) Regulations by virtue of this paragraph may include exceptions in the case of a person who—

(a) has a reason of a kind specified in the regulations for failing to implement or cooperate with arrangements made under paragraph 8, and

(b) satisfies any requirements of the regulations for proof of the reason.

Offences

13 (1) A person who leaves the United Kingdom in accordance with arrangements made under paragraph 8 commits an offence if he—

(a) returns to the United Kingdom, and

(b) requests that arrangements be made for him by virtue of paragraph 8, 9 or 10.

(2) A person commits an offence if he—

(a) requests that arrangements be made for him by virtue of paragraph 8, 9 or 10, and

(b) fails to mention a previous request by him for the making of arrangements under any of those paragraphs.

(3) A person who is guilty of an offence under this paragraph shall be liable on summary conviction to imprisonment for a term not exceeding six months.

Information

14 (1) If it appears to a local authority that paragraph 1 applies or may apply to a person in the authority's area by virtue of paragraph 6 or 7, the authority must inform the Secretary of State.

(2) A local authority shall act in accordance with any relevant guidance issued by the Secretary of State for the purpose of determining whether paragraph 1 applies or may apply to a person in the authority's area by virtue of paragraph 6 or 7.

Power to amend Schedule

15 The Secretary of State may by order amend this Schedule so as—

(a) to provide for paragraph 1 to apply or not to apply to a class of person;

(b) to add or remove a provision to or from the list in paragraph 1(1);

(c) to add, amend or remove a limitation of or exception to paragraph 1.

Orders and regulations

16 (1) An order or regulations under this Schedule must be made by statutory instrument.

(2) An order or regulations under this Schedule may—

(a) make provision which applies generally or only in specified cases or circumstances or only for specified purposes;

(b) make different provision for different cases, circumstances or purposes;

(c) make transitional provision;

(d) make consequential provision (which may include provision amending a provision made by or under this or another Act).

(3) An order under this Schedule, regulations under paragraph 2(1)(d) or (e) or other regulations which include consequential provision amending an enactment shall not be made unless a draft has been laid before and approved by resolution of each House of Parliament.

(4) Regulations under this Schedule to which sub-paragraph (3) does not apply shall be subject to annulment in pursuance of a resolution of either House of Parliament.

Interpretation

17 (1) In this Schedule—

"asylum-seeker" means a person—

(a) who is at least 18 years old,

(b) who has made a claim for asylum (within the meaning of section 18(3)), and

(c) whose claim has been recorded by the Secretary of State but not determined,

"Convention rights" has the same meaning as in the Human Rights Act 1998 (c 42),

"child" means a person under the age of eighteen,

"dependant" and "dependent" shall have such meanings as may be prescribed by regulations made by the Secretary of State,

"EEA State" means a State which is a contracting party to the Agreement on the European Economic Area signed at Oporto on 2nd May 1992 (as it has effect from time to time),

"local authority"—

(a) in relation to England and Wales, has the same meaning as in section 129(3),

(b) in relation to Scotland, has the same meaning as in section 129(4), and

(c) in relation to Northern Ireland, means a health service body within the meaning of section 133(4)(d) and the Northern Ireland Housing Executive (for which purpose a reference to the authority's area shall be taken as a reference to Northern Ireland),

"the Refugee Convention" means the Convention relating to the status of Refugees done at Geneva on 28th July 1951 and its Protocol, and

"removal directions" means directions under Schedule 2 to the Immigration Act 1971 (c 77) (control of entry, &c), under Schedule 3 to that Act (deportation) or under section 10 of the Immigration and Asylum Act 1999 (c 33) (removal of person unlawfully in United Kingdom).

(2) For the purpose of the definition of "asylum-seeker" in sub-paragraph (1) a claim is determined if—

(a) the Secretary of State has notified the claimant of his decision,

(b) no appeal against the decision can be brought (disregarding the possibility of an appeal out of time with permission), and

(c) any appeal which has already been brought has been disposed of.

(3) For the purpose of sub-paragraph (2)(c) an appeal is disposed of when it is no longer pending for the purpose of—

(a) Part 5 of this Act, or

(b) the Special Immigration Appeals Commission Act 1997 (c 68).

(4) The giving of directions in respect of a person under a provision of the Immigration Acts is not the provision of assistance to him for the purposes of this Schedule.

SCHEDULE 4
Immigration and Asylum Appeals: Adjudicators

Section 81

Term of office

1 (1) An adjudicator—

(a) may resign by notice in writing to the Lord Chancellor,

(b) shall cease to hold office on reaching the age of 70, and

(c) otherwise, shall hold and vacate office in accordance with the terms of his appointment.

(2) Sub-paragraph (1)(b) is subject to section 26(4) to (6) of the Judicial Pensions and Retirement Act 1993 (c 8) (extension to age 75).

Proceedings

2 The Chief Adjudicator shall arrange for adjudicators to sit at times and places determined by the Lord Chancellor.

3 The Chief Adjudicator may determine—

(a) that a specified appeal shall be heard by more than one adjudicator;

(b) that appeals of a specified kind shall be heard by more than one adjudicator;

(c) that proceedings of a specified kind in relation to an appeal shall be heard by more than one adjudicator.

4 An adjudicator shall undertake duties allocated to him by the Chief Adjudicator.

Staff

5 The Lord Chancellor may appoint staff for the adjudicators.

Money

6 The Lord Chancellor—

(a) may pay remuneration and allowances to adjudicators,

(b) may pay remuneration and allowances to staff of the adjudicators, and

(c) may defray expenses of the adjudicators.

7 The Lord Chancellor may pay compensation to a person who ceases to be an adjudicator if the Lord Chancellor thinks it appropriate because of special circumstances.

SCHEDULE 5
The Immigration Appeal Tribunal

Section 100

Membership

1 The Lord Chancellor shall appoint the members of the Tribunal.

2 (1) A member—
- (a) may resign by notice in writing to the Lord Chancellor,
- (b) shall cease to be a member on reaching the age of 70, and
- (c) otherwise, shall hold and vacate office in accordance with the terms of his appointment.

(2) Sub-paragraph (1)(b) is subject to section 26(4) to (6) of the Judicial Pensions and Retirement Act 1993 (c 8) (extension to age 75).

Presidency

3 The Lord Chancellor shall appoint as President of the Tribunal a member who holds or has held high judicial office within the meaning of the Appellate Jurisdiction Act 1876 (c 59).

4 (1) The Lord Chancellor shall appoint one legally qualified member of the Tribunal as its Deputy President.

(2) The Deputy President—
- (a) may act for the President if the President is unable to act or unavailable, and
- (b) shall perform such functions as the President may delegate or assign to him.

Proceedings

5 The Tribunal shall sit at times and places determined by the Lord Chancellor.

6 The Tribunal may sit in more than one division.

7 (1) The jurisdiction of the Tribunal may be exercised by such number of its members as the President may direct.

(2) A direction under this sub-paragraph—
- (a) may relate to specified proceedings or proceedings of a specified kind,
- (b) may enable jurisdiction to be exercised by a single member,
- (c) may require the member hearing proceedings, or a specified number of the members hearing proceedings, to be legally qualified, and
- (d) may be varied or revoked by a further direction.

Staff
8 The Lord Chancellor may appoint staff for the Tribunal.

Money
9 The Lord Chancellor—
(a) may pay remuneration and allowances to members of the Tribunal,
(b) may pay remuneration and allowances to staff of the Tribunal, and
(c) may defray expenses of the Tribunal.

10 The Lord Chancellor may pay compensation to a person who ceases to be a member of the Tribunal if the Lord Chancellor thinks it appropriate because of special circumstances.

Interpretation: legally qualified member
11 (1) For the purpose of this Schedule a member of the Tribunal is legally qualified if he—
(a) has a seven year general qualification within the meaning of section 71 of the Courts and Legal Services Act 1990 (c 41),
(b) is an advocate or solicitor in Scotland of at least seven years' standing,
(c) is a member of the Bar of Northern Ireland, or a solicitor of the Supreme Court of Northern Ireland, of at least seven years' standing, or
(d) is appointed by the Lord Chancellor as a legally qualified member.
(2) A person may be appointed by the Lord Chancellor under sub-paragraph (1)(d) only if he has legal or other experience which in the Lord Chancellor's opinion makes him suitable for appointment as a legally qualified member.

SCHEDULE 6
Immigration and Asylum Appeals: Transitional Provision

Section 114

"Commencement"
1 In this Schedule "commencement" means the coming into force of Part 5 of this Act.

Adjudicator
2 Where a person is an adjudicator under section 57 of the Immigration and Asylum Act 1999 (c 33) immediately before commencement his appointment shall have effect after commencement as if made under section 81 of this Act.

Tribunal

3 (1) Where a person is a member of the Immigration Appeal Tribunal immediately before commencement his appointment shall have effect after commencement as if made under Schedule 5.

(2) Where a person is a member of staff of the Immigration Appeal Tribunal immediately before commencement his appointment shall have effect after commencement as if made under Schedule 5.

Earlier appeal

4 In the application of section 96—

(a) a reference to an appeal or right of appeal under a provision of this Act includes a reference to an appeal or right of appeal under the Immigration and Asylum Act 1999,

(b) a reference to a requirement imposed under this Act includes a reference to a requirement of a similar nature imposed under that Act,

(c) a reference to a statement made in pursuance of a requirement imposed under a provision of this Act includes a reference to anything done in compliance with a requirement of a similar nature under that Act, and

(d) a reference to notification by virtue of this Act includes a reference to notification by virtue of any other enactment.

Saving

5 (1) This Schedule is without prejudice to the power to include transitional provision in an order under section 162.

(2) An order under that section may, in particular, provide for a reference to a provision of Part 5 of this Act to be treated as being or including a reference (with or without modification) to a provision of the Immigration and Asylum Act 1999 (c 33).

SCHEDULE 7
Immigration and Asylum Appeals: Consequential Amendments

Section 114

Immigration Act 1971 (c 77)

1 In section 33(4) of the Immigration Act 1971 (c 77) (pending appeal: interpretation) for paragraphs (a) and (b) substitute "in accordance with section 104 of the Nationality, Immigration and Asylum Act 2002 (pending appeals)".

2 In paragraph 2A(9) of Schedule 2 to that Act (control of entry: person with continuing leave) for "Part IV of the Immigration and Asylum Act 1999" substitute "Part 5 of the Nationality, Immigration and Asylum Act 2002 (immigration and asylum appeals)".

3 In paragraph 4(4) of that Schedule (examination and detention of documents) for "an appeal under this Act" substitute "an appeal under the Nationality, Immigration and Asylum Act 2002".

4 In paragraph 8(2) of that Schedule (time within which directions may be given) after "United Kingdom" insert "(ignoring any period during which an appeal by him under the Immigration Acts is pending)".

5 In paragraph 25 of that Schedule (rules) for "section 22 of this Act" substitute "section 106 of the Nationality, Immigration and Asylum Act 2002 (appeals)".

6 In paragraph 29 of that Schedule (bail pending appeal)—
- (a) in sub-paragraph (1), for the words from "section" to "1999" substitute "Part 5 of the Nationality, Immigration and Asylum Act 2002", and
- (b) for the words "Appeal Tribunal" substitute, in each place, "Immigration Appeal Tribunal".

7 In paragraph 2(2) of Schedule 3 to that Act (deportation) for "section 18 of this Act" substitute "section 105 of the Nationality, Immigration and Asylum Act 2002 (notice of decision)".

8 For paragraph 3 of that Schedule (deportation: effect of appeal) substitute—

"**3** So far as they relate to an appeal under section 82(1) of the Nationality, Immigration and Asylum Act 2002 against a decision of the kind referred to in section 82(2)(j) or (k) of that Act (decision to make deportation order and refusal to revoke deportation order), paragraphs 29 to 33 of Schedule 2 to this Act shall apply for the purposes of this Schedule as if the reference in paragraph 29(1) to Part I of that Schedule were a reference to this Schedule."

House of Commons Disqualification Act 1975 (c 24)

9 In Part III of Schedule 1 to the House of Commons Disqualification Act 1975 (disqualifying offices) for "Adjudicator appointed for the purposes of the Immigration and Asylum Act 1999." substitute "Adjudicator appointed for the purposes of Part 5 of the Nationality, Immigration and Asylum Act 2002.".

Northern Ireland Assembly Disqualification Act 1975 (c 25)

10 In Part III of Schedule 1 to the Northern Ireland Assembly Disqualification Act 1975 (disqualifying offices) for "Adjudicator appointed for the purposes of the Immigration and Asylum Act 1999." substitute "Adjudicator appointed for the purposes of Part 5 of the Nationality, Immigration and Asylum Act 2002.".

Race Relations Act 1976 (c 74)

11 In section 53(1) (restriction of proceedings) for "Part IV of the Immigration and Asylum Act 1999" substitute "Part 5 of the Nationality, Immigration and Asylum Act 2002".

12 Section 57A (immigration cases) shall be amended as follows—

(a) in subsection (1)(a) for "Part IV of the 1999 Act" substitute "Part 5 of the 2002 Act",

(b) in subsection (5) for the definition of "the Immigration Acts" substitute—

""the Immigration Acts" has the meaning given by section 158 of the 2002 Act;",

(c) in that subsection in the definition of "immigration appellate body" for "the 1999 Act" substitute "Part 5 of the 2002 Act",

(d) in that subsection for the definition of "immigration authority" substitute—

""immigration authority" means the Secretary of State, an immigration officer or a person responsible for the grant or refusal of entry clearance (within the meaning of section 33(1) of the Immigration Act 1971 (c 77));",

(e) in that subsection in the definition of "pending" for "Part IV of the 1999 Act" substitute "Part 5 of the 2002 Act",

(f) in that subsection in the definition of "relevant decision" for "Part IV of the 1999 Act" substitute "Part 5 of the 2002 Act",

(g) in that subsection in the definition of "relevant immigration proceedings" for "Part IV of the 1999 Act" substitute "Part 5 of the 2002 Act", and

(h) in that subsection for the definition of "the 1999 Act" substitute—

""the 2002 Act" means the Nationality, Immigration and Asylum Act 2002;".

13 In section 62(1)(ba) (persistent discrimination) for "Part IV of the Immigration and Asylum Act 1999" substitute "Part 5 of the Nationality, Immigration and Asylum Act 2002".

14 In section 65(7)(b) (help for aggrieved person) for "Part IV of the Immigration and Asylum Act 1999" substitute "Part 5 of the Nationality, Immigration and Asylum Act 2002".

15 In section 66 (assistance by Commission)—

(a) in subsection (8) for "Part IV of the Immigration and Asylum Act 1999" substitute "Part 5 of the Nationality, Immigration and Asylum Act 2002", and

(b) in subsection (9)—

(i) for "Part IV of the Act of 1999" substitute "Part 5 of the Act of 2002",

(ii) for "rules under section 5 or 8 of that Act;" substitute "rules under that Act;", and
(iii) for "rules under paragraph 3 or 4 of Schedule 4 to that Act." substitute "rules under that Act.".

Courts and Legal Services Act 1990 (c 41)
16 In Schedule 11 to the Courts and Legal Services Act 1990 (judges &c barred from legal practice) for "Adjudicator for the purposes of the Immigration and Asylum Act 1999 (other than Asylum Support Adjudicator)" substitute "Adjudicator appointed for the purposes of Part 5 of the Nationality, Immigration and Asylum Act 2002".

Tribunals and Inquiries Act 1992 (c 53)
17 In paragraph 22 of Schedule 1 to the Tribunals and Inquiries Act 1992 (tribunals under the supervision of the Council on Tribunals)—
(a) in sub-paragraph (a), for "section 57 of the Immigration and Asylum Act 1999" substitute "section 81 of the Nationality, Immigration and Asylum Act 2002", and
(b) in sub-paragraph (b), for "section 56 of that Act" substitute "section 100 of that Act".

Judicial Pensions and Retirement Act 1993 (c 8)
18 In Part II of Schedule 1 to the Judicial Pensions and Retirement Act 1993 (offices which may be qualifying judicial offices) for "Adjudicator for the purposes of the Immigration and Asylum Act 1999 (other than Asylum Support Adjudicator)" substitute "Adjudicator appointed for the purposes of Part 5 of the Nationality, Immigration and Asylum Act 2002".

19 In Schedule 5 to that Act (retirement provisions: the relevant offices) for "Adjudicator for the purposes of the Immigration and Asylum Act 1999 (other than Asylum Support Adjudicator)" substitute "Adjudicator appointed for the purposes of Part 5 of the Nationality, Immigration and Asylum Act 2002".

Special Immigration Appeals Commission Act 1997 (c 68)
20 The following shall be substituted for section 2 of the Special Immigration Appeals Commission Act 1997 (jurisdiction: appeals)—

"2 Jurisdiction: appeals
(1) A person may appeal to the Special Immigration Appeals Commission against a decision if—
(a) he would be able to appeal against the decision under section 82(1) or 83(2) of the Nationality, Immigration and Asylum Act 2002 but for a certificate of the Secretary of State under section 97 of that Act (national security, &c), or
(b) an appeal against the decision under section 82(1) or 83(2) of that Act lapsed under section 99 of that Act by virtue of a certificate of the Secretary of State under section 97 of that Act.

(2) The following provisions shall apply, with any necessary modifications, in relation to an appeal against an immigration decision under this section as they apply in relation to an appeal under section 82(1) of the Nationality, Immigration and Asylum Act 2002—

(a) section 3C of the Immigration Act 1971 (c 77) (continuation of leave pending variation decision),
(b) section 78 of the Nationality, Immigration and Asylum Act 2002 (no removal while appeal pending),
(c) section 79 of that Act (deportation order: appeal),
(d) section 82(3) of that Act (variation or revocation of leave to enter or remain: appeal),
(e) section 84 of that Act (grounds of appeal),
(f) section 85 of that Act (matters to be considered),
(g) section 86 of that Act (determination of appeal),
(h) section 87 of that Act (successful appeal: direction),
(i) section 96 of that Act (earlier right of appeal),
(j) section 104 of that Act (pending appeal),
(k) section 105 of that Act (notice of immigration decision), and
(l) section 110 of that Act (grants).

(3) The following provisions shall apply, with any necessary modifications, in relation to an appeal against the rejection of a claim for asylum under this section as they apply in relation to an appeal under section 83(2) of the Nationality, Immigration and Asylum Act 2002—

(a) section 85(4) of that Act (matters to be considered),
(b) section 86 of that Act (determination of appeal),
(c) section 87 of that Act (successful appeal: direction), and
(d) section 110 of that Act (grants).

(4) An appeal against the rejection of a claim for asylum under this section shall be treated as abandoned if the appellant leaves the United Kingdom.

(5) A person may bring or continue an appeal against an immigration decision under this section while he is in the United Kingdom only if he would be able to bring or continue the appeal while he was in the United Kingdom if it were an appeal under section 82(1) of that Act.

(6) In this section "immigration decision" has the meaning given by section 82(2) of the Nationality, Immigration and Asylum Act 2002."

21 Section 2A of that Act (human rights) shall cease to have effect.

22 Section 4 of that Act (determination of appeals) shall cease to have effect.

23 In section 5 of that Act (procedure)—

(a) in subsections (1)(a) and (b) and (2) omit "or 2A", and
(b) after subsection (2) insert—

"(2A) Rules under this section may, in particular, do anything which may be done by rules under section 106 of the Nationality, Immigration and Asylum Act 2002 (appeals: rules)."

24 Section 7A of that Act (pending appeals) shall cease to have effect.

25 In paragraph 5 of Schedule 1 to that Act—
- (a) in sub-paragraph (b)(i), for "section 57(2) of the Immigration and Asylum Act 1999" substitute "section 81(3)(a) of the Nationality, Immigration and Asylum Act 2002", and
- (b) in sub-paragraph (b)(ii), for "paragraph 1(3) of Schedule 2" substitute "paragraph 11 of Schedule 5".

26 Schedule 2 to that Act shall cease to have effect.

Immigration and Asylum Act 1999 (c 33)
27 In section 23(1) of the Immigration and Asylum Act 1999 (monitoring refusal of entry clearance) for "section 60(5)" there shall be substituted "section 90 or 91 of the Nationality, Immigration and Asylum Act 2002".

28 In section 53(4) of that Act (bail) for "this Act" there shall be substituted "the Nationality, Immigration and Asylum Act 2002".

29 (1) Paragraph 9 of Schedule 4 to that Act (appeals: procedure: Convention cases) shall be amended as follows—
- (a) in sub-paragraph (1)(a), omit "(4), (5)", and
- (b) omit sub-paragraphs (4) and (5).

(2) This paragraph is without prejudice to—
- (a) the effect after commencement of this paragraph of a certificate issued before commencement, or
- (b) the power of the Secretary of State after the commencement of this paragraph to issue a certificate in respect of a claim made before commencement.

Anti-terrorism, Crime and Security Act 2001 (c 24)
30 The following shall be substituted for section 27(10) of the Anti-terrorism, Crime and Security Act 2001 (grants)—
"(10) The reference in section 110 of the Nationality, Immigration and Asylum Act 2002 (immigration and asylum appeal: grant to voluntary organisation) to persons who have rights of appeal under Part 5 of that Act shall be treated as including a reference to suspected international terrorists."

Proceeds of Crime Act 2002 (c 29)
31 The following shall be substituted for paragraph 4 of Schedule 2 to the Proceeds of Crime Act 2002 (lifestyle offences: England and Wales: people trafficking)—

"4 (1) An offence under section 25, 25A or 25B of the Immigration Act 1971 (c 77) (assisting unlawful immigration etc).
(2) An offence under section 145 of the Nationality, Immigration and Asylum Act 2002 (traffic in prostitution)."

32 In paragraph 4 of Schedule 4 to that Act (lifestyle offences: Scotland: people trafficking) for "section 25(1) of the Immigration Act 1971 (assisting illegal entry etc)" there shall be substituted "section 25, 25A or 25B of the Immigration Act 1971 (assisting unlawful immigration etc)".

33 The following shall be substituted for paragraph 4 of Schedule 5 to that Act (lifestyle offences: Northern Ireland: people trafficking)—

"**4** (1) An offence under section 25, 25A or 25B of the Immigration Act 1971 (assisting unlawful immigration etc).
(2) An offence under section 145 of the Nationality, Immigration and Asylum Act 2002 (traffic in prostitution)."

SCHEDULE 8
Carriers' Liability

Section 125

1 The Immigration and Asylum Act 1999 (c 33) shall be amended as follows.

2 (1) Section 32 (penalty for carrying clandestine entrant) shall be amended as follows.
(2) After subsection (1)(a) insert—
"(aa) he arrives in the United Kingdom concealed in a rail freight wagon,".
(3) For subsection (2) substitute—
"(2) The Secretary of State may require a person who is responsible for a clandestine entrant to pay—
(a) a penalty in respect of the clandestine entrant;
(b) a penalty in respect of any person who was concealed with the clandestine entrant in the same transporter.
(2A) In imposing a penalty under subsection (2) the Secretary of State—
(a) must specify an amount which does not exceed the maximum prescribed for the purpose of this paragraph,
(b) may, in respect of a clandestine entrant or a concealed person, impose separate penalties on more than one of the persons responsible for the clandestine entrant, and
(c) may not impose penalties in respect of a clandestine entrant or a concealed person which amount in aggregate to more than the maximum prescribed for the purpose of this paragraph."
(4) For subsection (4) substitute—
"(4) Where a penalty is imposed under subsection (2) on the driver of a vehicle who is an employee of the vehicle's owner or hirer—
(a) the employee and the employer shall be jointly and severally liable for the penalty imposed on the driver (irrespective of whether a penalty is also imposed on the employer), and

(b) a provision of this Part about notification, objection or appeal shall have effect as if the penalty imposed on the driver were also imposed on the employer (irrespective of whether a penalty is also imposed on the employer in his capacity as the owner or hirer of the vehicle).

(4A) In the case of a detached trailer, subsection (4) shall have effect as if a reference to the driver were a reference to the operator."

(5) In subsection (5)—

(a) in paragraph (a) for the second "or" substitute "and", and

(b) in paragraphs (b) and (c) for "or" substitute "and".

(6) After subsection (5) insert—

"(5A) In the case of a clandestine entrant to whom subsection (1)(aa) applies, the responsible person is—

(a) where the entrant arrived concealed in a freight train, the train operator who, at the train's last scheduled stop before arrival in the United Kingdom, was responsible for certifying it as fit to travel to the United Kingdom, or

(b) where the entrant arrived concealed in a freight shuttle wagon, the operator of the shuttle-train of which the wagon formed part."

(7) In subsection (6)(a) and (b) for "or" substitute "and".

(8) After subsection (6) insert—

"(6A) Where a person falls within the definition of responsible person in more than one capacity, a separate penalty may be imposed on him under subsection (2) in respect of each capacity."

3 After section 32 insert—

"32A Level of penalty: code of practice

(1) The Secretary of State shall issue a code of practice specifying matters to be considered in determining the amount of a penalty under section 32.

(2) The Secretary of State shall have regard to the code (in addition to any other matters he thinks relevant)—

(a) when imposing a penalty under section 32, and

(b) when considering a notice of objection under section 35(4).

(3) Before issuing the code the Secretary of State shall lay a draft before Parliament.

(4) After laying the draft code before Parliament the Secretary of State may bring the code into operation by order.

(5) The Secretary of State may from time to time revise the whole or any part of the code and issue the code as revised.

(6) Subsections (3) and (4) also apply to a revision or proposed revision of the code."

4 The heading of section 33 (code of practice) becomes "Prevention of clandestine entrants: code of practice".

5 In section 33(2)(b) omit "both Houses of".

6 (1) Section 34 (defence) shall be amended as follows.
(2) For subsection (1) substitute—
"(1) A person ("the carrier") shall not be liable to the imposition of a penalty under section 32(2) if he has a defence under this section."
(3) In subsection (3)(c) omit the first "that".
(4) After subsection (3) insert—
"(3A) It is also a defence for the carrier to show that—
(a) he knew or suspected that a clandestine entrant was or might be concealed in a rail freight wagon, having boarded after the wagon began its journey to the United Kingdom;
(b) he could not stop the train or shuttle-train of which the wagon formed part without endangering safety;
(c) an effective system for preventing the carriage of clandestine entrants was in operation in relation to the train or shuttle-train; and
(d) on the occasion in question the person or persons responsible for operating the system did so properly."
(5) Omit subsection (5).
(6) For subsection (6) substitute—
"(6) Where a person has a defence under subsection (2) in respect of a clandestine entrant, every other responsible person in respect of the clandestine entrant is also entitled to the benefit of the defence."

7 (1) Section 35 (notification and objection) shall be amended as follows.
(2) In subsection (2)(d)(i) for "must" substitute "may".
(3) For subsections (3) to (8) substitute—
"(3) Subsection (4) applies where a person to whom a penalty notice is issued objects on the ground that—
(a) he is not liable to the imposition of a penalty, or
(b) the amount of the penalty is too high.
(4) The person may give a notice of objection to the Secretary of State.
(5) A notice of objection must—
(a) be in writing,
(b) give the objector's reasons, and
(c) be given before the end of such period as may be prescribed.
(6) Where the Secretary of State receives a notice of objection to a penalty in accordance with this section he shall consider it and—
(a) cancel the penalty,
(b) reduce the penalty,
(c) increase the penalty, or
(d) determine to take no action under paragraphs (a) to (c).
(7) Where the Secretary of State considers a notice of objection under subsection (6) he shall—
(a) inform the objector of his decision before the end of such period as may be prescribed or such longer period as he may agree with the objector,

(b) if he increases the penalty, issue a new penalty notice under subsection (1), and
(c) if he reduces the penalty, notify the objector of the reduced amount."

(4) In subsection (9)—
(a) for the first "served" substitute "issued", and
(b) for "served on" substitute "issued to".

(5) At the end add—

"(11) In proceedings for enforcement of a penalty under subsection (10) no question may be raised as to—
(a) liability to the imposition of the penalty, or
(b) its amount.

(12) A document which is to be issued to or served on a person outside the United Kingdom for the purpose of subsection (1) or (7) or in the course of proceedings under subsection (10) may be issued or served—
(a) in person,
(b) by post,
(c) by facsimile transmission, or
(d) in another prescribed manner.

(13) The Secretary of State may by regulations provide that a document issued or served in a manner listed in subsection (12) in accordance with the regulations is to be taken to have been received at a time specified by or determined in accordance with the regulations."

8 After section 35 insert—

"35A Appeal

(1) A person may appeal to the court against a penalty imposed on him under section 32 on the ground that—
(a) he is not liable to the imposition of a penalty, or
(b) the amount of the penalty is too high.

(2) On an appeal under this section the court may—
(a) allow the appeal and cancel the penalty,
(b) allow the appeal and reduce the penalty, or
(c) dismiss the appeal.

(3) An appeal under this section shall be a re-hearing of the Secretary of State's decision to impose a penalty and shall be determined having regard to—
(a) any code of practice under section 32A which has effect at the time of the appeal,
(b) the code of practice under section 33 which had effect at the time of the events to which the penalty relates, and
(c) any other matters which the court thinks relevant (which may include matters of which the Secretary of State was unaware).

(4) Subsection (3) has effect despite any provision of Civil Procedure Rules.

(5) An appeal may be brought by a person under this section against a penalty whether or not—

(a) he has given notice of objection under section 35(4);
(b) the penalty has been increased or reduced under section 35(6)."

9 (1) Section 36 (detention of vehicle) shall be amended as follows.
(2) In subsection (1)—
(a) for "given" substitute "issued",
(b) after paragraph (b) omit "or", and
(c) after paragraph (c) insert
"or
(d) rail freight wagon,".
(3) After subsection (2) insert—
"(2A) A vehicle may be detained under subsection (1) only if—
(a) the driver of the vehicle is an employee of its owner or hirer,
(b) the driver of the vehicle is its owner or hirer, or
(c) a penalty notice is issued to the owner or hirer of the vehicle.
(2B) A senior officer may detain a relevant vehicle, small ship, small aircraft or rail freight wagon pending—
(a) a decision whether to issue a penalty notice,
(b) the issue of a penalty notice, or
(c) a decision whether to detain under subsection (1).
(2C) That power may not be exercised in any case—
(a) for longer than is necessary in the circumstances of the case, or
(b) after the expiry of the period of 24 hours beginning with the conclusion of the first search of the vehicle, ship, aircraft or wagon by an immigration officer after it arrived in the United Kingdom."

10 After section 36 insert—

"36A Detention in default of payment
(1) This section applies where a person to whom a penalty notice has been issued under section 35 fails to pay the penalty before the date specified in accordance with section 35(2)(c).
(2) The Secretary of State may make arrangements for the detention of any vehicle, small ship, small aircraft or rail freight wagon which the person to whom the penalty notice was issued uses in the course of a business.
(3) A vehicle, ship, aircraft or wagon may be detained under subsection (2) whether or not the person to whom the penalty notice was issued owns it.
(4) But a vehicle may be detained under subsection (2) only if the person to whom the penalty notice was issued—
(a) is the owner or hirer of the vehicle, or
(b) was an employee of the owner or hirer of the vehicle when the penalty notice was issued.
(5) The power under subsection (2) may not be exercised while an appeal against the penalty under section 35A is pending or could be brought (ignoring the possibility of an appeal out of time with permission).

(6) The Secretary of State shall arrange for the release of a vehicle, ship, aircraft or wagon detained under this section if the person to whom the penalty notice was issued pays—

(a) the penalty, and

(b) expenses reasonably incurred in connection with the detention."

11 (1) Section 37 (effect of detention of transporter) shall be amended as follows.

(2) In subsection (1) for "section 36" substitute "section 36(1)".

(3) In subsection (2) for "claiming an interest in the transporter," substitute "whose interests may be affected by detention of the transporter,".

(4) In subsection (3)(c) omit "and the applicant has a compelling need to have the transporter released".

(5) After subsection (3) insert—

"(3A) The court may also release the transporter on the application of the owner of the transporter under subsection (2) if—

(a) a penalty notice was not issued to the owner or an employee of his, and

(b) the court considers it right to release the transporter.

(3B) In determining whether to release a transporter under subsection (3A) the court shall consider—

(a) the extent of any hardship caused by detention,

(b) the extent (if any) to which the owner is responsible for the matters in respect of which the penalty notice was issued, and

(c) any other matter which appears to the court to be relevant (whether specific to the circumstances of the case or of a general nature)."

(6) After subsection (5) insert—

"(5A) The power of sale under subsection (4) may be exercised only when no appeal against the imposition of the penalty is pending or can be brought (ignoring the possibility of an appeal out of time with permission).

(5B) The power of sale under subsection (4) shall lapse if not exercised within a prescribed period."

(7) After subsection (6) add—

"(7) This section applies to a transporter detained under section 36A as it applies to a transporter detained under section 36(1); but for that purpose—

(a) the court may release the transporter only if the court considers that the detention was unlawful or under subsection (3A) (and subsection (3) shall not apply), and

(b) the reference in subsection (4) to the period of 84 days shall be taken as a reference to a period prescribed for the purpose of this paragraph."

12 Section 39 (rail freight) shall cease to have effect.

13 For section 40 (charge in respect of passenger without proper documents) substitute—

"40 Charge in respect of passenger without proper documents

(1) This section applies if an individual requiring leave to enter the United Kingdom arrives in the United Kingdom by ship or aircraft and, on being required to do so by an immigration officer, fails to produce—

(a) an immigration document which is in force and which satisfactorily establishes his identity and his nationality or citizenship, and

(b) if the individual requires a visa, a visa of the required kind.

(2) The Secretary of State may charge the owner of the ship or aircraft, in respect of the individual, the sum of £2,000.

(3) The charge shall be payable to the Secretary of State on demand.

(4) No charge shall be payable in respect of any individual who is shown by the owner to have produced the required document or documents to the owner or his employee or agent when embarking on the ship or aircraft for the voyage or flight to the United Kingdom.

(5) For the purpose of subsection (4) an owner shall be entitled to regard a document as—

(a) being what it purports to be unless its falsity is reasonably apparent, and

(b) relating to the individual producing it unless it is reasonably apparent that it does not relate to him.

(6) For the purposes of this section an individual requires a visa if—

(a) under the immigration rules he requires a visa for entry into the United Kingdom, or

(b) as a result of section 41 he requires a visa for passing through the United Kingdom.

(7) The Secretary of State may by order amend this section for the purpose of applying it in relation to an individual who—

(a) requires leave to enter the United Kingdom, and

(b) arrives in the United Kingdom by train.

(8) An order under subsection (7) may provide for the application of this section—

(a) except in cases of a specified kind;

(b) subject to a specified defence.

(9) In this section "immigration document" means—

(a) a passport, and

(b) a document which relates to a national of a country other than the United Kingdom and which is designed to serve the same purpose as a passport.

(10) The Secretary of State may by order substitute a sum for the sum in subsection (2).

40A Notification and objection

(1) If the Secretary of State decides to charge a person under section 40, the Secretary of State must notify the person of his decision.

(2) A notice under subsection (1) (a "charge notice") must—

(a) state the Secretary of State's reasons for deciding to charge the person,

(b) state the amount of the charge,

(c) specify the date before which, and the manner in which, the charge must be paid,
(d) include an explanation of the steps that the person may take if he objects to the charge, and
(e) include an explanation of the steps that the Secretary of State may take under this Part to recover any unpaid charge.

(3) Where a person on whom a charge notice is served objects to the imposition of the charge on him, he may give a notice of objection to the Secretary of State.

(4) A notice of objection must—
(a) be in writing,
(b) give the objector's reasons, and
(c) be given before the end of such period as may be prescribed.

(5) Where the Secretary of State receives a notice of objection to a charge in accordance with this section, he shall—
(a) consider it, and
(b) determine whether or not to cancel the charge.

(6) Where the Secretary of State considers a notice of objection, he shall inform the objector of his decision before the end of—
(a) such period as may be prescribed, or
(b) such longer period as he may agree with the objector.

(7) Any sum payable to the Secretary of State as a charge under section 40 may be recovered by the Secretary of State as a debt due to him.

(8) In proceedings for enforcement of a charge under subsection (7) no question may be raised as to the validity of the charge.

(9) Subsections (12) and (13) of section 35 shall have effect for the purpose of this section as they have effect for the purpose of section 35(1), (7) and (10).

40B Appeal

(1) A person may appeal to the court against a decision to charge him under section 40.

(2) On an appeal under this section the court may—
(a) allow the appeal and cancel the charge, or
(b) dismiss the appeal.

(3) An appeal under this section—
(a) shall be a re-hearing of the Secretary of State's decision to impose a charge, and
(b) may be determined having regard to matters of which the Secretary of State was unaware.

(4) Subsection (3)(a) has effect despite any provision of Civil Procedure Rules.

(5) An appeal may be brought by a person under this section against a decision to charge him whether or not he has given notice of objection under section 40A(3)."

14 Section 42 (power to detain vehicle, &c carrying person without proper travel documents) shall cease to have effect.

15 In section 43 (interpretation) (which becomes subsection (1))—

(a) in the definition of "concealed" for "or aircraft" substitute ", aircraft or rail freight wagon",

(b) omit the definition of "court",

(c) after the definition of "equipment" insert—

""freight shuttle wagon" means a wagon which—

(a) forms part of a shuttle-train, and

(b) is designed to carry commercial goods vehicles;

"freight train" means any train other than—

(a) a train engaged on a service for the carriage of passengers, or

(b) a shuttle-train;",

(d) in the definition of "owner" omit paragraph (b) and the word "and" immediately preceding it,

(e) for the definition of "rail freight wagon" substitute—

""rail freight wagon" means—

(a) any rolling stock, other than a locomotive, which forms part of a freight train, or

(b) a freight shuttle wagon,

and for the purpose of this definition, "rolling stock" and "locomotive" have the meanings given by section 83 of the Railways Act 1993 (c 43);",

(f) after the definition of "ship" insert—

""shuttle-train" has the meaning given by section 1(9) of the Channel Tunnel Act 1987 (c 53);",

(g) in the definition of "transporter" for "or aircraft" substitute ", aircraft or rail freight wagon", and

(h) at the end insert—

"(2) A reference in this Part to "the court" is a reference—

(a) in England and Wales, to a county court,

(b) in Scotland, to the sheriff, and

(c) in Northern Ireland, to a county court.

(3) But—

(a) a county court may transfer proceedings under this Part to the High Court, and

(b) the sheriff may transfer proceedings under this Part to the Court of Session."

16 (1) Schedule 1 (sale of transporter) shall be amended as follows.

(2) In paragraph 1(2)(a) omit "or charge".

(3) After paragraph 2 insert—

"2A Where the owner of a transporter is a party to an application for leave to sell it, in determining whether to give leave the court shall consider—

(a) the extent of any hardship likely to be caused by sale,

(b) the extent (if any) to which the owner is responsible for the matters in respect of which the penalty notice was issued, and

(c) any other matter which appears to the court to be relevant (whether specific to the circumstances of the case or of a general nature)."

(4) In paragraph 5(1) omit "or 42".

(5) In paragraph 5(2)(d) omit "or charge".

17 (1) This paragraph applies to a code of practice which—

(a) has effect, before the coming into force of paragraph 12 of this Schedule, by virtue of sections 33 and 39 of the Immigration and Asylum Act 1999 (c 33) (power to apply provisions about carriers' liability to rail freight), and

(b) could be issued under section 33 of that Act after the coming into force of paragraph 2 of this Schedule.

(2) A code of practice to which this paragraph applies—

(a) shall continue to have effect after the coming into force of paragraph 12 of this Schedule, and

(b) shall be treated after that time as if made and brought into operation under section 33 alone.

SCHEDULE 9
Repeals

Section 161

Short title and chapter	*Extent of repeal*
Immigration Act 1971 (c 77)	In section 3(9)(b), the words "issued by or on behalf of the Government of the United Kingdom certifying that he has such a right of abode".
	Section 7(1)(a).
	Section 24A(4).
	Section 25A(7).
	In section 26(3) the word "or" after paragraph (c).
	In section 28(1) the words ", 24A, 25".
	In section 28A—
	subsection (4),
	in subsection (10), ", (4)(b)", and
	in subsection (11), ", (4)".
	Section 29.
	Section 31(d).
Race Relations Act 1976 (c 74)	Section 19E(7).
	In section 71A(1), the words "(within the meaning of section 19D(1))".

Short title and chapter	*Extent of repeal*
British Nationality Act 1981 (c 61)	In section 3(6), paragraph (c) and the word "and" immediately preceding it. Sections 7 to 9. In section 10— in subsection (1), the words ", if a woman,", and in subsection (2), the words "if a woman,". In section 17(6), paragraph (c) and the word "and" immediately preceding it. Sections 19 to 21. In section 22— in subsection (1), the words ", if a woman,", and in subsection (2), the words "if a woman,". Section 27(2). Section 28. Section 33. Section 44(2) and (3). Section 47. In Schedule 1— in paragraph 4(c), the words "and (e)", and in paragraph 8(c), the words "and (e)". In Schedule 2— in paragraphs 1(1)(b) and 2(1)(b), the words "he is born legitimate and", and in paragraph 3(1)(b), the words "had attained the age of ten but". In Schedule 4— in paragraph 2, in the second column of the Table, the entry relating to section 29(1) of the Immigration Act 1971, and paragraph 6.
British Nationality (Falkland Islands) Act 1983 (c 6)	Section 4(3)(b).
British Nationality (Hong Kong) Act 1990 (c 34)	Section 1(5).
Asylum and Immigration Act 1996 (c 49)	Section 5.
Special Immigration Appeals Commission Act 1997 (c 68)	Section 2A.

Short title and chapter	*Extent of repeal*
	Section 4. In section 5(1)(a) and (b) and (2), the words "or 2A". Section 7A. Schedule 2.
Immigration and Asylum Act 1999 (c 33)	In section 10(1)(c), the words "("the first directions")" and "("the other person")". Section 15. Section 29. In section 33(2)(b), the words "both Houses of". In section 34— in subsection (3)(c), the first "that", and subsection (5). In section 36(1), the word "or" immediately preceding paragraph (c). In section 37(3)(c), the words "and the applicant has a compelling need to have the transporter released". Section 38(1) and (3). Section 39. Section 42. In section 43, in the definition of "owner" paragraph (b) and the word "and" immediately preceding it. Sections 44 to 52. Section 53(5). Section 55. Sections 56 to 81. Section 94(5) and (6). Section 96(4) to (6). In section 147, the definition of "detention centre". Section 166(4)(e). In Schedule 1— in paragraph 1(2)(a), the words "or charge", in paragraph 5(1), the words "or 42", and in paragraph 5(2)(d), the words "or charge". In paragraph 9 of Schedule 4, the words "(4), (5)" in sub-paragraph (1)(a), and sub-paragraphs (4) and (5). Schedules 2 to 4.

Short title and chapter	*Extent of repeal*
	In Schedule 8, paragraphs 2 and 6. In Schedule 14, paragraphs 46(a), 51, 53, 66, 96, 98(2) and (3), 120 to 121 and 126 to 129.
Race Relations (Amendment) Act 2000 (c 34)	In Schedule 2, paragraphs 23 to 29 and 32 to 40.

Immigration and Asylum Appeals (Procedure) Rules 2003

2003 No 652

Made . . . . *10th March 2003*
Laid before Parliament . . . . *11th March 2003*
Coming into force . . . . *1st April 2003*

The Lord Chancellor, in exercise of the powers conferred by sections 106(1)–(3) and 112(3) of the Nationality, Immigration and Asylum Act 2002 and section 40A(7) of the British Nationality Act 1981, after consulting with the Council on Tribunals in accordance with section 8 of the Tribunals and Inquiries Act 1992, makes the following Rules:

Part 1
Introduction

1 Citation and commencement
These Rules may be cited as the Immigration and Asylum Appeals (Procedure) Rules 2003 and shall come into force on 1st April 2003.

2 Interpretation
In these Rules—

"the 2002 Act" means the Nationality, Immigration and Asylum Act 2002;

"adjudicator" means an adjudicator appointed for the purposes of Part 5 of the 2002 Act;

"appellant" in relation to an appeal to an adjudicator has the meaning given by rule 5(2), and in relation to an appeal to the Tribunal has the meaning given by rule 14(2);

"appellate authority" in relation to an appeal or application to an adjudicator means an adjudicator or the adjudicators' staff, and in relation to an appeal or application to the Tribunal means the Tribunal or its staff;

"appropriate prescribed form" means the appropriate form in the Schedule to these Rules, or that form with any variations that the circumstances may require;

"asylum claim" has the meaning given in section 113(1) of the 2002 Act;

"the Immigration Acts" means the Acts referred to in section 158(1) of the 2002 Act;
"immigration decision" means a decision of a kind listed in section 82(2) of the 2002 Act;
"immigration rules" means the rules referred to in section 1(4) of the Immigration Act 1971;
"party", in relation to an appeal where the appellant or respondent has made a claim for asylum, includes the United Kingdom Representative, if he has given written notice to the appellate authority that he wishes to be treated as a party;
"relevant decision", subject to rule 61(2), means—

(i) an immigration decision;
(ii) a decision to reject an asylum claim against which there is a right of appeal under section 83 of the 2002 Act; or
(iii) a decision to make an order under section 40 of the British Nationality Act 1981 (deprivation of citizenship);

"respondent" in relation to an appeal to an adjudicator has the meaning given by rule 5(2), and in relation to an appeal to the Tribunal has the meaning given by rule 14(2);
"senior adjudicator" means the Chief Adjudicator, the Deputy Chief Adjudicator, a Regional Adjudicator or a Deputy Regional Adjudicator;
"Tribunal" means the Immigration Appeal Tribunal;
"United Kingdom Representative" means the United Kingdom Representative of the United Nations High Commissioner for Refugees.

3 Scope of these Rules

(1) These Rules apply to the following appeals and applications—

(a) appeals to an adjudicator against a relevant decision;
(b) appeals (including applications for permission to appeal) to the Tribunal against an adjudicator's determination;
(c) applications to the Tribunal for permission to appeal to the Court of Appeal or the Court of Session; and
(d) applications to an adjudicator or the Tribunal for bail.

(2) These Rules apply subject to any other Rules made under section 106 of the 2002 Act which apply to specific classes of appeals and applications.

(3) Any provision of these Rules which specifies who is permitted or required to exercise the jurisdiction of the Tribunal for a particular purpose is subject to any contrary direction of the President of the Tribunal under paragraph 7 of Schedule 5 to the 2002 Act.

4 Overriding objective

The overriding objective of these Rules is to secure the just, timely and effective disposal of appeals and applications in the interests of the parties to the proceedings and in the wider public interest.

Part 2
Appeals to an Adjudicator

5 Scope of this Part and interpretation

(1) This Part applies to appeals to an adjudicator against a relevant decision.

(2) In this Part, and in Part 6 insofar as it applies to appeals to an adjudicator—

(a) "appellant" means a person appealing to an adjudicator;

(b) "respondent" means the decision maker specified in the notice of decision against which the appellant is appealing.

6 Giving notice of appeal

(1) An appeal to an adjudicator against a relevant decision must be instituted by giving notice of appeal in accordance with these Rules.

(2) Subject to paragraph (3), notice of appeal must be given by serving it on the respondent at the address specified in the notice of decision.

(3) A person who is in detention under the Immigration Acts may give notice of appeal either—

(a) in accordance with paragraph (2); or

(b) by serving it on the person having custody of him.

(4) Where notice of appeal is given in accordance with paragraph (3)(b), the person having custody of the appellant must endorse on the notice the date that it is served on him and forward it to the respondent.

7 Time limit for appeal

(1) A notice of appeal by a person who is in the United Kingdom must be given—

(a) if the person is in detention under the Immigration Acts when he is served with notice of the decision against which he is appealing, not later than 5 days after he is served with that notice; and

(b) in any other case, not later than 10 days after he is served with notice of the decision.

(2) A notice of appeal by a person who is outside the United Kingdom must be given—

(a) if the person—

(i) was in the United Kingdom when the decision against which he is appealing was made; and

(ii) may not appeal while he is in the United Kingdom by reason of a provision of the 2002 Act,

not later than 28 days after his departure from the United Kingdom; or

(b) in any other case, not later than 28 days after he is served with notice of the decision.

(3) Where a person—

(a) is served with notice of a decision to reject an asylum claim; and

(b) on the date of being served with that notice does not satisfy the condition in section 83(1)(b) of the 2002 Act, but later satisfies that condition, paragraphs (1) and (2)(b) apply with the modification that the time for giving notice of appeal under section 83(2) runs from the date on which the appellant is served with notice of the decision to grant him leave to enter or remain in the United Kingdom by which he satisfies the condition in section 83(1)(b).

8 Form and contents of notice of appeal

(1) The notice of appeal must be in the appropriate prescribed form and must—

- (a) state the name and address of the appellant; and
- (b) state whether the appellant has authorised a representative to act for him in the appeal and, if so, give the representative's name and address.

(2) The notice of appeal must set out the grounds for the appeal and give reasons in support of those grounds.

(3) The notice of appeal must be signed by the appellant or his representative, and dated.

(4) If a notice of appeal is signed by the appellant's representative, the representative must certify in the notice of appeal that he has completed the notice of appeal in accordance with the appellant's instructions.

9 Respondent's duty to file appeal papers

(1) Subject to rule 10, the respondent must file with the appellate authority any notice of appeal which is served on him, together with a copy of—

- (a) the notice of the decision against which the appellant is appealing, and any other document which was served on the appellant giving reasons for that decision;
- (b) any—
  - (i) record of an interview with the appellant; or
  - (ii) other unpublished document,

  which is referred to in a document mentioned in sub-paragraph (a); and
- (c) the notice of any other immigration decision made in relation to the applicant in respect of which he has a right of appeal under section 82 of the 2002 Act.

(2) The respondent must serve on the appellant, as soon as practicable after filing documents under paragraph (1)—

- (a) a copy of all the documents filed with the appellate authority; and
- (b) notice of the date on which they were filed.

10 Late notice of appeal

(1) Where a notice of appeal is given outside the applicable time limit in rule 7, the appellant must—

- (a) state in the notice of appeal his reasons for failing to give the notice within that period; and
- (b) attach to the notice of appeal any written evidence upon which he relies in support of those reasons.

(2) Where the respondent receives a notice of appeal outside the applicable time limit, he may treat the notice as if it had been given in time, if satisfied that by reason of special circumstances it would be unjust not to do so.

(3) Where the respondent receives a notice of appeal which he contends has been given outside the applicable time limit, and does not treat the notice as if it had been given in time, he must—

- (a) file with the appellate authority—
  - (i) the notice of appeal;
  - (ii) a copy of the notice of the decision against which the appellant is appealing and any document served on the appellant giving reasons for that decision; and
  - (iii) a copy of the notice which he serves on the appellant under sub-paragraph (b); and
- (b) at the same time, serve on the appellant a notice stating that—
  - (i) he is treating the notice of appeal as being given out of time; and
  - (ii) he is sending the notice of appeal to the appellate authority for an adjudicator to decide whether to extend the time for appealing.

(4) If the appellant contends that the notice of appeal was given in time he may file with the appellate authority written evidence in support of that contention.

(5) Written evidence under paragraph (4) must be filed—

- (a) if the appellant is in the United Kingdom, not later than 3 days; or
- (b) if the appellant is outside the United Kingdom, not later than 10 days,

after the appellant is served with a notice under paragraph (3)(b).

(6) If the appellant files evidence under paragraph (4), an adjudicator must decide whether the notice of appeal was given in time.

(7) Where the notice of appeal was given out of time, the adjudicator may extend the time for appealing if satisfied that by reason of special circumstances it would be unjust not to do so.

(8) The adjudicator must decide the issues in paragraphs (6) and (7)—

- (a) without a hearing; and
- (b) on the basis of the documents filed by the respondent and any written evidence filed by the appellant.

(9) The appellate authority must serve notice of the adjudicator's decision on the parties.

(10) If the adjudicator decides that the notice of appeal was given in time, or he extends the time for appealing, rule 9 shall apply.

11 Variation of grounds of appeal

(1) This rule applies where documents have been filed with the appellate authority in accordance with rule 9.

(2) Subject to section 85(2) of the 2002 Act, the appellant may vary his grounds of appeal only with the permission of an adjudicator.

12 Hearing of appeal

Every appeal must be considered at a hearing before an adjudicator, except where—

(a) the appeal—

(i) lapses pursuant to section 99 of the 2002 Act;

(ii) is treated as abandoned pursuant to section 104(4) of the 2002 Act;

(iii) is treated as finally determined pursuant to section 104(5) of the 2002 Act; or

(iv) is withdrawn by the appellant in accordance with rule 42; or

(b) a provision of these Rules or of any other enactment permits or requires an adjudicator to dispose of an appeal without a hearing.

13 Closure date

(1) Rule 40 applies to the adjournment of an appeal to an adjudicator, subject to the following provisions of this rule.

(2) Subject to paragraph (3), where an adjudicator adjourns the hearing of an appeal, the adjudicator must give directions fixing a date (the "closure date") by which an adjudicator must either—

(a) hear the appeal; or

(b) determine the appeal without a hearing.

(3) Paragraph (2) does not apply where the appellate authority has fixed and notified the parties of a first hearing date and a subsequent hearing date, and the first hearing is adjourned.

(4) The closure date—

(a) must be fixed according to the individual circumstances of the case; but

(b) subject to paragraphs (6) and (8), must be not more than 6 weeks after the date of the adjourned hearing.

(5) The new date fixed for the hearing in accordance with rule 40(4) must be on or before the closure date.

(6) An adjudicator may fix a closure date which is more than 6 weeks after the date of the adjourned hearing, or may vary a closure date—

(a) if all the parties consent; or

(b) in exceptional circumstances, if the adjudicator is satisfied by evidence filed or given by or on behalf of a party that—

(i) the appeal cannot be justly determined within 6 weeks, or by the closure date where one has already been fixed; and

(ii) there is an identifiable future date by which the appeal can be justly determined.

(7) A senior adjudicator may (either before or after the closure date has passed) vary the closure date for an appeal if no adjudicator is or was available to hear or determine the appeal by that date.

(8) The Chief Adjudicator may in exceptional circumstances—

(a) direct that, in such classes of case as he shall specify, the time within which pending appeals must be heard or determined in accordance with paragraph (2) shall be extended by such period as he shall specify; and

(b) accordingly modify the orders fixing a closure date which have been made in those appeals.

Part 3
Appeals to the Tribunal

14 Scope of this Part and interpretation

(1) This Part applies to appeals to the Tribunal from the determination of an adjudicator.

(2) In this Part, and in Part 6 insofar as it applies to appeals to the Tribunal—

(a) "appellant" means a party appealing to the Tribunal against an adjudicator's determination, and includes a party applying to the Tribunal for permission to appeal; and

(b) "respondent" means the person who was the opposite party in the proceedings before the adjudicator.

15 Applying for permission to appeal to the Tribunal

(1) An appeal from the determination of an adjudicator may only be made with the permission of the Tribunal upon an application made in accordance with these Rules.

(2) Subject to paragraph (3), an application for permission to appeal must be made by filing an application notice with the appellate authority.

(3) A person who is in detention under the Immigration Acts may apply for permission to appeal either—

(a) in accordance with paragraph (2); or

(b) by serving an application notice on the person having custody of him.

(4) Where an application notice is served in accordance with paragraph (3)(b), the person having custody of the appellant must endorse on the notice the date that it is served on him and forward it to the appellate authority.

(5) As soon as practicable after an application notice for permission to appeal is filed, the appellate authority must notify the respondent that it has been filed.

16 Time limit for application for permission to appeal

(1) An application notice for permission to appeal must be filed in accordance with rule 15(2) or served in accordance with rule 15(3)(b)—

(a) if the appellant is in detention under the Immigration Acts when he is served with the adjudicator's determination, not later than 5 days after he is served with that determination;

(b) in any other case where the appellant is in the United Kingdom, not later than 10 days after he is served with the adjudicator's determination; and

(c) where the appellant is outside the United Kingdom, not later than 28 days after he is served with the adjudicator's determination.

(2) The Tribunal may extend the time limits in paragraph (1) if it is satisfied that by reason of special circumstances it would be unjust not to do so.

17 Form and contents of application notice

(1) An application notice for permission to appeal must be in the appropriate prescribed form and must—

(a) state the appellant's name and address; and

(b) state whether the appellant has authorised a representative to act for him in the appeal and, if so, give the representative's name and address.

(2) The application notice must state all the grounds of appeal and give reasons in support of those grounds.

(3) The grounds of appeal must—

(a) identify the alleged errors of law in the adjudicator's determination; and

(b) explain why such errors made a material difference to the decision.

(4) The application notice must be signed by the appellant or his representative, and dated.

(5) If an application notice is signed by the appellant's representative, the representative must certify in the application notice that he has completed the application notice in accordance with the appellant's instructions.

(6) There must be attached to the application notice a clear and complete copy of the adjudicator's determination together with a copy of any other material relied on.

18 Determining the permission application

(1) An application for permission to appeal to the Tribunal must be decided by a legally qualified member of the Tribunal without a hearing.

(2) The Tribunal is not required to consider any grounds of appeal other than those included in the application.

(3) The Tribunal may grant or refuse permission to appeal.

(4) The Tribunal may grant permission to appeal only if it is satisfied that—

(a) the appeal would have a real prospect of success; or

(b) there is some other compelling reason why the appeal should be heard.

(5) Where the Tribunal grants permission to appeal it may limit the permission to one or more of the grounds of appeal specified in the application.

(6) The Tribunal's determination must include its reasons, which may be in summary form.

(7) Where the Tribunal grants permission to appeal—

(a) its determination must indicate the grounds upon which permission to appeal is granted; and

(b) the appellate authority must serve on the respondent, together with the determination, a copy of the application notice and the documents which were attached to it.

19 Respondent's notice

(1) A respondent who wishes to—

(a) apply for permission to appeal to the Tribunal against the adjudicator's determination; or

(b) ask the Tribunal to uphold the adjudicator's determination for reasons different from or additional to those given by the adjudicator,

must file a respondent's notice with the appellate authority.

(2) A respondent's notice must be filed—

(a) within such period as the Tribunal may direct; or

(b) where the Tribunal makes no such direction, within 10 days,

after the respondent is served with notice that the appellant has been granted permission to appeal.

(3) A respondent's notice must be served on the appellant at the same time as it is filed.

20 Variation of grounds of appeal

(1) A party may vary his grounds of appeal only with the permission of the Tribunal.

(2) Where the Tribunal has refused permission to appeal on any ground, it must not grant permission to vary the grounds of appeal to include that ground unless it is satisfied that, because of special circumstances, it would be unjust not to allow the variation.

21 Evidence

(1) The Tribunal may consider as evidence any note or record made by the adjudicator of any hearing before him in connection with the appeal.

(2) If a party wishes to ask the Tribunal to consider evidence which was not submitted to the adjudicator, he must file with the appellate authority and serve on the other party written notice to that effect, which must—

(a) indicate the nature of the evidence; and

(b) explain why it was not submitted to the adjudicator.

(3) A notice under paragraph (2) must be filed and served as soon as practicable after the parties have been notified that permission to appeal has been granted.

(4) If the Tribunal decides to admit additional evidence, it may give directions as to—

(a) the manner in which; and

(b) the time by which,

the evidence is to be given or filed.

22 Remitting an appeal

(1) The Tribunal may remit an appeal to an adjudicator for him to determine in accordance with any directions given by the Tribunal.

(2) The power in paragraph (1) may be exercised by a legally qualified member of the Tribunal without a hearing.

23 Hearing of appeal

Where permission to appeal is granted, the grounds of appeal in respect of which permission is granted must be considered by the Tribunal at a hearing, except where—

(a) the appeal—
 (i) lapses pursuant to section 99 of the 2002 Act;
 (ii) is treated as abandoned pursuant to section 104(4) of the 2002 Act;
 (iii) is treated as finally determined pursuant to section 104(5) of the 2002 Act; or
 (iv) is withdrawn by the appellant in accordance with rule 42;

(b) the Tribunal decides without a hearing to remit the appeal to an adjudicator; or

(c) a provision of these Rules or of any other enactment permits or requires the Tribunal to dispose of an appeal without a hearing.

24 Certificates of no merit

(1) If, when it determines an appeal or an application for permission to appeal under this Part, the Tribunal considers that—

(a) the appeal or application to the Tribunal is vexatious or unreasonable; or

(b) where the appellant was the party who appealed to an adjudicator, that appeal was vexatious or unreasonable,

it must issue a certificate to that effect (a "certificate of no merit").

(2) Where the Tribunal issues a certificate of no merit, the appellate authority must—

(a) serve a copy of the certificate on—
 (i) every party; and
 (ii) any legal representative acting for the party against whom the certificate is issued; and

(b) serve on the body specified in paragraph (3) a copy of—
 (i) the certificate; and
 (ii) the determination of the Tribunal upon the appeal or application for permission to appeal.

(3) The body referred to in paragraph (2)(b) is—

(a) the Legal Services Commission, if the certificate relates to an appeal or application which was determined in England and Wales;

(b) the Scottish Legal Aid Board, if the certificate relates to an appeal or application which was determined in Scotland; and

(c) the Legal Aid Committee of the Law Society of Northern Ireland, if the certificate relates to an appeal or application which was determined in Northern Ireland.

25 Costs of applications for statutory review

(1) This rule applies where—

(a) a party has applied to the High Court or the Court of Session under section 101(2) of the 2002 Act for a review of a decision of the Tribunal; and

(b) the High Court or the Court of Session has reserved the costs (or, in Scotland, expenses) of that application to the Tribunal.

(2) The Tribunal has discretion whether to order one party to pay the costs or expenses of that application to another.

(3) If the Tribunal orders one party to pay costs of an application to the High Court to another, it must refer the case to a costs judge to assess the amount of costs to be paid.

(4) If the Tribunal orders one party to pay expenses of an application to the Court of Session to another, it must refer the case to an Auditor of the Court of Session for the taxation of those expenses.

(5) In paragraph (3), "costs judge" means a taxing master of the Supreme Court of England and Wales.

Part 4
Applications for Permission to Appeal from Tribunal

26 Scope of this Part

This Part applies to applications to the Tribunal for permission to appeal on a point of law to the Court of Appeal or the Court of Session from a determination of an appeal by the Tribunal.

27 Applying for permission to appeal

(1) Subject to paragraph (2), an application to the Tribunal under this Part must be made by filing with the appellate authority an application notice for permission to appeal.

(2) A person who is in detention under the Immigration Acts may apply for permission to appeal either—

(a) in accordance with paragraph (1); or

(b) by serving an application notice on the person having custody of him.

(3) Where an application notice is served in accordance with paragraph (2)(b), the person having custody of the applicant must endorse on the notice the date that it is served on him and forward it to the appellate authority.

(4) As soon as practicable after an application notice for permission to appeal is filed, the appellate authority must notify the other party to the appeal to the Tribunal that it has been filed.

28 Time limit for application

(1) An application notice under this Part must be filed in accordance with rule 27(1) or served in accordance with rule 27(2)(b)—

(a) if the applicant is in detention under the Immigration Acts when he is served with the Tribunal's determination, not later than 5 days after he is served with that determination; and

(b) in any other case, not later than 10 days after he is served with the Tribunal's determination.

(2) The Tribunal may not extend the time limits in paragraph (1).

29 Form and contents of application notice

(1) The application notice must—

(a) be in the appropriate prescribed form;

(b) state the grounds of appeal; and

(c) be signed by the applicant or his representative, and dated.

(2) If the application notice is signed by the applicant's representative, the representative must certify in the application notice that he has completed the application notice in accordance with the applicant's instructions.

30 Determining the application

(1) An application for permission to appeal must be determined by a legally qualified member of the Tribunal without a hearing.

(2) The Tribunal may—

(a) grant permission to appeal;

(b) refuse permission to appeal; or

(c) subject to paragraph (3), set aside the Tribunal's determination and direct that the appeal to the Tribunal be reheard.

(3) An order under paragraph (2)(c)—

(a) may only be made by the President or Deputy President of the Tribunal; and

(b) may not be made without first giving every party an opportunity to make written representations.

(4) The Tribunal's determination must include its reasons, which may be in summary form.

Part 5
Bail

31 Scope of this Part and interpretation

(1) This Part applies to applications under the Immigration Acts to an adjudicator or the Tribunal, by persons detained under those Acts, to be released on bail.

(2) In this Part, and in Part 6 insofar as it applies to applications for bail, "applicant" means a person applying to an adjudicator or the Tribunal to be released on bail.

(3) The parties to a bail application are the applicant and the Secretary of State.

32 Applications for bail

(1) An application to be released on bail must be made by filing with the appellate authority an application notice in the appropriate prescribed form.

(2) The application notice must contain the following details—
- (a) the applicant's—
  - (i) full name;
  - (ii) date of birth; and
  - (iii) date of arrival in the United Kingdom;
- (b) the address of the place where the applicant is detained;
- (c) whether an appeal by the applicant to an adjudicator or the Tribunal is pending;
- (d) the address where the applicant will reside if his application for bail is granted, or, if he is unable to give such an address, the reason why an address is not given;
- (e) the amount of the recognizance in which he will agree to be bound;
- (f) the full names, addresses, occupations and dates of birth of any persons who have agreed to act as sureties for the applicant if bail is granted, and the amounts of the recognizances in which they will agree to be bound;
- (g) the grounds on which the application is made and, where a previous application has been refused, full details of any change in circumstances which has occurred since the refusal; and
- (h) whether and in what respect an interpreter will be required at the hearing.

(3) The application must be signed by the applicant or his representative or, in the case of an applicant who is a child or is for any other reason incapable of acting, by a person acting on his behalf.

33 Bail hearing

(1) Where an application for bail is filed, the appellate authority must—
- (a) as soon as reasonably practicable, serve a copy of the application on the Secretary of State; and
- (b) fix a hearing.

(2) If the Secretary of State wishes to contest the application, he must file with the appellate authority and serve on the applicant a written statement of his reasons for doing so—
- (a) not later than 2.00 pm the day before the hearing; or
- (b) if he was served with notice of the hearing less than 24 hours before that time, as soon as reasonably practicable.

(3) The appellate authority must serve written notice of the adjudicator or the Tribunal's decision on—
- (a) the parties; and
- (b) the person having custody of the applicant.

(4) Where bail is granted, the notice must include—
- (a) the conditions of bail; and
- (b) the amount in which the applicant and any sureties are to be bound.

(5) Where bail is refused, the notice must include reasons for the refusal.

34 Recognizances

(1) The recognizance of an applicant or a surety must be in writing and must state—

(a) the amount in which he agrees to be bound; and

(b) that he has read and understood the bail decision and that he agrees to pay that amount of money if the applicant fails to comply with the conditions set out in the bail decision.

(2) The recognizance must be—

(a) signed by the applicant or surety; and

(b) filed with the appellate authority.

35 Release of applicant

The person having custody of the applicant must release him upon—

(a) being served with a copy of the decision to grant bail; and

(b) being satisfied that any recognizances required as a condition of that decision have been entered into.

36 Application of this Part to Scotland

This Part applies to Scotland with the following modifications—

(a) in rule 32, for paragraph (2)(e) and (f) substitute—

"(e) the amount, if any, to be deposited if bail is granted;

(f) the full names, addresses and occupations of any persons offering to act as cautioners if the application for bail is granted;";

(b) in rule 33, for paragraph (4)(b) substitute—

"(b) the amount (if any) to be deposited by the applicant and any cautioners.";

(c) rule 34 does not apply; and

(d) in rule 35, for sub-paragraph (b) substitute—

"(b) being satisfied that the amount to be deposited, if any, has been deposited.".

Part 6
General Provisions

37 Conduct of appeals and applications

The appellate authority may, subject to these Rules and to any other enactment, decide the procedure to be followed in relation to any appeal or application.

38 Directions

(1) The appellate authority may give directions to the parties relating to the conduct of any appeal or application.

(2) The power to give directions is to be exercised subject to any specific provision of these Rules and of any other enactment.

(3) Directions under this rule may be given orally or in writing.

(4) The appellate authority must serve notice of any written directions on every party.

(5) Directions given under this rule may, in particular—

(a) relate to any matter concerning the preparation for a hearing;

(b) specify the length of time allowed for anything to be done;

(c) vary any time limit;

(d) provide for—

(i) a particular matter to be dealt with as a preliminary issue;

(ii) a pre-hearing review to be held;

(iii) a party to provide further details of his case, or any other information which appears to be necessary for the determination of the appeal or application;

(iv) the witnesses, if any, to be heard; and

(v) the manner in which any evidence is to be given (for example by directing that witness statements are to stand as evidence in chief);

(e) require any party to file and serve—

(i) statements of the evidence which will be called at the hearing;

(ii) a paginated and indexed bundle of all the documents which will be relied on at the hearing;

(iii) a skeleton argument which summarises succinctly the submissions which will be made at the hearing and cites all the authorities which will be relied on, identifying any particular passages to be relied on;

(iv) a time estimate for the hearing;

(v) a list of witnesses whom any party wishes to call to give evidence;

(vi) a chronology of events; and

(vii) details of whether and in what respect an interpreter will be required at a hearing;

(f) limit—

(i) the number or length of documents upon which a party may rely at a hearing;

(ii) the length of oral submissions;

(iii) the time allowed for the examination and cross-examination of witnesses; and

(iv) the issues which are to be addressed at a hearing;

(g) require the parties to take any steps to enable two or more appeals or applications to be heard together under rule 51;

(h) provide for a hearing to be conducted or evidence given or representations made by video link or by other electronic means; and

(i) make provision to secure the anonymity of a party or witness.

(6) The appellate authority must not direct an unrepresented party to do something unless it is satisfied that he is able to comply with the direction.

39 Notification of hearings

(1) When the appellate authority fixes a hearing it must serve notice of the date, time and place of the hearing on—

(a) every party; and
(b) any representative acting for a party.

(2) The appellate authority may bring forward the date of a hearing, but must serve notice of the new date, time and place of the hearing on the persons specified in paragraph (1).

40 Adjournment of hearings

(1) Subject to any provision of these Rules or of any other enactment, an adjudicator or the Tribunal may adjourn the hearing of any appeal or application.

(2) An adjudicator or the Tribunal must not adjourn a hearing on the application of a party, unless satisfied that the appeal or application cannot otherwise be justly determined.

(3) Where a party applies for an adjournment of a hearing, he must—
(a) if practicable, notify all other parties of the application;
(b) show good reason why an adjournment is necessary; and
(c) produce evidence of any fact or matter relied upon in support of the application.

(4) Where a hearing is adjourned, the appellate authority—
(a) must fix a new date, time and place for the hearing; and
(b) may give directions for the future conduct of the appeal or application.

41 Certification of pending appeals

(1) If the Secretary of State or an immigration officer issues a certificate under section 96, 97 or 98 of the 2002 Act which relates to a pending appeal, subject to paragraph (4) he must file notice of the certification with the appellate authority.

(2) Where a notice of certification under section 96(1) or (2), 97 or 98 of the 2002 Act is filed, the appellate authority must notify the parties that the appeal has lapsed in accordance with section 99.

(3) Where a notice of certification under section 96(3) of the 2002 Act is filed, the appellate authority must notify the parties that the appellant may not rely on any ground of appeal specified in the notice.

(4) This rule does not apply where the certificate is issued before the respondent has forwarded the appeal papers to the appellate authority under rule 9.

42 Withdrawal of appeal

(1) An appellant may withdraw an appeal—
(a) orally, at a hearing; or
(b) at any time, by filing written notice with the appellate authority.

(2) If an appellant withdraws an appeal, the appellate authority must serve on the parties a notice that the appeal has been recorded as having been withdrawn.

43 Abandonment of appeal

(1) The parties to a pending appeal must notify the appellate authority if an event specified in section 104(4) or (5) of the 2002 Act takes place.

(2) Where the appellate authority treats an appeal as abandoned pursuant to section 104(4) of the 2002 Act, or finally determined pursuant to section 104(5) of the 2002 Act, it must—

- (a) serve on the parties informing them that the appeal is being treated as abandoned or finally determined; and
- (b) take no further action in relation to the appeal.

44 Hearing of appeal in absence of a party

(1) An adjudicator or the Tribunal must hear an appeal in the absence of a party or his representative, if satisfied that the party or his representative—

- (a) has been given notice of the date, time and place of the hearing; and
- (b) has given no satisfactory explanation for his absence.

(2) Where paragraph (1) does not apply, an adjudicator or the Tribunal may hear an appeal in the absence of a party if satisfied that—

- (a) a representative of the party is present at the hearing;
- (b) the party is outside the United Kingdom;
- (c) the party is suffering from a communicable disease or there is a risk of him behaving in a violent or disorderly manner;
- (d) the party is unable to attend the hearing because of illness, accident or some other good reason;
- (e) the party is unrepresented and it is impracticable to give him notice of the hearing; or
- (f) the party has notified the appellate authority that he does not wish to attend the hearing.

45 Determining the appeal without a hearing

(1) An adjudicator or the Tribunal may, subject to paragraphs (2) and (3) of this rule, determine an appeal without a hearing if—

- (a) all the parties to the appeal consent;
- (b) the party appealing against a relevant decision is outside the United Kingdom or it is impracticable to give him notice of a hearing and, in either case, he is unrepresented;
- (c) a party has failed to comply with a provision of these rules or a direction of the appellate authority, and the adjudicator or Tribunal is satisfied that in all the circumstances, including the extent of the failure and any reasons for it, it is appropriate to determine the appeal without a hearing; or
- (d) the adjudicator or Tribunal is satisfied, having regard to the material before him or it and the nature of the issues raised, that the appeal can be justly determined without a hearing.

(2) Where paragraph (1)(c) applies and the appellant is the party in default, the adjudicator or Tribunal may dismiss the appeal without substantive consideration, if satisfied that it is appropriate to do so.

(3) Where paragraph (1)(d) applies, the adjudicator or Tribunal must not determine the appeal without a hearing without first giving the parties notice of his or its intention to do so, and an opportunity to make written representations as to whether there should be a hearing.

46 Representation

(1) A party appealing against a relevant decision or applying for bail may act in person or be represented by any person not prohibited from providing immigration services by section 84 of the Immigration and Asylum Act 1999.

(2) Where the Secretary of State, an immigration officer, an entry clearance officer or the United Kingdom Representative is a party to an appeal, he may be represented by any person authorised to act on his behalf.

(3) If a party to whom paragraph (1) applies is represented by a person not permitted by that paragraph to represent him, any determination given or other step taken by the appellate authority in the appeal or application shall nevertheless be valid.

(4) Where a representative begins to act for a party, he must immediately notify the appellate authority of that fact.

(5) Where a representative is acting for a party, he may on behalf of that party do anything that these Rules require or permit that party to do.

(6) Where a representative is acting for a party appealing against a relevant decision, the party is under a duty—

(a) to maintain contact with his representative until the appeal is finally determined; and

(b) to notify the representative of any change of address.

(7) Where a representative ceases to act for a party, the representative and the party must notify the appellate authority and every other party of that fact, and of the name and address of any new representative (if known).

(8) Until the appellate authority is notified that a representative has ceased to act for a party, any document served on that representative shall be deemed to be properly served on the party he was representing.

47 Summoning of witnesses

(1) An adjudicator or the Tribunal may, by issuing a summons ("a witness summons"), require any person in the United Kingdom—

(a) to attend as a witness at the hearing of an appeal; and

(b) subject to rule 48(2), at the hearing to answer any questions or produce any documents in his custody or under his control which relate to any matter in issue in the appeal.

(2) A person is not required to attend a hearing in obedience to a witness summons unless—

(a) the summons is served on him; and

(b) the necessary expenses of his attendance are paid or tendered to him.

(3) If a witness summons is issued at the request of a party, that party must pay or tender the expenses referred to in paragraph (2)(b).

48 Evidence

(1) An adjudicator or the Tribunal may allow oral, documentary or other evidence to be given of any fact which appears to be relevant to an appeal or an application for bail, even if that evidence would be inadmissible in a court of law.

(2) An adjudicator or the Tribunal may not compel a party or witness to give any evidence or produce any document which he could not be compelled to give or produce at the trial of a civil claim in the part of the United Kingdom in which the hearing is taking place.

(3) An adjudicator or the Tribunal may require the oral evidence of a witness to be given on oath or affirmation.

(4) In an appeal to which section 85(5) or section 102(3) of the 2002 Act applies, an adjudicator or the Tribunal must only consider evidence relating to matters which he or it is not prevented by those sections from considering.

(5) An adjudicator or the Tribunal must not consider any evidence which is not filed or served in accordance with time limits set out in these Rules or directions given under rule 38, unless satisfied that there are good reasons to do so.

(6) Subject to section 108 of the 2002 Act, an adjudicator or the Tribunal must not take account of any evidence that has not been made available to all the parties.

49 Burden of proof

(1) If—

- (a) a party appealing against a relevant decision asserts that the decision ought not to have been taken against him; or
- (b) an applicant for bail asserts that he ought not to have been detained,

on the ground that the statutory provision under which that decision or action was taken does not apply to him, it is for that party to prove that the provision does not apply to him.

(2) If in any appeal or application—

- (a) a party asserts any fact; and
- (b) by virtue of an Act, statutory instrument or immigration rules, if the party had made such an assertion to the Secretary of State, an immigration officer or an entry clearance officer, it would have been for the party to satisfy the Secretary of State or officer that the assertion was true,

it is for that party to prove that the fact asserted is true.

50 Admission of public to hearings

(1) Subject to the following provisions of this rule, every hearing before an adjudicator or the Tribunal must be held in public.

(2) Where an adjudicator or the Tribunal is considering an allegation referred to in section 108 of the 2002 Act, all members of the public must be excluded from the hearing.

(3) An adjudicator or the Tribunal may exclude any or all members of the public from any hearing or part of a hearing if it is necessary—

(a) in the interests of public order or national security; or

(b) to protect the private life of a party or the interests of a minor.

(4) An adjudicator or the Tribunal may also, in exceptional circumstances, exclude any or all members of the public from any hearing or part of a hearing to ensure that publicity does not prejudice the interests of justice, but only if and to the extent that it is strictly necessary to do so.

(5) A member of the Council on Tribunals or of its Scottish Committee acting in that capacity is entitled to attend any hearing and may not be excluded pursuant to paragraph (2), (3) or (4) of this rule.

51 Hearing two or more appeals together

(1) Where two or more appeals to an adjudicator or to the Tribunal are pending at the same time, an adjudicator or the Tribunal may direct them to be heard together if it appears that—

(a) some common question of law or fact arises in each of them;

(b) they relate to decisions or action taken in respect of persons who are members of the same family; or

(c) for some other reason it is desirable for the appeals to be heard together.

(2) An adjudicator or the Tribunal must give all the parties an opportunity to make representations before determining appeals together under this rule.

52 Transfer of proceedings

(1) Where—

(a) an adjudicator has started to hear an appeal but has not completed the hearing or given his determination; and

(b) a senior adjudicator decides that it is not practicable for that adjudicator to complete the hearing or to give his determination justly or without undue delay,

a senior adjudicator may direct the appeal to be heard by another adjudicator.

(2) Where an appeal is transferred to another adjudicator ("the new adjudicator") in accordance with paragraph (1)—

(a) any document sent to or given by the adjudicator from whom the appeal was transferred shall be deemed to have been sent to or given by the new adjudicator; and

(b) the new adjudicator shall have power to deal with the appeal as if it had been commenced before him.

(3) The powers of a senior adjudicator under this rule shall, with the appropriate modifications, also apply to the President of the Tribunal in relation to proceedings before the Tribunal.

53 Giving of determination

(1) This rule applies where an adjudicator or the Tribunal determines an appeal or an application for permission to appeal under any of Parts 2, 3 or 4 of these Rules.

(2) The appellate authority must record the decision of the adjudicator or the Tribunal and the reasons for it.

(3) Unless a rule provides otherwise, the appellate authority must serve on—

(a) every party; and

(b) any representative acting for a party,

a written determination containing the decision of the adjudicator or the Tribunal and the reasons for it.

(4) The reasons for a decision may be given and recorded in summary form where a rule so provides.

54 Filing and service of documents

(1) Any document which is required or permitted by these Rules or by a direction of the appellate authority to be filed with the appellate authority, or served on any person may be—

(a) delivered or sent by post to an address;

(b) sent by fax to a fax number; or

(c) sent by e-mail to an e-mail address,

specified for that purpose by the person or authority to whom the document is directed.

(2) A document to be served on an individual may be served personally by leaving it with that individual.

(3) Subject to paragraph (4), if any document is served on a person who has notified the appellate authority that he is acting as the representative of a party, it shall be deemed to have been served on that party.

(4) Paragraph (3) does not apply where—

(a) a rule; or

(b) a direction of an adjudicator or the Tribunal,

requires a document to be served on both a party and his representative.

(5) Subject to paragraph (6), any document that is served on a person in accordance with this rule shall, unless the contrary is proved, be deemed to be served—

(a) where the document is sent by post from and to a place within the United Kingdom, on the second day after it was sent;

(b) where the document is sent by post from or to a place outside the United Kingdom, on the twenty-eighth day after it was sent; and

(c) in any other case, on the day on which the document was sent or delivered to, or left with, that person.

(6) Any document which is filed with the appellate authority, and any notice of appeal or application notice which is served on a person under rule 6(2), 6(3)(b), 15(3)(b) or 27(2)(b), shall be treated as being filed or served on the day on which it is received by that authority or person.

(7) Where the United Kingdom Representative is a party to an appeal, any document which is required by these Rules or by a direction of the

appellate authority to be served on the appellant or the respondent must also be served on the United Kingdom Representative.

55 Address for service

(1) Every party, and any person representing a party, must notify the appellate authority of a postal address at which documents may be served on him and of any changes to that address.

(2) Until a party or representative notifies the appellate authority of a change of address, any document served on him at the most recent address which he has given to the appellate authority shall be deemed to have been properly served on him.

56 Calculation of time

(1) Where a period of time for doing any act is specified by these Rules or by a direction of the appellate authority, that period is to be calculated—

(a) excluding the day on which the period begins; and

(b) where the period is 10 days or less, excluding any day which is not a business day.

(2) Where the time specified by these Rules or by a direction of the appellate authority for doing any act ends on a day which is not a business day, that act is done in time if it is done on the next business day.

(3) In this rule, "business day" means any day other than a Saturday or Sunday, a bank holiday, Christmas Day, 27th to 31st December or Good Friday.

57 Signature of documents

Any requirement in these Rules for a document to be signed shall be satisfied, in the case of a document which is filed or served by e-mail in accordance with these Rules, by the person who is required to sign the document typing his name in it.

58 Errors of procedure

Where, before an adjudicator or the Tribunal has determined an appeal or application, there has been an error of procedure such as a failure to comply with a rule—

(a) subject to these Rules, the error does not invalidate any step taken in the proceedings, unless an adjudicator or the Tribunal so orders; and

(b) an adjudicator or the Tribunal may make an order, or take any other step, that he or it considers appropriate to remedy the error.

59 Correction of orders and determinations

(1) An adjudicator or the Tribunal may at any time amend an order or determination to correct a clerical error or other accidental slip or omission.

(2) The power in paragraph (1) includes power for the Tribunal to amend an order or determination of an adjudicator, after consulting the adjudicator concerned.

(3) Where an order or determination is amended under this rule—

(a) the appellate authority must serve an amended order or notice of determination on every party; and

(b) the time within which a party may apply for permission to appeal against an amended determination runs from the date on which the party is served with the amended determination.

Part 7
Revocation and Transitional Provisions

60 Revocation

The Immigration and Asylum Appeals (Procedure) Rules 2000 are revoked.

61 Transitional provisions

(1) Subject to paragraphs (4) to (9), these Rules apply with the modification in paragraph (2) and such other modifications as are appropriate to—

(a) any appeal or application to an adjudicator or the Tribunal pending on 1st April 2003 to which, immediately before that date, the Immigration and Asylum Appeals (Procedure) Rules 2000 ("the 2000 Rules") applied;

(b) any appeal or application to an adjudicator or the Tribunal made on or after 1st April 2003 under an enactment other than the 2002 Act, to which the 2000 Rules would have applied if they had not been revoked.

(2) In relation to an appeal or application to which these Rules apply by virtue of paragraph (1), references in these Rules to a relevant decision shall be interpreted as including any decision of the Secretary of State, an immigration officer or an entry clearance officer against which there is a right of appeal to an adjudicator or the Tribunal under any enactment.

(3) In relation to an appeal or application to an adjudicator or the Tribunal which is pending on 1st April 2003, anything done or any direction given before 1st April 2003 under the 2000 Rules (including anything which, pursuant to rule 4(2) of the 2000 Rules, was treated as if done or given under those Rules) shall be treated as if done or given under these Rules.

(4) In relation to an appeal to an adjudicator against a relevant decision made before 1st April 2003—

(a) rules 7 and 10 of these Rules shall not apply; and

(b) rules 6, 7 and 12 of the 2000 Rules shall continue to apply as if those Rules had not been revoked.

(5) In relation to an application for permission to appeal to the Tribunal against an adjudicator's determination made before 1st April 2003—

(a) rule 16 of these Rules shall not apply; and

(b) rules 18(2), 18(3) and 19 of the 2000 Rules shall continue to apply as if those Rules had not been revoked.

(6) In relation to an application to the Tribunal for permission to appeal to the Court of Appeal or the Court of Session against a determination made by the Tribunal before 1st April 2003—

(a) rule 28 of these Rules shall not apply; and
(b) rule 27(1) of the 2000 Rules shall continue to apply as if those Rules had not been revoked.

(7) In relation to an adjudicator's determination against which there is no right of appeal to the Tribunal because of a certificate made by the Secretary of State before 1st April 2003 under paragraph 9 of Schedule 4 to the Immigration and Asylum Act 1999, rule 16 of the 2000 Rules shall continue to apply as if those Rules had not been revoked.

(8) Where, before 1st April 2003, written notice of a decision or determination was sent to the Secretary of State under rule 15(2), 16(5)(b), 18(9A), 19(3) or 19(6)(b) of the 2000 Rules, the Secretary of State must deal with the written notice in accordance with those Rules as if they had not been revoked.

(9) Rule 24 (certificates of no merit) shall not apply in relation to an appeal or application for permission to appeal where the notice of appeal or application notice was given or filed before 1st April 2003.

Irvine of Lairg, C

Dated 10th March 2003

SCHEDULE
Forms

Rule 2

N1
Notice of Appeal to Adjudicator (United Kingdom)
[Form not reproduced here.]

N2
Notice of Appeal to Adjudicator (Overseas)
[Form not reproduced here.]

N3
Notice of Appeal to Adjudicator (Right of Appeal that can Only be Exercised upon Leaving the United Kingdom)
[Form not reproduced here.]

T1
Application for Permission to Appeal to Tribunal (United Kingdom)
[Form not reproduced here.]

T2
Application for Permission to Appeal to Tribunal (Overseas)
[Form not reproduced here.]

C1

Application for Permission to Appeal to the Court of Appeal (Court of Session where Original Decision of Adjudicator made in Scotland)

[Form not reproduced here.]

B1

Application to be Released on Bail

[Form not reproduced here.]

EXPLANATORY NOTE

(This note is not part of the Rules)

These Rules prescribe the procedure to be followed for appeals and applications to an adjudicator and to the Immigration Appeal Tribunal under Part 5 of the Nationality, Immigration and Asylum Act 2002, which comes into force on 1st April 2003, and under section 40A of the British Nationality Act 1981, as inserted by section 4 of the 2002 Act. The Rules also prescribe the procedure to be followed for applications to an adjudicator or the Tribunal for bail.

Part 1 of these Rules contains introductory provisions.

Part 2 contains rules about appeals to an adjudicator. Subject to various exceptions and limitations in Part 5 of the 2002 Act, a right of appeal lies to an adjudicator—

(a) under section 82 of the 2002 Act, against an immigration decision;

(b) under section 83 of the 2002 Act, in certain circumstances, against a decision to reject an asylum claim; and

(c) under section 40A of the British Nationality Act 1981, against a decision to make an order depriving a person of a British citizenship status.

Part 3 contains rules about appeals (including applications for permission to appeal) to the Tribunal. Section 101(1) of the 2002 Act and section 40A(3) of the 1981 Act provide that a party to an appeal to an adjudicator may, with the permission of the Immigration Appeal Tribunal, appeal to the Tribunal against an adjudicator's determination on a point of law.

Part 4 contains rules about applications to the Tribunal for permission to appeal to the Court of Appeal or (in Scotland) to the Court of Session.

Part 5 contains rules about applications to an adjudicator or the Tribunal for bail. Such applications may be made under Schedule 2 to the Immigration Act 1971 and section 9A of the Asylum and Immigration Appeals Act 1993.

Part 6 contains general provisions which apply to appeals and applications under these Rules.

Part 7 revokes the Immigration and Asylum Appeals (Procedure) Rules 2000 and contains transitional provisions for appeals and applications pending on 1st April 2003.

Immigration and Asylum Appeals (Fast Track Procedure) Rules 2003

2003 No 801

Made . . . . *20th March 2003*
Laid before Parliament . . . . *20th March 2003*
Coming into force . . . . *10th April 2003*

The Lord Chancellor, in exercise of the powers conferred by sections 106(1)–(3) and 112(3) of the Nationality, Immigration and Asylum Act 2002, after consulting with the Council on Tribunals in accordance with section 8 of the Tribunals and Inquiries Act 1992, makes the following Rules:

Part 1
Introduction

1 Citation and commencement
These Rules may be cited as the Immigration and Asylum Appeals (Fast Track Procedure) Rules 2003 and shall come into force on 10th April 2003.

2 Interpretation
(1) In these Rules—
"the Principal Rules" means the Immigration and Asylum Appeals (Procedure) Rules 2003;
"appellant", in relation to an appeal to an adjudicator has the same meaning as it is given in rule 5(2)(a) of the Principal Rules, and in relation to an appeal to the Tribunal has the same meaning as it is given in rule 14(2)(a) of the Principal Rules;
"respondent", in relation to an appeal to an adjudicator has the same meaning as it is given in rule 5(2)(b) of the Principal Rules, and in relation to an appeal to the Tribunal has the same meaning as it is given in rule 14(2)(b) of the Principal Rules.
(2) Other words and expressions used in these Rules which are defined in rule 2 of the Principal Rules have the same meaning in these Rules as in the Principal Rules.
(3) Where a provision of the Principal Rules applies by virtue of these Rules—

(a) any reference in that provision to the Principal Rules is to be interpreted as including a reference to these Rules; and
(b) any reference in that provision to a specific Part or rule in the Principal Rules is to be interpreted as including a reference to any equivalent Part or rule in these Rules.

(4) For the purposes of rules 4, 9 and 15 of these Rules, a party does not cease to satisfy a condition that he must have continuously been in detention under the Immigration Acts at a place or places specified in the Schedule to these Rules by reason only of—
(a) being transported from one place of detention specified in the Schedule to another place which is so specified; or
(b) leaving and returning to such a place of detention for any purpose between the hours of 7 am and 7 pm.

3 Scope of these Rules

(1) The following Parts of these Rules apply to appeals and applications to an adjudicator or the Tribunal to the following extent—
(a) Parts 2 and 5 apply to appeals to an adjudicator, in the circumstances specified in rule 4;
(b) Parts 3 and 5 apply to appeals (including applications for permission to appeal) to the Tribunal against an adjudicator's determination, in the circumstances specified in rule 9;
(c) Parts 4 and 5 apply to applications to the Tribunal for permission to appeal to the Court of Appeal or the Court of Session, in the circumstances specified in rule 15; and
(d) Part 6 applies to pending appeals and applications to which any of Parts 2, 3, 4 and 5 apply or have applied.

(2) In appeals and applications to which these Rules apply, the Principal Rules also apply, but only to the extent specified in rules 5, 10, 16 and 20 of these Rules.

Part 2
Appeals to an Adjudicator

4 Scope of this Part

This Part applies to an appeal to an adjudicator against an immigration decision which was made on or after 10th April 2003, where—
(a) the appellant was in detention under the Immigration Acts at a place specified in the Schedule to these Rules when notice of that immigration decision was served on him; and
(b) the appellant has continuously been in detention under the Immigration Acts at a place or places specified in the Schedule since that notice was served on him.

5 Application of Part 2 of the Principal Rules

The following rules in Part 2 of the Principal Rules apply to an appeal to an adjudicator to which this Part applies—

(a) rule 5;
(b) rule 6;
(c) rule 8;
(d) rule 10(1);
(e) rule 11; and
(f) rule 12, except for sub-paragraph (b).

6 Time limits

(1) A notice of appeal to an adjudicator must be given in accordance with rules 6 and 8 of the Principal Rules not later than 2 days after the day on which the appellant is served with notice of the decision against which he wishes to appeal.

(2) An adjudicator may not extend the time limit in paragraph (1) unless he is satisfied that, because of circumstances outside the control of the appellant or his representative, it was not practicable for notice of appeal to be given within that time limit.

(3) The respondent must (whether or not the notice of appeal is given within the time specified in paragraph (1))—

(a) file with the appellate authority the documents specified in rule 9(1) of the Principal Rules; and
(b) serve on the appellant the documents specified in rule 9(2) of the Principal Rules,

not later than 2 days after the day on which notice of appeal is given.

7 Listing

(1) The appellate authority must fix a hearing date as soon as practicable after the respondent files the documents under rule 6(3)(a).

(2) The hearing date must be not later than 2 days after the day on which the respondent files those documents, or as soon as practicable thereafter if the appellate authority is unable to arrange a hearing within that time.

(3) The appellate authority must serve notice of the date, time and place of the hearing on—

(a) every party; and
(b) subject to rule 21, any representative acting for a party,

not later than noon on the day before the hearing.

8 Determining the appeal

(1) An adjudicator must consider the appeal at the hearing fixed under rule 7(1), and give a written determination following that hearing, except where—

(a) the notice of appeal was given out of time, and the adjudicator does not grant an extension of time;
(b) rule 12(a) of the Principal Rules applies; or
(c) the adjudicator adjourns the hearing on a ground specified in paragraph (2).

(2) An adjudicator may only adjourn the hearing of an appeal where—

(a) it is necessary to do so because there is insufficient time to hear the appeal;

(b) a party has not been served with notice of the hearing in accordance with these Rules;
(c) the adjudicator is satisfied by evidence filed or given by or an behalf of a party that—
  (i) the appeal cannot be justly determined on the date on which it is listed for hearing; and
  (ii) there is an identifiable future date, not more than 10 days after the date on which the appeal is listed for hearing, by which the appeal can be justly determined; or
(d) the adjudicator makes an order under rule 23.

(3) The appellate authority must serve the adjudicator's written determination of the appeal on—
(a) every party; and
(b) subject to rule 21, any representative acting for a party,

not later than one day after the day on which the hearing of the appeal finishes.

Part 3
Appeals to the Tribunal

9 Scope of this Part

This Part applies to an appeal (including an application for permission to appeal) to the Tribunal where—
(a) the appeal is against the determination of an adjudicator upon an appeal to which Part 2 of these Rules applied; and
(b) the party appealing against an immigration decision has, since being served with notice of that immigration decision, continuously been in detention under the Immigration Acts at a place or places specified in the Schedule to these Rules.

10 Application of Part 3 of the Principal Rules

The following rules in Part 3 of the Principal Rules apply to an appeal to the Tribunal to which this Part applies—
(a) rule 14;
(b) rule 15, except for paragraph (5);
(c) rule 17;
(d) rule 18, except for paragraph (7)(b);
(e) rule 19(1) and (3);
(f) rule 20;
(g) rule 21(1), (2) and (4);
(h) rule 22;
(i) rule 23;
(j) rule 24; and
(k) rule 25.

11 Applying for permission to appeal

(1) An application for permission to appeal to the Tribunal against an adjudicator's determination must be made, in accordance with rules 15(1)–

(4) and 17 of the Principal Rules, not later than 2 days after the day on which the appellant is served with the adjudicator's determination.

(2) The appellant must—

(a) state in his application notice whether he seeks an oral hearing of the appeal if permission to appeal is granted, giving reasons if he does so; and

(b) file with the application notice (whether or not he seeks an oral hearing)—

(i) any written submissions upon which he wishes to rely if the Tribunal grants permission to appeal and decides to determine the appeal without a hearing; and

(ii) any notice under rule 21(2) of the Principal Rules asking the Tribunal to consider additional evidence.

(3) When the appellate authority receives the application notice, it must serve a copy of the notice and any accompanying documents on the respondent as soon as practicable.

(4) The Tribunal may extend the time limit in paragraph (1) if it is satisfied that, by reason of special circumstances, it would be unjust not to do so.

12 Documents to be filed by respondent

(1) The respondent must, not later than one day after the day on which he is served with a copy of the application notice—

(a) file with the appellate authority a statement of whether he seeks an oral hearing of the appeal if permission is granted, giving reasons if he does so; and

(b) file with that statement (whether or not he seeks an oral hearing)—

(i) any written submissions upon which he wishes to rely if the Tribunal grants permission to appeal and decides to determine the appeal without a hearing;

(ii) any respondent's notice under rule 19 of the Principal Rules; and

(iii) any notice under rule 21(2) of the Principal Rules asking the Tribunal to consider additional evidence.

(2) The Tribunal may extend the time limit in paragraph (1) if it is satisfied that, by reason of special circumstances, it would be unjust not to do so.

13 Determining the permission application

The Tribunal must determine the application for permission to appeal, and the Tribunal's written determination must be served on—

(a) every party; and

(b) subject to rule 21, any representative of a party,

not later than one day after the expiry of the time for the respondent to file documents under rule 12.

14 Determining the appeal

(1) This rule applies where the Tribunal grants permission to appeal under rule 18 of the Principal Rules.

(2) The Tribunal must, having regard to any written representations made by the parties, decide whether to—

(a) determine the appeal without a hearing in accordance with rule 45(1) of the Principal Rules; or

(b) fix a hearing.

(3) If the Tribunal decides to determine an appeal without a hearing, it must determine it—

(a) at the same time as granting permission to appeal; or

(b) as soon as practicable afterwards.

(4) If the Tribunal fixes a hearing—

(a) the hearing date must be not later than 2 days after the grant of permission to appeal, or as soon as practicable thereafter if the appellate authority is unable to arrange the hearing within that time; and

(b) the appellate authority must serve notice of the date, time and place of the hearing on—

(i) every party; and

(ii) subject to rule 21, any representative acting for a party,

not later than noon on the day before the hearing.

(5) The Tribunal may only adjourn the hearing of an appeal only where—

(a) it is necessary to do so because there is insufficient time to hear the appeal;

(b) a party has not been served with notice of the hearing in accordance with these Rules;

(c) the Tribunal is satisfied by evidence filed or given by or on behalf of a party that—

(i) the appeal cannot be justly determined on the date on which it is listed for hearing; and

(ii) there is an identifiable future date, not more than 10 days after the date on which the appeal is listed for hearing, by which the appeal can be justly determined; or

(d) the Tribunal makes an order under rule 23.

(6) The appellate authority must serve the Tribunal's written determination of the appeal upon—

(a) every party; and

(b) subject to rule 21, any representative acting for a party,

not later than one day after the day on which the hearing of the appeal finishes, or the Tribunal determines the appeal without a hearing.

Part 4

Applications for Permission to Appeal from Tribunal

15 Scope of this Part

This Part applies to an application to the Tribunal for permission to appeal to the Court of Appeal or the Court of Session where—

(a) the application is for permission to appeal against the determination of the Tribunal upon an appeal to which Part 3 of these Rules applied; and
(b) the party appealing against an immigration decision has, since being served with notice of that immigration decision, continuously been in detention under the Immigration Acts at a place or places specified in the Schedule to these Rules.

16 Application of Part 4 of the Principal Rules
The following rules in Part 4 of the Principal Rules apply to an application to which this Part applies—
(a) rule 26;
(b) rule 27;
(c) rule 29; and
(d) rule 30.

17 Time limit for application
(1) An application notice to the Tribunal for permission to appeal to the Court of Appeal or the Court of Session must be given, in accordance with rules 27 and 29 of the Principal Rules, not later than 2 days after the day on which the appellant is served with the Tribunal's determination.
(2) The Tribunal may not extend the time limit in paragraph (1).

18 Determining the application
The Tribunal must determine the application, and its determination must be served on—
(a) every party; and
(b) subject to rule 21, any representative acting for a party,
not later than one day after the day on which the appellate authority receives the application notice.

Part 5
General Provisions

19 Scope of this Part
This Part applies to an appeal or application to which any of Parts 2, 3 and 4 of these Rules apply.

20 Application of Part 6 of the Principal Rules
Part 6 of the Principal Rules applies to an appeal or application to which this Part applies, except that—
(a) rule 39(1) (notification of hearings) applies subject to rules 7(3), 14(4)(b) and 21 of these Rules;
(b) rule 40 (adjournment of hearings) does not apply;
(c) rule 45 (determining the appeal without a hearing) does not apply

in relation to an appeal to an adjudicator, and paragraph (3) of that rule does not apply in relation to an appeal to the Tribunal; and

(d) rule 53(3) (giving of determination) applies subject to rule 21 of these Rules.

21 Service of documents on representatives

Any requirement in these Rules, or in the Principal Rules as applied by these Rules, to serve any document on a party's representative in addition to serving it on that party, shall not apply unless the representative provides a fax number for service.

22 Validity of determinations

Any determination made in an appeal or application under these Rules shall be valid notwithstanding that—

(a) a hearing did not take place; or

(b) the determination was not made or served,

within a time period specified in these Rules.

Part 6
Removal of Pending Proceedings from Fast Track

23 Transfer of appeal out of fast track procedure

(1) Where Part 2 or 3 of these Rules applies to a pending appeal, an adjudicator or the Tribunal may order that that Part shall cease to apply to the appeal—

(a) if all the parties consent;

(b) in exceptional circumstances, if the adjudicator or the Tribunal is satisfied by evidence filed or given by or on behalf of a party that the appeal cannot otherwise be justly determined; or

(c) if—

(i) the respondent has failed to comply with a provision of these Rules, or the Principal Rules as applied by these Rules, or a direction of the appellate authority; and

(ii) the adjudicator or the Tribunal is satisfied that the appellant would be prejudiced by that failure if the appeal were determined in accordance with these Rules.

(2) An adjudicator or the Tribunal may, when making an order under paragraph (1)—

(a) adjourn any hearing of the appeal; and

(b) give directions relating to the further conduct of the appeal.

(3) Where an adjudicator adjourns a hearing in accordance with paragraph (2), rule 13 of the Principal Rules (closure date) shall apply.

24 Application of the Principal Rules

(1) This rule applies where any of Parts 2 to 4 of these Rules ceases to apply to a pending appeal or application because—

(a) the conditions in rule 4, 9 or 15 cease to apply; or
(b) an adjudicator or the Tribunal makes an order under rule 23.

(2) Subject to paragraph (3), the Principal Rules shall apply to the appeal or application from the date on which that Part of these Rules ceases to apply.

(3) Where—
(a) a time period for something to be done has started to run under a provision of these Rules; and
(b) that provision ceases to apply,

if the Principal Rules contain a time limit for the same thing to be done, the time period in the Principal Rules shall apply, and shall be treated as running from the date on which the time period under these Rules started to run.

Irvine of Lairg, C
20th March 2003

SCHEDULE

Immigration Removal Centre, Harmondsworth, Middlesex.

EXPLANATORY NOTE

(This note is not part of the Rules)

These Rules prescribe a fast track procedure to be followed for appeals to an adjudicator or the Immigration Appeal Tribunal against immigration decisions, where the appellant is in detention under the Immigration Acts at a specified location. The Rules will initially only apply to appellants who are detained at Harmondsworth Immigration Removal Centre, but it is intended that they may subsequently be amended to apply to appellants who are detained at other locations.

These Rules specify the extent to which the Immigration and Asylum Appeals (Procedure) Rules 2003 (SI 2003/652) ("the Principal Rules") are to apply to fast track appeals. They modify certain provisions of the Principal Rules and make different provision for certain matters. In particular these Rules:

—specify shorter time limits for appealing and applying for permission to appeal;

—specify the times within which appeals are to be listed and heard, and determinations are to be served on the parties;

—limit the powers of adjudicators and the Tribunal to extend the time for appealing and to adjourn hearings;

—enable the Tribunal to determine an appeal without an oral hearing at the same time as granting permission to appeal; and

—specify the circumstances in which an adjudicator or the Tribunal may direct that an appeal is to be taken out of the fast track procedure, and how an appeal is to be dealt with when the fast track procedure ceases to apply.

Civil Procedure (Amendment) Rules 2003

2003 No 364

Made . . . . *20th February 2003*
Laid before Parliament . . . . *24th February 2003*
Coming into force . . . . *in accordance with rule 1*

The Civil Procedure Rule Committee, having power under section 2 of the Civil Procedure Act 1997 to make rules of court under section 1 of that Act, after consulting in accordance with section 2(6)(a) of that Act, make the following Rules—

1 Citation, commencement and interpretation
These Rules may be cited as the Civil Procedure (Amendment) Rules 2003 and shall come into force on the commencement of Part 5 of the Nationality, Immigration and Asylum Act 2002.

2
In these Rules, "the Rules" means the Civil Procedure Rules 1998 and a reference to a Part or rule by number alone means the Part or rule so numbered in the Rules.

3 Amendments to Civil Procedure Rules 1998
In Part 54, the title is amended to "JUDICIAL REVIEW AND STATUTORY REVIEW".

4
For the list of contents in Part 54, substitute the list of contents and insert the section heading as set out in Part 1 of the Schedule to these Rules.

5
In Part 54
- (a) in rule 54.1, in paragraph (1), for "This Part" substitute "This Section of this Part";
- (b) in rule 54.1, in paragraph (2)—
  - (i) at the beginning, for "In this Part" substitute "In this Section"; and

(ii) in sub-paragraph (e), for "this Part" substitute "this Section";

(c) in the headings of rules 54.2 and 54.3, for "Part" substitute "Section";

(d) in rule 54.4, and in rule 54.16, for "Part" substitute "Section";

(e) in rule 54.20, in sub-paragraph (a), for "Part" substitute "Section"; and

(f) after rule 54.20, insert Section II as set out in Part 2 of the Schedule to these Rules.

Phillips of Worth Matravers, M R
Andrew Morritt, V-C
Anthony May, L J
Stephen Oliver-Jones
Carlos Dabezies
Steven Whitaker
Michael Black
Michelle Stevens-Hoare
Philip Rainey
Tim Parker
Juliet Herzog
Nicholas Burkill
Alan Street
Ahmad Butt
I allow these Rules
Irvine of Lairg, C
20th February 2003

SCHEDULE

Rules 4 and 5

Part 1
Judicial Review and Statutory Review

Contents of this Part

Contents of this Part

Section I—Judicial Review

Part 2

Section II—Statutory Review under the Nationality, Immigration and Asylum Act 2002

54.21 Scope and interpretation

(1) This Section of this Part contains rules about applications to the High Court under section 101(2) of the Nationality, Immigration and Asylum Act 2002 for a review of a decision of the Immigration Appeal Tribunal on an application for permission to appeal from an adjudicator.

(2) In this Section—

(a) "the Act" means the Nationality, Immigration and Asylum Act 2002;

(b) "adjudicator" means an adjudicator appointed for the purposes of Part 5 of the Act;

(c) "applicant" means a person applying to the High Court under section 101(2) of the Act;

(d) "other party" means the other party to the proceedings before the Tribunal; and
(e) "Tribunal" means the Immigration Appeal Tribunal.

54.22 Application for review

(1) An application under section 101(2) of the Act must be made to the Administrative Court.
(2) The application must be made by filing an application notice.
(3) The applicant must file with the application notice—
(a) the decision to which the application relates, and any document giving reasons for the decision;
(b) the grounds of appeal to the adjudicator;
(c) the adjudicator's determination;
(d) the grounds of appeal to the Tribunal together with any documents sent with them;
(e) the Tribunal's determination on the application for permission to appeal; and
(f) any other documents material to the application which were before the adjudicator.
(4) The applicant must also file with the application notice written submissions setting out—
(a) the grounds upon which it is contended that the Tribunal made an error of law; and
(b) reasons in support of those grounds.
(5) In paragraph (3)(a) of this rule, "decision" means an immigration decision within the meaning of section 82 of the Act, or a decision to reject an asylum claim to which section 83 of the Act applies.

54.23 Time limit for application

(1) The application notice must be filed not later than 14 days after the applicant is deemed to have received notice of the Tribunal's decision in accordance with rules made under section 106 of the Act.
(2) The court may extend the time limit in paragraph (1) in exceptional circumstances.
(3) An application to extend the time limit must be made in the application notice and supported by written evidence verified by a statement of truth.

54.24 Service of application

(1) The applicant must serve on the Tribunal copies of the application notice and written submissions.
(2) Where an application is for review of a decision by the Tribunal to grant permission to appeal, the applicant must serve on the other party copies of—
(a) thc application noticc;
(b) the written submissions; and

(c) all the documents filed in support of the application, except for documents which come from or have already been served on that party.

(3) Where documents are required to be served under paragraphs (1) and (2), they must be served as soon as practicable after they are filed.

54.25 Determining the application

(1) The application will be determined by a single judge without a hearing, and by reference only to the written submissions and the documents filed with them.

(2) If the applicant relies on evidence which was not submitted to the adjudicator or the Tribunal, the court will not consider that evidence unless it is satisfied that there were good reasons why it was not submitted to the adjudicator or the Tribunal.

(3) The court may affirm or reverse the Tribunal's decision.

(4) Where the Tribunal refused permission to appeal, the court will reverse the Tribunal's decision only if it is satisfied that—

(a) the Tribunal may have made an error of law; and

(b) either—

(i) the appeal would have a real prospect of success; or

(ii) there is some other compelling reason why the appeal should be heard.

(5) Where the Tribunal granted permission to appeal, the court will reverse the Tribunal's decision only if it is satisfied that—

(a) the appeal would have no real prospect of success; and

(b) there is no other compelling reason why the appeal should be heard.

(6) If the court reverses the Tribunal's decision to refuse permission to appeal—

(a) the court's order will constitute a grant of permission to appeal to the Tribunal; and

(b) the court may limit the grant of permission to appeal to specific grounds.

(7) The court's decision shall be final and there shall be no appeal from that decision or renewal of the application.

54.26 Service of order

(1) The court will send copies of its order to—

(a) the applicant, except where paragraph (2) applies;

(b) the other party; and

(c) the Tribunal.

(2) Where—

(a) the application relates, in whole or in part, to a claim for asylum;

(b) the Tribunal refused permission to appeal; and

(c) the court affirms the Tribunal's decision,

the court will send a copy of its order to the Secretary of State, who must serve the order on the applicant.

(3) Where the Secretary of State has served an order in accordance with paragraph (2), he must notify the court on what date and by what method the order was served.

(4) If the court issues a certificate under section 101(3)(d) of the Act, it will send a copy of the certificate together with the order to—

(a) the persons to whom it sends the order under paragraphs (1) and (2); and

(b) if the applicant is in receipt of public funding, the Legal Services Commission.

54.27 Costs

The court may reserve the costs of the application to be determined by the Tribunal.

EXPLANATORY NOTE

(This note is not part of the Rules)

These Rules amend the Civil Procedure Rules 1998 by inserting a new Section II of Part 54, containing rules about applications to the High Court under section 101(2) of the Nationality, Immigration and Asylum Act 2002. That section provides that a party to an application to the Immigration Appeal Tribunal for permission to appeal against an adjudicator's determination may apply to the High Court for a review of the Tribunal's decision on the ground that the Tribunal made an error of law.

The title of Part 54 is changed to "Judicial Review and Statutory Review" and consequential amendments are made to the existing rules in Part 54.

APPENDIX 5

The Surendran Guidelines

1. Where the Home Office is not represented, we do not consider that a special adjudicator is entitled to treat a decision appealed against as having been withdrawn. The withdrawal of a decision to refuse leave to enter and asylum requires a positive act on the part of the Home Office in the form of a statement in writing that the decision has been withdrawn. In the instant case, and in similar cases, this is not the position. The Home Office, on the contrary, requests that the special adjudicator deals with the appeal on the basis of the contents of the letter of refusal and any other written submissions which the Home Office makes when indicating that it would not be represented.
2. Nor do we consider that the appeal should be allowed simpliciter. The function of the adjudicator is to review the reasons given by the Home Office for refusing asylum within the context of the evidence before him and the submissions made on behalf of the appellant, and then come to his own conclusions as to whether or not the appeal should be allowed or dismissed. In doing so he must, of course, observe the correct burden and standard of proof.
3. Where an adjudicator is aware that the Home Office is not to be represented, he should take particular care to read all the papers in the bundle before him prior to the hearing and, if necessary, in particular in those cases where he has only been informed on the morning of the hearing that the Home Office will not appear, he should consider the advisability of adjourning for the purposes of reading the papers and therefore putting the case further back in his list for the same day.
4. Where matters of credibility are raised in the letter of refusal, the special adjudicator should request the representative to address these matters, particularly in his examination of the appellant or, if the appellant is not giving evidence, in his submissions. Whether or not these matters are addressed by

the representative, and whether or not the special adjudicator has himself expressed any particular concern, he is entitled to form his own view as to credibility on the basis of the material before him.

5. Where no matters of credibility are raised in the letter of refusal but, from a reading of the papers, the special adjudicator himself considers that there are matters of credibility arising therefrom, he should similarly point these matters out to the representative and ask that they be dealt with, either in examination of the appellant or in submissions.
6. It is our view that it is not the function of a special adjudicator to adopt an inquisitorial role in cases of this nature. The system pertaining at present is essentially an adversial system and the special adjudicator is an impartial judge and assessor of the evidence before him. Where the Home Office does not appear the Home Office's argument and basis of refusal, as contained in the letter of refusal, is the Home Office's case purely and simply, subject to any other representations which the Home Office may make to the special adjudicator. It is not the function of the special adjudicator to expand upon that document, nor is it his function to raise matters which are not raised in it, unless these are matters which are apparent to him from a reading of the papers, in which case these matters should be drawn to the attention of the appellant's representative who should then be invited to make submissions or call evidence in relation thereto. We would add that this is not necessarily the same function which has to be performed by a special adjudicator where he has refused to adjourn a case in the absence of a representative for the appellant, and the appellant is virtually conducting his own appeal. In such event, it is the duty of the special adjudicator to give every assistance, which he can give, to the appellant.
7. Where, having received the evidence or submissions in relation to matters which he has drawn to the attention of the representatives, the special adjudicator considers clarification is necessary, then he should be at liberty to ask questions for the purposes of seeking clarification. We would emphasise, however, that it is not his function to raise matters which a Presenting Officer might have raised in cross-examination had he been present.

8. There might well be matters which are not raised in the letter of refusal which the special adjudicator considers to be relevant and of importance. We have in mind, for example, the question of whether or not, in the event that the special adjudicator concludes that a Convention ground exists, internal flight is relevant, or perhaps, where, from the letter of refusal and the other documents in the file, it appears to the special adjudicator that the question of whether or not the appellant is entitled to Convention protection by reason of the existence of civil war (matters raised by the House of Lords in the case of Adan). Where these are matters which clearly the special adjudicator considers he may well wish to deal with in his determination, then he should raise these with the representative and invite submissions to be made in relation thereto.
9. There are documents which are now available on the Internet and which can be considered to be in the public domain, which may not be included in the bundle before the special adjudicator. We have in mind the US State Department Report, Amnesty Reports and Home Office Country Reports. If the special adjudicator considers that he might well wish to refer to these documents in his determination, then he should so indicate to the representative and invite submissions in relation thereto.
10. We do not consider that a special adjudicator should grant an adjournment except in the most exceptional circumstances and where, in the view of the special adjudicator, matters of concern in the evidence before him cannot be properly addressed by examination of the appellant by his representative or submissions made by that representative. If, during the course of a hearing, it becomes apparent to a special adjudicator that such circumstances have arisen, then he should adjourn the case part heard, require the Home Office to make available a Presenting Officer at the adjourned hearing, and prepare a record of proceedings of the case, which should be submitted to both parties up to the point of the adjournment, and such record to be submitted prior to the adjourned hearing.

Contact Details

HOME OFFICE

Immigration and Nationality Directorate (IND)

Lunar House
40 Wellesley Road
Croydon CR9 2BY
Open for applications and enquiries from 9 a.m. – 4.00 p.m.
Mondays to Fridays (excluding public holidays)
General enquiries
Tel: 0870 606 7766
Application forms
Tel: 0870 241 0645
Further information
Tel: 020 8649 7878
Website (including Asylum Policy Instructions, Operational Guidance Notes, CIPU reports and Bulletins)
www.ind.homeoffice.gov.uk

Nationality Directorate

India Buildings
(3rd Floor)
Water Street
Liverpool L2 0QN
General enquiries
Tel: 0151 237 5200
Fax: 0151 237 5385
Application forms
Tel: 0151 237 0143/ 0163

National Asylum Support Service (NASS)

Voyager House
30 Wellesley Road
Croydon CR0 2AD
Tel: 0845 602 1739
Fax: 0845 601 1143

Secretary of State for the Home Department

(Minister's Private Office)
Queen Anne's Gate
London SW1H 9AT
Tel: 020 7273 4599
Fax: 020 7273 2043

Treasury Solicitor

Queen Anne's Chambers
28 Broadway
London SW1H 9JS
Tel: 020 7210 3318
Fax: 020 7210 3433

IMMIGRATION DETENTION/ REMOVAL CENTRES

Campsfield House

Langford Lane
Kiddlington
Oxford OX5 1RE
Tel: 01865 845 700/ 377 712
Fax: 01865 377 723

Dungavel Removal Centre

Dungavel House Immigration Centre
Strathaven
South Lanarkshire ML10 6RF
Tel: 01698 395 000

Harmondsworth Removal Centre

Colnbrook Bypass
Longford
West Drayton
Middlesex UB7 0HB
Tel: 020 8283 3850
Fax: 020 8283 3851

Haslar Removal Centre

2 Dolphin Way
Gosport
Hampshire PO12 2AW
Tel: 02392 604 000/ 528 636
Fax: 02392 528 631

Lindholme Removal Centre

Bawtry Road
Hatfield
Woodhouse
Doncaster DN7 6WZ
Tel: 01302 848 666
Fax: 01302 423 221

Tinsley House Removal Centre

Perimeter Road South
Gatwick Airport
West Sussex RH6 0PQ
Tel: 01293 434 800
Fax: 01293 434 800

IMMIGRATION SERVICE ENFORCEMENT UNITS

UK Immigration Service

Eton House

581 Staines Road
Hounslow TW4 5DL
Tel: 020 8814 5060
Fax: 020 8814 5345

Becket House

66–68 St Thomas Street
London SE1 3QU
Tel: 020 7238 1300
Fax: 020 7378 9110/ 9113

Bedford Enforcement Unit

Twinwood Road
Clapham
Bedfordshire MK41 6BL
Tel: 01234 821 600
Fax: 01234 821 607

Leeds/ Bradford Enforcement Unit

Waterside Court
Kirkstall Road
Leeds
West Yorkshire LS4 2QB
Tel: 0113 386 5735
Fax: 0113 386 5756

Midlands Enforcement Unit

Dominion Court
41 Station Road
Solihull B91 3RT
Tel: 0121 606 7300
Fax: 0121 606 7325

North-West Enforcement Unit

Dallas Court
(Units 1–2)
South Langworthy Road
Salford Quays
Salford M50 2GF
Tel: 0161 888 4100
Fax: 0161 888 4119

Stansted Enforcement Unit

Enterprise House
Stansted Airport
Stansted
Essex CM24 1QW
Tel: 01279 680 691
Fax: 01279 680 041

South-East Ports Surveillance Team

Dover Hoverport
Dover
Kent CT17 9TF
Tel: 01304 200 400
Fax: 01304 216 303

HOME OFFICE PRESENTING OFFICER UNITS (POUs)

2308 Coventry Road
Sheldon
Birmingham B26 3JS
Tel: 0121 700 1616
Fax: 0121 706 1694

Hanover House

Plane Tree Crescent
Feltham
Middlesex TW13 7JJ
Tel: 020 8917 2039
Fax: 020 8890 6489

Eagle Building

(10th Floor)
215 Bothwell Street
Glasgow G2 7ED
Tel: 0141 221 4218
Fax: 0141 204 5987

Springfield House

(2nd Floor)
76 Wellington Street
Leeds LS1 2AY
Tel: 0113 244 4205
Fax: 0113 245 3472

Building 1

(2nd Floor)
Angel Square
1 Torrens Street
London EC1V 1SX
Tel: 020 7239 1701
Fax: 020 7239 1683

West Point

(15th Floor)
501 Chester Road
Old Trafford
Manchester M16 9HU
Tel: 0161 877 6322
Fax: 0161 877 5955

COURTS

Immigration Appellate Authority (IAA)

General enquiries:
0845 600 0877
Website (including daily listings)
www.iaa.gov.uk

IAA main hearing centres

Sheldon Court

(2nd Floor)
1 Wagon Lane
Birmingham B26 3DU
Tel: 0845 600 0877
Fax: 0121 742 4142

Phoenix House

Rushton Avenue
Thornbury
Bradford BD3 7BH
Tel: 0845 600 0877
Fax: 01274 267 045

Croydon Magistrates' Court

(1st Floor)
Barclay Road
Croydon
CR9 3NG
Tel: 0845 600 0877
Fax: 020 8662 4627/ 4648

York House

2–3 Duke's Green Avenue
Feltham
Middlesex TW14 0LS
Tel: 0845 600 0877
Fax: 020 8831 3500

Eagle Building

(4th Floor)
215 Bothwell Street
Glasgow G2 7EZ
Tel: 0845 600 0877
Fax: 0141 242 7555

Coronet House

(4th Floor)
Queen Street
Leeds LS1 2SH
Tel: 0845 600 0877
Fax: 0113 244 6260

Taylor House

88 Rosebery Avenue
Islington
London EC1R 4QU
Tel: 0845 600 0877
Fax: 020 7862 4211

Piccadilly Exchange

(1st Floor)
2 Piccadilly Plaza
Piccadilly
Manchester M1 4AH
Tel: 0845 600 0877
Fax: 0161 234 2035/ 2036

Aldine House

(3rd Floor)
New Bailey Street
Salford
Manchester M3 5RN
Tel: 0845 600 0877
Fax: 0161 839 3793

Nottingham Magistrates' Court

Carrington Street
Nottingham NG2 1EE
Tel: 0845 600 0877
Fax: 0115 955 8216

Bennett House

Town Road
Hanley
Stoke-on-Trent ST1 2QB
Tel: 0845 600 0877
Fax: 0178 220 0144

Kings Court

Royal Quays
Earl Grey Way
North Shields
Tyne & Wear NE29 6AR
Tel: 0845 600 0877
Fax: 0191 298 2247/ 2248

Bridge House

(2nd Floor)
Bridge Street
Walsall WS1 1HZ
Tel: 0845 600 0877
Fax: 0192 262 6056

IAA satellite hearing centres

Barnet County Court

St Mary's Court
Regent Park Road
Finchley
London N3 1BQ
Tel: 0845 600 0877
Fax: 020 7862 4290

Blackwood County Court

Blackwood Road
Blackwood NP2 2XB
Tel: 0845 600 0877
Fax: 0163 341 6734

Bromley Magistrates' Court

The Court House
London Road
Bromley
Kent BR1 1BY
Tel: 0845 600 0877
Fax: 020 7862 4290

Cardiff Magistrates' Court

Fitzalan Place
Cardiff CF24 0RZ
Tel: 0845 600 0877
Fax: 0163 341 6734/ 6735

Epsom Magistrates' Court

Epsom Court House
Ashley Road
Epsom
Surrey RH4 1SX
Tel: 0845 600 0877
Fax: 020 8831 3500

Newport Magistrates' Court

Pentonville
Newport NP20 5XQ
Tel: 0845 600 0877
Fax: 0163 341 6734/ 6735

Pontypool County Court

Park Road
Riverside
Pontypool NP4 6NZ
Tel: 0845 600 0877
Fax: 0163 341 6734/ 6735

Stratford Magistrates' Court

389–397 High Street
Stratford
London E15 1DL
Tel: 0845 600 0877
Fax: 0207 862 4290

Sessions House

17 Ewell Road
Surbiton KT6 6AQ
Tel: 0845 6000 877
Fax: 020 8786 2949

Immigration Appeal Tribunal (IAT)

Field House
15 Bream's Buildings
London EC4A 1DZ
Tel: 020 7073 4200
Fax: 020 7073 4090/ 4091

Tribunal applications:

Secretary to the Immigration Appeal Tribunal
Arnhem House Tribunal
Arnhem Support Centre (Tribunal)
PO Box 6987
Leicester LE1 6ZX
Tel: 0845 600 0877
Fax: 0116 249 4214/ 4215/ 4216/ 4130

Administrative Court Office

Room C315
Royal Courts of Justice
Strand
London WC2A 2LL
General Office
Tel: 020 7947 6205/ 7335
Fax: 020 7947 6802/ 7845
List Office
Tel: 020 7947 6304/ 6297
Fax: 020 7947 6330

Civil Appeals Office

Room E307
Royal Courts of Justice
Strand
London WC2A 2LL
General Office
Tel: 020 7947 6195/ 6917
Fax: 020 7947 6621

ORGANISATIONS & RESOURCES

Amnesty International UK

99–119 Rosebery Avenue
London EC1R 4RE
Tel: 020 7814 6200
Fax: 020 7833 1510
www.amnesty.org.uk

Asylum Aid

28 Commercial Street
London E1 6LS
Tel: 020 7377 5123
Fax: 020 7247 7789
www.asylumaid.org.uk

Bail for Immigration Detainees

28 Commercial Street
London E1 6LS
Tel: 020 7247 3590
Fax: 020 7247 3550
www.biduk.org

BBC News

www.bbc.co.uk/news

Casetrack

www.casetrack.com

Electronic Immigration Network (EIN)

The Progress Centre
Charlton Place
Ardwick Green
Manchester M12 6HS
Tel: 0845 458 4151/ 0161 273 7515
Fax: 0845 458 0051/ 0161 274 3159
www.ein.org.uk

Foreign and Commonwealth Office

King Charles Street
London SW1A 2AH
Tel: 020 7008 1500
www.fco.gov.uk

Free Representation Unit (FRU)

Peer House
8–14 Verulam Street
London WC1X 8LZ
Tel: 020 7831 0692
Fax: 020 7831 2398
www.fru.org.uk

HUDOC (ECtHR case law)

www.echr.coe.int/hudoc.htm

Human Rights Watch (HRW)

2–12 Pentonville Road
(2nd Floor)
London N1 9HF
Tel: 020 7713 1995
Fax: 020 7713 1800
www.hrw.org

Immigration Advisory Service (IAS)

County House
(3rd Floor)
190 Great Dover Street
London SE1 4YB
Tel: 020 7357 7511
Fax: 020 7403 5875
www.iasuk.org

Immigration Law Practitioners' Association (ILPA)

Lindsey House
40–42 Charterhouse Street
London EC1M 6JN
Tel: 020 7251 8383
Fax: 020 7251 8384
www.ilpa.org.uk

Legal Action Group (LAG)

242 Pentonville Road
London N1 9UN
Tel: 020 7833 2931
Fax: 020 7837 6094
www.lag.org.uk

Joint Council for the Welfare of Immigrants (JCWI)

115 Old Street
London EC1V 9JR
Tel: 020 7251 8708
Fax: 020 7251 8707
www.jcwi.org.uk

Lawtel

www.lawtel.com

Medical Foundation for the Care of Victims of Torture

96–98 Grafton Road
London NW5 3EJ
Tel: 020 7813 7777
Fax: 020 7813 0011
www.torturecare.org.uk

Refugee Action

Old Fire Station
(3rd Floor)
150 Waterloo Road
London SE1 8SB
Tel: 020 7654 7700
Fax: 020 7401 3699
www.refugee-action.org.uk

Refugee Council

3 Bondway
London SW8 1SJ
Tel: 020 7820 3000
Fax: 020 7582 9929
www.refugeecouncil.org.uk

Refugee Legal Centre (RLC)

Nelson House
153–157 Commercial Road
London E1 2DA
Tel: 020 7780 3200
Fax: 020 7780 3201
www.refugee-legal-centre.org.uk

Southall Black Sisters

52 Norwood Road
Southall
Middlesex UB2 4DW
Tel: 020 8571 9596
Fax: 020 8574 6781

United Nations High Commissioner for Refugees (UNHCR)

Millbank Tower
(21st Floor)
21–24 Millbank
London SW1P 4QP
Tel: 020 7828 9191
Fax: 020 7630 5349
www.unhcr.org.uk

US State Department

www.state.gov

Index

B

I

S

T